DATA PROTECTION AND PRIVACY

The subjects of Privacy and Data Protection are more relevant than ever, and especially since 25 May 2018, when the European General Data Protection Regulation became enforceable.

This volume brings together papers that offer conceptual analyses, highlight issues, propose solutions, and discuss practices regarding privacy and data protection. It is one of the results of the eleventh annual International Conference on Computers, Privacy, and Data Protection, CPDP 2018, held in Brussels in January 2018.

The book explores the following topics: biometrics and data protection in criminal justice processing, privacy, discrimination and platforms for men who have sex with men, mitigation through data protection instruments of unfair inequalities as a result of machine learning, privacy and human-robot interaction in robotized healthcare, privacy-by-design, personal data protection of deceased data subjects, large-scale face databases and the GDPR, the new Europol regulation, rethinking trust in the Internet of Things, fines under the GDPR, data analytics and the GDPR, and the essence of the right to the protection of personal data.

This interdisciplinary book was written while the reality of the General Data Protection Regulation 2016/679 was becoming clear. It discusses open issues and daring and prospective approaches. It will serve as an insightful resource for readers with an interest in computers, privacy and data protection.

Computers, Privacy and Data Protection

Previous volumes in this series (published by Springer)

2009
Reinventing Data Protection?
Editors: Serge Gutwirth, Yves Poullet, Paul De Hert, Cécile de Terwangne, Sjaak Nouwt
ISBN 978-1-4020-9497-2 (Print) ISBN 978-1-4020-9498-9 (Online)

2010
Data Protection in A Profiled World?
Editors: Serge Gutwirth, Yves Poullet, Paul De Hert
ISBN 978-90-481-8864-2 (Print) ISBN: 978-90-481-8865-9 (Online)

2011
Computers, Privacy and Data Protection: An Element of Choice
Editors: Serge Gutwirth, Yves Poullet, Paul De Hert, Ronald Leenes
ISBN: 978-94-007-0640-8 (Print) 978-94-007-0641-5 (Online)

2012
European Data Protection: In Good Health?
Editors: Serge Gutwirth, Ronald Leenes, Paul De Hert, Yves Poullet
ISBN: 978-94-007-2902-5 (Print) 978-94-007-2903-2 (Online)

2013
European Data Protection: Coming of Age
Editors: Serge Gutwirth, Ronald Leenes, Paul de Hert, Yves Poullet
ISBN: 978-94-007-5184-2 (Print) 978-94-007-5170-5 (Online)

2014
Reloading Data Protection
Multidisciplinary Insights and Contemporary Challenges
Editors: Serge Gutwirth, Ronald Leenes, Paul De Hert
ISBN: 978-94-007-7539-8 (Print) 978-94-007-7540-4 (Online)

2015
Reforming European Data Protection Law
Editors: Serge Gutwirth, Ronald Leenes, Paul de Hert
ISBN: 978-94-017-9384-1 (Print) 978-94-017-9385-8 (Online)

2016
Data Protection on the Move
Current Developments in ICT and Privacy/Data Protection
Editors: Serge Gutwirth, Ronald Leenes, Paul De Hert
ISBN: 978-94-017-7375-1 (Print) 978-94-017-7376-8 (Online)

2017
Data Protection and Privacy: (In)visibilities and Infrastructures
Editors: Ronald Leenes, Rosamunde van Brakel, Serge Gutwirth, Paul De Hert
ISBN: 978-3-319-56177-6 (Print) 978-3-319-50796-5 (Online)

Previous volumes in this series (published by Hart Publishing)

2018
Data Protection and Privacy: The Age of Intelligent Machines
Editors: Ronald Leenes, Rosamunde van Brakel, Serge Gutwirth, Paul De Hert
ISBN: 978-1-509-91934-5 (Print) 978-1-509-91935-2 (EPDF) 978-1-509-91936-9 (EPUB)

Data Protection and Privacy

The Internet of Bodies

Edited by

Ronald Leenes

Rosamunde van Brakel

Serge Gutwirth

and

Paul De Hert

·HART·

OXFORD · LONDON · NEW YORK · NEW DELHI · SYDNEY

HART PUBLISHING

Bloomsbury Publishing Plc

Kemp House, Chawley Park, Cumnor Hill, Oxford, OX2 9PH, UK

HART PUBLISHING, the Hart/Stag logo, BLOOMSBURY and the Diana logo are
trademarks of Bloomsbury Publishing Plc

First published in Great Britain 2018

A catalogue record for this book is available from the British Library.

Library of Congress Cataloging-in-Publication data

Names: Computers, Privacy and Data Protection (Conference) (11th : 2018 : Brussels, Belgium) |
Leenes, Ronald, editor. | van Brakel, Rosamunde, editior. | Gutwirth, Serge, editor. |
Hert, Paul de, editor.

Title: Data protection and privacy : the internet of bodies / edited by Ronald Leenes,
Rosamunde van Brakel, Serge Gutwirth & Paul De Hert.

Description: Oxford ; Portland, Oregon : Hart Publishing, 2018.

Identifiers: LCCN 2018040592 (print) | LCCN 2018041420 (ebook) |
ISBN 9781509926220 (Epub) | ISBN 9781509926206 (hardback : alk. paper)

Subjects: LCSH: Data protection—Law and legislation—European Union countries—Congresses. |
European Parliament. General Data Protection Regulation—Congresses.

Classification: LCC KJE6071.A8 (ebook) | LCC KJE6071.A8 C66 2018 (print) | DDC 343.2409/99—dc23

LC record available at https://lccn.loc.gov/2018040592

ISBN: HB: 978-1-50992-620-6
        ePDF: 978-1-50992-621-3
        ePub: 978-1-50992-622-0

Typeset by Compuscript Ltd, Shannon
Printed and bound in Great Britain by CPI Group (UK) Ltd, Croydon CR0 4YY

MIX
Paper from
responsible sources
FSC® C013604

To find out more about our authors and books visit www.hartpublishing.co.uk.
Here you will find extracts, author information, details of forthcoming events
and the option to sign up for our newsletters.

PREFACE

It is the end of June 2018 as we write this preface. Data Protection D-Day is behind us and we are still here. Whereas it seems that until 2017, data protection was only on the radar of a limited number of people, including readers of books such as these, this has clearly changed during 2017 and the beginning of 2018. Everyone suddenly became aware that the new (European) Data Protection Regulation was coming and that (significant) action had to be taken. Never mind the fact that the GDPR builds on the Data Protection Directive which had only been in force since the late 1990s.

Certainly, up to 25 May 2018, the buzz was clearly noticeable. We have all received numerous e-mails from organisations claiming they value us highly and asking for our permission to keep in touch. Well, it is a start: now they should also make sure they comply with the rest of the GDPR. Indeed, terms such as data protection impact assessment, data protection officer and certification can now be heard from people who were by and large ignorant of the whole concept of data protection a few years ago. Times do seem to be changing.

In the meantime, the international privacy and data protection crowd, gathered in Brussels for the eleventh time to engage in the International Conference on Computers, Privacy and Data Protection Conference (CPDP) from 24–26 January 2018. An audience of 1,100 people had the chance to discuss a wide range of contemporary topics and issues with over 400 speakers in the 70 panels, during the breaks, side events, and ad-hoc dinners and pub crawls. Striving for diversity and balance, CPDP gathers academics, lawyers, practitioners, policy-makers, computer scientists and civil society from all over the world to exchange ideas and discuss the latest emerging issues and trends. This unique multi-disciplinary formula has served to make CPDP one of the leading data protection and privacy conferences in Europe and around the world.

Although 25 May clearly was on everyone's mind, the conference almost seemed to have moved beyond the launch date of the GDPR coming into full force. The discussions moved towards what is wrong with the GDPR, what can be improved, and what now? As data collection increasingly focuses on the physical body and bodies are increasingly connected, digitised and informatised the conference theme was 'The internet of bodies', nodding at the Internet of Things, which is ultimately just about information about humans. And indeed, many sessions at the conference focused on the ubiquitous networks of objects and devices increasingly entering our lives.

The CPDP conference is definitely the place to be, but we are also happy to produce a tangible spin-off every year: the CPDP book volumes. CPDP papers are cited very frequently and the series has a significant readership. The conference cycle starts with a call for papers in the summer preceding the conference. The paper submissions are peer reviewed, and those authors whose papers are accepted can present their work in the various academic panels at the conference. After the conference, speakers are also invited to submit papers on the basis of the panel discussions. All papers submitted on the basis of these calls are then (again) double-blinded peer reviewed. This year we have received 18 papers in the second round, of which 12 were accepted for publication. It is these 12 papers that you will find in this volume, complemented by the conference closing speech, which is traditionally given by the EDPS chair (currently Giovanni Buttarelli).

The conference addressed many privacy and data protection issues in its 70 panels ranging from the implementation of the GDPR, wearables, IoT, blockchain, border control to data breaches, privacy and security by design, health data, algorithmic accountability. Far too many topics to all be listed here. We refer the interested reader to the conference website www.cpdpconferences.org.

The current volume can only offer a very small part of what the conference has to offer. Nevertheless, the editors feel the current volume represents a very valuable set of papers describing and discussing contemporary privacy and data protection issues.

All the chapters of this book have been peer reviewed and commented on by at least two referees with expertise and interest in the subject matters. Since their work is crucial for maintaining the scientific quality of the book we would explicitly take the opportunity to thank them for their commitment and efforts:

Meg Ambrose, Jef Ausloos, Emre Bayamlıoglu, Bibi van den Berg, Michael Birnhack, Gergely Biczók, Franziska Boehm, Hans Buitelaar, Johann Cas, Damien Clifford, Colette Cuijpers, Lorenzo Dalla Corte, Silvia De Conca, Claudia Diaz, Denis Duez, Michael Friedewald, Lothar Fritsch, Masa Galic, Raphaël Gellert, Inge Graef, Serge Gutwirth, Marit Hansen, Joris van Hoboken, Chris Hoofnagle, Kristina Irion, Irene Kamara, Els Kindt, Eleni Kosta, Daniel Le Métayer, Marc van Lieshout, Arno Lodder, Bastiaan van Loenen, Alessandro Mantelero, Nicholas Martin, Bryce Newell, Akiko Orita, Rene Peralta, Robin Pierce, Jo Pierson, Nadya Purtova, Charles Raab, Arnold Roosendaal, Maurice Schellekens, Bart van der Sloot, Sophie Stalla-Bourdillon, Ivan Szekely, Linnet Taylor, Mistale Taylor, Yung Shin Van Der Sype, Joseph Savirimuthu, Hosna Skeikhattar, Ivan Skorvanek, Brendan Van Alsenoy, Gabriela Zanfir Fortuna, Nicolo Zingales.

A special word of thanks goes to the new European Data Protection Supervisor, Giovanni Buttarelli. We have incorporated Mr Buttarelli's speech as the final chapter in this volume.

Ronald Leenes, Rosamunde van Brakel,
Serge Gutwirth & Paul De Hert
1 July 2018

CONTENTS

LIST OF CONTRIBUTORS

Natalie Bertels is a senior legal researcher in privacy and data protection. She specialises in new technologies and the development of data-driven services and products. Her research focuses on the data protection challenges of a big data/cloud/IoT/HPC setting and the methodologies and implementation of privacy by design. Currently, she is involved in the PRiSE project (Privacy-by-Design Regulation in Software Engineering, internal KUL funding, 2017–2021), working on an integrated (legal-technical) risk assessment methodology and in the imec Smart City initiative City of Things. She is the vice-chair of the Policy and Societal Task Force of the Big Data Value Association (BDVA, www.bdva.eu). Before joining CiTiP, Natalie practiced law as an IP and ICT law attorney.

Giovanni Buttarelli was appointed European Data Protection Supervisor on 4 December 2014 by a joint decision of the European Parliament and the Council for a term of five years. Before joining the EDPS, he worked as Secretary General to the Italian Data Protection Authority, a position he occupied between 1997 and 2009. A member of the Italian judiciary with the rank of Cassation judge, he has been involved in many initiatives and committees on data protection and related issues at international level. His experience on data protection includes the participation in many bodies at European Union level (including Art. 31 Committee of Directive n. 95/46/EC and Taiex programmes), and at the Council of Europe (in particular, as a consultant, T-PD; CJ-PD, DH-S-Ac, Venice Commission), as well as contributing to many hearings, meetings and workshops held by Parliaments and to specialised book journals and papers. He currently teaches on privacy at the Luiss University, Rome.

Fanny Coudert is a legal officer at the European Data Protection Supervisor (EDPS), Supervision and Enforcement Unit and a researcher in data protection privacy law within EU research projects. She has started her PhD on the topic of 'The Purpose Specification Principle in the Area of Freedom, Security and Justice: Towards Renewed Data Protection Principles for Information-based Practices in the Field of Security'. Fanny also has experience as a lawyer and consultant.

Silvia de Conca is a PhD Candidate at the Tilburg Institute for Law, Technology, and Society of the University of Tilburg, (the Netherlands). She holds an LLM in IT Law from the London School of Economics (UK), an LLM cum honoris and an LLB from Roma Tre University (Italy). She has years of experience practicing the law in international law firms in Milan and Rome, as well as teaching IT and IP law at the Monterrey Tech Institute (Mexico).

Aviva de Groot is a PhD candidate at the Tilburg Institute for Law, Technology, and Society of the University of Tilburg (The Netherlands). She holds an LLM in Information Law from the Institute for Information Law (IViR) of the University of Amsterdam and an LLB from the University of Amsterdam. Her professional experience includes administrative law, human rights law and data protection and she coordinated the interdisciplinary Minor Privacy Studies for the University of Amsterdam.

Ivo Emanuilov is a researcher at the Centre for IT & IP Law of KU Leuven. He carries out fundamental and practical research on the legal and ethical issues of artificial intelligence, cognitive, autonomous and decentralised technologies. Ivo is experienced in interdisciplinary research at the interface of computer science and law focusing on issues of computational models of law, cognitive computing, privacy and data protection, cybersecurity, liability, safety and certification of autonomous systems in transport. He holds an LLM Intellectual Property and ICT Law from KU Leuven and has formal training and qualifications in software engineering and system programming.

Heike Felzmann is a lecturer in Philosophy, School of Humanities, at NUI Galway. She holds a Dr phil from Philipps-University Marburg, a MA in Philosophy from SUNY Stony Brook, a Dipl psych in Psychology and Magister Artium in Philosophy from the University of Hamburg. Currently much of her work focuses on robot ethics; she is a contributor to the H2020 MARIO project, the H2020 ROCSAFE project, the COST Action Wearable Robots and the ERASMUS PROSPERO Project.

Eduard Fosch-Villaronga is with the Microsoft Cloud Computing Research Center and Center for Commercial Law Studies at Queen Mary University of London, and holds an LLB from the Autonomous University of Barcelona (Spain); an LLM from Université de Toulouse (France); an MA from Polytechnic School at Autonomous University of Madrid (Spain); and the Erasmus Mundus Joint Doctorate (PhD) (EMJD) in Law, Science and Technology (coordinated by the University of Bologna). His expertise lies at the intersection between law, healthcare and robotics.

Georgy Ishmaev is a PhD candidate in the Ethics/Philosophy of Technology section of Values Technology and Innovation department at TBM faculty TU Delft. His doctoral thesis research in ethics of technology is focused on the explication and evaluation of normative assumptions embedded in blockchain solutions relevant to the issues of private data protection.

Catherine Jasserand is a PhD researcher at the University of Groningen, Faculty of Law within the Security, Technology and e-Privacy (STeP) Research Group. She is doing research in data protection and biometrics. Besides her PhD project, she has carried out research for the EU FP7 funded-project INGRESS (Innovative Technology for Fingerprint Live Scanners, available at www.ingress-project.eu).

Before joining the University of Groningen, she worked for several years at the Institute for Information Law (IViR), University of Amsterdam, as a researcher in intellectual property and new technology law. She holds a Master's degree in European law from the University of Paris and an LLM in intellectual property and new technology law from the University of California (Berkeley). She is qualified as a lawyer in France and in the United States (New York State)

Wouter Joosen is full professor at the Department of Computer Science of the KU Leuven in Belgium, where he teaches courses on software architecture and component-based software engineering, distributed systems and the engineering of secure service platforms. His research interests are in aspect-orientated software development, focusing on software architecture and middleware, and in security aspects of software, including security in component frameworks and security architectures.

Alison Knight qualified as a Solicitor in 2001 after completing her training contract with Dechert LLP in London. She subsequently joined Dechert's European Group in Brussels, specialising in Competition Law (in particular, the defence of European Commission investigations and multi-jurisdictional merger notifications). While working for the Office of Fair Trading from 2004 to 2007, she investigated high-profile mergers, acted as a project leader on the revision of its merger control guidelines and participated in dawn raids on suspected cartelists. During this time, Alison undertook in-house training at the Competition Commission and King's College, London. She subsequently worked as an Associate with the Competition Team at Bond Pearce LLP until 2010, giving full-line advice and training to clients primarily from retail, energy and postal sectors. Alison is now a senior compliance lawyer at the University of Southampton in charge of data governance, an academic researcher affiliated to the Institute for Law and the Web and an editor in IT, Data Protection, and Privacy Laws.

Joanna Kulesza, PhD is an assistant professor of international law and internet governance at the University of Lodz, Poland. She is also a Scientific Committee member of EU Fundamental Rights Agency. She serves as an expert on human rights online for the Council of Europe and European Commission. Kulesza has been involved with the Sino-European Cybersecurity Dialogue (SECD) and the Global Commission on the Stability of Cyberspace (GCSC) working on international cybersecurity and human rights. She is involved in various research projects focused on privacy and cybersecurity, including a fundamental rights review pilot project for the European Parliament, where she is responsible for the fundamental rights review of European agencies policies, including Europol and Eurojust. She serves as Membership Committee Chair for the Global Internet Governance Academic Network (GigaNet).

Gianclaudio Malgieri is a Doctoral Researcher at the Law, Science, Technology and Society Studies (LSTS) Research Group of the Free University of Brussels (VUB). He is lecturer of data protection law and intellectual property for undergraduate and post-graduate courses at the University of Pisa and Sant'Anna School of Advanced Studies; he is also Senior Associate for a law firm specialising in privacy compliance. He received an LLM with honours from the University of Pisa and a JD with honours Sant'Anna School of Advanced Studies of Pisa (Italy). He also studied cyberlaw at the London School of Economics; international trade law at the World Trade Institute of the University of Bern and he was also a research student at École Normale Supérieure de Paris. He was visiting researcher at the Oxford University. He has published more than 20 articles in leading international law reviews, including the *Italian Handbook of Personal Data Protection*.

Laurens Naudts is a Doctoral Researcher and researcher in law at the KU Leuven Centre for IT & IP Law. His research interests focus on the interrelationship between artificial intelligence, ethics, justice, fairness and the law. Laurens' PhD research reconsiders the concepts of equality and data protection within the context of machine learning and algorithmically guided decision making. As a researcher, Laurens has also been actively involved in several national and EU funded (FP7 and H2020) research projects, including, inter alia, iLINC, Preemptive and VICTORIA. Laurens was formerly appointed as a researcher at the European University Institute (Centre for Media Pluralism and Media Freedom) where he performed scientific research for the project 'Strengthening Journalism in Europe: Tools, Networking, Training'.

Paul Nemitz is the Principal Adviser in the Directorate General for Justice and Consumers of the European Commission. He previously was the Director for Fundamental Rights in the European Commission, in the lead on the Reform of Data Protection in Europe. Nemitz is a Member of the World Council on Extended Intelligence and a Visiting Professor at the College of Europe in Bruges. He was recently appointed a Fellow of the Free University of Brussels (VUB), where he is a Member of the Brussels Privacy Hub.

Guido Noto La Diega is Senior Lecturer in cyber law and intellectual property at the Northumbria University (School of Law), where is European Research Partnerships Coordinator and Co-convenor of NINSO, The Northumbria Internet & Society Research Group. Alongside the post at Northumbria, Dr Noto La Diega is Fellow of the Nexa Center for Internet & Society and Director of Ital-IoT Centre of Multidisciplinary Research on the Internet of Things. In terms of practice, he is Of Counsel of Damiani and Damiani International Law Firm and co-founder of DPA2018, a boutique consultancy firm specialising in GDPR compliance. Author of dozens of peer-reviewed publications and speaker at national and international conferences, Dr Noto La Diega is a world-renowned expert in cyber law, with considerable expertise in data protection, privacy, consumer protection, and copyright.

Robin L. Pierce is with the Tilburg Institute of Law and Technology at Tilburg University, and holds a PhD from Harvard University, a JD from the University of California, Berkeley School of Law, and a BA from Princeton University.

Dr Aida Ponce del Castillo is a senior researcher at the European Trade Union in Brussels. She obtained a PhD 'Doctor Europaeus' in Law and a master in Bioethics.

Maria Grazia Porcedda is a Research Fellow at the School of Law of the University of Leeds, where she is a member of the EPSRC-funded CRITiCal project. Her research and publications focus on EU law and technology, particularly data protection and cyber security matters. She was a member of EDEN (Europol Data Experts Network) and of the EUISS Task Force on Cyber Capacity Building until July 2018. She holds a PhD in Law from the European University Institute, where she worked on the CharterClick! (DG Just), SurPRISE and SURVEILLE FP7 projects. Her research has been recognised by grants and prizes from the Accademia Nazionale dei Lincei and the Italian Association of Information Security (CLUSIT).

Scott Robbins is currently a PhD Researcher in the ethics of technology at the Delft University of Technology, the Netherlands (TU Delft). He graduated with a Bachelors in Computer Science (cum laude) at California State University, and with a Masters in Ethics and Technology (cum laude) at the University of Twente, the Netherlands.

Jessica Schroers is a legal researcher working at the KU Leuven Centre for IT and IP Law. She started working at its predecessor, the Interdisciplinary Centre for Law & ICT (ICRI) in 2013. Her research focuses mainly on data protection and identity management, but she also has experience in security and trust and blockchain and has been working on various EU and Belgian projects, among others FutureID, ECOSSIAN and BOSS. She conducts PhD research on the responsibility of users for their electronic identity.

Sophie Stalla-Bourdillon is Professor in Information Technology Law and Data Governance and Director of the Institute for Law and the Web, University of Southampton. She is also a nonexecutive Director of the Web Science Institute and a member of the Southampton Cybersecurity Centre of Excellence. Sophie is at the forefront of interdisciplinary research in the fields of content regulation and data protection. She has been working on value-by-design approaches to regulation for FP7 OPTET, electronic identification (Horizon 2020 FutureTrust) and data sharing relying upon anonymisation techniques. She is currently supporting data-driven start-ups within the Data Pitch innovation accelerator (a Horizon 2020 innovation programme). Sophie has acted as an expert for several international organisations (eg OCSE, OEDC). She was part of the expert group formed by the Council of Europe on intermediary liability MSI-NET (2016–2018) and will be part of the expert group for the Observatory on the Online Platform Economy formed by the European Commission (2018–2020).

Peggy Valcke is a full-time research professor and lecturer in ICT law at KU Leuven. She is a visiting professor at Tilburg University and member of the scientific committee of the Florence School of Regulation at EUI. She is a leading

European expert in media and communications law, fundamental rights of the digital citizen, data protection and media freedoms, data portability, right to be forgotten, big data etc. She was a member of Google's Advisory Council on the Right to be Forgotten and is currently a member of Digital Minds for Belgium, a working group convened by Belgium's Minister for Telecommunications and Digital Agenda. She has served as an expert for organisations such as the European Commission, the Council of Europe, national media regulators (including the German Media Concentration Commission and the Broadcasting Authority of Ireland), as well as administrations and authorities in Belgium (such as the BIPT and CSA).

Dimitri Van Landuyt is a Research Manager in Software Engineering at DistriNet, in the Language technology and Middleware task force. His research focuses on topics related to core software engineering principles, software architecture, software quality by design, security and privacy by design, requirements engineering and its role in the early stages of the software development life-cycle (domain analysis, requirements, architecture), multi-concern engineering, software product line engineering, model-driven development, development of cloud applications, software-engineering-as-a-service and empirical studies. His PhD focused on the topic of Robust and Reusable Interfaces in Aspect-Oriented Software Architectures. Dimitri is actively coaching four PhD researchers within the DistriNet research group.

Kim Wuyts is a postdoctoral researcher at the Department of Computer Science at KU Leuven (Belgium). She has more than 10 years' experience in security and privacy in software engineering. Kim is one of the main forces behind the development and extension of LINDDUN, a privacy-by-design framework that provides systematic support to elicit and mitigate privacy threats in software systems.

Erik Zouave an Analyst with the Swedish Defense Research Agency FOI, researching legal aspects of technology and security. He is a Research Fellow with the Citizen Lab, Munk School of Global Affairs, at the University of Toronto, Google Policy Fellow and former Researcher with KU-Leuven CiTiP – imec.

1

You've been Measured, You've been Weighed and You've been Found Suspicious

Biometrics and Data Protection in Criminal Justice Processing

ERIK ZOUAVE AND JESSICA SCHROERS

Abstract

Biometrics, the measurement of life or living beings, has been applied within criminal intelligence and investigations for over a century. Since early law enforcement biometrics, the techniques and sources for biometric processing have increased dramatically. More than ever, personal data is collected from public fora, in particular the Internet, to infer suspects' physical, physiological and behavioural characteristics. This raises concerns of burgeoning databases with increasingly complex, heterogeneous biometric data impacting the rights of individuals. In this chapter, we assess the current state of the art of legal recommendations on how to *demonstrate compliance* with the regulation of biometric data under European data protection law. Our assessment focuses especially on the automation of second generation biometrics and *technical by design* measures to minimise data protection risks in police biometrics based on online identifiers. We find that most of the scholarship and interpretation has focused on providing general recommendations in the civilian context, and that these recommendations frequently reflect situations of one-to-one verification rather than one-to-many identification. Only some recommendations are suitable in the way ahead under Directive (EU) 2016/680. We therefore argue that the adoption of the Directive necessitates a reinvigorated focus on *technical by design* compliance.

Keywords

Biometrics, biometric data, data protection, law enforcement, Directive (EU) 2016/680

1. Introduction

Biometrics, the measurement of life or living beings has been applied within criminal intelligence and investigations for over a century for uses such as the unique identification of suspects of crimes or threats to public security. Dactyloscopy, or fingerprinting, used by the Bengali Inspector General already in the late 1800s[1] and the U.S. Federal Bureau of Investigation since 1924,[2] quickly became widespread biometric investigative methods together with DNA sampling.[3] Biometrics is a powerful and fact-based[4] means to authenticate identities and match them to events, locations, groups and concepts of interests.

However, since early police biometrics, the techniques and sources for biometric processing have increased dramatically. While first-generation biometrics were generally "strong" biometrics such as fingerprint, or iris, second-generation biometrics include technologies that measure "motor skills," electromagnetic body signals and human-computer interaction patterns (eg walking patterns, dynamic facial features, voice recognition, online behaviour recognition etc.) and require less user cooperation.[5] Increasingly, embedded systems, ambient intelligence and distant sensors aggregate the volumes of available data.[6] More than ever, personal data is collected from public fora, particularly in the form of *online identifiers* from the Internet, to infer suspects' physical, physiological and behavioural characteristics. Consider, for example, ubiquitous social media where image, audio and video data are shared and where biometrics are even incorporated into services such as "tagging" or "suggesting" people in photos.

This diversification and increase of biometric data poses discrete risks to the privacy and protection of personal data that must be balanced against security interests. Firstly, this trend raises concerns that the collection, generation and

---

[1] Simon Cole, *Suspect Identities a History of Fingerprinting and Criminal Identification*, London: Harvard University Press, 2002; Carlo Ginzburg, 'Morelli, Freud, and Sherlock Holmes: Clues and Scientific Method,' *History Workshop*, No 9 (Spring, 1980): 25–27.

[2] Cole, n 1. Federal Bureau of Investigations, 'Fingerprints and Other Biometrics.' FBI, 2017, accessed 18 July 2017. Available at: www.fbi.gov/services/cjis/fingerprints-and-other-biometrics.

[3] Article 29 Data Protection Working Party, *Working document on biometrics* (12168/02/EN, WP80, Adopted 1 August 2003): 1.

[4] See Simon A. Cole, 'The 'Opinionisation' of Fingerprint Evidence,' *BioSocieties* 3 (2008): 105–113.

[5] Emilio Mordini, Dimitros Tzovaras, ed. *Second Generation Biometrics: The Ethical, Legal and Social Context* (Dordrecht: Springer, 2012), 9–11.

[6] Paul De Hert, 'Biometrics and the Challenge to Human Rights in Europe. Need for Regulation and Regulatory Distinctions,' in *Security and Privacy in Biometrics* edited by P. Campisi (London: Springer, 2013).

storage of biometric data will become increasingly associated to *disproportionate* Big Data practices.[7] Secondly, the heterogeneity of data sources, formats and data quality may further impact the *accuracy* of biometric data underpinning criminal evidence, seriously affecting the rights of data subjects.[8] Thirdly, the diversification and increasing use of biometrics also increases the *sensitivity* of the data and the risk and likelihoods of adverse impacts for affected individuals when the *security and confidentiality* of the processing proves insufficient. Finally, the scale and complexity of this processing necessarily leads to increased reliance on semi-automated and automated techniques, making the overall process more "opaque" and less foreseeable.[9]

In view of such concerns, the European Union data protection reforms have updated the laws applying to civilian research and development of police biometrics on the one hand – through Regulation (EU) 2016/679 – and to police and criminal justice authorities as end-users of such systems on the other hand – through Directive (EU) 2016/680. However, we argue that guidance on technical implementation has been and remains focused on civilian identity management to the detriment of data subjects processed by police biometric systems for the identification of suspects of crime.

In this chapter, we assess the state of the art of legal recommendations on how to *demonstrate compliance* with the regulation of biometric data under European data protection law, especially with respect to *technical by design* measures to minimise data protection risks in police biometrics based on online identifiers. We find that only some of the widely accepted recommendations are suitable in the way ahead under Directive (EU) 2016/680 when combined with novel implementation methods. Given the significant values and rights at stake, we argue for reinvigorated research into technical by design compliance measures for police biometrics.

Demonstrating compliance is a principle of data protection. It entails both *organisational measures*, such as the adoption of data protection policies and carrying out data protection impact assessments, as well as *technical measures* implemented in processing systems to comply with all data protection principles

---

[7] Article 29 Data Protection Working Party, *Opinion 3/2012 on developments in biometric technologies* (00720/12/EN, WP103, Adopte 27 April 2012); Els J. Kindt, 'The Processing of Biometric Data: A Comparative Legal Analysis with a Focus on the Proportionality Principle and Recommendations for a Legal Framework' (PhD diss., KU Leuven, May 2012); Els J. Kindt, *Privacy and Data Protection Issues of Biometric Applications: A Comparative Legal Analysis* (Springer, 2013); Paul De Hert and Hans Lammerant, 'Predictive Profiling and its Legal Limits: Effectiveness gone Forever?' in *Exploring the Boundaries of Big Data* ed Bart Van der Sloot et.al (Amsterdam: University Press, 2016).

[8] Article 29 Data Protection Working Party, *Opinion 3/2012* n 7; Els J. Kindt, 'Biometric Applications and the Data Protection Legislation,' *Datenschutz und Datensicherheit* 31, no 3 (2007):168; CoE T-PD, *Progress report on the application of the principles of Convention 108 to the collection and processing of biometric data* (T-PD, February 2005), paras 67–70.

[9] CoE *T-PD Progress report*, n 8, para 70; Article 29 Data Protection Working Party, *Opinion 02/2010 on facial recognition in online and mobile services* (00727/12/EN WP192, Adopted 22 March 2012), 8; *Opinion 3/2012* above n 7 at 4.

by design through the entirety of operations. We focus on the technical aspects of compliance as these are more contextual, frequently elude generalisation, yet are essential for data protection law in practice. Indeed, the European Data Protection Supervisor emphasises the need for specific by design safeguards or technical measures to resolve, for example, proportionality and accuracy problems in biometric data.[10] We derive our insights from Directive 2016/680, its commonalities with the Regulation, and soft law guidance from the Article 29 Working Party and the (European) Data Protection Supervisor. Following Jasserand's terminology clarification, we understand biometrics as the automatic recognition of individuals, while biometric data is considered as "a type of personal data relating to biometric characteristics and linked to the identification or identifiability of an individual."[11] The term "biometric systems" is used synonymously with biometrics.

This chapter also draws on contextual learning from law enforcement to supplement established recommendations with novel means of mitigating complexity and heterogeneity. We draw on the conceptual research of Coudert et al regarding digital evidence in legal proceedings and the practical biometric case studies in the Horisons 2020 DANTE project, its system, and law enforcement practitioners. The DANTE project aims to deliver effective biometrics, notably physical facial, silhouette, and voice metrics as well as behavioural analysis of stylometrics, logos, objects and concepts, from online sources and *identifiers*, while applying legal best practices to avoid unwanted societal impacts.[12] However, in doing so, we observe and propose solutions to common problems in the automation of policing and biometrics.

2. A History of Police Biometrics

As mentioned previously, biometrics have featured as an investigatory tool since the nineteenth century. Cole observes that biometric procedures allowed police to "link bodies ... across time and space" and "to track the body" of a criminal rather than just signs of criminality.[13] Early police biometrics were particularly useful for establishing recidivism within precincts.[14] Two types of early police biometrics became particularly prevalent; dactyloscopy, or fingerprinting, and anthropometry, or the measurement of body proportions.[15]

---

[10] EDPS, *Opinion 3/2016: Opinion on the exchange of information on third country nationals as regards the European Criminal Records Information System (ECRIS)* (13 April 2016).

[11] Catherine A. Jasserand, 'Avoiding Terminological Confusion between the Notions of 'Biometrics' and 'Biometric Data': An Investigation into the Meanings of the Terms from a European Data Protection and a Scientific Perspective' *International Data Privacy Law* 6, no 1 (2016): 63.

[12] Dante, 'Dante' Dante 2018. Available at: www.h2020-dante.eu/ last accessed 28 May 2018.

[13] See Cole, n 1 at 3.

[14] Ibid at 32–33.

[15] Ibid at 32; Stephen Mayhew, 'History of Biometrics' Biometric update, 14 January 2015. Available at: www.biometricupdate.com/201501/history-of-biometrics, last accessed 18 July 2017; See Kindt *Privacy and Data Protection* above n 7 at 15–16.

The fact that criminal justice biometrics can be *physical*, *physiological* as well as *behavioural*, and that their perceived reliability will vary according to context, is recorded in early European case law. As accounted by Cole, sixteenth-century French courts relied on the peculiarities of a cobbler's measurement of feet, testimonial accounts of dialect and outward appearance, such as hair color and scars, in determining whether Martin Guerre was, in fact, Martin Guerre or an impostor.[16] The French court relied less on the quantitative measurements of the cobbler and more on the (fleeting) qualitative memories of witnesses.

Nineteenth-century investigative biometrics sought to standardise the description of qualitative physical features such as whether fingerprints have arches or whirls and whether lips are pouty, by which reproducible methods the data should be collected, and in which order and format it should be presented. In other words, the idea of biometric templates were introduced to policing.[17] However, these early biometrics were limited by the constraints of manual labor and, frequently, the need to physically take measurements from suspects.

Contemporary (and future) police biometrics are significantly impacted by modern technology, allowing for the pluralisation and automation of data collection and analysis.[18] Urban spaces are surveilled with CCTV and thermal cameras[19] and online spaces allow for massive sharing of data in text, audio, image and video formats. It is in this online context that the DANTE project, our primary source of contextual learning, appears. DANTE delivers automated data mining and analytics solutions to detect, retrieve, collect and analyze heterogeneous and complex multimedia and multi-language terrorist-related contents, from both the Surface and the Deep Web. It detects and monitors terrorist-related fundraising, propaganda, training and disinformation. It seeks to link online pseudonyms, identify publishers of terrorist content and suspects that are identifiable through textual, image, audio and video data.

3. The Legal Framework for Police Biometrics

The EU data protection reforms have attempted to resolve several problems with biometric data processing. Firstly, the Regulation and Directive encompass a common, binding definition to biometric data, clarifying its scope.[20]

---

[16] See Cole, above n 1 at 6–7.

[17] Ibid at 32–59.

[18] See, eg, Michael Choras, 'Emerging Methods of Biometrics Human Identification,' *Innovative Computing, Information and Control, 2007. ICICIC '07. Second International Conference* (September 2007).

[19] Samuel Nunn, 'Police Technology in Cities: Changes and Challenges,' *Technology in Society* 3 (2001): 11–27.

[20] Regulation (EU) 2016/679 on the protection of natural persons with regard to the processing of personal data and on the free movement of such data, and repealing Directive 95/46/EC [2016]

In this respect, biometric data encompasses personal data, i.e. data relating to an individual, subjected to *specific technical processing* to *uniquely identify* that individual. However, identification is not necessarily precise and correct. Biometrics, even in the meaning of the law, are rather probabilistic and relate to *physical, physiological, and behavioural* features that are distinct to the data subject.[21] The peculiarities and commonalities of these features can be exemplified through certain functions of the DANTE system:

- *Physical features* include outwardly observable traits (e.g. extraction of metrics from facial features in images and videos).

- *Physiological features* encompass both physical, external and internal traits such as voice metrics for speaker identification and the registering of intensity of radicalisation.

- *Behavioural features* include peculiar conducts or demeanors (e.g. a specific stylometric of writing). It can also significantly overlap with physical features such as the adoption of group insignias as tattoos, or physiological features such as sentiments connected to certain concepts of interest to an individual.

Secondly, additional legal certainty was introduced regarding the status of biometric data as special (or sensitive) categories of data and the restricted purposes for which it can be processed.[22] However, this clarification affects police to a lesser degree than developers of police biometrics as the *detection and suppression of crime* is their default purpose for legitimate processing. Research (and development) moreover, while a legitimate purpose in itself, will further rely on, for example, the data subject's *consent*, enrolling only data that was *manifestly made public* by the data subject, most likely the *substantial public interest* of crime prevention to ensure the legality of processing.[23]

Thirdly, the reforms established that the processing of biometric data entail high risks to the rights and freedoms of data subjects.[24] As such, the safeguards and measures to address risks to data subjects' rights in the design[25] of biometric systems and the processing of biometric data should be based on a data protection

---

OJ L 119/1 (Regulation (EU) 2016/679), Article 4; Directive (EU) 2016/680 on the protection of natural persons with regard to the processing of personal data by competent authorities for the purposes of the prevention, investigation, detection or prosecution of criminal offences or the execution of criminal penalties, and on the free movement of such data, and repealing Council Framework Decision 2008/977/JHA [2016] OJ L 119/89 (Directive (EU) 2016/680), Art 3.

[21] Article 29 Data Protection Working Party, *Opinion 4/2007 on the concept of personal data* (01248/07/EN WP 136, Adopted 20 June), 9; see *Opinion 3/2012* at 4–5; CoE T-PD, *Progress report* n 8 at paras 16–18, 28, 29; Article 29 Data Protection Working Party, *Working document on biometrics* n 3.

[22] Regulation (EU) 2016/679, Art 9; Directive (EU) 2016/680, Art 10.

[23] Ibid, Art 9.

[24] Directive (EU), 2016/680, recital 51, Art 27.

[25] Regulation (EU) 2016/679, Art 25, Directive (EU) 2916/680, Art 20.

impact assessment (DPIA).[26] Additionally, if during the DPIA it is found that there will be residual high risks to the rights of the data subject, despite applied safeguards, then it is also necessary to consult the national Supervisory Authority prior to any processing.[27] This chapter details risks and technical mitigations that may be considered through such processes.

Finally, the sum of these legal requirements is that there are fewer and stricter circumstances where a person can lawfully be uniquely identified.

4. The Applicability of Current Recommendations to Criminal Justice Biometrics

Both developers and end-users of biometric systems must account for the measures and safeguards both from the outset of their design and during their use. In other words, they must ensure data protection by *design* and by *default*.[28] To this end, much of the scholarly debates and guidance from interpretative bodies such as the Article 29 Working Party have focused on explaining which types of measures are appropriate for biometric data. However, the primary inspiration for these recommendations is generally not police use-cases but rather civilian processing, often within the scope of identity management, with occasional excursions and references to the world of police biometrics.

4.1. Policing versus Identity Management

So, to what extent are these recommendations applicable in a law enforcement context? To answer this, we compare how biometric data are used in identity management and law enforcement respectively. We then analyse the general recommendations, given by the Article 29 Working Party, European courts, and scholars, especially their applicability in the law enforcement context to identify differences and point out gaps. We focus specifically on biometrics using *online identifiers* or traces of online activities by which natural persons can be identified. As will be explained, these sources and identifiers of the biometric data frequently have a lower probabilistic *accuracy* than physical fingerprints or DNA traces, or at the very least, require complex technical processing methods.

---

[26] Article 29 Data Protection Working Party, *Guidelines on Data Protection Impact Assessment (DPIA) and determining whether processing is 'likely to result in a high risk' for the purposes of Regulation 2016/679* (17/EN, WP 248), 6.

[27] Regulation (EU) 2016/679, Art 36, recital 94 Directive (EU) 2016/680, Art 28.

[28] Ibid, Art 25, Ibid, Art 20.

4.2. Differences between Identity Management and Police Biometrics

As the Article 29 Working Party explains in Opinion 3/2012, the processing of biometric data within a biometric system generally involves enrolment, storage, and matching.

While in civilian identity management the data subject, usually, personally and willingly enrolls into the biometric system, and can be informed, this is not always the case in policing. The primary goal in identity management is to reliably assign identity attributes to authenticate the identity of an individual in the context of an (online) transaction.[29] At the stage of enrolment, the data subject is identified, and the biometric data and template is connected to the person or the authorisation of the person. The matching therefore only needs one-to-one verification (e.g. the fingerprint matches the stored template) and the biometric data can be stored in a decentralised manner, which generally reflects the main recommendations found in the literature. In police use of second-generation biometrics, the data is not actively enrolled by the data subject, which is uninformed of enrolment. The aim is not to link data for authentication, but to link the biometric data to an identity or biometric data already in the database, generally in the context of an investigation. In this context, one-to-one verification is not possible, but one-to-many identification (comparing the biometric information with all biometric information available in the database) is necessary, with the higher failure rate that this entails.[30] However, police must still ensure the lawfulness and the veracity of processing both in terms of data protection and evidentiary standards.[31]

4.3. Principal Differences and Similarities

The data protection principles are similar in Regulation 2016/679 and Directive 2016/680 with slight differences. While the Regulation requires that processing needs to be *lawful, fair,* and *transparent,* the Directive only requires it to be lawful and fair. The Directive also enacts this principle concomitant to the criminal procedural law principle of evidentiary *admissibility;* that the processing of evidentiary data does not breach any general principles of law. Hence, while it may be argued

---

[29] Thomas J. Smedinghoff, 'Solving the Legal Challenges of Trustworthy Online Identity', *Computer Law & Security Review* 28, no. 5 (2012): 532.

[30] EDPS, *Opinion on three proposals regarding the Second Generation Schengen Information System (SIS II)* (COM (2005)230 final, COM (2005)236 final and COM (2005)237 final), OJ C 91, 19.04.2006.

[31] Fanny Coudert et al, 'Pervasive Monitoring: Appreciating Citisen's Surveillance as Digital Evidence in Legal Proceedings,' in *4th International Conference on Imaging for Crime Detection and Prevention 2011* (ICDP 2011) (London: IET, 2011).

that lawfulness in general data protection should be understood in the narrow sense of having a *lawful ground* for processing, a narrow reading is not contextually appropriate in policing.[32]

Certain recommendations of the Article 29 Data Protection Working Party can be directly applied to the law enforcement context. For example, a clear definition of the purpose is necessary, whether the context is identity management or law enforcement. Accordingly, the principle of purpose limitation specified in the GDPR and the Directive is the same. Furthermore, a legitimate ground is needed as biometric data is now considered sensitive data, and data security must always be ensured. Moreover, the Directive specifically requires the execution of certain security controls, such as an equipment access control.

The main differences between civilian identity management and investigatory identification, as will be explained below, are particularly noteworthy with respect to *proportionality* and *data minimisation, accuracy, transparency* and the *information on the processing*, as well as *security*. However, it is especially noteworthy that conflicting interests in the by design approach to data protection, not only arise out of the contextual difference of purpose between general and police processing (e.g. ensuring legal evidentiary standards) but also out of conflicts between the data protection principles themselves.

4.4. Proportionality and Data Minimisation

The principle of proportionality applies through the entire lifecycle of processing, from the design and selection of the technical means to the erasure of collected data.[33] In essence, it aims to prohibit behaviours that would otherwise result in indiscriminate, irrelevant, or excessive processing. The European Court of Justice applied the principle of proportionality to biometric passports in *Schwarz v Stadt Bochum*, reviewing the legality, the respect for the essence of privacy and protection of personal data, necessity and proportionality, as well as the objectives and interests at stake.[34] Moreover, with respect to proportionality specifically, several solutions for biometric data processing have been posited.

Limiting the types of crimes and investigations that can motivate the activation of biometric functions is a technical-organisational precondition to enrolling biometric systems in policing. Both the case of *S and Marper v the United Kingdom* and the Working Party's recent Opinion on Directive 2016/680, indicate that

---

[32] Jef Ausloos, 'Giving meaning to lawfulness under the GDPR,' CiTiP Blog, KU Leuven, 2 May 2017. Available at: www.law.kuleuven.be/citip/blog/2761-2/, last accessed 4 March 2018.

[33] Article 29 Data Protection Working Party, *Opinion 01/2014 on the application of necessity and proportionality concepts and data protection within the law enforcement sector* (536/14/EN, WP 211, Adopted 27 February 2014).

[34] C-291/12 *Schwarz v Stadt Bochum* [2013] (CJEU); Article 29 Data Protection Working Party, *Opinion 01/2014,* n 33 at 11–12.

invasive forms of processing should be reserved for serious crimes and situations of imminent danger. Decisions to process for additional biometric data should always be made by a human operator, not via automated decisions by a technical system.[35] Interpretive bodies are also looking at the relative invasiveness of various biometric methods used by police. This was, for example, considered in *S and Marper, Schwarz* and *Opinion 03/2015*, in which the Article 29 Working Party held that genetic profiles should only be generated for the purposes of a specific investigation.[36]

Proportionate collection of data for biometric enrolment is one of the great challenges for proportionality in contemporary policing. It is inherent to the procedure of biometric data processing that the data subject is only identified, and the purpose achieved, at the end of the process, after (i) raw data and sample data is *collected*, (ii) biometric data is *enrolled* by extracting relevant metrics into, (iii) a *biometric template* which can then be (iv) *stored* and (v) *matched* to make the final determination whether templates are similar. This makes it difficult to limit automated collection to certain predefined data subjects[37] and creates a normative conflict between the principles of necessity and proportionality. A dataset contains data with varying degrees of necessity or usefulness for the investigation, but all of it should not be indiscriminately processed. We suggest that novel safeguards based on common normative components to necessity and proportionality, namely *relevance, quality,* and *adequacy* can resolve the conflict between the two principles:

(a) *Explainability* so that the human operator of the biometric system can understand how the system determines the relevance of sources and data that it enrolls.[38]

(b) *Vetting* by a human operator to ensure the relevance and adequacy of the sources and data.

(c) *Homogeneity* so data is derived from similar and predictable sources where the quality, accuracy and reliability of the source can be documented and scaled.

---

[35] Article 29 Data Protection Working Party, *Opinion on some key issues of the Law Enforcement Directive (EU 2016/680)* (17/EN, WP 258, Adopted 29 November 2017).

[36] Article 29 Data Protection Working Party, *Opinion 03/2015 on the draft directive on the protection of individuals with regard to the processing of personal data by competent authorities for the purposes of prevention, investigation, detection or prosecution of criminal offences or the execution of criminal penalties, and the free movement of such data* (3211/15/EN, WP 233, Adopted 1 December 2015), 8.

[37] Speaker Identification Integrated Project, 'D2.1 – Interim Report on PbD (Privacy by Design) design and operations guidelines' SiiP 18 May 2015 (Project Deliverable). Available at: www.siip.eu/filesystem/D2.1.pdf: 44, accessed 3 June 2018.

[38] Erik Zouave and Thomas Marquenie, 'An Inconvenient Truth: Algorithmic Transparency and Accountability in Criminal Intelligence Profiling' *Intelligence and Security Informatics Conference (EISIC)* Athens, Greece 2017; Speaker Identification Integrated Project, n 37 at 46; see De Hert and Lammerant, n 7 at 166.

Deletion of raw data and biometric samples is a prevalent minimisation technique.[39] The suggestion is essentially that the data used in generating a biometric template and associated data should be struck once the template is created. However, it can be particularly difficult for police to determine whether associated data will be valuable to an investigation at the outset of processing. The deletion of raw data can prejudice the *reliability* and the "court-proofness" of online data. As explained by Coudert et al, courts frequently require additional evidence to the biometric data itself, such as indicators of time, location, and surrounding context.[40] As such, there is no easy solution but to address the need of associated data on a case-by-case basis. Deletion may only be possible after the fact (e.g. after a prosecutor has decided the data will not be used) and to restrict the processing of associated data through other mechanisms such as limited user credentials.

Limiting the template scope is a potent design feature which allows a system to store only the necessary metrics for biometric matching.[41] These measurements should also have a plausible, if not empirically supported relevance for achieving identification. In many cases, especially in physical and physiological biometrics such as face and voice recognition, it may be foreseeable which metrics system designers will opt for as the algorithms need to use consistent measurement methods. These biometrics can also have a relatively high degree of automation. Behavioural biometrics through object recognition on the other hand may be better suited for manual processing and is likely to be subject to more flexible and diverse valuation. For example, while ISIS members may wear similar garbs and logos, only a few may have a strong preference for certain sneakers. This type of manual biometric processing will not always correlate neatly to specific biometric template data. Such indicators must also pass over a high contextual threshold and be peculiar to the data subject to become behavioural identifiers in a biometric sense. To the degree that behaviours can be automatically *analyzed*, *evaluated*, or *predicted*, it is likely that such processing will amount to *profiling* in the meaning of data protection law, prior to reaching the threshold for biometric data, resulting in additional risks for the data subject.

Limited and unlinkable biometric matching protects the data subject from unduly recurring and extensive matching of their templates and re-use across different biometric systems.[42] Similarly biometric templates should only have a limited amount of necessary and relevant keywords associated to them so that they are only accessed and matched under strictly necessary conditions.[43] Whereas

---

[39] See Kindt, n 7 at 353; CoE T-PD, *Progress report*, n 8 at para 64; Article 29 Data Protection Working Party, *Opinion 3/2012* n 7 at 7.

[40] See Coudert et al, n 31.

[41] Article 29 Data Protection Working Party, *Opinion 3/2012* n 7 at 4 and 8.

[42] See Kindt, n 7 at 347, 353; Article 29 Data Protection Working Party, *Opinion 3/2012* n 7 at 8 and 22; Speaker Identification Integrated Project, 'D2.1 – Interim Report on PbD (Privacy by Design) Design and Operations Guidelines' SiiP 18 May 2015 (Project Deliverable). Available at: www.siip.eu/filesystem/D2.1.pdf: 20, last accessed 3 June 2018.

[43] CoE T-PD, *Progress report* n 8 at paras 64–65.

it is possible to, for example, encrypt templates to avoid linkability, it would be inconvenient if this irrevocably barred any sharing of templates, such as for international police cooperation and mutual legal assistance.[44] However, the concept of unlinkability should account for the *Schwarz* decision and criminal procedure. Biometric data, as a rule, should be unlinkable between investigations, such as by restricting user credentials, and matching should be based on *urgency*, such as an imminent threat to life, and *seriousness*, such as indicators of criminal behavioural patterns and recurrence of such patterns. In practice, this means that the unlinkability criterion of biometric data proportionality both converges with and informs the criminal procedural requirement of evidentiary admissibility, thus working towards mutual data management goals.

Multiple and revocable identities and pseudonymity should be used as appropriate to ensure that system users have access to relevant information without necessarily identifying data subjects.[45] It should also be possible to revoke pseudonyms and identities that have been compromised or are no longer necessary for investigations.[46]

Safeguards for persons with special needs can be particularly challenging to implement by design. While it may not always be reasonable to train a system to recognise and protect data from minors for example, it must also be noted that such data, even that regarding special disabilities can be crucial in identifying a criminal suspect.

Automated deletion or anonymisation of biometric and associated data necessary for investigations should be pursued according to predetermined time limits. When national data protection law or operational policy does not provide storage limits, predetermined review dates and reminders should be implemented.[47] As emphasised in *S and Marper*, storage periods must be limited and adjusted to the *category* of data subject in question (e.g. whether they are a convicted criminal, a charged suspect, or an uncharged suspect). Deletion is particularly relevant where no charge is brought or where suspects have been acquitted.

As mentioned throughout the recommendations, *access restriction* is an important measure. Comparably to what the court found in *Digital Rights Ireland*, the access to biometric databases should be based upon objective criteria "by which the number of persons authorised to access and subsequently use the data retained is limited to what is strictly necessary in the light of the objective pursued," which then can be implemented by the mentioned technical approaches.[48]

---

[44] Europol, 'Europol Information System (EIS)' Europol, 2017. Available at: www.europol.europa.eu/activities-services/services-support/information-exchange/europol-information-system, last accessed 26 September 2017.

[45] See Kindt, n 7 at 349.

[46] Directive (EU) 2016/680, Arts 4 and 16; Kindt, n 7 at 351.

[47] Article 29 Data Protection Working Party, *Opinion on some key issues of the Law Enforcement Directive* n 35.

[48] C-293/12 *Digital Rights Ireland v Minister for Communications and others* [2014] (CJEU).

4.5. Accuracy

The probabilistic aspect of biometric features is particularly significant in the automation of biometrics as it is frequently focused on reliability in terms of quantifiable, measurable and reproducible outcomes. However, the probabilistic accuracy of biometric data can be impacted by several variables. Consider, for example, external variables such as varying data quality or reliability, including differing angles, lighting, resolution and pixilation of images,[49] changes in physical features due to aging, illness, and injury,[50] or even biometric similarities between individuals such as between twins.[51]

Some biometric operations are inherently less complicated than others and this is clearly reflected in the peculiarities of physical, physiological, and behavioural biometrics. For example, for the physical metrics of facial and silhouette recognition it may comparatively straightforward to determine which physical features to measures (e.g. metrics of spatial relationships such as width of eyebrows and nose length).[52] They are impacted by external interventions and natural processes, such as wounds or aging. The physiological–behavioural spectrum entails a wider array observable characteristics and features, which also entails a greater variance in reliability. On the emotional spectrum, it may be simple to teach machines to classify the words "awful" and "brilliant" as positive and negative sentiments. However, negative context and sarcasm is more complex (e.g. "this 2015 Syrah vintage has the hallmarks of a wine best served to the kitchen drain") as the words may be perceived as neutral or even positive (i.e. "best").[53] As such, Pennebaker observes that automated analysis of theme patterns in language content holds more promise than automated emotion detection.[54] It may be impossible to fully foresee which behaviours sets an individual apart in a group and to build a system that can account for individual peculiarities. In this respect, behavioural analysis of terrorism may be focused on group identities, such as the use of common insignias or logos or preference for certain propagandistic music. Not all distinct behaviours can be reliably translated into metrics.[55] However, behavioural features that can be quantified are often frequently occurring, consistent and comparable data points,

---

[49] Article 29 Data Protection Working Party, *Opinion 3/2012* n 7 at 6 and 22.

[50] CoE T-PD, *Progress report* n 8 at paras 67–70; Anil K. Jain et al, 'Face Matching and Retrieval in Forensics Applications,' *IEEE MultiMedia* 19 no. 1 (2012): 20–28.

[51] Elisa Strickland, 'Can Biometrics ID an Identical Twin?' *IEEE Spectrum: Technology, Engineering, and Science News*, March 2011. Available at: https://spectrum.ieee.org/computing/software/can-biometrics-id-an-identical-twin, last accessed 26 September 2017; Simon A. Cole and Michael Lynch, 'The Social and Legal Construction of Suspects,' *Annual Review of Law and Social Sciences* 2 (2006): 53.

[52] Anil K Jain et al, 'Biometric Identification' *Communications of the ACM 95 43no.2* (2000).

[53] Bo Pang and Lillian Lee, 'Opinion Mining and Sentiment Analysis,' *Foundations and Trends in Information Retrieval* 2 no. 1–2 (2016).

[54] James W Pennebaker, 'Psychological Aspects of Natural Language Use: Our Words, Our Selves,' *Annual Review of Psychology* 54 no. 1 (2003).

[55] Ahmed Awad E Ahmed and Issa Traore, 'Detecting Computer Intrusions Using Behavioral Biometrics,' IEEE Transactions on Pattern Analysis and Machine Intelligence 28, no.2 (2005).

such as author preferences for content themes and grammatical constructs, or the stride length, step cycle and joint angles in analysis of gait.[56]

It is also possible that inaccuracies arise out of variables that are internal to the biometric system. The ground rules and protocols for measuring similarities and establishing identity can be flawed.[57] Moreover, whereas basic statistical and logical assumptions can be correct, the algorithms may have been taught to recognise features with insufficient training data.[58]

Data protection law regulates both aspects of accuracy and collates closely to the procedural law requirement of *reliability*. Firstly, the Regulation and Directive require that the data controllers must take *every reasonable step* to ensure that personal data is accurate and up to date.[59] This implies a general obligation to ensure the correctness in fact as well as correctness in assessment.[60] Secondly, Regulation (EU) 2016/679 also recommends ensuring the appropriateness of algorithms (i.e. mathematical or statistical procedures carried out on data, in particular to ensure accuracy).[61] Finally, the Directive requires that police and criminal justice authorities arrange for clear distinctions between data relating to various categories of data subjects, such as known criminals, suspects, and third parties, and between fact and personal assessment.[62] As such, the law reflects an attempt to ensure factual correctness, methodological faithfulness and consequential accuracy of results. Similarly, the concept of reliability generally reflects the need to establish the veracity of data from which evidence is drawn, that the data is appropriately managed, and consequently can be believed by a court.[63]

Furthermore, the accuracy of biometric systems is related to the principle of proportionality with respects to the *appropriateness* of an interference, the *minimisation* of processing and the *comprehensiveness* of evidence. Again, in *Schwarz*, the European Court of Justice noted that the possibility of spoofing or mistaken identification is not decisive in determining the appropriateness of an identification method. However, this presupposes that law enforcement takes further action and applies additional measures to verify the identity of the individual, or as stated by the Court:

> *A mismatch of that kind will simply draw the competent authorities' attention to the person concerned and will result in a more detailed check of that person in order definitively to establish his identity.*[64]

---

[56] Imed Bouchrika, Michaela Goffredo, John Carter, and Mark Nixon 'On Using Gait in Forensic Biometrics,' *Journal of Forensic Sciences* 56 no. 4 (2011).

[57] See Zouave and Marquenie, 'An Inconvenient Truth: Algorithmic Transparency and Accountability in Criminal Intelligence Profiling,' n 38; Thomas Marquenie and Erik Zouave, 'Speaking Truth to Computational Power: Coding Non-Discrimination by Design in Police Technology,' Presentation, Heraklion, Crete, Next Generation Community Policing, 2017.

[58] CoE T-PD, *Progress report* n 8 at paras 67–70.

[59] Regulation (EU) 2016/679, Art 5; Directive (EU) 2016/680, Art 4.

[60] Ibid, recital 63; Ibid, Art 7.

[61] Ibid, recital 71.

[62] Ibid, Arts 6 and 7.

[63] See Coudert et al, n 31.

[64] C-291/12 *Schwarz v Stadt Bochum*: para 44.

This leads to important conclusions about proportionality and accuracy in biometrics. Firstly, police may rely on less accurate methods for an initial identification if *reasonable*. Secondly, the necessity of verifying that identity can justify additional collection and processing for sounder matching and identification. Thirdly, by way of criminal procedural law, the biometric data can then be comprehensively shared with a court but may not be indiscriminately reused for additional investigations.

Whereas the reasonableness of measures is legally ambiguous, there are practicable industry standards on both the developer side and end-user side that address methodological reliability and information reliability. For example, algorithms can be adjusted to reflect accuracy dilemmas by modifying the degree of confidence in algorithmic outputs,[65] employing the recommendation that legal scholars refer to as *tunable trust*.[66] Trust ultimately reflects the level of confidence in the accuracy of the matching, which is made tunable both through system features such as the amount, varieties, as well as the quality of metrics that are matched, as implied in *Schwarz*. In the legal sense, tunable trust should not only reflect the risk of factually incorrect outputs, but also the varying likelihood and severity of risk that inaccuracy would entail for the rights of the data subject. However, we suggest that while tunable trust is one of few concrete legal recommendations to improve accuracy, it should not only be output- and methods-focused but also input-focused and *scalable*. For example, many law enforcement agencies rely on reliability scales to grade the trustworthiness of sources and information, as well as the content of the information.[67] The scalability reflects the fact that human software designers and system end-users make assumptions about the trustworthiness of the matching (ie. the tunability, as well as the reliability of associated data) and the fact that these assumptions must be made visible by the investigatory process. Hence, *scalable trust* through the entire biometric process can be facilitated by design.

[65] Michael D Breitenstein, Bastian Leibe, Esther Koller-Meier and Luc Van Gool, 'Robust Tracking-by-Detection using a Detector Confidence Particle Filter,' in *2009 IEEE 12th International Conference on Computer Vision (ICCV)*, (IEEE, Kyoto, September 2009) 1515–1522; Sarah Hajian, et al, 'Discrimination- and Privacy-aware Patterns,' *Data Mining and Knowledge Discovery* 29, no.6 (2015): 1740–1741; Krishna Kumar Tripathi, 'Pre-Post Processing of Discriminated Data,' *Special Issue of International Journal of Electronics, Communication & Soft Computing Science and Engineering (National Conference on 'Advanced Technologies in Computing and Networking'-ATCON-2015)* 4, no. 4 (April 2015): 137; Krishna Kumar Tripathi, 'Analysis of Direct and Indirect Discrimination Discovery and Prevention Algorithms in Data Mining,' *International Journal of Engineering Research & Technology* 3, no. 2 (2014): 2422.

[66] See Kindt, n 7 at 354.

[67] United Kingdom College of Policing, 'Intelligence management: Intelligence report' Police UK 2015. Available at: www.app.college.police.uk/app-content/intelligence-management/intelligence-report/, last accessed 26 September 2017.

4.6. Security

Security is a requirement[68] to ensure the overall proportionality, accuracy, and integrity of biometric data processing. The legal imperative for security is the prevention of accidental or unlawful destruction, loss, alteration, disclosure, or transmission of personal data (i.e. *personal data breaches*). Moreover, police data protection law further obligates the execution of certain security controls, such as *equipment access control* to deny unauthorised access to processing equipment.[69] Both of these security imperatives converge with the data management aspects of the reliability requirement under criminal procedural law.

Some of the substantive recommendations to come from the Article 29 Data Protection Working Group and the Council of Europe include:

- *Enrolment security* to ensure that the enrolment process is secure and does not facilitate personal data breaches.[70] This aspect of security can be particularly important in public security processing such as counter-terrorist operations where external third parties may be interested in monitoring or interfering with the processing.[71]

- *Template security* by *limiting the scope of biometric templates* to avoid data and identity overlap between templates so that they can be reproduced and reused indiscriminately or for incompatible purposes.[72] Moreover, templates can further be kept secure by means of encryption and by applying *encryption key security* to keep keys and access to templates secure and confidential.[73]

- *Anti-spoofing* measures ensure that the biometric system can't be tricked to accept wrongful data.[74] A related type of security is *algorithmic security* which aims to prevent algorithms involved in reasoning and matching from unauthorised access, tampering, and duping.[75]

4.7. Transparency and Information on the Processing

As mentioned earlier, while the Regulation requires that processing needs to be lawful, fair, and transparent, the Directive only requires it to be lawful and fair, which already shows a significant difference between civil applications data processing in law enforcement.

---

[68] Regulation (EU) 2016/679, Art 5; Directive (EU) 2016/680, Art 4.
[69] Ibid, Art 29.
[70] Article 29 Data Protection Working Party, *Opinion 3/2012* n 7 at 5.
[71] Ibid at 14–15.
[72] Ibid at 4.
[73] Article 29 Data Protection Working Party, *Working document on biometrics* n 3 at 9.
[74] Article 29 Data Protection Working Party, *Opinion 3/2012* n 7 at 24.
[75] CoE T-PD, *Progress report* n 8 at paras 9, 77.

While it is possible to *inform the data subject* in civil identity management, it is not always possible in policing as it could be detrimental for the outcome of investigations. This does not mean that transparency is completely left out. For example, chapter III of the Directive provides several rights to the data subject, and recital 26 provides that "natural persons should be made aware of risks, rules, safeguards and rights in relation to the processing of their personal data and how to exercise their rights in relation to the processing." However, these rights can be restricted under the Directive to avoid prejudicing legal inquiries, investigations, public or national security, or the rights and freedoms of others. As the EDPS notes, the limitations should be interpreted restrictively, on a case-by-case basis and only for the time necessary; as soon as the limitation is not no longer applicable, the data subjects should be able to exercise their right.[76]

Similarly, researchers can limit the information afforded by not collecting personal data directly from the data subjects themselves. Specifically, Article 14 of the GDPR provides that duties to inform the data subject do not apply to researchers collecting data from another source than the data subject, such as the Internet, if the provision of such information proves impossible or involves a disproportionate effort; potentially limiting transparency already prior to a system's inception. Information regarding biometric data kept to train a police system could facilitate spoofing by informing circumvention methods.

Moreover, transparency measures can and should also be exercised towards additional stakeholders such as the *Data Protection Officers*, the *Supervisory Authorities*, and even courts. In this respect, by design measures to facilitate audits of processing justifications, storage times and statistics, data and data subject categories and statistics, and processing logs, are particularly useful tools of demonstrating oversight towards internal and external oversight mechanisms.[77]

The *right to explanation* and obligations for *algorithmic transparency* are subject to noteworthy debate. Articles 13 to 15 of the GDPR, regarding data subject rights to information and access to processing, further provide that in cases of profiling and automated decisions, the data subject has, what Wachter et al categorise as a right to "*ex ante*" and "*ex post*" information about the *logic* involved; frequently conflated with a right to *explanation of decisions* reached by automated means (recital 71 and Articles 21 to 22).[78] Provisions for logical transparency are not present in the Directive as Article 13 does not require informing the data subject about the existence of profiling, automated decisions, or the logic involved in these. It may therefore be tempting to conclude that there

---

[76] Article 29 Data Protection Working Party, *Opinion on some key issues of the Law Enforcement Directive* n 35.

[77] Erik Zouave and Thomas Marquenie, 'An Inconvenient Truth: Algorithmic Transparency and Accountability in Criminal Intelligence Profiling' n 38.

[78] Sandra Wachter et al, 'Why a Right to Explanation of Automated Decision-making Does Not Exist in the General Data Protection Regulation,' *International Data Privacy Law* 7, no. 2 (2017); Andrew D Selbst and Julia Powles, 'Meaningful Information and the Right to Explanation,' *International Data Privacy Law* 7, no. 4 (2017).

is no obligation to actively ensure "*ex ante*" transparency of algorithmic logic. However, controllers must inform the data subject about their rights of access and rectification. Moreover, while the Directive does not provide for an explicit right to object to automated decisions as in the GDPR, it echoes the obligations for appropriate safeguards, including human intervention. Recital 38 of the Directive further connects the "*ex ante*" and "*ex post*" rights to information, rectification, and human intervention with an explanation to facilitate hearing the subject's view on decisions.

By design compliance relates to mitigations throughout the entirety of processing operations, not just before and after. As posited by the Article 29 Working Party, explanation should be approached as a safeguard not just a right. This makes an *ex ante– ex post* distinction normatively and practically unwork-able for several reasons. Firstly, automation of processing operations, especially (sensitive) biometric data, will not always be provided by law. Human interven-tion must then preempt automation and the *human operator* who intervenes must have an *ex ante* explanation of the system decision logic anyway to know where to intervene. Secondly, when automation is permissible, the data subject, the data protection officer, a supervisory authority and possibly a court may all require *ex post* explanations to determine wrongdoing, arrive at a means of rectifica-tion or provide for legal remedy. Thirdly, both the human operator and a data protection officer may require *continual in-explanations* of, for example, the data sources, logical, and decisions components during the processing to avail them-selves of the appropriateness of sources and correctness of data and assessments. In complex processing of heterogeneous data, it is unlikely that data protection compliance can be automated. Data protection in practice necessarily requires high degrees of human involvement through the entirety of the life cycles of processing operations.

However, algorithmic transparency raises security concerns which must be evaluated before biometric processing techniques are applied. If the logic of biomet-ric systems is publicly divulged, such as through a court or supervisory authority, malicious third parties may predict which sources and data are processed by the system, thus reducing enrollment security, increasing the likelihood of spoofing, and reducing the algorithmic security. This means that the content and form of explanations are not trivial, but require thorough evaluation to ensure an honest, correct and secure rendition.

5. Conclusion

Modern police biometrics, by virtue of its complexity and heterogeneity, chal-lenges the current state of the art for legal recommendations on how to *demonstrate compliance*. The problem is especially prevalent in *technical* compliance with the *by design* obligation that is present in both civilian and police data protection law.

While most of the scholarship and interpretation has focused on providing general recommendations in the civilian context and situations of one-to-one verification rather than one-to-many identification, only some of them can be applied in the police context, and innovative implementation solutions will be needed. The adoption of Directive 2016/679 necessitates reinvigorated efforts from both, interpretative bodies such as the EDPS and academia, in understanding the peculiarities of police data protection and biometrics. The highly contextual and underdeveloped research into by design compliance is especially pressing, as, when developers and end-users of police systems lack appropriate guidance to implement technological safeguards, data subjects exposed to the highest of risks suffer. Moreover, additional research into data protection and criminal procedural law and practice is needed with respects to raw data associated to biometric data, to arrive at more sound data management and prevent unwanted burgeoning biometric databases. The close relationship between behavioural profiling and behavioural biometrics significantly increases the risk to the data subject, necessitating additional comparisons of best practices to decrease the invasiveness of processing operations. Finally, increasing scholarly, policy-maker, and practitioner interests in the right to explanation and logic or algorithmic transparency has readily informed discussions on automated profiling and Big Data processing. However, the issue of transparency and explanation modalities in the security-sensitive context of policing is deserving of research unto itself.

Acknowledgement

This research received funding from the European Union Horison 2020 Framework Programme through DANTE (Detecting and analysing terrorist-related online contents and financing activities) project, H2020- FCT-2015-700367.

2

Grinding Privacy
in the Internet of Bodies

An Empirical Qualitative Research
on Dating Mobile Applications
for Men Who Have Sex with Men

GUIDO NOTO LA DIEGA*

Abstract

The 'Internet of Bodies' (IoB) is the latest development of the Internet of Things. It encompasses a variety of phenomena, from implanted smart devices to the informal regulation of body norms in online communities. This article presents the results of an empirical qualitative research on dating mobile applications for men who have sex with men ('MSM apps'). The pair IoB-privacy is analysed through two interwoven perspectives: the intermediary liability of the MSM app providers and the responsibility for discriminatory practices against the users' physical appearance (aesthetic discrimination). On the one hand, privacy constitutes the justification of the immunities from intermediary liability (so-called safe harbours). Indeed, it is believed that if online intermediaries were requested to play an active role (eg by policing their platforms to prevent their users from carrying out illegal activities) this would infringe the users' privacy. This article calls into question this justification. On the other hand, in an age of ubiquitous surveillance, one may think that the body is the only place where the right to be left alone can be effective. This article contests this view by showing that the users' bodies are

* Guido Noto La Diega, PhD is Senior Lecturer in Cyber Law and Intellectual Property at Northumbria University, where he is European Research Partnerships Coordinator (Law) and Co-convenor of NINSO The Northumbria Internet & Society Research Group. He is also Fellow of the Nexa Center for Internet & Society and Director of Ital-IoT Centre of Multidisciplinary Research on the Internet of Things. The author thanks the anonymous reviewers for the most helpful comments. The Ethics Committee of Northumbria University, Faculty of Business and Law, approved this research.

no longer the sanctuary of privacy. Bodies are observed, measured, and sometimes change as a result of the online experience. This research adopted an empirical qualitative multi-layered methodology which included a focus group, structured interviews, an online survey and the text analysis of the Terms of Service, privacy policies and guidelines of a number of MSM apps.

Keywords

Dating apps, men who have sex with men, privacy, intermediary liability, online discrimination, body image, online platforms

> Beare part with me most straight and pleasant Tree,
> And imitate the Torments of my smart
> Which cruell Love doth send into my heart,
> Keepe in thy skin this testament of me:
>
> Which Love ingraven hath with miserie,
> Cutting with griefe the unresisting part,
> Which would with pleasure soone have learnd loves art,
> But wounds still curelesse, must my rulers bee.
>
> Thy sap doth weepingly bewray thy paine,
> My heart-blood drops with stormes it doth sustaine,
> Love sencelesse, neither good nor mercy knowes
> Pitiles I doe wound thee, while that I
> Unpitied, and unthought on, wounded crie:
> Then out-live me, and testifie my woes.
>
> Lady Mary Wroth, The Countess of Montgomeries Urania (1621)

1. Introduction

This chapter presents the results of an empirical qualitative research on dating mobile apps[1] for men who have sex[2] with men ('MSM apps').[3] The main findings

---

[1] Even though the relevant providers increasingly market these apps as social networks and even though this approach is followed by some scholars (eg Brandon Miller, "'They're the Modern-day Gay Bar": Exploring the Uses and Gratifications of Social Networks for Men who have Sex with Men' *Computers in Human Behavior* 51 (2015): 476), the way most of the analysed apps are designed suggest to prefer the generic 'app' and 'platform' terms, because they often lack dedicated communal spaces where users can actually socialise and interact. Of the analysed apps, only Hornet has proper social features. Chad van de Wiele and Stephanie Tom Tong, 'Breaking Boundaries: The Uses and Gratifications of Grindr' (2014) *UbiComp '14 Proceedings of the 2014 ACM International Joint Conference on Pervasive and Ubiquitous Computing* 619 refer to 'people-nearby applications'. Though it correctly emphasises the geographical element of these apps, it does not take account of those apps (such as PlanetRomeo) that enable users to set up a fictional location. Moreover, with minor exceptions (Joey Chiao-Yin Hsiao

regard privacy as the common denominator of the intermediary liability of the MSM app providers and their responsibility in discriminatory behaviours against the users' physical appearance (aesthetic discrimination). On the one hand, privacy constitutes the justification of the immunities from intermediary liability (so-called safe harbours).[4] Indeed, it is believed that if online intermediaries were requested to play an active role (eg by policing their platforms to prevent their users from carrying out illegal activities, this would infringe the users' privacy).[5] This chapter calls into question this justification. On the other hand, in an age of ubiquitous surveillance, one would think that the body is the only place where the right to be left alone can be effective. This chapter contests this view by showing that the users' bodies and their perceptions are no longer the sanctuary of privacy. Bodies are observed, measured and, more importantly, change as a result of the online experience.

and Tawanna R. Dillahunt, 'People-Nearby Applications: How Newcomers Move Their Relationships Offline and Develop Social and Cultural Capital' (2017) *CSCW '17 Proceedings of the 2017 ACM Conference on Computer Supported Cooperative Work and Social Computing* 26), it does not seem that this phrase has been adopted in the relevant literature.

[2] This is not to say that sex or dating are the only reasons why users engage with this kind of app. Indeed, users resort to these apps (which one can call 'dating apps' for ease of reference) for many reasons, including seeking friendship, entertainment, and preparing for travelling. Elisabeth Timmermans and Elien De Caluwé, 'Development and Validation of the Tinder Motives Scale (TMS)' *Computers in Human Behavior* 70 (2017): 341 present 13 motives for using Tinder. See also Mitchell Hobbs, Stephen Owen, and Livia Gerber, 'Liquid Love? Dating Apps, Sex, Relationships and the Digital Transformation of Intimacy' *Journal of Sociology* 53, no 2 (2017): 271; Sindy R Sumter, Laura Vandenbosch and Loes Ligtenberg, 'Love me Tinder: Untangling Emerging Adults' Motivations for Using the Dating Application Tinder' *Telematics and Informatics* 34, no 2, (2017): 67; Christopher J Carpenter and Bree McEwan, 'The Players of Micro-dating: Individual and Gender Differences in Goal Orientations Toward Micro-dating Apps' *First Monday* 21, no 5 (2016): 1–13.

[3] 'Men who have sex with men' (MSM) is a definition used traditionally in the medical research on HIV (see Michael W. Ross, 'Men Who Have Sex with Men' 4, no 4 *AIDS Care* (1992): 457. Here it is preferred to LGBT (or similar acronyms) because it does not make the assumption that those who use MSM apps identify themselves as gay or bisexual. It is increasingly accepted that two men can have sexual intercourse without necessarily being considered (or considering themselves) as homo- or bisexual (see, for instance, Jane Ward, *Not Gay: Sex Between Straight White Men* (New York: NYU Press, 2015), who shows that sex between men has always been a regular feature of heterosexual life). Queer is equally problematic because originally it was a derogatory term and many people still feel offended by it (one of the respondents to the survey used for this chapter openly complained about the use of the term 'queer', which was initially used as the title of the survey). There is no umbrella term which encompasses all the nuances of sexuality and gender. MSM, for instance, may be seen as exclusive of agender and asexual people. However, apps like Grindr, Hornet and Romeo are hypersexualised and gender-polarised. Therefore, MSM seems the label that better encompasses the vast majority of the users of the analysed apps.

[4] *Scarlet Extended SA v SABAM* [2011] ECR I-11959.

[5] See, for instance, Daphne Keller, 'The Right Tools: Europe's Intermediary Liability Laws and the 2016 General Data Protection Regulation' *SSRN* (8 February 2017): 64. Available at: www.ssrn.com/abstract=2914684, last accessed 25 September 2017, according to whom 'the eCommerce rule against making [online service providers] monitor users' communications protects both information and privacy rights of Internet users'.

1.1. The Internet of Bodies

This research sheds light on a broader phenomenon, that is the Internet of Bodies (IoB),[6] the newest phase of the Internet of Things. It may be natural to think that personal data is that data that we provide (eg when creating a Facebook account) or that third parties can otherwise infer from our behaviour (eg Google's targeted advertising).[7] One may be surprised, however, to discover that our body is becoming one of the most important sources of personal data. Facial recognition is the obvious example, with the iPhone X set to make it ubiquitous.[8] One may, then, realise that with the Internet of Things, our body is increasingly monitored and treated by smart devices (mainly wearables and implantables).[9] Lastly, with artificial enhancement one is witnessing the seamless development from human beings into cyborgs (so-called cyborgisation).[10] These are only some examples of the privacy issues in the IoB, the pair body/privacy gives rise to a number of privacy issues[11]

[6] This seems to be the latest development of the Internet of Things. The IoB was the theme of the Computers, Privacy Data Protection conference of January 2018 (CPDP 2017). The idea of an 'Internet of Bodies' had been suggested, for instance, by Meghan Neal, 'The Internet of Bodies Is Coming, and You Could Get Hacked' (Motherboard Vice, 13 March 2014). Available at: www.motherboard. vice.com/en_us/article/gvyqgm/the-internet-of-bodies-is-coming-and-you-could-get-hacked, last accessed 25 September 2017, who predicted that in 25 years traditional smart devices will be obsolete because '[c]omputers will become so tiny they can be embedded under the skin, implanted inside the body, or integrated into a contact lens and stuck on top of your eyeball.' An example of the increasing demand for an expertise in this field is provided by the research carried out by Ghislaine Boddington at the University of Greenwich (see, for instance, her pioneering workshop on 'Virtual Physical Bodies' (17–19 September 1999), ResCen, Middlesex University, London).

[7] This dichotomy shapes also the Regulation (EU) 2016/679 of the European Parliament and of the Council of 27 April 2016 on the protection of natural persons with regard to the processing of personal data and on the free movement of such data, and repealing Directive 95/46/EC (General Data Protection Regulation or GDPR) [2016] OJ L119/1. See, for instance, Art 13 on the information to be provided where personal data are collected from the data subject and Art 14 on the information to be provided where personal data have not been obtained from the data subject. Building on the GDPR's approach, Gianclaudio Malgieri, 'Property and (Intellectual) Ownership of Consumers' Information: A New Taxonomy for Personal Data' PinG 4, (2016): 133 suggests to distinguish between strong relationship data (data provided directly by customers), intermediate relationship data (data observed or inferred and related to the present life of consumers), and weak relationship data (predictive data).

[8] For some critical remarks, see Jesse Emspak, 'Should Apple iPhone X Trust Facial Recognition for Security?' *Scientific American* (22 September 2017). Available at: www.scientificamerican.com/article/ should-apple-iphone-x-trust-facial-recognition-for-security/, last accessed 25 September 2017.

[9] Even though smart devices are increasingly implanted in our bodies, Katina Michael, 'Mental Health, Implantables, and Side Effects' *IEEE Technology and Society Magazine* 34, no 2 (2015): 5, 6, denounces the 'lack of qualitative research being conducted across the spectrum of implantable devices in the health sector'. On biometrics and physical privacy, see Nancy Yue Liu, *Bio-Privacy: Privacy Regulations and the Challenge of Biometrics* (Abingdon: Routledge, 2012) 79–81.

[10] cf Deborah Lupton, 'Donna Haraway: The Digital Cyborg Assemblage and the New Digital Health Technologies' in *The Palgrave Handbook of Social Theory for the Sociology of Health and Medicine* edited by Fran Collyer (Basingstoke: Palgrave Macmillan, 2015) 567.

[11] See, for instance, Jeffrey H. Reiman, 'Privacy, Intimacy, and Personhood' *Philosophy & Public Affairs* 6, no 1 (1976): 26, 43, where he says 'I come to view myself as the kind of entity that is entitled to the social ritual of privacy. That is, I come to believe that this body is mine in the moral sense.'

and much research is needed to give 'form to the amorphous by joining it to the inchoate'.[12]

What one would have not expected until recent times is that artificial intelligence may enable researchers to extract personal data from one's appearance. A first, ethically questionable, step was made by those scholars[13] who used supervised machine learning to infer criminal tendencies from the facial traits, thus allegedly showing that 'criminals have a significantly higher degree of dissimilarity in facial appearance than *normal* (*sic!*) population'.[14] This kind of research may resemble Cesare Lombroso's theories[15] whereby 'criminals were inherently and physically different from others'.[16] Suffice to say that those theories were greatly valued during Mussolini's fascist administration.[17] Taking a Law and Literature approach, then, one may think of *Minority Report*'s[18] mutants whose clairvoyance powers allowed the Precrime Division to arrest suspects before they committed any crime.

More recently, it has been claimed[19] that, thanks to deep neural networks, it is possible to identify sexual orientation just by analysing one's traits. According to those authors, if one has small jaw and chin, slim eyebrows, long nose, and large foreheads, one is likely to be a homosexual man, while the opposite would apply to homosexual women (bigger jaws, thicker eyebrows, etc.).[20] Even leaving aside accuracy issues, it is not clear how this research copes, if at all, with ethnic minorities. A late nineteenth-century precedent of this approach is constituted by Havelock Ellis'[21] effort to position the 'homosexual' body as visually

---

[12] Moira Gatens, 'Privacy and the Body: The Publicity of Affect' in *Privacies: Philosophical Evaluations* edited by Beate Rössler (Palo Alto: Stanford University Press, 2004) 113 (the amorphous referring to privacy and the inchoate to the body). Gatens' analysis, albeit interesting, is here overlooked because of its philosophical and literary take.

[13] Xiaolin Wu and Xi Zhang, 'Automated Inference on Criminality using Face Images' *arXiv*, 13 November 2016. Available at: www.arxiv.org/pdf/1611.04135v1.pdf, last accessed 25 September 2017.

[14] Ibid at 2.

[15] The main reference is to Cesare Lombroso, *L'uomo delinquente* (Milan: Hoepli, 1876). For a scholarly translation, see Cesare Lombroso, *Criminal man* (Durham: Duke University Press, Eng tr, 2006).

[16] Suzanne Bell, 'Lombroso, Cesare (1835–1909), in *A Dictionary of Forensic Science* (Oxford: OUP, 2012). The system was refined by Alphonse Bertillon, who developed the first systematic biometric method to supposedly identify criminals.

[17] See Mary Gibson, 'Forensic Psychiatry and the Birth of the Criminal Insane Asylum in Modern Italy' *International Journal of Law and Psychiatry* 37, no 1 (2014): 117, 118.

[18] Philip K. Dick, *The Minority Report* (1956; Gollancz: London, 2002).

[19] Yilun Wang and Michal Kosinski, 'Deep Neural Networks are More Accurate Than Humans at Detecting Sexual Orientation from Facial Images' (Open Science Framework, 7 September 2017). Available at: www.osf.io/zn79k/, last accessed 25 September 2017. On some shortcomings and biases of this research see Antonio Casilli, 'Une intelligence artificielle révèle les préjugés anti-LGBT (et anti-plein d'autres gens) des chercheurs de Stanford' (*Casilli*, 9 September 2017). Available at: www.casilli.fr/2017/09/09/une-intelligence-artificielle-revele-les-prejuges-des-chercheurs-de-stanford-envers-gays-biais-racisme/, last accessed 25 September 2017.

[20] See Wang and Kosinski, n 19 at 6.

[21] Henry Havelock Ellis and John Addington Symonds, *Sexual Inversion* (1897, Basingstoke: Palgrave Macmillan, 2008).

distinguishable from the 'normal' body through anatomical markers.[22] One can only imagine how these technologies could be used in any of the 15 countries where homosexuality is still punished with the death penalty.[23]

In the IoB, the online presence of the bodies is changing the Internet. However, the opposite applies as well. For instance, recently, researchers[24] have shown that looking at photos of underweight women affects the viewer's mind in 15 minutes. In the IoB, the Internet changes bodies and their perception.

This research focuses on two aspects of the IoB. First, how the body and beauty ideals are affected by online dating platforms. Second, to what extent the privacy and freedom of expression of the users of these platforms is violated by the latter's behaviour. This topic is interwoven with the one of the intermediary liability, since the traditional justification for the immunities and the absence of a general monitoring obligation revolves around privacy and freedom of expression.

1.2. Relevance and Contribution to Knowledge

Location-based (or geo-networking) dating apps are an increasingly important part of the IoB and of the Internet of Things; they are, indeed, 'a form of ubiquitous computing".[25] The choice of dating apps over other mobile apps is justified because they 'encourage the sharing of more personal information than conventional social media apps, including continuous location data'.[26] The case study presented in this chapter regards MSM apps, because they constitute the ideal leans through which to look at privacy as both the justification for the immunities from intermediary liability, as well as bodily privacy. As to the first point, there are some high-profile cases regarding the intermediary liability of MSM apps.[27] As to the second, while the body and its perception are at the centre of the mating ritual in general,[28]

---

[22] Siobhan Somerville, 'Scientific Racism and the Emergence of the Homosexual Body' *Journal of the History of Sexuality*, 5, no 2 (1994): 243, 248–249.

[23] Homosexuality is punished with the death penalty in Afghanistan, Brunei, Mauritania, Sudan, Northern Nigeria, Yemen, Saudi Arabia, Somalia, Iran, Pakistan, Islamic State of Iraq and the Levant, Somaliland, Palestine (Gaza), United Arab Emirates, and Qatar. However, there is no evidence of enforcement in the last two countries; see, Aengus Carroll (ed), *State-sponsored Homophobia* (Geneva: ILGA, 11th edn, 2016) 37.

[24] Jean-Luc Jucker et al, 'The Effect of the Thin Body Ideal in a Media-naïve Population' *bioXriv*, 14 August 2017. Available at: www.biorxiv.org/content/biorxiv/early/2017/08/14/176107.full.pdf, last accessed 25 September 2017.

[25] See Van de Wiele, n 1 at 619.

[26] Jody Farnden, Ben Martini, and Kim-Kwang Raymond Choo, 'Privacy Risks in Mobile Dating Apps' (2015). Available at: www.arxiv.org/abs/1505.02906, last accessed 3 June 2018.

[27] See, eg, *Herrick v Grindr, LLC*, No 1:2017cv00932 – Document 63 (SDNY 2018); *Saponaro v Grindr, LLC*, 93 F Supp 3d 319, 323 (DNJ 2015).

[28] This seems to be true both for human beings and some animals; cf Michelle E.H. Helinski and Laura C. Harrington, 'Male Mating History and Body Size Influence Female Fecundity and Longevity of the Dengue Vector *Aedes aegypti*' *J Med Entomol* 48, no 2 (2011): 202.

this seems particularly true for most MSMs.[29] Indeed, it has been noted that the 'body image issues of gay men are wildly out of control'.[30] Many MSMs believe they do not deserve a relationship because their body is not attractive enough; it would seem that it is 'all about the body'.[31] Scholars have consistently found that there is 'greater appearance potency in the gay subculture'.[32] This research leaves out lesbian users because it has been proved that the physical appearance plays a key role in men's dating, less so in women's.[33] Finally, the choice of this case is justified not only by the importance of the body within the MSM community, but also by the role of dating apps in the said community. Indeed, most same-sex couples met online,[34] and '(t)he most striking difference between the way same-sex couples meet and the way heterosexual couples meet is the dominance of the Internet among same-sex couples'.[35,36] The online dating market is growing, generating revenues of US$1,383 million in 2018.[37] In the US, which is the main market,[38]

---

[29] Suffice to say, that studies that compared homosexual and heterosexual men found that in homosexual men the discrepancy between their current body and the body they believed they should have to attract a dating partner is significantly greater than the discrepancy between their current and ideal body types. See Lauren M. Fussner and April R. Smith, 'It's Not Me, It's You: Perceptions of Partner Body Image Preferences Associated with Eating Disorder Symptoms in Gay and Heterosexual Men' *Journal of Homosexuality* 62, no 10 (2015): 1329. On a pop note, it is no coincidence that Grindr's first web series – 'What the Flip' – is focusing on body shaming and discrimination against Asian men. See INTO Editors, 'Dating as a Different Body Type' *Into*, 14 September 2017. Available at: intomore.com/videos/dating-as-a-different-body-type/57402b4c71dc4258, last accessed 27 September 2017.

[30] Alan Downs, *The Velvet Rage: Overcoming the Pain of Growing Up Gay in a Straight Man's World* (Cambridge: Da Capo Press, 2012) 190.

[31] Ibid at 190.

[32] Glen S. Jankowski et al, "Appearance Potent'? A Content Analysis of UK Gay and Straight Men's Magazines' *Body Image* 11, no 4 (2014): 474.

[33] Participant to a recent survey indicated that it was 'desirable' or 'essential' that their potential partner was good-looking (92% vs 84%) and had a slender body (80% vs 58%). Melissa R. Fales et al, 'Mating Markets and Bargaining Hands: Mate Preferences for Attractiveness and Resources in Two National U.S. Studies' *Personality and Individual Differences* 88 (2016): 78.

[34] Michael J. Rosenfeld and Reuben J. Thomas, 'Searching for a Mate: The Rise of the Internet as a Social Intermediary' *American Sociological Review* 77, no 4 (2012): 523. They also found that partnership rate has increased during the internet era for same-sex couples, but '(u)nlike the partnership rate of gays and lesbians, overall adult partnership appears not to have changed during the Internet era' (ibid at 542).

[35] Ibid at 532. The cited study would probably need an update; it would not be surprising if the situation had changed due to the use of apps like Tinder and OKCupid becoming commonplace. Future research will address these questions.

[36] The relationship between privacy and MSM can be analysed from other angles. For instance, it has been noted that the European Court of Human Rights has advanced the protection of LGBT people mainly relying on the right to privacy (eg European Convention of Human Rights, Art 8. See, for instance, *Oliari v Italy* Apps nos 18766/11 and 36030/11 (ECHR, 31 July 2015). This is the very reason why the court never recognised the right to marriage, which is a right on the public stage. See Frances Hamilton, 'The Case for Same-Sex Marriage Before the European Court of Human Rights' *Journal of Homosexuality*, 26 September 2017. Available at: www.tandfonline.com/doi/full/10.1080/00918369.2017.1380991, last accessed 27 September 2017.

[37] 'Online dating' (*Statista*, 2018). Available at: www.statista.com/outlook/372/100/online-dating/worldwide#, last accessed 2 June 2018.

[38] Revenues of US$590 million have been generated in the US in 2018 (ibid).

the only MSM app in the top 10 is Grindr (Fig. 1). The focus on this app is also explained by the fact that while Tinder and Grindr are the dating apps with more weekly active users in the world, Grindr is ranked higher than Tinder in terms of users' engagement.[39] Additionally, it has been recently uncovered that Grindr shares HIV status data and sexual preferences data with third parties,[40] which raised the question to what extent can long and illegible Terms of Service, privacy policies, guidelines, etc. (collectively 'legals') justify such practices, especially now that the General Data Protection Regulation (GDPR)[41] is in force.

Figure 2.1 Online dating market share in the US[42]

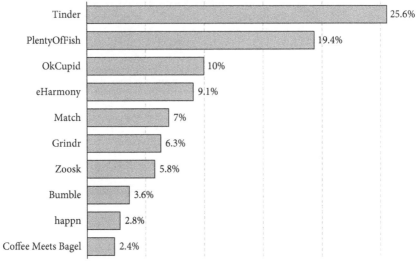

[39] 7Park Data 'Love in the Time of Apps: Dating. (*7Park Data*, February 2017) Available at: info.7parkdata.com/dating-report 2017?portalId=447976&hsFormKey=e8588e233d311b2c5434d589 9dfe5b99&submissionGuid=d751da3e-09d9-4aeb-9503-db6b1f8271ae#wizard_module_2450048960 88576082163332572113761706729, last accessed 25 September 2017.

[40] The Norwegian Consumer Council filed a complaint against Grindr because of this. *Forbrukerrådet*, complaint of 3 April 2018. The text is available in English at www.fil.forbrukerradet.no/wp-content/uploads/2018/04/2018-04-03-complaint-grindr.pdf, last accessed 3 May 2018.

[41] Regulation (EU) 2016/679 of the European Parliament and of the Council of 27 April 2016 on the protection of natural persons with regard to the processing of personal data and on the free movement of such data, and repealing Directive 95/46/EC (General Data Protection Regulation) [2016] OJ L 119/1.

[42] 'Most Popular Dating Apps in the United States as of April 2016, by Market Share' (*Statista*, 2016). Available at; www.statista.com/statistics/737081/popular-online-dating-market-share-users-monthly/, last accessed 2 June 2018.

This chapter contributes to the advancement of existing literature in a twofold way. First, by assessing the privacy implications of location-based online services beyond the location data[43] or the cross-border issues.[44] Second, more generally socio-legal research on MSM apps is still in its infancy,[45] and the findings regarding traditional dating sites do not necessarily apply to mobile apps, which privilege picture-based selection, minimise room for textual self-description and draw upon existing Facebook profile data.[46] Even though some scholars[47] are carrying

[43] For the focus on location data and purpose limitation, see the interesting work of Michael Herrmann et al, 'Privacy in Location-Based Services: An Interdisciplinary Approach' SCRIPTed 13, no 2 (2016): 144. On trilateration to figure out the location of the targeted victim even when the 'hide distance' function is enabled see Nguyen Phong Hoang, Yasuhito Asano, and Masatoshi Yoshikawa, 'Your Neighbors are My Spies: Location and other Privacy Concerns in Dating Apps' 18th International Conference on Advanced Communication Technology (2016): 715. See also Hao Dang, Stephanie Cai, and Xuanning Lang, 'Location-based Gay Communication: An Empirical Study of Smartphone Gay Apps Use in Macau' (*SSRN*, 27 April 2013). Available at: ssrn.com/abstract=2257253, last accessed 27 September 2017 about location-based services for MSM, but they overlook the privacy-related issues.

[44] See Arno R. Lodder, 'When 'There' Can be Everywhere: On the Cross-Border Use of WhatsApp, Pandora, and Grindr' *European Journal of Law and Technology* 5, no 2, (2014): 1. A partial exception is Kristian Møller Jørgensen, 'The Mediatization of Public Sex Cultures in the Case of the Hook-up App Grindr' (ECREA 2016 conference, Prague, November 2016), in that he states that '(a)long with the normalisation of geo-locative dating and hook-up practices in the mainstream public (…) imaginations of sexual privacy and indeed publicness seem to be changing'. However, in that paper privacy is understood as a sociological concept and the real focus is on publicness. Similarly, Evangelos Tziallas, 'Gamified Eroticism: Gay Male 'Social Networking' Applications and Self-Pornography' *Sexuality & Culture* 19 (2015): 759, 769 conceptualises the interactions on MSM apps as porn and asserts that this fundamentally altered inter alia the meaning of privacy.

[45] Conversely, health-related research is already quite developed. In particular, some scholars underline that Grindr and similar apps increase the risk of HIV/STIs transmission. See, for instance, ER Burrell et al, 'Use of the Location-based Social Networking Application GRINDR as a Recruitment Tool in Rectal Microbicide Development Research' *AIDS and Behavior* 16 (2012): 1816; Raphael Landovitz et al, 'Epidemiology, Sexual Risk Behavior, and HIV Prevention Practices of Men who Have Sex with Men Using GRINDR in Los Angeles, California' *Journal of Urban Health* 90, no 4 (2013): 729; Hailey Winetrobe et al, 'Associations of Unprotected Anal Intercourse with Grindr-met Partners among Grindr-using Young Men who have Sex with Men in Los Angeles' *AIDS Care* (2014): 1. More recently, Lixuan Zhang, Iryna Pentina and Wendy Fox Kirk, 'Who Uses Mobile Apps to Meet Strangers: The Roles of Core Traits and Surface Characteristics' *Journal of Informational Privacy and Security* 19 (2017): 1–19 have underlined that there are mainly two streams of research around dating apps. On the one hand, studies of the motivations for using this kind of apps (eg Hobbs, n 2)). On the other hand, research on who uses dating apps (eg Barış Sevi, Tuğçe Aral and Terry Eskenazi, 'Exploring the Hook-Up App: Low Sexual Disgust and High Sociosexuality Predict Motivation to use Tinder for Casual Sex' *Personality and Individual Differences* 133 (2017): 17–20.

[46] Christoph Lutz and Giulia Ranzini, 'Where Dating Meets Data: Investigating Social and Institutional Privacy Concerns on Tinder' *Social Media + Society* 3, no 1 (2017): 1.

[47] See Chris Ashford, 'Queer Theory, Cyber-ethnographies and Researching Online Sex Environments' *C.T.L.* 18, no 3 (2009): 297; see Dang (n 43); Lodder (n 44); Kyle Jamie Fisher, 'Grindr: An Investigation into How the Remediation of Gay 'Hook Up' Culture is Converging Homosexual Digital Spaces and Heterosexual Physical Spaces' (*Academia.edu*). Available at: www.academia.edu/29176885/Grindr_An_investigation_into_how_the_remediation_of_gay_hook_up_culture_is_converging_homosexual_digital_spaces_and_heterosexual_physical_spaces, last accessed 27 September 2017; Joseph Lawless, 'The Politicizing of the Femme Fatale: Negotiations of Gender Performativity in the Digital Space' (Columbia Law School, Autumn 2015). Available at: www.academia.edu/28712568/

out socio-legal research on MSM apps, no academic research has ever explored privacy and intermediary liability in MSM dating apps,[48] not even with regard to non-MSM[49] dating apps.[50] Third, by reflecting on exclusionary practices that go beyond the traditional categories taken into account by discrimination laws.

1.3. Research Methods

The chapter adopts a multi-layered empirical qualitative methodology. The first was a study of privacy, intermediary liability, and discrimination laws in the EU, seen from the perspective of the UK implementations. Second, a focus group was organised with users of MSM apps to understand the main issues they encountered during the online dating experience, with particular regard to privacy, intermediary liability and aesthetic discrimination. Third, text analysis was conducted with regards to the legals of 14 apps (47 documents). Alongside a content analysis, this measured the readability of the legals of Grindr, PlanetRomeo and Hornet using the tests performed by the software Readable.io (ie the Flesch-Kincaid Grade Level, the Flesch-Kincaid Reading Ease, the Gunning-Fog Score, the Coleman-Liau Index, the SMOG Index, the Automated Readability test, the Spache Score, and the New Dale-Chall Score).[51] The purpose of this phase was to assess whether the practices lamented by the participants to the focus group as a contractual basis and whether the legals were enforceable in light of their readability and content. The fourth methodological layer was an online survey (hereinafter the 'MSM survey') distributed over a semester[52] to 54 users of MSM apps recruited passively[53] via

The_Politicizing_of_the_Femme_Fatale_Negotiations_of_Gender_Performativity_in_the_Digital_ Space, last accessed 27 September 2017; Kristian Møller Jørgensen, 'Boundary Works of Grindr Research: Sociological and Queer Perspectives on Shame and Intimacy' (AoIR 2016 conference, Berlin, October 2016).

[48] On privacy and MSM apps, however, see Hoang, n 43.

[49] Since MSMs do not necessarily identify as non-heterosexual, it would be inaccurate to describe apps such as Tinder and POF as 'heterosexual' dating apps.

[50] However, privacy and non-MSM dating apps there is a growing body of literature. See, for instance, Rory D. Bahadur, 'Individual Sovereignty, Freer Sex and Diminished Privacy: How an Informed and Realistic Modern Sexual Morality Provides Salvation from Unjustified Shame' *Elon Law Review* 8, no 2 (2016): 245, on the increasingly publicised heterosexual female sexuality, mainly related to dating apps and, more generally, the internet. See also Farnden (n 26); Lutz (n 46); Kath Albury et al, 'Data Cultures of Mobile Dating and Hook-up Apps: Emerging Issues for Critical Social Science Research' *Big Data & Society* 4, no 2 (2017): 1.

[51] Once the test, was performed, it became clear that the Spache Score and the New Dale-Chall Score are not suitable for the analysis of the legals because they are designed with elementary school children in mind.

[52] From 20 March 2017 to 20 September 2017.

[53] The participation to the survey has not been actively solicited. The potential participants contacted this author, whose profile clearly stated the research-related purpose of the account. After some introductory explanations on the survey, the relevant link was sent only after the potential respondent expressed their agreement. The survey could not be completed without reading and accepting the participant information and debrief sheet.

an ad-hoc account active on Grindr,[54] PlanetRomeo, Hornet and Scruff.[55] The questionnaire had 17 questions about three main points: the users' expectations about privacy and liability of platforms; users' attitude towards and experience of the legals; and their aesthetic discrimination experiences. Lastly, structured interviews were carried out with spokespeople of two MSM app providers. This had a twofold function. First, to collect data on practices which are not documented in the 'legals' (eg in terms of take-down policies). Second, to inform the MSM app providers of the users' concerns to raise awareness and in an attempt to have them adopt fairer policies.

The sample and the research are not and do not aim to be representative of the whole MSM population. Unlike quantitative research, qualitative methods do not aim to be representative of the entire relevant population, nor to present results that could be universally generalised.[56] Therefore, despite the sample not being representative, the findings are worth presentation because clear trends have been emerging during the collection and analysis of the data. Future research should attempt to broaden the sample by using a larger number of apps to recruit participants and by changing the location from where these are accessed. The possibility of a comparison between MSM apps and non-MSM apps may also be explored. Qualitative methods focus on saturation, as in obtaining a comprehensive understanding by continuing to sample until no new substantive information is acquired.[57] In terms of sampling method, purposive sampling was chosen, a'a technique widely used in qualitative research for the identification and selection of information-rich cases for the most effective use of limited resources'.[58]

2. The Internet Entering the Body Aesthetic Discrimination

Traditionally, the body and the home are the main examples of private 'places' where people are entitled to their privacy. The body is seen as a place of privacy,

---

[54] The main focus is on Grindr, which is the most important MSM app, described as 'the hook-up app that my sexual biography as a gay man is inseparable from' (Jørgensen, n 44 at 1).

[55] A poll with over 2,000 respondents found that Grindr, Scruff, Hornet, Tinder, Jack'd, and PlanetRomeo are the most used MSM apps (Travel Gay Asia and Gay Star News, 'Gay dating apps survey 2016' (*Travel Gay Asia*, 1 December 2016). Available at: www.travelgayasia.com/gay-dating-apps-survey-2016/, last accessed 28 September 2017. This author had created an ad hoc profile to also study Jack'd, but the company suspended his account, possibly because it was deemed to be an attempt at unauthorised advertising. Tinder was left out because it is not limited to MSM dating.

[56] See, eg, BL Berg and H Lune, *Qualitative Research Methods for the Social Sciences* (8th edn, Boston: Pearson 2011).

[57] M.B. Miles and A.M. Huberman, *Qualitative Data Analysis: An Expanded Sourcebook* (2nd edn, London: Sage 1994) 26.

[58] MQ Patton, *Qualitative Research and Evaluation Methods* (3rd edn, London: Sage 2002) 36 as cited by Lawrence A Palinkas et al, 'Purposeful Sampling for Qualitative Data Collection and Analysis in Mixed Method Implementation Research' *Administration and Policy in Mental Health and Mental Health Services Research* 42, no 5 (2015): 533.

for instance in those countries where nudity is restricted to private environments or where security checks cannot be overly invasive.[59] It has been underlined, moreover, that many aspects of the body are privacy sensitive, though there are significant changes depending on the cultural context (eg the female body in most Islamic cultures).[60] In an age of surveillance and ubiquitous computing, however, the privacy expectations are changing profoundly, to the point that people have to endure privacy invasions even in their own bodies, be it in the form of implanted smart devices or, more broadly, as an intrusion in the perception of one's own body. In the IoB, the online presence of bodies is changing the Internet and, accordingly, the Internet is changing bodies. The focus of this section is on exclusionary practices based on the physical appearance, going under the name of aesthetic discrimination.

One of the main issues which emerged during this research is that MSM apps are places of exclusion base on the users' physical appearance. Profile descriptions on MSM apps are significantly characterised by the exclusion of entire segments of population based on their race and appearance (see Figure 2.1).[61] It is, therefore, questionable why racist profile descriptions on dating apps are considered unacceptable (and rightly so) but 'using an automatic "filter" to exclude certain kinds of bodies does not'.[62] Even more problematic than the filters, used to view only users that reflect certain characteristics (eg 'twinks'), are the profile descriptions that overtly exclude users both for racist and aesthetic reasons. This research shows that these facts have important consequences in terms of body image and self-esteem. This is in line with the research on the use of nudity in advertising, which proves that '(s)carcely dressed models had a negative effect on individuals' body esteem compared to dressed model'.[63] It has been shown[64] that there is an abundance of MSM users who rely on photos where their flesh and skin are

---

[59] See Judee K. Burgoon, 'Privacy and Communication' in *Communication Yearbook* 6 edited by Michael Burgoon (London: Routledge, 1982) 206, 213; J.L. Cohen, 'Rethinking Privacy: Autonomy, Identity, and the Abortion Controversy' in Jeff Alan Weintraub and Krishan Kumar, *Public and Private in Thought and Practice: Perspectives on a Grand Dichotomy* (Chicago: University of Chicago Press, 1997) 161; Rosamund Scott, *Rights, Duties and the Body. Law and Ethics of the Maternal-Fetal Conflict* (Oxford: Hart, 2002) 195.

[60] Philip Brey, 'The Importance of Workplace Privacy' in *The Ethics of Workplace Privacy* edited by Sven Ove Hansson and Elin Palm (Bern: Pieter Lang, 2005) 97, 102.

[61] As noted by Tom Penney, 'Faceism and Fascism in Gay Online Dating' (*32 Queer Networks*, 2017) Available at: ww.dpi.studioxx.org/en/no/32-queer-networks/faceism-and-fascism-gay-online-dating per centE2 per cent80 per centA8, last accessed 27 September 2017, it 'is startling how aggressively defensive and entitled profiles are; 'masc only, no fems', 'don't contact me if ...', 'no Asians', which altogether constructs an environment of hostility and exclusion before-the-fact.'

[62] Senthorun Raj, 'Grindring for Justice' (Right Now, 21 March 2016). Available at: www.rightnow. org.au/essay/grindring-for-justice/, last accessed 27 September 2017.

[63] Nathalie Dens, Patrick De Pelsmacker and Wim Jannsens, 'Effects of Scarcely Dressed Models in Advertising on Body Esteem for Belgian Men and Women' *Sex Roles* 60, nos 5–6 (2009): 366.

[64] Carl Bonner-Thompson, "The Meat Market': Production and Regulation of Masculinities on the Grindr Grid in Newcastle upon-Tyne, UK' *Gender, Place & Culture* (2017): 3.

exposed (so-called hypersexualised masculinities).[65] Along the same lines, a study found that MSM magazines feature 'more images of men that were appearance ideal, nude and sexualized than the straight men's magazines'.[66] And dating has become akin to advertising; to put it in a user of MSM apps' words 'any dating profile sort of thing is a place for advertising, it's selling yourself essentially, you obviously, you're using that profile with an aim in mind, so it's a market, it's a meat market essentially'.[67] In conclusion, both in dating and in advertising the common exposition of nudity produce negative effects on the body and self-esteem.[68]

Figure 2.2 Screenshot of a Scruff's user profile description

This research started with a focus group where some users of MSM apps informed this author that these apps were making them feel as if their bodies were wrong. One of them, a self-perceived 'stocky' guy in his thirties, stated that his profile pictures were blocked because he showed his torso and tummy, but similar pictures of users whom he considered 'fitter' were accepted by the same apps. A virtual tour carried out by this author on Grindr seemed to confirm that fit shirt-less torsos constituted a significant number of the profile pictures displayed. One of the aspects that this research aimed at finding out was whether the participants to the focus group had been merely unlucky or whether these apps were actually discriminating against users with a certain kind of body.

---

[65] Ibid.
[66] See Jankowski et al, n 33 at 474.
[67] See Bonner-Thompson, n 64 at 1.
[68] This is not to say that nudity in itself cannot be considered positive in terms of liberation from social constructions and taboos.

As to the other participants of the focus group, who stated that they did not feel at ease with their own body as a consequence of the use of MSM apps,[69] this work endeavoured to resolve a dilemma. In simple terms, do MSM exclude interactions with users whose body is not fit, young, white, (at least seemingly) abled, and masculine because they are naturally inclined to do so or do the apps play a role in creating or at least reinforcing a specific type of body which is deemed acceptable and sexually desirable, while excluding those who do not conform to the proposed model? Recently, research confirmed that 'exclusion is found in the way users celebrate and reinforce ideas of traditional masculinity and denigrate and reinforce stereotypic ideas about femininity embodied by some gay men'.[70] While treating a person differently on the basis of the colour of their skin is the paradigm of discrimination (and, therefore, discrimination laws may provide some protection to users belonging to ethnic minorities), no such thing is accepted with regards to the 'aesthetic discrimination', that is unfavourable treatment based on a person's appearance. There is a growing discussion about phenomena such as body shaming,[71] fat shaming/fattism,[72] ageism,[73]

---

[69] Body dissatisfaction associated with dating is not exclusive to MSM relationships. For instance, it was found that there is 'a relationship between importance of popularity with boys and body dissatisfaction (which is) fully mediated by the belief that boys see thinness as important in rating girls' attractiveness.' (Susan J. Paxton et al, 'Body Dissatisfaction, Dating, and Importance of Thinness to Attractiveness in Adolescent Girls' *Sex Roles* 53, nos 9–10 (2005): 663; similarly, see Carolyn Tucker Halpern et al, 'Effects of Body Fat on Weight Concerns, Dating, and Sexual Activity: A Longitudinal Analysis of Black and White Adolescent Girls' *Sex Roles* 35, no 3 (1999): 721. Research suggests that 'homosexual men and women have similar mate preferences to heterosexual men and women by showing more dating desire for attractive and high social status persons' (Thao Ha et al, 'Effects of Attractiveness and Status in Dating Desire in Homosexual and Heterosexual Men and Women' *Archives of Sexual Behavior* 41, no 3 (2012): 673.) Future research should further address similarities and differences between MSM and heterosexual dating.

[70] Michael D. Bartone, 'Jack'd a Mobile Social Networking Application and Gender Performance: A Site of Exclusion within a Site of Inclusion' *Journal of Homosexuality* 65, no 4 (2018): 501. The cited research, however, does not clearly allocate the responsibility for this phenomenon.

[71] For a recent research that sheds new light on the issue, see Karen Lumsden and Heather Morgan, 'Media Framing of Trolling and Online Abuse: Silencing Strategies, Symbolic Violence, and Victim Blaming' *Feminist Media Studies* 17, no 6 (2017): 926–940, that focus on online behaviours related to trolling including body shaming. For an application to the MSM realm, see Supercup, 'The Ugly Truth of Body Shaming in the Gay Press' (*Huffington Post*, 18 April 2017). Available at: www.huffingtonpost.com/entry/the-ugly-truth-of-body-shaming-in-the-gay-press_us_58f63545e4b048372700dba, last accessed 25 September 2017.

[72] Jason S. Wrench and Jennifer L. Knapp, 'The Effects of Body Image Perceptions and Sociocommunicative Orientations on Self-Esteem, Depression, and Identification and Involvement in the Gay Community' *Journal of Homosexuality* 55, no 3 (2008): 471 denounced the negative effects of this phenomenon and noted that males report 'higher levels of image fixation, anti-fat attitudes, dislike of fat people, weight locus of control (indicating internal loci), physical discrimination, weight discrimination, and depression' (ibid, 496).

[73] See the pioneering work of Raul C. Schiavi, *Aging and Male Sexuality* (Cambridge: CUP, 1999) and the more recent Imani Woody, 'Aging Out: A Qualitative Exploration of Ageism and Heterosexism Among Aging African American Lesbians and Gay Men' *Journal of Homosexuality* 61, no 1 (2013): 145.

internalised homophobia[74] (that usually victimises camp or feminine guys), and ableism.[75] However, they are treated as something radically and ontologically different to racial discrimination. An analysis of the responses to the MSM survey made clear, however, that users do not perceive racial discrimination and aesthetic discrimination as intrinsically different things. This chapter argues that, even though aesthetic discrimination and the racial one have differences, they overlap and are closely related, because they are not a matter of mere taste:[76] in excluding certain bodies, one is embodying and expressing heteronormative and capitalist values and power dynamics.[77] Heteronormative because it 'is through the overwhelming and felicitous norms of heterosexuality that queers understand and resignify desire'.[78] This confirms the findings[79] according to which the present heteronormative cultural and legal framework reflects a focus upon the 'good gay' as opposed to the 'bad queer'.[80] 'Capitalist' because the data collected suggests that the 'acceptable' MSM is a highly productive and respectable member of his community who embraces and even exacerbates the male/female binary.[81] Similarly, it has been noted that 'gay men's place within the hierarchy of society is below that of heterosexual males and those presenting traditional masculinities, and thus social-dominance orientation can be attributed with a preference

---

[74] Internalised homophobia can be described as the internalisation of the mythology and opprobrium which characterise current social attitudes towards homosexuality. See Alan K. Malyon, 'Psychotherapeutic Implications of Internalized Homophobia in Gay Men' *Journal of Homosexuality* 7, nos 2–3 (1982): 59, 60. For the relation of this concept to shame and self-esteem see David J. Allen and Terry Oleson, 'Shame in Internalized Homophobia in Gay Men' Journal of Homosexuality 37, no 3 (1999): 33.

[75] Some authors claim that asexual people reinforce ableism by distancing themselves from people with disabilities. See Karen Cuthbert, 'You Have to be Normal to be Abnormal: An Empirically Grounded Exploration of the Intersection of Asexuality and Disability' Sociology 51, no 2 (2017): 241.

[76] The classical 'no fats, no femmes, no Asians' slogan, that one can find in many profile descriptions of users of MSM apps, does not seem a mere expression of taste (which may be something along lines of 'I am looking for' or 'I am into'). Conversely, the focus of these profile descriptions is to exclude entire segments of the community in the essentialist belief that, say, all non-masculine users are the same. The writer-director Vince Ha turned that sadly popular phrase into the film No Fats, No Femmes, No Asians, presented in Toronto on 14 June 2017. Similarly, it has been noted that '(w)e tend to think our preferences are natural and fixed when, in fact, they may be more plastic and susceptible to structural influences than we imagine'. See Russell K. Robinson, 'Structural Dimensions of Romantic Preferences' *Fordham Law Review* 76 (2008): 2787.

[77] This author is not affirming, however, that one should oblige oneself to change whom one is attracted to. One can agree with Raj (n 62), where he says that 'we will always find specific features about a person sexy. But, it is how we express those desires and the space we give others to shape their own pleasures that we must be more vigilant about and attentive towards'.

[78] See Lawless, n 47 at 1.

[79] Chris Ashford, 'Barebacking and the 'Cult of Violence': Queering the Criminal Law' *The Journal of Criminal Law* 74 (2010): 339 at 343.

[80] For the distinction, see C. F. Stychin, *A Nation by Rights* (Temple University Press: Philadelphia, 1998) 200.

[81] It has been said that the effeminate queer man is 'the perceived impediment to queer male social ascension' (see Lawless, n 47 at 3).

of men presenting as masculine over those with queer masculinities'.[82] Along the same lines, one can observe that '(f)ar from being spaces of experimentation, exploration, and play in regard to gender, these online collectives maintain many of the dominant and oppressive notions of how individuals should act based on their biological sex'.[83] The erasure of bodily differences, moreover, has been read as a new form of fascism.[84] Less critically, one may see the preference for a masculine as the confirmation of that literature[85] according to which highly sex-typical faces are considered more attractive.

Moving on to closely analyse the MSM survey distributed by this author, of the 54 users who were surveyed, 90 per cent of the respondents were white and more than half were British. As to the sexuality, 80 per cent identified themselves as gay, 6 per cent as bisexual, 2 per cent as queer, 2 per cent as questioning, and 2 per cent as straight/gay.[86] While nearly 90 per cent described themselves as males (or men, masculine, cisgender), only 2 per cent identified as queer.[87] A vast majority reported experiences of direct discrimination while using MSM apps (88%), but 10 per cent declared not to be discriminated against. In descending order, the reported forms of online discrimination were homophobia (28%), fat shaming (20%), ageism (14%), generic aesthetic discrimination (12%), racism (12%), femme-phobia[88] (6%), internalised discrimination[89] (6%), queer-phobia[90] (4%), biphobia (2%). Some other forms of discrimination, such as transphobia and ableism, were not reported probably because of the limited sample. Some of these categories overlap. For instance, femme-phobia, internalised homophobia, and queer-phobia regard, by definition, male individuals perceived as feminine or gender non-conforming. On this aspect, recent studies found that 'smartphone applications for gay men are reinforcing ideas of masculinity'.[91] This is in line with the works that observe that 'it is through the erasure of the effeminate

---

[82] See Bartone, n 70 at 517. For the theory of social-dominance orientation, see Felicia Pratto et al, 'Social Dominance Orientation: A Personality Variable Predicting Social and Political Attitudes' *Journal of Personality and Social Psychology* 67, no 4 (1994): 741 at 742.

[83] John E. Campbell, *Getting It On Online: Cyberspace, Gay Male Sexuality and Embodied Identity* (New York: Harrington Park, 2004) 68.

[84] According to Penney (n 61), when 'enough people together make demands publicly for only gym-fit, white men, or even if all believe that they are entitled to nothing less, difference flees from what is essentially a user-generated fascistic model of participation'.

[85] See, for instance, Isabel Scott et al, 'Context-dependent Preferences for Facial Dimorphism in a Rural Malaysian Population' *Evolution and Human Behaviour* 29, no 4 (2008): 289.

[86] 6 per cent of the respondents did not indicate their sexuality.

[87] 8 per cent of the respondents did not indicate their gender.

[88] By femme-phobia, we mean a discriminatory or otherwise intolerant behaviour against men whose gender performance is perceived as feminine.

[89] Internalised homophobia is the often-subconscious adoption of homophobic beliefs and behaviours by non-heterosexual men.

[90] By queerphobia, we mean a discriminatory or otherwise intolerant behaviour against men whose gender performance is perceived as non-binary or otherwise gender non-conforming.

[91] See Bartone, n 70 at 517.

queer male as a desirable and desiring subject that the masculine Grindr user reveals the overwhelming anxiety linked to his sexual legibility'.[92] The analysed phenomena do not manifest themselves only in dating platforms; indeed, it has been pointed out that misogyny and homophobia characterise most online interactions, including social networks and videogames.[93]

Most responses show that there is a certain body which is perceived as right and one which is deemed wrong.[94] For instance, some respondents say '[i]f you don't fit a mould, then don't even bother',[95] or 'I don't have the right body'[96] and 'I felt discriminated by other app's users for my physical aspect'.[97] Not fitting the acceptable aesthetic model can lead to being ignored or to verbal or physical violence. In one of the responses one reads: '[o]ften have people call me fat, ugly, disgusting etc. I've had obscenities shouted at me on the street due to my apperences (sic)'.[98] This can have dangerous consequences. A participant was discriminated against because he was perceived as feminine and, therefore, he 'stopped going out to dance for a long time, in the fear of being targeted as gay in heteronormative spaces, and as an undesirable-bodied individual in homonormative spaces'.[99] Other respondents could not find a job because of their gender

---

[92] See Lawless n 37 at 2.

[93] See, eg, Alice Marwick Alice, 'Gender, Sexuality and Social Media' in *The Social Media Handbook* edited by Jeremy Hunsinger and Theresa M. Senft (Abingdon: Routledge 2013) 59; Noémie Marignier, "Gay ou pas gay?' Panique énonciative sur le forum jeuxvideo.com' (Genre, sexualité & société, 1 June 2017). Available at: gss.revues.org/3964, last accessed 31 October 2017.

[94] One of the internal reviewers pointed out that there are also 'alternative' spaces such as Growlr (app designed for the 'bear' population), where unfit bodies are sought after. However, this research analysed only the main apps used by the general MSM population, leaving out the apps that target specific subgroups, for which different rules and aesthetic standards may apply. Nonetheless, the critique may be placed in the broader context of those studies that claim that online practices give rise to new expressions of gender and sexuality (see, eg, Sébastien François, 'Fanf(r)ictions. Tensions identitaires et relationnellles chez les auteurs de récits de fans' *Réseaux* 1, no 153 (2009): 157; Céline Metton-Gayon, *Les adolescents, leur téléphone et Internet. « Tu viens sur MSN? »* (Paris: L'Harmattan 2009).

[95] Respondent 262768-262760-23304805, response to the MSM survey.

[96] Ibid, Respondent 262768-262760-21618126.

[97] Ibid, Respondent 262768-262760-22124066.

[98] Ibid, Respondent 262768-262760-22435340. This respondent did not answer the question about the difference between online and offline aesthetic discrimination. However, it is believed that while offline discrimination may be perceived as more violent, the online one may be equally damaging because anonymous and because the online/offline divide does not seem any longer tenable. It has been noted that anonymous, spontaneous, disinhibited, and impersonal nature of online interaction will increase the likelihood that prejudice will be expressed more overtly. See Jack Glaser and Kimberly Kahn, 'Prejudice, Discrimination, and the Internet' in *The Social Net: Understanding Human Behavior in Cyberspace* edited by Y. Amichai-Hamburger (Oxford: OUP, 2005) 247. According to Brendesha M. Tynes et al, 'Online Racial Discrimination and Psychological Adjustment Among Adolescents' *Journal of Adolescent Health* 43, no 6 (2008): 565, '(c)onsistent with offline studies, online racial discrimination was negatively associated with psychological functioning'. More recently, on online-offline dichotomy as problematic see Lina Eklund, 'Bridging the online/offline divide: The example of digital gaming' *Computers in Human Behavior* 53 (2015): Ibid, 527.

[99] Respondent 262768-262760-21641632, response to the MSM survey.

non-conforming appearance or were victims of mobbing in the workplace, particularly in traditionally male-dominated industries.[100] Others wished to be able to afford plastic surgery and one expressed suicidal tendencies. This constitutes an advance in the existing literature, which has hitherto focused the effects of weight discrimination on the willingness to adopt unhealthy behaviours and eating disorders.[101] These findings are in line with those of recent research[102] about Tinder, that found that the popular app's users have low levels of satisfaction with their faces and bodies and have high levels of shame about their bodies. The same study found that men report lower levels of self-esteem;[103] future research should investigate whether the level of body-related self-esteem varies according to the sexuality of the user.

Overall, the contention is that given the pervasiveness of exclusionary practices based on the physical appearance and due to their negative consequences, there are good reasons to rethink discrimination laws. If this chapter's suggestion were accepted, this could lead to an extension of discrimination laws to encompass new protected characteristics[104] and new scenarios.[105] However, even in the event of a rejection of the parallel between these forms of discrimination, it is hoped that this research will shed new light on the aesthetic discrimination, with consequences at least in terms of a change in the apps' policies and the users' behaviour, as well as a consistent application of hate speech laws to these phenomena. This research already produced a positive impact, in that one of the platforms amended its legals after its spokesperson was interviewed by the author. Indeed, this author brought to the spokesperson's attention that it was unacceptable to invite users to 'take it like a man' when another user rejected them. The day after the interview the spokesperson confirmed that 'after our call I had that *problematic language* removed from our

---

[100] Ibid, Respondents 262768-262760-22758557 and 262768-262760-22767053.

[101] See Aliza Friedman et al, 'Effects of Weight Stigma Concerns, Perceived Discrimination, and Weight Bias Internalization on Disordered Eating in Bariatric Surgery Patients' *Canadian Journal of Diabetes* 39, S1 (2015): S46; Janine B. Beekman et al, 'Effects of Perceived Weight Discrimination on Willingness to Adopt Unhealthy Behaviors: Influence of Genomic Information' *Psychol Health* 31, no 3 (2015): 334.

[102] Jessica Strubel and Trent A Petrie, 'Love Me Tinder: Body Image and Psychosocial Functioning Among Men and Women' *Body Image* (2017): 21 at 34.

[103] Ibid at 38.

[104] In the UK, for instance, the protected characteristics are race, age, sex (including being or becoming a transsexual person), civil status, pregnancy, disability, religion, belief, and sexual orientation (Equality Act 2010, ss 4–12). Therefore, whereas discrimination based on homophobia, ageism and ableism is illegal, fattism, body shaming, slut shaming, queer-phobia, etc. are not.

[105] Currently, in the UK, discrimination is illegal if carried out at work, in education, as a consumer, when using public services, when buying or renting a property, and as a member or guest of a private club or association. On fattism and employment see Mark V. Roehling, 'Weight-based Discrimination in Employment: Psychological and Legal Aspects' *Pers Psychol* 52 (1999): 969; more generally see Elizabeth E. Theran, 'Legal Theory on Weight Discrimination' in *Weight Bias: Nature, Consequences, and Remedies* edited by Kelly D. Brownell et al. (New York: Guilford, 2005) 195.

etiquette guide. We are in the process of *updating all the language* but I at least wanted to make sure that that part was removed'.[106]

With the Internet entering one's own body, the traditional assumption of the body as the paradigm of the place of the right to be left alone should be revisited.

2.1. The Responsibility for Aesthetic Discrimination

While over 90 per cent of the respondents to the MSM survey feel pressured to look different from how they normally look, they are divided as to where these pressures come from. Four out of 10 users feel that MSM apps are exerting pressures to change their bodies. However, 33 per cent of the respondents blame it on society as a whole and 25 per cent on other users or the MSM community. In the latter view, one can hear the echo of the 'gay clone' theory,[107] whereby the gay culture produces its own stereotypical identity and rules of power. More recently, it has been observed that 'men are producing their own standards of participation that exclude differences from within their own community'.[108] While it seems true that the norms regulating the MSM online environment reproduce heteronormative dynamics and that differences tend to be erased,[109] it is debatable that this is a case of pure autonomy in the literal sense of self-production of norms. The platforms, indeed, seem to play a critical role in setting a standard of aesthetic acceptability (eg with their use of muscled models in advertising) but also by allowing body-related exclusionary practices.

Prima facie, it might seem that MSM apps are not responsible for aesthetic discrimination. Some of them declare it publicly. So, for instance, Hornet 'will never accept any rejection that refers to a person's age, religion, race, or size'.[110] When the issue was brought to their attention, spokespeople for two important MSM apps accept that the phenomenon exists, but either they claim that it would be incorrect to label it as discrimination or that the app should not be

---

[106] E-mail of MSM app No 1's spokesperson to this author, 2 March 2017. For ethical reasons, full anonymity was ensured; therefore the reference will be to MSM app No 1 and No 2. The participants to the survey were not requested to disclose personal data and were allocated a unique code for ease of analysis.

[107] Martin P. Levine, 'The Gay Clone' in *Sexuality* edited by Robert A. Nye (Oxford: OUP, 1999) 376.

[108] See Penney, n 61.

[109] One of the internal reviewers raised the point that many MSM apps enable their users to identify as belonging to a tribe (eg 'twinks', 'daddies', etc.). This may suggest that differences are encouraged. However, the apps provide a predefined architecture of choice, ie the user needs to identify in one of the pre-designed tribes, they cannot create a new tribe; this does not seem to encourage real diversity. Second, many tribes do not have much to do with the body (eg discreet, geek, jock, leather, poz, rugged).

[110] Hornet Etiquette Guide. Available at: love.hornetapp.com/etiquette-guide/, last accessed 25 September 2017 (the website does not clarify when the guide was last updated).

considered responsible because 'we are just platforms'.[111] Some users, in turn, see the MSM apps as responsible because '[t]hey create the platform and create the presumption that they'll police it accordingly. Once you do that, you're responsible'.[112]

The survey did not confirm – yet did not refute[113] – the hypothesis put forward by one of the participants in the focus group stage, according to whom there would be a pattern whereby only profile pictures of fit and young bodies go through the filtering system of MSM apps. However, most respondents to the MSM survey do believe that these apps are promoting a fit, young, white and masculine aesthetic model. This is consistent with the existing literature[114] pointing out that the way MSM apps are designed reinforces aesthetic discrimination. For instance, by requiring (and sometimes forcing) users to fill in the information on height, weight and body type, these apps are contributing to the creation of a standard of beauty in the MSM community.[115] More generally, another study[116] found that 35 per cent of MSM users experience abuse and harassment online.[117]

Many respondents infer the said promotion of an aesthetic model from the pictures used by MSM apps in advertising. They mostly show 'fit muscly guys',[118] 'fit masculine men',[119] etc. Some participants, however, say that these apps 'just mirror those social norms'[120] and even if it is true that the model proposed is that of the 'white muscular fit men, very masculine looking',[121] this happens because people would not use the apps 'if they were marketed through pictures of fat, or feminine-looking, or traditionally conceived as "ugly men"'.[122] The issue is resolved by this user by saying that 'Grindr, Romeo, and Hornet are definitely not queer activist apps. They try to sell, and masculinity and fitness are what sells'.[123] While the depiction of dating as a market confirms previous studies,[124] a clarification

---

[111] Interview of this author to a spokesperson for the MSM app No 2.

[112] Respondent 262768-262760-21618126, response to the MSM survey.

[113] Confirming and refuting hypothesis may be seen as quantitative pursuit. What the author intends to say it that the no other participants reported the problem of having the profile pictures suspended because they did not meet certain aesthetical standards.

[114] See Dang, n 43 at 19–20.

[115] It has been noted that '*Jack'd* suggests the users to choose whether their body type is 'bear' or 'not bear', 'masculine' or 'not masculine', which may lead its users to think 'bear and masculine is the mainstream body type'" (ibid at 20).

[116] See Travel Gay Asia and Gay Star News, n 55.

[117] The cited study does not specify whether the said abuse and harassment relate to body image.

[118] Respondent 262768-262760-21617248, response to MSM survey.

[119] Ibid, Respondent 262768-262760-21633723.

[120] Ibid, Respondent 262768-262760-21641632.

[121] Ibid.

[122] Ibid.

[123] Ibid.

[124] The idea of dating as a new economic market was presented by Marie Bergström, *Au bonheur des rencontres. Classe, sexualité et rapports de genre dans la production et l'usage des sites de rencontres en France* (Paris: SciencesPo, PhD Dissertation, 2014).

is needed with regard to the latter response. This author does not expect profit-maximising entities to become queer advocate groups;[125] however, it would be surprising if they did not play any role in the setting of body standards, given the importance of these apps in the everyday life of MSM.[126] Moreover, it is not necessarily true that fit bodies sell more than average ones. It has been found[127] that while the exposure to thin ideals harms an individual's body esteem, it is not a more effective marketing strategy.

Along the same lines, another respondent says that the 'discrimination comes from within the community. The only way in which MSM apps promote it is by not being vigilant enough to users who abuse it.'[128] If the lack of vigilance were true, it may be explained with the fact that if the app provider were vigilant, it would not be able to invoke the safe harbour in the event of an intermediary liability claim. Therefore, let us look into this intricate regime.

3. The Intermediary Liability of Online Dating Platforms for Men Who Have Sex with Men

It must be said that being responsible for imposing or reinforcing a certain aesthetic model is not the same[129] as being liable for the illegal activities carried out by the users (eg unauthorised use of personal data, hate speech, stalking, etc.). Liability is responsibility's legal *species*. Privacy, however, plays an equally important role in both the scenarios, because it is eroded in an IoB world where one loses control over one's body; at the same time, privacy is invoked as a justification to the immunities from intermediary liability.[130] This refers to the liability of online intermediaries (eg a social networking website) for illegal activities carried out by third parties using the platform made available by the intermediaries

---

[125] This is mirrored in the near absence of sexuality-related diversity in the corporate social responsibility policies. See João Bôsco Góis and Kamila Cristina de Silva Teixeira, 'Diversity in Corporate Social Responsibility: The (Almost Invisible) Place of Homosexuality' *Culture Health & Sexuality* 13(S1) (2011): S130.

[126] See 7Park Data, n 39.

[127] H Dittmar and S Howard, 'Thin-ideal Internalization and Social Comparison Tendency as Moderators of Media Models' Impact on Women's Body-focused Anxiety' *Journal of Social and Clinical Psychology* 23 (2004): 747. For a contrary opinion, see B Martin, E Veer and S Pervan, 'Self-referencing and Consumer Evaluations of Larger-sized Female Models: A Weight Locus of Control Perspective' *Marketing Letters* 18, no 3 (2007): 197.

[128] Respondent 262768-262760-21766224, response to MSM survey.

[129] This is due to the current restrictions to discrimination laws, that allow a number of discriminatory practices if carried out against categories that the legislators and the courts do not think to deserve protection (eg against obese people or queer individuals). Needless to say, however, that a discriminatory act can qualify as illegal under laws that are not related to discrimination (eg hate speech).

[130] See *Scarlet*, n 4.

themselves. Hosting providers[131] are immune from liability if they do not have actual knowledge of the illegal activities or information and, as regards claims for damages, are not aware of facts or circumstances from which the illegal activity or information is apparent.[132] Alternatively, they can invoke the safe harbour if they act expeditiously to remove or disable access to illegal information that they store upon obtaining said knowledge or awareness.[133] Moreover, they will be liable in damages only if there is evidence of awareness of facts or circumstances from which the illegal activity or information is apparent.[134] The current legal framework does not provide a clear answer to a number of questions raised by user-generated content and, more generally, user behaviour. It is unclear, for instance, what happens if terrorism-related videos are shared on Facebook and the company does not promptly remove the content, lacking a proper take-down notice.

The sections above showed that MSM apps can be used for illegal activities such as hate speech as well as for discriminatory practices. This is not the only illegal use of these apps. Other examples may include the creation of fake profiles for the purposes of stalking and harassment. An example of this is provided by *Herrick v Grindr*.[135] In February 2017, a US court found in favour of Grindr in a case where a user had been stalked and harassed by 400 men and the platform had ignored his requests to block the fake profile that invited Grindr's users to have sexual encounters with him.[136] The passive attitude of the app provider persisted even after the lawsuit began (see Figure 2.3).

Another instance of illegal use of MSM apps became famous when a man stalked, drugged, raped and killed three teenagers hooked-up on Grindr.[137] As before,[138] Grindr did not cooperate; one may imply that this is because

---

[131] The eCommerce Directive provides partly different rules for the immunities of different providers of an information provider service, namely mere conduit, caching, hosting. In this chapter, the focus will be on hosting because MSM app providers are likely to fall under said regime, if they are not publishers in the first place.

[132] eCommerce Directive, Art 14(1)(a).

[133] Ibid, Art 14(1)(b). The notice-and-takedown mechanisms have not yet been harmonised. Some countries have sector-specific rules (on terrorism, child porn, etc), only a few Member States have detailed the timescale of the takedown. Moreover, national courts take different approaches when deciding whether an intermediary has actual knowledge. See Commission, 'Commission Staff Working Document 'Bringing e-commerce benefits to consumers'' (SEC(2011) 1640 final).

[134] See, eg, Commission Recommendation of 1 March 2018 on measures to effectively tackle illegal content online (C(20181177 final), para 8.

[135] See *Herrick v Grindr, LLC*, n 27.

[136] The US Court of the Southern District of New York denied an application for extension of temporary restraining order (TRO). The parties will appear for an initial pre-trial conference on 10 March 2017.

[137] See Daniel De Simone, 'The killer the police missed' (*BBC News*, 25 November 2016). Available at: www.bbc.co.uk/news/resources/idt-d32c5bc9-aa42-49b8-b77c-b258ea2a9205, last accessed 25 September 2017.

[138] See Graham Gremore, 'Why is Grindr refusing to cooperate more in the search for this missing grad student?' (Queerty, 6 March 2017). Available at; www.queerty.com/grindr-refusing-cooperate-search-missing-grad-student-20170306, last accessed 25 September 2017.

Matthew Herrick
@MatthewSHerrick

Let it be known this company still has done nothing. The profiles still exist and I'm still being subjected to this torture. Disgusting.

WIRED ✪ @WIRED
Strangers started showing up at this man's home and work, all because of fake
Grindr accounts. Then it got dangerous bit.ly/2jS7fJ6

RETWEETS   LIKES
3   3

Figure 2.3 Tweet by the plaintiff in *Herrick v Grindr*[139]

cooperating might be seen as an admission that the platform has knowledge of the illegal activities carried out by its users or that it is in the position to stop them or prevent further consequences from happening. Consequently, in the said cases, if Grindr knew, it would have not be able to invoke the immunity from intermediary liability.[140]

In the EU, the intermediary liability regime was harmonised by the eCommerce Directive and Brexit will not have an immediate direct impact in this field. In the UK, the main references in terms of intermiadiary liability are the eCommerce Regulations, the Defamation Act 1996,[141] and the Defamation Act 2013.[142] To add to the complexity, it is not clear if the common law defence of innocent dissemination survives or if it has been replaced by the statutory defences.[143] The European and English laws on intermediary liability revolve around three safe harbours: mere conduit, caching, and hosting. However, unlike the European matrix, the English implementation does not provide for an absolute exclusion of liability. Indeed, the main difference seems to be that they do

---

[139] Matthew Herrick (@MatthewSHerrick), tweet of 6 February 2017, 1:14AM. Available at; twitter. com/MatthewSHerrick/status/828411528441372672, last accessed 28 September 2017.

[140] One of the internal reviewers underlined that this is a speculative exercise, but other explanations may apply. It may be that Grindr did not have any information that could help the investigations. This may well be, but it would be surprising, given the amount and granularity of data MSM apps collect for a number of reasons, including advertising.

[141] Defamation Act 1996, s 1.

[142] Defamation Act 2013, ss 5 and 10. Under s 5 of this Act, the Defamation (Operator of Websites) Regulations 2013 were made.

[143] According to *Metropolitan International Schools Ltd v Designtechnica Corporation, Google UK Ltd & Google Inc* [2009] EWHC 1765 (QB), it does.

not exclude intermediaries' liability altogether. Conversely, they allow injunctive relief, while excluding damages, any other pecuniary remedy, and criminal sanctions.[144] Another notable addition is that regulation 22 presents a non-exhaustive list of factors to help courts assessing if the intermediary has actual knowledge as required by regulations 18 and 19 on caching and hosting. Courts shall have regard to, inter alia, whether a service provider has received a notice through a means of contact made available in accordance with regulation 6(1)(c)[145] and the extent to which the notice includes the full name and address of the sender of the notice, details of the location of the information in question, and details of the unlawful nature of the activity or information in question. Thus, on this point, the eCommerce Regulations provide a regime, which is even more favourable to intermediaries, if compared to the eCommerce Directive. Suffice to say that there is no sanction for an intermediary that does not provide an easy way to contact them. For instance, this author unsuccessfully tried to find a way to contact with one of the selected MSM apps, but it was not possible to find their e-mail or any other point of contact. Therefore, it may be argued that intermediaries could shield themselves by making it difficult for users to issue a notice. This does not seem fair. More generally, the formal emphasis on the notice – as opposed to a more flexible approach where knowledge can be inferred by a number of factors – leads to abuses, such as those recently uncovered with regards to eBay, which removes listings against mere allegations of patent infringement, without actual proof, let alone court orders.[146] This change of policy may be seen also as a reaction to the increased pressures on intermediaries to take a more active role in policing the Internet.[147]

In the UK, like in the rest of Europe and in other jurisdictions, the intermediary liability regime was designed to favour intermediaries[148] in a twofold way. First, by allowing them to escape liability when they play a merely passive role in the intermediation and/or have no knowledge of the illegal activities carried out by the third parties. Second, by pointing out that one cannot impose on them a general obligation of monitoring. Otherwise, so the rationale goes, there would be a violation of fundamental rights such as privacy

---

[144] eCommerce Regulations, regs 17–19.

[145] Intermediaries shall make available the details of the service provider, including their email address, which make it possible to contact them rapidly and communicate with them in a direct and effective manner.

[146] For more information, see Open Rights Group, 'eBay must stop Epson's patent abuse' (*Open Rights Group*, 25 October 2017). Available at: www.openrightsgroup.org/press/releases/2017/ebay-must-stop-epson-patent-abuse, last accessed 25 October 2017.

[147] For a recent expression of this trend, see, for instance, Michał Sałajczyk, 'Poland: File hosting platform ordered to monitor its resources for pirated films' (*MediaWrites*, 11 October 2017). Available at: www.mediawrites.law/file-hosting-platform-ordered-to-monitor-its-resources-for-pirated-films/, last accessed 25 October 2017.

[148] See Centre for Democracy and Technology, 'Intermediary liability: protecting internet platforms for expression and innovation' (*CDT*, April 2010). Available at: www.cdt.org/files/pdfs/CDT-Intermediarypercent20Liability_(2010).pdf, last accessed 24 October 2017.

and freedom of expression.[149] The leading case is *Scarlet Extended SA v SABAM*,[150] which stated that the European regime of intermediary liability is rooted in the online users' 'right to protection of their personal data and their freedom to receive or impart information, which are rights safeguarded by Articles 8 and 11 of the Charter'[151] of Fundamental Rights of the EU. In the lobbying battle to secure their own immunity, Internet service providers argued that 'nor was it desirable or possibly legal for them to (manually check all the material which passed through their servers) without invading the privacy and confidentiality of their subscribers'.[152] Along the same lines, in September 2017 the European Commission underlined that the operation of technical systems of protection and identification of illegal content online 'must however take place within the limits of the applicable rules of EU and national law, in particular on the protection of privacy and personal data and the prohibition on Member States to impose general monitoring obligations'.[153] All in all, the privacy-based justification for the immunity from liability already sounded spurious at the time of the adoption of the eCommerce Directive, but now, in light of the actual practices of most online intermediaries, there is further evidence that it is untenable.

Intermediaries are increasingly asked to take on a policing role through responses to legal requirements, industry self-regulation, as well as through their business practice.[154] Concerns have been expressed that Internet service providers could be become 'copyright cops', thus compressing privacy, freedom of expression, and due process.[155] Similarly, other authors[156] affirm that the implementation

---

[149] In some instances, privacy may be a serious concern, see *CG v Facebook Ireland Ltd* [2015] NIQB 11, where Facebook was ordered to pay damages to a convicted sex offender, and to remove a page from its website which had been set up with the purpose of driving sex offenders in Northern Ireland from their homes and exposing them to vilification and the risk of serious harm. The sex offender had had an expectation of privacy in respect of his personal information. See also *J20 v Facebook Ireland Ltd* [2016] NIQB 98.

[150] See *Scarlet,* n 4.

[151] Ibid at [50].

[152] Lilian Edwards, 'The Fall and Rise of Intermediary Liability Online' in Lilian Edwards and Charlotte Waelde, *Law and the Internet* (Oxford: Hart, 3rd edn, 2009) 47, 59.

[153] Commission, 'Tackling Illegal Content Online. Towards an Enhanced Responsibility of Online Platforms' (Communication) COM (2017) 555 final, para 3(3)(2). This is consistent with the eCommerce Directive, recital 40, whereby 'the provisions of this Directive relating to liability should not preclude the development and effective operation, by the different interested parties, of technical systems of protection and identification and of technical surveillance instruments made possible by digital technology within the limits laid down by Directives 95/46/EC and 97/66/EC'.

[154] cf Lilian Edwards, 'The Role of Internet Intermediaries in Advancing Public Policy Objectives Forging Partnerships for Advancing Policy Objectives for the Internet Economy, Part II' (*SSRN*, 22 June 2011). Available at: ssrn.com/abstract=1875708, last accessed 28 September 2017.

[155] Lilian Edwards, 'Should ISPs Be Compelled to Become Copyright Cops? File-Sharing, the Music Industry and Enforcement Online' (*SSRN*, 16 July 2009). Available at: https://ssrn.com/abstract=1435115, last accessed 28 September 2017.

[156] Felipe Romero-Moreno, 'The Digital Economy Act 2010: Subscriber Monitoring and the Right to Privacy under Article 8 of the ECHR' *International Review of Law, Computers, & Technology* 30, no 3 (2016): 229.

of the 'initial obligations'[157] of the Digital Economy Act 2010[158] would allegedly conflict with the European Convention on Human Rights.[159] More recently, in September 2017, the European Commission presented a set of guidelines for online intermediaries 'to step up the fight against illegal content online in cooperation with national authorities, Member States and other relevant stakeholders'.[160] Unsurprisingly, the European trade association representing online platforms reacted with utter disappointed to the Commission's approach to the regulation on online intermediaries.[161] Even though this trend may lead to a further compression of the freedom of expression and of the right to privacy,[162] it is recognised that the level and extent of intermediaries' duties is a matter of balancing policy needs, so the regime of immunities may fluctuate.[163] There may be good reasons for a reassessment of the balance today. Illegal activities (also beyond copyright infringement) are increasingly carried out online.[164] Online intermediaries appear more and more powerful. Intermediaries tend not to prevent, nor to react to illegal activities carried out by their users; what is worse, is that this could be a reaction to the intermediary liability regime that protects them if they appear to be neutral. Additionally, this study confirms that there is a degree of hypocrisy in rooting the immunity from liability in the right to privacy, which is then clearly violated by the same intermediaries.

---

[157] Internet service providers shall notify their subscribers if their IP address has been reported as associated to copyright infringement. Moreover, they must monitor the reports and compile an anonymous 'copyright infringement list' of those who have received three or more notifications in one year.

[158] Digital Economy Act 2010, s. 3.

[159] European Convention on Human Rights, Art. 8.

[160] Commission, 'Tackling Illegal Content Online. Towards an enhanced responsibility of online platforms' (Communication) COM (2017) 555 final, para 1.

[161] EDiMA, 'EDiMA strongly disappointed at the European Commission announcements regarding new Platform Regulation initiatives' (*EDiMA*, 10 May 2017). Available at: www.europeandigitalmediaassociation.org/pdfs/latest_news/Press%20Release%20-%20EDiMA%20Mid-term%20review%20reaction.pdf, last accessed 13 November 2017.

[162] In replying to this communication, it has been underlined that '(a)ny regime for tackling illegal content on the internet has to be carefully calibrated to ensure respect for the fundamental rights on which our society and our democracy are based' (European Digital Rights, 'Letter to the Digital Economy Commissioner Mariya Gabriel 'A coherent and rights-based approach to dealing with illegal content'' (EDRI, 20 October 2017). Available at; https://edri.org/files/letter_coherent_rightsbasedapproach_illegalcontent_20171020.pdf, last accessed 12 November 2017. This author agrees with the statement according to which 'not acceptable for governments to encourage or coerce internet intermediaries to take measures 'voluntarily' that would not be permitted by international law or national constitutions, if they were provided for by law' (ibid at 2).

[163] Charlotte Waelde and Lilian Edwards, 'Online Intermediaries and Copyright Liability' (2005) WIPO Workshop Keynote Paper. Available at: www.ssrn.com/abstract=1159640.

[164] See, eg, Office for National Statistics, 'Crime in England and Wales: Year ending May 2017' (ONS, 20 July 2017). Available at: www.ons.gov.uk/peoplepopulationandcommunity/crimeandjustice/bulletins/crimeinenglandandwales/yearendingmar2017, alst accessed 25 September 2017, which states that: '(a)dults aged 16 and over experienced an estimated 3.4 million incidents of fraud in the survey year ending March 2017 (…), with over half of these (57%; 1.9 million incidents) being cyber-related'.

Coming back to the MSM survey, the respondents were asked question about intermediary liability and the role of privacy. Twenty per cent of the participants believe that MSM apps should be held liable because they create the expectation of policing the platform. Those who disagree, however, point out that MSM apps should be more active in preventing and reacting to illegal activities. The passive attitude of MSM apps may be explained in light of the intermediary liability regime, because the app providers may fear that if they were proactive they could not invoke the immunity from liability analysed below.[165]

The respondent quoted above, who linked the policing of the platform to the liability is right in believing that if a platform polices the user-generated content and users' behaviour they cannot claim immunity,[166] but these apps deny that they have any actual control and therefore knowledge. For instance, Grindr declares that it 'does not control the content of User Accounts and profiles'.[167] From this supposed lack of control the app makes follow a lack of obligation to monitor users (but a right to do so) and, correspondingly, an absolute disclaimer of liability.[168] The lack of control seems excluded by the fact, for instance, that the MSM apps access and store private messages and all materials (including photos, location, and videos) 'for archival purposes or as otherwise allowed by law'.[169]

---

[165] On the relevance of the active role in finding intermediary liability see, for instance, Case C-324/09 *L'Oréal SA and Others v eBay International AG and Others* [2011] ECR I-6011, para 116, where the Court of Justice stated that intermediaries cannot claim immunity under the eCommerce Directive (Art 14(1)), if they 'have played an active role of such a kind as to give it knowledge of, or control over, the data' relating to the allegedly illegal activity carried out by the platform's users.

[166] While discriminatory practices online are not illegal per se (eg if not related to employment, education, etc.), they may become illegal, for instance if they qualify as hate speech. In the event of theft of the profile picture for the creation of fake profiles, then the platform may be found liable, inter alia, for copyright infringement (leaving aside criminal law, see the Crown Prosecution Service, 'Guidelines on Prosecuting Cases Involving Communications Sent via Social Media' (*CPS*, 3 March 2016). Available at: www.cps.gov.uk/legal/a_to_c/communications_sent_via_social_media/, last accessed 26 September 2017).

[167] Grindr Terms and Conditions of Service (hereinafter Grindr Terms), clause 10(4). The text is available at: www.grindr.com/terms-of-service, last accessed 25 September 2017 (the website does not clarify when the terms were last updated).

[168] Ibid, cl 10(4). See also cl 12(4). Similar provisions can be found in other platforms; see, for instance, the Hornet Terms of Service (hereinafter 'Hornet Terms'), cl 7(c). Available at: www.love.hornetapp.com/terms-of-service/, last accessed 26 September 2017: 'Hornet assumes no responsibility whatsoever in connection with or arising from User Submissions (…) reserves the right to prevent you from submitting User Submissions.'

[169] Grindr Privacy Policy. Available at: www.grindr.com/privacy-policy, last accessed 28 September 2017. These data are shared, inter alia, with the Chinese parent company; one may doubt, however, that the users are aware of this and that the Chinese privacy laws ensure the same level of protection as the European ones, let alone the same level of protection for LGBT rights. See, respectively, Bo Zhao and G.P. (Jeanne) Mifsud Bonnici, 'Protecting EU Citizens' Personal Data in China: A Reality or a Fantasy?' *International Journal of Law and Information Technology* 24, no 2 (2016): 28 and Talha Burki, 'Health and Rights Challenges for China's LGBT Community' *The Lancet* 389, no 10076 (2017): 1286. Hornet is not clear on the point of which data are collected and with whom they are shared, but the reference to 'habits, characteristics and user patterns' may well include

These data are used, inter alia, for marketing purposes,[170] therefore the apps should at least allow an opt-out mechanism, which is not provided.[171] Moreover, the user-generated content is preliminarily filtered[172] and both spokespersons confirmed that this operation is not automated. In other words, there is a team manually overviewing all user-generated content and this puts the app provider in the position to know if the platform is being used for illegal purposes.[173] Over 40 per cent of the users said their profile pictures had been rejected and their accounts had been suspended at least once. The main reason for this seemed to be suggestive photos (though this was interpreted broadly, as encompassing for instance the showing of navel hair),[174] followed by vulgar language. This shows that MSM apps have control over their users' activities (in defiance of the right to privacy) therefore, they know if something potentially illegal happens on the platform. If this is the case, they cannot invoke the immunity from intermediary liability analysed below. One may wonder why MSM apps control (if not police) their users' activities. The answer provided by both the spokespeople interviewed was that they are required to do so by the app stores[175] (ie mainly

private messages (Hornet Privacy Policy. Available at: www.love.hornetapp.com/privacy-policy/, last accessed 28 September 2017). Likewise, PlanetRomeo stores the personal data provided when creating an account 'as well as other personal data provided by you when you use the Service.' PlanetRomeo Privacy Statement. Available at: www.planetromeo.com/en/privacy/, last accessed 28 September 2017.

[170] Ibid.

[171] While direct marketing is a legitimate use under the GDPR, recital 47, the consent is still required by the Privacy and Electronic Communications (EC Directive) Regulations 2003, SI 2003/2426. The draft ePrivacy Regulation (Proposal for a Regulation of the European Parliament and of the Council concerning the respect for private life and the protection of personal data in electronic communications and repealing Directive 2002/58/EC) keeps consent as a requirement for direct marketing (recital 33), save the right to withdraw consent 'at any time in an easy manner' (recital 34). See also ePrivacy Regulation, Art 16.

[172] Whilst the profile pictures are subject to an *ex-ante* control, profile descriptions are monitored mostly *ex post*.

[173] Filtering or human moderation give 'providers knowledge of a variety of different kinds of illegality' (Christina Angelopoulos, 'MTE v Hungary: A New ECtHR Judgment on Intermediary Liability and Freedom Of Expression' *Journal of Intellectual Property Law & Practice* 11, no 8 (2016): 582 at 584.

[174] One of the internal reviewers suggested that this might explain the rejection of Figure 1. Arguably, one photo arguably 'suggests' nudity, in the other the towel slips 'suggestively'.

[175] There is a clear imbalance of power between the app stores (at least those provided by Google and Apple) and the app providers. This may explain the imposition of the very strict legals of the MSM apps, that ban every user-generated content that is even vaguely inappropriate or even immoral. Apple's guidelines, however, do not seem as strict. They exclude only '(o)vertly sexual or pornographic material' (Apple App Store Review Guidelines, para 1.1.4. Available at: www.developer.apple.com/app-store/review/guidelines/, last accessed 27 September 2017), which is quite different to Hornet's ban, covering even '(p)hotos with only underpants being worn' (Hornet Usage Guidelines. Available at:love.hornetapp.com/usage-guidelines/, last accessed 27 September 2017). A middle way, Google does not allow explicit content, such as pornography, and that which is 'sexually gratifying' (Google Play Developer Program Policies. Available at: https://play.google.com/intl/None/about/developer-content-policy-print/, last accessed 12 November 2017).

For a discussion on the vagueness of Apple's developer guidelines and the uncertainty and opaqueness of its approval process see Luis E. Hestres, 'App Neutrality: Apple's App Store and Freedom of Expression Online' *International Journal of Communication* 7 (2013): 1265.

by Google and Apple).[176] This trend dates back to the agreement between the Attorney-General of California (the 'California agreement) and six app store providers;[177] from that document stemmed the obligation for these providers to include 'a field for privacy statements or links in the application submission/ approval process for apps'.[178] More recently, legal scholars have suggested that, since app developers and users are located around the world, thus making it difficult for privacy laws to be enforced, app stores play a 'central role in determining the standard of data privacy which is afforded to users'.[179] A spokesperson of an MSM app provider[180] said that, to allow the app store providers to monitor compliance with their content policies, they provide the app store providers with a username and password; Apple and Google then log in as a normal user and monitor the enforcement of their guidelines.[181] From the data collected in the MSM survey, it seems clear that this practice is not consistent with the privacy expectations of the users. This back door left to app store providers may be considered in the context of the California agreement to rely 'to a great extent on the store as a protector of privacy'.[182] Reportedly,[183] finally, the app stores would be responsible for imposing very strict terms to the MSM apps and would be required to police the platforms so as not to be banned by the app stores. Funnily enough, however, the MSM apps' terms are usually stricter than those of the app stores, with the only exclusion discriminatory content, which is absolutely prohibited by Apple's app store guidelines,[184] but not Grindr, PlanetRomeo or Hornet.[185]

[176] All the MSM apps' legals refer to the app stores guidelines, but only Grindr expressly incorporates, at the end of its Terms, the 'Apple Store Additional Terms and Conditions.' In the Hornet Usage Guidelines, then, one can read that '(w)e have to honor some guidelines by our partners Apple and Google, among others. If we don't – bam – Hornet gets pulled quicker than a quick thing on National Quick Day'.

[177] State of California Office of the Attorney General (Kamala D. Harris), 'The Joint Statement of Principle' (*California Office of Attorney General*, 22 February 2012). *International Journal of Communication* Available at: www.oag.ca.gov/system/files/attachments/press_releases/n2630_signed_agreement.pdf, last accessed 27 September 2017.

[178] Daithí Mac Síthigh 'App law Within: Rights and Regulation in the Smartphone Age' *International Journal of Law and Information Technology* 21, no 2 (2013): 154 at 179.

[179] Adrian Fong, 'The Role of App Intermediaries in Protecting Data Privacy' *International Journal of Law and Information Technology* 25, no 2 (2017): at 85.

[180] The other spokesperson preferred not to disclose information about how the app store providers ensure that the MSM app providers comply with their content policies.

[181] There may be different mechanisms to ensure the app providers' compliance with the app store's guidelines. For instance, developers that wish that their apps be available on Google Play are required to fill in a questionnaire about the nature of the app's content and in case of misrepresentation that app may be removed or suspended (Google Play Developer Program Policies, para 'Content Ratings'). However, it is not clear how Google ensures that the app providers do not make any misrepresentation.

[182] See Síthigh, n 178 at 180.

[183] Interview with spokesperson of MSM app no 1 and no 2.

[184] App Store Review Guidelines, para 1.1.1.

[185] While PlanetRomeo Terms of Use (hereinafter PlanetRomeo Terms see www.planetromeo.com/en/terms-of-use/, last accessed 27 September 2017) do not provide anything on the point, Grindr makes a generic mention to 'racially or ethnically or otherwise offensive' content (Grindr Terms clause 8(3)(12)) and Hornet to 'racially or ethnically offensive' content (Hornet Terms, clause 5(i)).

The fact that MSM apps have filtering mechanisms in place, while endangering their immunity from intermediary liability, may be explained in light of the app store guidelines, which require MSM apps to have a method in place for filtering objectionable material.[186]

Now, let us assume that MSM apps do not, in fact, monitor or have control over their users and the content they generate. If this were the case, MSM apps should at least react promptly upon receiving a notice where the user reports some illegal activity. If the illegal content is not taken down nor its access disabled, under the intermediary liability regime the MSM app provider will be found liable. Surprisingly, therefore, the MSM apps' legals provide that 'under no circumstances, including negligence, will Grindr be liable (for the) interactions with Grindr or any other user (…) even if Grindr or a Grindr authorized representative has been advised of the possibility of such damages'.[187] Or that PlanetRomeo's 'liability for consequential damages (…) arising out of, or in connection with the Agreement or these Terms of Use (…) independent of whether the User provides notice to (PlanetRomeo) of such potential injury, damages or loss, is excluded'.[188] Such clauses go against the letter and purpose of the eCommerce Directive[189] and UK Regulations[190] whereby immunity cannot be claimed if there is knowledge of the illegal activities carried out by the platforms' users.[191] These clause are, therefore, unenforceable, notwithstanding the attempts of the MSM apps to make the user believe that the only remedy is to refrain from using the service.[192]

The EU, in regulating intermediary liability, sought to strike a balance between competing interests such as reputation, freedom of speech, privacy, and competitiveness.[193] It would seem that the operation was not entirely successful.

---

[186] App Store Review Guidelines, para 1.2. Google Play Store's guidelines are not explicit on the point, but they state that '(a)pps that contain or feature user-generated content (UGC) must take additional precautions in order to provide a policy compliant app experience' (Developer Program Policies, para 'User Generated Content').

[187] Grindr Terms, clause 18(1). Similarly, see Hornet Terms, clause 13(4).

[188] PlanetRomeo Terms, clause 10(4).

[189] Directive 2000/31/EC of the European Parliament and of the Council of 8 June 2000 on certain legal aspects of information society services, in particular electronic commerce, in the Internal Market [2000] OJ 178. The withdrawal of the UK from the EU is unlikely to directly affect the regimes introduced as a consequence of EU Directives, because they were transposed into national legislation. However, after the completion of the leaving process, the UK will be free to introduce diverging eCommerce legislation and case law.

[190] Electronic Commerce (EC Directive) Regulations 2002, SI 2001/2555 (eCommerce Regulations); see, in particular, regs 17–19.

[191] Under the eCommerce Directive, for instance, '(i)n order to benefit from a limitation of liability, the provider of an information society service, consisting of the storage of information, upon obtaining actual knowledge or awareness of illegal activities has to act expeditiously to remove or to disable access to the information concerned' (recital 46).

[192] 'The User's only remedy in the event of an attributable failure or unlawful acts of PlanetRomeo, is to discontinue the use of the Service' (Romeo Terms, 10(2)).

[193] See *Scarlet*, n 4.

Artificial intelligence and big data, often produced by connected devices (Internet of Things), enable online intermediaries to control a vast amount of information on the users' activities and predict future behaviours. Monitoring, in the form of tracking and profiling (eg for behavioural advertising purposes) is commonplace. This questions the assumption whereby it would not be feasible for intermediaries to actively monitor all their users in to prevent[194] or react to unlawful activities. It is no coincidence that the European Commission recently presented guidelines to 'facilitate and intensify the implementation of good practices for preventing, detecting, removing and disabling access to illegal content'.[195] Moroever, the European Court of Human Rights made clear that intermediaries are often in a position to know about their users' activities regardless of a formal notice.[196] This study brings empirical evidence that online platforms try to avoid liability even when they have knowledge of the illegal activities of their users. More importantly, they violate privacy and freedom of expression, the same rights that would justify their immunity from liability.

4. Privacy in the Online Private Ordering of the Internet of Bodies

In the IoB, privacy plays a key role in justifying the intermediary liability of the platforms, as well as the platform's responsibility in terms of aestheric discrimination. Therefore, it is crucial to understand how privacy is regulated in the IoB.

Even though data protection and privacy are the object of hard laws,[197] the 'legals' play an increasing role in the regulation of the relevant rights. Due to the pace of the technological evolution, the law cannot keep up.[198] A consequence of

---

[194] In countries where homosexuality is stigmatised or criminalised, MSM apps may send the users a warning, but it 'is questionable whether such a built-in feature can be demanded from the provider of the app' (Lodder, n 44 at 12).

[195] Commission, 'Tackling Illegal Content Online. Towards an enhanced responsibility of online platforms' (Communication) COM (2017) 555 final, para 1.

[196] *Delfi AS v Estonia* [GC], No. 64569/09 [2015] ECHR [159].

[197] At the European level, see the Data Protection Directive, the GDPR, and the ePrivacy Directive (Directive 2002/58/EC of the European Parliament and of the Council of 12 July 2002 concerning the processing of personal data and the protection of privacy in the electronic communications sector (2002) OJ L 201). In the UK, see, mainly, the Data Protection Act 1998 and the Privacy and Electronic Communications (EC Directive) Regulations 2003, SI 2003/2426. See also the Data Protection HL Bill (2017–19) 66. Introduced in September 2017 to implement the GDPR, it is currently at the committee stage at the House of Lords

[198] The principle of technological neutrality, whereby laws should not deal with specific technologies, is only a partial solution to the problem. First, there are several exceptions. For instance, under Art 8(1) of the Vienna Convention on Road Traffic, '(e)very moving vehicle or combination of vehicles shall have a driver'. Therefore, currently if a party to this convention authorised driverless cars on its territory, they would be in breach of their international obligations. See Hans-Heinrich

this delay is that private actors fill the gaps (and sometimes purport to circumvent existing laws) by means of their 'legals', thus creating a private ordering of online relations.[199] Most of the legals are US contracts rarely adapted to the EU context; more importantly, they are hardly legible, obscure and often non-enforceable.[200] This is particularly alarming, since 'data privacy law has been subsumed by consumer contract law'.[201] The said features explain the so-called rational ignorance of those who do not read the privacy policies; indeed, it may be 'rational to refrain from reading privacy policies if the costs of reading exceed the expected benefits of ignorance'.[202] The readability has also immediate legal consequences in terms of remedies since, under the Unfair Terms Directive,[203] the assessment of the unfair nature of the terms shall relate to the definition of the main subject matter of the contract and to the adequacy of the price or remuneration only insofar as the contract is not drafted in plain intelligible language.

Nearly 70 per cent of the respondents to the MSM survey admit that they do not read the 'legals',[204] because they are too long, full of jargon, boring,

Trute, 'The Internet of Things: Remarks from the German Perspective' *Journal of Law & Economic Regulation* 5 (2016): 118 at 135. More generally, even when the law does not target a specific technology, it is adopted with a specific technological context in mind. An example may be copyright law, which was designed for a world of books and photocopies and, therefore, struggles in an era of Snapchat selfies and cloud storage. Ysolde Gendreau, 'A Technologically Neutral Solution for the Internet: Is It Wishful Thinking?' in *Science, Truth and Justice* edited by Joost Blom and Hélène Dumont (Canadian Institute for the. Administration of Justice, Themis, 2000) 199, 214 notes that what 'may today be considered technologically neutral may at a later date be viewed as technologically specific'. She believes that the solution could be found in favouring 'general principles over arcane technicalities' (ibid 214–215), in other terms a *'droit d'auteur'* approach over a copyright one. Cf, more recently, Kelvin Sum, 'Syncing copyright with the online digital environment' (SLS 2017 conference, 8 September 2017, Dublin).

[199] By private ordering, traditionally, one means the delegation of regulatory powers to private actors (the ICANN being the classic example). However, here by private ordering it is meant the *de-facto* delegation of the regulation of the online environment to contractual and quasi-contractual agreements that fill the gaps left by traditional regulation and legislation, that often is already old in the moment when it is adopted. On the traditional concept, see Steven L. Schwarcz, 'Private Ordering' *Northwestern University Law Review* 97, no 1 (2002): 319. For a range of possible meanings of 'private ordering' see *The Role of Intellectual Property Rights in Biotechnology Innovation* edited by David Castle (Cheltenham: Edward Elgar, 2009) 312 fn 42–44.

[200] For a deeper analysis of online private ordering, see Guido Noto La Diega and Ian Walden, 'Contracting for the 'Internet of Things': Looking into the Nest' *European Journal of Law & Technology* 2 (2016) 1. On the importance of plain and legible terms see Council Directive 93/13/EEC of 5 April 1993 on unfair terms in consumer contracts [1993] OJ L95/29, recital 20, arts 4(2) and 5; Case C-26/13 *Árpád Kásler and Hajnalka Káslerné Rábai v OTP Jelzálogbank Zrt* [2014] ECR, paras 60–75.

[201] Omri Ben-Shahar and Lior Jacob Strahilevitz, 'Contracting over Privacy: Introduction' *Journal of Legal Studies* 45(S2) (2016): S1.

[202] Yoan Hermstrüwer, 'Contracting Around Privacy: The (Behavioral) Law and Economics of Consent and Big Data' 8, no 1 JIPITEC (2017): 9, 17, referring to Omri Ben-Shahar and Carl E. Schneider, 'The Failure of Mandated Disclosure' *University of Pennsylvania Law Review* 159 (2011) 647.

[203] Council Directive 93/13/EEC of 5 April 1993 on unfair terms in consumer contracts (1993) OJ L 95/29, art 4. Similarly, in the UK, the Unfair Terms in Consumer Contracts Regulations 1994, SI 1994/3159, reg 3.

[204] This is consistent with the existing literature. For instance, it is deemed well-established that 'readership of terms and conditions, privacy notices, end-user licence agreements and other click-through

irrelevant, and complicated (two of them blamed their own laziness or lack of patience). These features affect the core of privacy online; indeed 'ambiguous language (…) undermines the purpose and value of privacy notices for site users'.[205] Those who read the legals do so to be sure about their rights and obligations vis-à-vis the platform and other users (especially with regards to blocking and/or reporting other users). However, the same respondents are sometimes aware that 'they're never run the way they say they are. I just like to know how well they pretend to protect you and how protected my data is'.[206]

Those who read the legals claim to understand them or, at least, to be aware of the existence of the relevant policies, but they justify this with their education (PhD in Law) or the specific background and area of work. This is in line with the studies that found that 'courts and laypeople can understand the same privacy policy language quite differently'.[207] However, this could also be seen as another instance of when users' self-perceived knowledge of their rights is high, but their actual knowledge is limited.[208] While maintaing that they understand the legals of the MSM apps they use, they accept that '[t]hey're often extremely inaccessible in the way they're created and can still be full of holes'.[209] It seems clear that the online social contract has weak foundations. However, one of the users suggests re-designing the legals by getting rid of the link to the Terms of Service and Privacy Policy and, instead, 'to give the user a few brief points of what terms they are agreeing to, especially ones relating to privacy'. This solution can be seen as an expression of the broader 'awareness by design'[210] trend.

agreements is generally low' (Maartje Elshout et al, 'Study on Consumers' Attitudes Towards Online Terms and Conditions (T&Cs)' (*European Commission*, 21 March 2016) 9 Available at: www.ec.europa.eu/consumers/consumer_evidence/behavioural_research/docs/terms_and_conditions_final_report_en.pdf, last accessed 26 September 2017). See also Stuart Moran, Ewa Luger, and Tom Rodden, 'Literatin: Beyond Awareness of Readability in Terms and Conditions' (Ubicomp '14 Adjunct, Seattle, September 2014), who suggest a way to solve a problem with a Chrome extension that compares the complexity of popular fictional literature to the legals to sensitise people to their complexity. See also Ewa Luger, Stuart Moran, and Tom Rodden, 'Consent for All: Revealing the Hidden Complexity of Terms and Conditions' (CHI 2013: Changing Perspectives, Paris, April–May 2013).
[205] Joel R. Reidenberg et al, 'Ambiguity in Privacy Policies and the Impact of Regulation' *Journal of Legal Studies* 45 (S2) (2016): S163.
[206] Respondent 262768-262760-21618126, response to the MSM survey.
[207] Lior Jacob Strahilevitz and Matthew B. Kugler, 'Is Privacy Policy Language Irrelevant to Consumers?' *Journal of Legal Studies* 45(S2) (2016): S69.
[208] See Elshout et al, n 204 at 10.
[209] Respondent 262768-262760-21618126, response to the MSM survey.
[210] Guido Noto La Diega, 'Uber Law and Awareness by Design. An Empirical Study on Online Platforms and Dehumanised Negotiations' *European Journal of Consumer Law* 2 (2016): 383, 410, defines 'awareness by design' as 'the use of technologies (especially design) to empower the user and make them aware of risks, rights, and obligations.' He makes the example of the replacement of the usual pre-ticked box ('I have read/I have understood') boxes with a box whose default option is 'I have not read/I have not understood.'

Hopefully, the privacy-by-design requirement under the GDPR[211] will also be interpreted as encompassing the drafting of the legals. Embedding privacy in the design in this sense would mean short, clear, consistent, and engaging legals. Gamified interactions[212] may constitute an important strategy.

This might help to explain the so-called privacy paradox, whereby 'despite apparent high levels of concern about privacy risks, consumers often give up their privacy, sometimes for relatively low-level rewards'.[213] Users do care about their privacy but, nonetheless, give away their personal data also because they are not in the position to understand their rights and obligations.[214] The online social contract should be founded on a clear pact as to the parties' rights and obligations; the readability of the legals may play an important role. Therefore, this author measured readability level, readability score, and text quality.[215] The readability formulas taken into account as to the readability levels are the Flesch-Kincaid Grade Level,[216] the Gunning-Fog Score,[217] the Coleman-Liau Index,[218]

---

[211] GDPR, Art 25.

[212] Gamifying privacy seems pivotal to making users take privacy seriously. Indeed, given the tendency not to read the privacy policies, gamification can lead to increased interactivity and thus alertness. See, for instance, Centre for Democracy and Technology 'The Gamification of Privacy' (*CDT*, 11 July 2011) Available at: www.cdt.org/blog/the-gamification-of-privacy/. Some authors distinguish between serious games and gamified interactions (Cristina Rottondi and Giacomo Verticale, 'A Privacy-Friendly Gaming Framework in Smart Electricity and Water Grids' (2017) 5 IEEE Access 14221). The former refers to games designed for purposes others than entertainment, the latter to 'the use of game design elements in non-game contexts'. In this chapter, it is believed that using game design elements in the drafting and presentation of privacy policies can be a good way to increase the users' awareness thus making it more likely that they will have privacy-preserving behaviours. Unlike that study, this author is more concerned with the use of games to protect privacy, rather than with the privacy risks of online gaming.

[213] Competition & Markets Authority, 'The commercial use of consumer data. Report on the CMA's call for information' (*GovUK*, June 2015) 130. Available at: www.gov.uk/government/uploads/system/uploads/attachment_data/file/435817/The_commercial_use_of_consumer_data.pdf, last accessed 25 September 2017.

[214] Certainly, the belief of not having any other choice but accepting the legals plays an important in making users give away their rights.

[215] The software used was Readable.io.

[216] The Flesch-Kincaid Grade Level rates texts on a US school grade level. For instance, a score of 8.0 means that an eighth grader (Year 9 in England) can understand the document. For most documents, the desirable score is between 7.0 and 8.0. The parameters of this test are word length and sentence length. Cf Glenda M. McClure, 'Readability Formulas: Useful or useless?' *IEEE Transactions on Professional Communication* PC30(1) (1987) at 12.

[217] The parameters of this test are sentence length and hard words (words with more than two syllables). The desirable score is 8 and it should never go beyond 12 (High School senior). For more details, see Robert Gunning, *The Technique of Clear Writing* (New York: McGraw-Hill, 1952).

[218] Unlike the two tests above, the Colemain-Liau Index considers the length of the words with regards to the letters, not to the syllables. It looks at the average number of letters and the average number of sentences per 100 words. Like the other tests, the scores approximate the US levels. Therefore, the desirable score is between 7 and 8. For more information, see Meri Coleman and T.L. Liau, 'A Computer Readability Formula Designed for Machine Scoring' *Journal of Applied Psychology* 60, no 2 (1975): 283.

the SMOG Index,[219] and Automated Readability.[220] As to the readability score, I have referred to the Flesch-Kincaid Reading Ease,[221] the Spache Score,[222] and the New Dale-Chall Score.[223] Considering the Terms of Service in isolation would be incorrect, since these incorporate also the privacy policy[224] and the usage guidelines.[225] The results are as follows.

Grindr's, PlanetRomeo's, and Hornet's legals consist respectively of 14,189, 7,537, and 6,342 words. The first and the last are very similar, including entire sentences which are taken *verbatim* from the other app's legals. PlanetRomeo's legals are quite different (probably because they are a European company) and do not include separate usage guidelines.

Table 2.1 Readability level

Readability formula	Grindr	PlanetRomeo	Hornet
Flesch-Kincaid Grade Level	13	10	10.6
Gunning-Fog Score	14.1	11.7	11.6
Coleman-Liau Index	13.8	13.6	13.3
SMOG Index	15.1	12.4	13.3
Automated readability	13.3	9.1	9.9
Average Grade Level	13.9	11.4	11.7

[219] This test looks at the words of three or more syllables in three 10-sentence samples. Grades 13-16 require college education, 17–18 graduate training, and 19 and above, higher professional qualification. According to Paul Fitzsimmons et al, 'A Readability Assessment of Online Parkinson's Disease Information' *J R Coll Physicians Edinb* 40 (2010): 292, the SMOG index is better than the Flesch-Kincaid test because the latter would underestimate reading difficulties. For more information, see G. Harry Mc Laughlin, 'SMOG Grading – A New Readability Formula' *Journal of Reading* May (1969) 639.

[220] This index looks at characters (relevant only here and in the Coleman-Liau Index), words, and sentences. Like most of the tests, it approximates the US grade level. A score of 8 means that a seventh grader would be able to understand the document. The desirable score would be between 8 and 9. See E.A. Smith and R.J. Senter, 'Automated Readability Index' (US Defense Technical Information Center, November 1967). Available at: www.dtic.mil/dtic/tr/fulltext/u2/667273.pdf, last accessed 29 September 2017.

[221] The Flesch-Kincaid Reading Ease rates texts on a 100-point scale. The higher the score, the easier it is to understand the document. The desirable score is between 60 and 70 (8th–9th grade, plain English, easily understood by 13- to 14-year-old students). The parameters of this test are word and sentence length. For more details, see www. support.office.com/en-gb/article/Test-your-document-s-readability-85b4969e-e80a-4777-8dd3-f7fc3c8b3fd2#__toc342546557, last accessed 29 September 2017.

[222] This formula looks at the average sentence length and the percentage of unique unfamiliar words. It was designed for children up to the fourth grade. See George Spache, 'A New Readability Formula for Primary-grade Reading Materials' *The Elementary School Journal* 53, no 7 (1952): 410.

[223] This formula focuses on words, difficult words and sentences. Words are difficult if US fourth graders are not familiar with them. It is suitable for children not beyond the ninth grade. See Jeanne S. Chall and Edgar Dale, *Readability Revisited: The New Dale-Chall Readability Formula* (Brookline: Brookline Books, 1995).

[224] Grindr Terms, clause 5.

[225] Ibid clause 8(1).

Table 2.2 Readability score

Readability formula	Grindr	PlanetRomeo	Hornet
Flesch-Kincaid Reading Ease	41.1	48.4	48.2
Spache Score	4.1	3.3	3.9
New Dale-Chall Score	6.8	6.1	6.2

The desirable score would be 8. One can see that the Grindr legals are less readable according to all the tests, requiring at least college education. Since 59 per cent of the users of dating apps do not have the sufficient level of education,[226] one can infer that the majority of the users of MSM apps cannot understand the terms of their contractual relation with the platform. PlanetRomeo has the most readable legals, although Hornet performs better with regards to the Gunning-Fog Score and the Coleman-Liau Index. Even though Hornet does not score the highest in terms of readability *per se*, they have the shortest legals, which seems particularly important given the information over-load that users experience online.[227]

Given that the desirable score would be between 60 and 70, the Flesch-Kincaid Reading Ease shows that the legals of these apps are all difficult to read (college level). However, PlanetRomeo is, albeit not by much, the best, being the closest to 'fairly difficult to read' (tenth to twelfth grade). The Spache score should be disregarded because it is designed for children in the fourth grade and because using other calculators the output is radically different.[228] Similarly, the New Dale-Chall Schore deems difficult the words that are not familiar to a US fourth grader, which one can imagine is not the typical user of MSM apps.[229]

Therefore, the ranking as shown in Table 2.2 is the same as the one in Table 2.1. It is confirmed that Grindr's legals are the least readable and PlanetRomeo's ones are the most readable.

[226] Aaron Smith, '15% of American adults have used online dating sites or mobile dating apps' (Pew Research Centre, 11 February 2016). Available at: http://assets.pewresearch.org/wp-content/uploads/sites/14/2016/02/PI_2016.02.11_Online-Dating_FINAL.pdf, last accessed 14 November 2017.

[227] See Chun-Ying Chen, Susan Pedersen and Karen L. Murphy, 'Learners' Perceived Information Overload in Online Learning via Computer-mediated Communication' *Research in Learning Technology* 19, no 2 (2011): 101.

[228] For instance, if one uses the calculator available at www.readabilityformulas.com/dalechall-formula/spache-formula.php, last accessed 29 September 2017, as opposed to the one provided by Readable.io, one finds that Grindr Terms score 20.

[229] Using Dale-Chall calculators different to the one provided by Readable.io, the results are different (even though not as much as the one regarding the Spache Formula). For instance, Grindr Terms score 8.2 using the calculator available at www.readabilityformulas.com/dalechallformula/dale-chall-formula.php, last accessed 29 September 2017.

Table 2.3 Text quality

Parameter	Grindr	PlanetRomeo	Hornet
Sentences > 30 syllables	327	175	123
Sentences > 20 syllables	413	275	171
Words > 4 syllables	391	641	129
Words > 12 letters	151	79	61
Passive voice count	114	77	58
Adverb count	394	227	206

Again, Grindr is the worst performer across the board, while PlanetRomeo has the best text quality. The fact that it has more words with more than four syllables is probably due to the name of the app itself being longer than its rivals, as well as to the use of some words in Dutch.[230] Hornet's text quality is superior to the competitors, but this may be due primarily to the quantitative datum of the length of its legals.

The above results present only a partial picture as only the three companies' legals were assessed. However, by accessing the relevant services, the user will be bound also to other legals (eg Google's as to analytics and/or advertising). Therefore, supposedly, the user should read and understand also a number of third-party legals, which means that the overall readability would further decrease.

In the unlikely event of a user reading and understanding the legals, the effort would soon be useless. Indeed, the legals are updated quite often and without proper notice.[231] Of the legals analysed, Grindr was the only one clarifying the date of the terms and the main updated, but they did not made available the previous versions (unlike Google, for instance).[232]

The low readability of the legals and the structural inequality of bargaining power also explain the privacy paradox. A European report[233] found that the number of users who read the 'legals' would more than double if they contained simple language and short text. One may object, however, that even though the legals are hard to understand and potentially unfair, this has no practical consequences because they are enforced fairly or they are not enforced at all. For instance, one could imagine that even though immoral behaviour is

---

[230] See, eg, '*Databankenwet*' and '*toerekenbare tekortkoming*', referring to, respectively, the Dutch Database Act and the liability for attributably failing to perform the agreement.

[231] See, for instance, Hornet Terms, clause 4, according to which 'Hornet reserves the right to change, modify, add, or remove portions of this Agreement or any guidelines at any time with or without notice. Your continued use of the Hornet Services after the posting of any modifications or changes constitutes your binding acceptance of such changes'. See also Grindr Terms, clause 8(1).

[232] The 21 versions of Google's Privacy Policy are available at www.google.com/policies/privacy/archive/, last accessed 29 September 2017.

[233] Elshout et al. (n 204).

outlawed in law, in reality the app providers will allow this type of behaviour.[234] The findings of this study suggest otherwise. Amongst the respondents who have an opinion and/or knowledge on the issue, 60 per cent believe that the legals are unfairly enforced.[235] The rest believe that they are enforced, but fairly (half of them state that there is an element of arbitrariness to the private enforcement). In turn, no one believes that the legals are not enforced in the first place.[236]

4.1. Beyond the Form: Do MSM App Providers Respect their Users' Privacy?

While the form of the legals can in itself be in breach of the GDPR,[237] it is important to assess if their content confirms that the analysed intermediaries do not respect their users' privacy. It has been already noted that MSM app providers betray their users' privacy expectations by providing app store providers with a back-door. A recent complaint[238] lodged by the Norwegian Consumer Council (*Forbrukerrådet*) against Grindr confirms that MSM app providers' behaviour may not be privacy friendly.

First, an analysis of the functioning of Grindr and a number of interviews evidenced that Grindr screens each profile picture ex ante and reviews the profile descriptions (see Figure 2.2).[239] The focus group confirmed that the practice of not authorising profile pictures is commonplace, which suggests that Grindr and similar apps put in place a strict filter.

The screening activities have a direct impact on the liability regime, because the intermediary is aware of the illegal activities carried out by the users in their

---

[234] Under the PlanetRomeo Terms of Use, '(t)he use of the Service may not (…) involve any illegal activities or activities that are contrary to morality or public order' (clause 2(4(j)). Likewise, under Grindr Terms 'You will NOT post, store, send, transmit, or disseminate any information or material which a reasonable person could deem to be objectionable …, or otherwise inappropriate, regardless of whether this material or its dissemination is unlawful' (clause 8(12).

[235] In the US, privacy policies can be enforced by the Federal Trade Commission as promises to consumers under the Federal Trade Commission Act, 15 U.S.C. § 45(a), s 5 on unfair methods of competition and unfair or deceptive acts or practices. See Gautam S Hans, 'Privacy Policies, Terms of Service, and FTC Enforcement: Broadening Unfairness Regulation for a New Era' *Michigan Telecommunications and Technology Law Review* 19, no 1 (2012): 163. In Europe, the 'legals' may be found unenforceable under consumer legislation or sectoral one (see, for instance, *Spreadex Ltd v Cochrane* (2012) *The Times*, 24 August, [2012] EWHC 1290 (Comm)).

[236] With regards to massively multiplayer online games (MMO games), Megan Rae Blakely, 'Subject to Terms and Conditions: User Concepts of Ownership and Intellectual Property in MMOs' (SLS2017 conference, Dublin, September 2017), found that the relevant legals are not enforced.

[237] Opaque legals hardly deliver GDPR-compliant consent. More generally, the distinction between form and substance is blurred in the data protection field.

[238] See *Forbrukerrådet* (n 40).

[239] Screen shown to Grindr's users after uploading a profile picture. Screenshot taken from an android device accessed on 7 April 2018 at 17:47 GMT.

profile descriptions or with their profile pictures. Now, prima facie one may think that if the national implementation of the eCommerce Directive is based on the notice-and-takedown system, then MSM app providers would not be liable for illegal content – even if they have actual knowledge of it – without needing a notice. However, under *Kaschke v Gray*,[240] blog owners cannot avail themselves of the hosting immunity if they can infer the existence of the infringing content from the checking of the spelling and grammar of the user-generated content. Applying this case to our scenario, it seems clear that MSM app providers filtering their users' content cannot invoke the safe harbours. Conversely, a defensive strategy for said providers might be that their operation is entirely automatic; without humans in the loop, no knowledge is possible.[241] While one of the spokespersons of the MSM apps affirmed that there was a team of human beings reviewing the content,[242] there is evidence that at least some platforms do put in place automated screening systems.[243]

In light of the increased use of AI and automated systems, it is arguable that *Davison* is no longer good law in that respect, otherwise every intermediary could escape all liability by automating the way they monitor their users and/or screen the user-generated content.

Second, regrettably, instead of precisely listing the data that Grindr accesses, they provide mere 'examples of the types of data that we collect'.[244] The interviewed users were surprised to find out that this data encompasses all the (supposedly) private messages, including all photos, location, audio and video. From a purpose limitation[245] and data retention perspective, it is noteworthy

---

[240] [2010] EWHC 690 (QB).

[241] *Davison v Habeeb* [2011] EWHC 3031 (QB) applied *Metropolitan International Schools* (n 143), and, therefore, did not held Google liable for their search services, despite their listings and snippets including defamatory content. The reason for that was that 'the operation of the Google search engine is entirely automatic' (*Davison* [40]).

[242] Interview to MSM spokesperson No 1, who said that 'there is usually a human being, but not for fake profiles. All the pictures are 'voted' as non-sexual, illegal, a little bit sexual, etc.' The spokesperson of the MSM app No 2 did not know if the screening was human or not. However, on 26 April 2018, the customer support of said spokesperson's company confirmed that they 'have a team of dedicated staff members who reviews and double-checks all profile pictures and profile descriptions'.

[243] As one can read in *Herrick* (n 126), Grindr's website stated 'we have a system of digital and human screening tools to protect our users.' Such assertion is no longer present. Grindr's customer support observed that they have a 'Review Team conducted by humans that review the content of Grindr profiles.' (B. – Grindr Customer Support, email of 26 April 2018). However, they did not answer this researcher's question whether 'the review of the profile pictures and profile descriptions is automated, semi-automated, or entirely human.' (E-mail to Grindr Customer Support of 26 April 2018). PlanetRomeo's customer support pointed out that only profile pictures are reviewed manually, whereas the rest 'on demand manually and partly automatically' (S. – PlanetRomeo Customer Support, e-mail of 2 May 2018).

[244] Grindr Privacy Policy.

[245] GDPR, Art 5.

that the messages are retained indefinetely[246] not only for archival purposes, but also 'as otherwise allowed by law'. Processing of personal data for purposes other than those for which consent was originally sought is allowed only for archiving, scientific, historical or statistical purposes.[247] However, archiving falls within the scope only if 'in the public interest',[248] which does not seem to apply to Grindr's archiving. Moreover, this exception requires the putting in place of appropriate safeguards to ensure data minimisation, whilst Grindr seems to collect data way beyond what is strictly necessary for its operation.

It is impossible to fully understand which data Grindr is processing. To this end, this author sent Grindr a data subject access request in January 2018. As of May 2018, they have not granted this access.[249]

Third, the GDPR strengthens the conditions for valid consent,[250] as it must be given freely, informed, unambiguous, specific, granular, clear, prominent, opt-in, properly documented and easily withdrawn.[251] The only GDPR-compliant consent 'is a tool that gives data subjects control over whether or not personal data concerning them will be processed'.[252] This does not seem the case with Grindr. Indeed, the consent is expressed simply 'by accessing'[253] the service.

---

[246] To put it in legalese, 'for the period necessary to fulfill the purposes outlined in this Privacy Policy, *unless a longer retention period is required for the operation of the Grindr Services or permitted by law*' (Grindr Privacy Policy, italics added). Since the purposes are not clearly outlines, the retention risks being indefinite. Different terms apply to some jurisdictions. The only special terms that provide a limit to the data retention are the Brazilian Grindr Terms: 'We will keep the application logs under confidentiality, in a controlled and safe environment, for six (6) months' (Grindr Special Terms for International Users, 8(5)). The special terms are available below the regular terms.

[247] GDPR, Art 89. It should be kept in mind, however, that further processing may be lawful also outside said exception, if personal data is processed in a manner that is compatible with the original purposes (GDPR, Art 5(1)(b)).

[248] GDPR, Art 89(1).

[249] On 8 April 2018, this author reiterated the request. As of 4 May 2018, Grindr has not followed up on the data subject request.

[250] Consent is not the only legal basis for processing. From the outset, one should assess if Grindr may rely on the necessity for the performance of a contract or on the legitimate interest of the data controller (GDPR, art 6(1)(b) and (f)). It is implausible that the sharing of personal data including sexual data and health data with advertisers and other third parties is necessary for the performance of the contract. This justification may cover, conversely, the processing of geolocation data, since the purpose of the service is to enable users to get in contact with other users based on the respective location. It is unlikely, then, that the company can avail itself of the legitimate interest justification because in light of the type of data processed, the processing should be regarded as very intrusive. Moreover, the MSM survey and the reaction to the HIV status data's leak confirm that data is not used 'in ways (data subjects) would reasonably expect' (Information Commissioner's Office, *Guide to the General Data Protection Regulation (GDPR)* (v. 1.0.17, ICO 2018) 40. For a recent failure of the legitimate interest defence for availability of less instrusive alternatives see Commission Nationale de l'Informatique et des Libertés (CNIL), *Décision MED n° 2018- 007 du 5 mars 2018 mettant en demeure la société Direct Energie.*

[251] GDPR, Arts 4(11) and 7; recitals 32, 33, 42, and 43.

[252] Article 29 Working Party, 'Guidelines on Consent under Regulation 2016/679' (WP259, 28 November 2017) 4.

[253] Grindr Privacy Policy.

While this is hardly freely given[254] and opt-in consent, this mechanism is particularly problematic with regards to the data on sex, sexual orientation, and health that Grindr processes. Indeed, the main legal basis for the processing of such sensitive personal data is *explicit* consent, which is the opposite of the *per-facta-concludentia* consent that seems the industry practice. Since regular consent requires already an affirmative action, it is unclear what explicit consent means. The Article 29 Working Party suggests that data subjects may explicitly consent 'by filling in an electronic form, by sending an email, by uploading a scanned document carrying the signature of the data subject, or by using an electronic signature'.[255] The fact that Grindr processes both sensitive and non-sensitive personal data has an impact on its obligations with regards to both types of data. Indeed, consent is presumed not to be freely given if the data controller does not allow separate consent to different personal data operations, 'despite it being appropriate in the individual case'.[256] The processing of both sensitive and non-sensitive data seems an obvious example of separate consent. This said, whereas conduct (as opposed to statements or declaration) cannot deliver explicit consent, it could nonetheless be a form of expressing (non-explicit) consent.[257] While the check box is not in itself invalid consent must be informed, therefore a long and illegible[258] document would not deliver GDPR-compliant consent, particularly if it is not clear for which purpose each type of data is processed.[259]

Another problem with Grindr's check box is that 'consent must always be obtained before the controller starts processing personal data for which consent is needed'.[260] However, this screen follows the request of the e-mail address and the date of birth, which can constitute personal data (see Figure 2.3).[261]

Granularity is another critical point. The Article 29 Working Party clarifies that if 'consent is bundled up as a non-negotiable part of terms and conditions it is presumed not to have been freely given'.[262] Grindr asks the users' to accept the privacy policy separately to the terms of service. However, it is questionable whether non-negotiable privacy policies can ensure that consent is freely given.

---

[254] Consent is not freely given, for instance, if 'the data subject has no genuine or free choice or is unable to refuse or withdraw consent without detriment' (GDPR, recital 42).

[255] See Article 29 Working Party, n 252 at 19. They suggest also a two-stage verification process, where the data controller informs of the intent of processing sensitive personal data explaining the purposes and the data subject is required to reply 'I agree.'

[256] GDPR, recital 43.

[257] Ibid, recital 32.

[258] Article 29 Working Party, n, 252 at 14.

[259] For the requirement of informed consent, see ibid at 13.

[260] Ibid at 18. Even though the GDPR does not expressly require prior consent, this is implied in Art 6 and recital 40.

[261] First screen shown to Grindr's new users before accessing the service. The screenshot was taken on 4 April 2018 at 16:23 GMT with an android device.

[262] Article 29 Working Party, n 252 at 6. This is in line with the GDPR, Art 7(4).

This is particularly evident with the data Grindr collects without them being necessary for the provision of the service, for instance the sharing of HIV status data with third parties.[263]

Moreover, Grindr limits or even denies the exercise of the right to withdraw not only 'if the law permits or requires us to do so',[264] which it does not in the EU, but also 'if we are unable to adequately verify your identity'.[265] Aside from the fact that the GDPR does not provide any exceptions or limitations to the right of withdrawal, it is noteworthy that '(i)t shall be as easy to withdraw as to give consent'.[266] Since it is not required to prove one's identity when giving consent, this requirement does not apply to its withdrawal. Moreover, data controllers should provide the same interface for giving and withdrawing consent,[267] but it is unclear which interface one should use to exercise this right.

In April 2018, a complaint filed by the Norwegian Consumer Council against Grindr exposed these issues, particularly with regard to the sharing of (a) data on sexual preferences with advertisers[268] and (b) HIV status data with two analytics service providers. There are three strong arguments. First, Grindr declares that its users' personal data may be processed in countries with weak data protection laws therefore, 'you might be left without a legal remedy in the event of a privacy breach'.[269] This chapter joins the Consumer Council[270] in considering unfortunate the contractual provision on transnational data transfers because neither Grindr nor its parent company Beijing Kunlun Tech Co, Ltd. signed up to the Privacy Shield.[271] Additionally, it is crucial to keep in mind that one of the main innovations of the GDPR is its extraterritorial application when goods or services are offered to data subjects in the EU or when these subjects' behaviour

---

[263] GDPR, Art 7(4). The Article 29 Working Party makes the example of photo editing app collecting geolocation data for behavioural advertising purposes. Since this goes beyond what is necessary for the provision of the service and since 'users cannot use the app without consent (…) consent cannot be considered as being freely given.' (ibid at 7).

[264] Grindr Privacy Policy.

[265] Ibid.

[266] GDPR, Art 7(3).

[267] Article 29 Working Party, n 252 at 21.

[268] The sharing of sensitive personal data for advertising purposes is not unprecedented. For instance, Facebook was fined €1.2 million in Spain for this reason. José González Cabañas, Ángel Cuevas, Rubén Cuevas, 'Facebook Use of Sensitive Data for Advertising in Europe' (*ArXiv*, 14 February 2018) found that Facebook labelled 73% of EU users in association to sensitive personal data. Available at: arxiv.org/abs/1802.05030, last accessed 18 April 2018. The authors developed a browser extension that Facebook users can use to discover how the social networking site is monetising their data. The tool is available at www.fdvt.org/, last accessed 18 April 2018.

[269] Grindr Privacy Policy.

[270] *Forbrukerrådet* (n 40) 4.

[271] Available at: www.privacyshield.gov/list, last accessed 5 April 2018. The main legal bases for the international data transfers are adequacy decisions, bespoke arrangements, Standard Contractual Clauses, and Binding Corporate Rules. To the knowledge of this author, none of these legal bases applies to the Grindr's scenario.

is monitored.[272] It would seem that Grindr both offers services to data subjects in the EU and monitors them, therefore it cannot leave these subjects without legal recourse.

The second argument is that data Grindr shares data about sexual orientation and sexual preferences through unencrypted data flows.[273] This is in line with its privacy policy, whereby the company takes reasonable efforts to protect personal data from unauthorised access, yet 'Grindr cannot guarantee the security of your Personal Data'.[274] While the GDPR is technologically neutral, therefore, it does not mandate encryption, 'the controller or processor should evaluate the risks inherent in the processing and implement measures to mitigate those risks, such as encryption'.[275] In selecting the adequate security measures, companies must take into account the 'state of the art, the costs of implementation and the nature, scope, context and purposes of processing as well as the risk of varying likelihood and severity for the rights and freedoms of natural persons'.[276] When processing sensitive data, arguably, encryption should be the default security measure.

A third strong argument put forward by the Norwegiam Consumer Council is that 'information about sensitive personal data being shared with third parties should not be hidden away in long terms of service and privacy policies'.[277] This is in line with the Article 29 Working Party's guidelines on consent according to which 'information relevant for making informed decisions on whether or not to consent may not be hidden in general terms and conditions'.[278] While users were surprised to find out that the data about their HIV status and sexual preferences were shared with third parties, this practice is not in itself unlawful. Therefore, the main issue is assessing if the consent asked by Grindr is of the quality required by the GDPR. As said above, arguably this is not the case, with the consent neither informed, freely given, granular or specific, let alone explicit.

The outrage[279] that followed the news that Grindr shares HIV status and sexual preferences data with third parties is both a testament to the fact that the legals

---

[272] GDPR, Art 3(2).

[273] The evidence of this is the experiment reported in SVT and SINTEF, 'Grindr Privacy Leaks' (*GitHub*, 2018) Available at: www.github.com/SINTEF-9012/grindr-privacy-leaks, last accessed 4 May 2018.

[274] Grindr Privacy Policy. Grindr's CTO, however, ensures that at least the transmission of HIV status data is encrypted. Scott Chen, 'Here's What You Should Know Regarding your HIV Status Data' (*Grindr Tumblr*, 3 April 2018). Available at: www.grindr.tumblr.com/post/172528912083/heres-what-you-should-know-regarding-your-hiv, last accessed 6 April 2018.

[275] GDPR, recital 83.

[276] GDPR, Art 32.

[277] *Forbrukerrådet* (n 40) 5.

[278] Article 29 Working Party (n 252) para 3.3.2.

[279] See, for instance, Brian Moylan, 'Grindr was a safe space for gay men. Its HIV status leak betrayed us' (*The Guardian*, 4 April 2018). Available at: www.theguardian.com/commentisfree/2018/apr/04/grindr-gay-men-hiv-status-leak-app, last accessed 4 April 2018.

are not read or understood, as well as the fact that bottom-up pressures can be a very effective tool to improve data protection practices. Indeed, after claiming that this kind of sharing was industry practice, Grindr stated that they will refrain from it in the future.[280] Interestingly, another justification put forward by the company was that if a user decides to disclose in their profile description, then this data is public.[281] One should keep in mind that sensitive personal data is lawfully processed if manifestly made available to the public.[282] However, the MSM survey confirmed that Grindr users see the platform as a private space.[283] Grindr's argument risks making people hide their HIV status, thus reinforcing the stigma surrounding it.

Grindr's response, moreover, is only partly convincing. First, the company will keep sharing data on sexual preferences with third parties including advertisers. Second, they have offered reassurance that no third parties can access profile data on Grindr; only 'appropriate Grindr employees and trusted contractors'[284] can and they are 'bound by appropriate privacy and confidentiality terms'.[285] This is at odds with the section of the privacy policy providing that both advertisers and partners use their own cookies or other tracking technology to collect personal data within the Grindr Services, while Grindr does 'not control use of these tracking technologies'.[286] It is not clear which data these third parties have access to, if not the profile data. One might conjecture that they have access to the 'private' messages, including any photographic content shared by the users.[287]

---

[280] Kristine Phillips, 'Grindr says it will stop sharing users' HIV data with third-party firms amid backlash' (*The Washington Post*, 3 April 2018). Available at:www.washingtonpost.com/news/to-your-health/wp/2018/04/03/grindr-says-it-will-stop-sharing-users-hiv-data-with-third-party-firms-amid-backlash/?utm_term=.a3beb24b874d, last accessed 4 April 2018.

[281] See the Grindr Privacy Policy and Chen (n 274).

[282] GDPR, Art 9(2)(e).

[283] It has been argued, however, that MSM apps refigure conceptualisations of public/private boundaries. Sam Miles, 'Sex in the Digital City: Location-Based Dating Apps and Queer Urban Life' *Gender, Place & Culture* 24, no 11 (2017): 1595.

[284] Chen (n 274).

[285] Ibid.

[286] Grindr Privacy Policy. In the app, it was found the code signature of the following trackers: AdColony, AppsFlyer, Apptimize, Braze, Facebook Ads, Facebook Login, Facebook Share, Google Ads Google CrashLytics, Google DoubleClick, Google Firebase Analytics, Inmobi, Localytics, Millennial Media, Moat, Smaato, Twitter MoPub. See 'Grindr – Gay Chat, Meet & Date' (*Exodus*, 26 March 2018) Available at: reports.exodus-privacy.eu.org/reports/5323/, last accessed 4 May 2018.

[287] This would seem excluded by SVT (n 273). According to said report, Grindr shares with third parties the following data: Grindr (app name), precise GPS position, gender, HIV status, 'last tested' date, e-mail address, age, height, weight, body type, position (sexual), Grindr profile ID, 'tribe' (Bear, Clean Cut, Daddy, Discreet, Geek, Jock, Leather, Otter, Poz, Rugged, Trans, Unknown), 'Looking for' (Chat, Dates, Friends, Networking, Relationship, Right Now, Unknown), ethnicity, relationship status, phone ID, advertising ID, phone characteristics, language, activity.

The first challenge of the web, according to its inventor Sir Tim Berners-Lee, is the loss of control over personal data, which he relates to the fact that 'T&Cs are all or nothing'.[288] This study showed that the quality of the legals of the MSM apps is an important element of this loss of control over one's own personal data. The low quality of the 'legals' has practical consequences; one need only mention that consumers report problems with purchases related to the fact that they did not read and/or understand the terms of service.[289] Ultimately, a fairer approach to data privacy and security would positively affect the consumers' trust in the IoB (with increased profitability for the IoB providers).[290] In the IoB environment, there are mostly data-fuelled, asymmetric, mass transactions; therefore, the main way to have a fairer private ordering of privacy is to make IoB providers understand that being privacy-friendly is a competitive advantage.[291] If, in application of a joint interpretation of Data Protection by Design,[292] accountability,[293] and transparency,[294] these providers changed the way they present the information about their users' privacy (eg with visualisation tools and gamified interactions), they would contribute to laying the foundations for a more balanced online social contract. Thus, IoB providers would take up the recent Commission's suggestion to provide a 'clear, easily understandable and sufficiently detailed explanation of their content policy in their terms of service',[295] consistent the enhanced transparency principle as restated in the GDPR.[296]

---

[288] Web Foundation, 'Three Challenges for the Web, According to its Inventor' (*WebFoundation*, 12 March 2017) Available at: webfoundation.org/2017/03/web-turns-28-letter/, last accessed 19 September 2017.

[289] Elshout et al (n 204).

[290] On the relation between privacy, trust, and purchasing behaviour see Carlos Flavian and Miguel Guinaliu, 'Consumer Trust, Perceived Security and Privacy Policy' *Industrial Management & Data Systems* 106, no 5 (2006): 601.

[291] See, for instance, David Hoffman, 'Privacy is a Business Opportunity' (*Harvard Business Review*, 18 April 2014) Available at; hbr.org/2014/04/privacy-is-a-business-opportunity, last accessed 26 September 2017 and Sören Preibusch, Dorothea Kübler, and Alastair R. Beresford, 'Price Versus Privacy: An Experiment into the Competitive Advantage of Collecting Less Personal Information' *Electronic Commerce Research* 13, no 4 (2013): 42. It has been pointed out that two solutions to the lack of bargaining power of users of online platforms may be to develop efforts to incentivise service providers to adopt consumer-friendly legals and to raise the awareness of users with regard to the content thereof (Ellen Wauters, Eva Lievens and Peggy Valcke, 'Towards a Better Protection of Social Media Users: A Legal Perspective on the Terms of Use of Social Networking Sites' *Int J Law Info Tech* 22, no 3 (2014): 254, 293.

[292] GDPR, Art 25.

[293] GDPR, Art 5(2).

[294] GDPR, Arts 5(1)(a) and 12.

[295] Commission, 'Tackling Illegal Content Online. Towards an enhanced responsibility of online platforms' (Communication) COM (2017) 555 final, para 4(2).

[296] GDPR, Art 12, recital 58.

5. Conclusion

In an IoB world, the body is becoming a key source of personal data. The body is changing the Internet like the Internet is changing the body (eg in terms of cyborgisation and aesthetic discrimination). The body is no longer the sanctuary of the right to be left alone, which used to be the core of the right to privacy. In the IoB, as shown by this research, privacy has a fundamentally rhetorical function. On the one hand, it justifies the platforms' immunity from liability, whilst on the other hand, these same platforms force users to give away their privacy in the context of opaque and often unfair online transactions.

This research confirmed that in the online MSM community the body is heavily influenced by other users' attitudes as well as by the MSM apps themselves. That profile descriptions openly exclude entire segments of the population based on their appearance (eg no fats, no 'femmes') and the fact that specific types of picture are used to advertise the services provided by MSM apps are just some examples of this.

MSM feel pressured to adapt to a certain model of body (ie fit, young, masculine and white). By excluding certain bodies, MSM users and apps reproduce heteronormative and capitalist values and power dynamics. The acceptable MSM is a highly productive and respectable member of the community who embraces and even exacerbates the male/female binary. The Internet would seem to offer an opportunity to dissociate physical body and gender identity, to the point that it was declared that 'in cyberspace the transgendered body is the natural body'[297] and that, thanks to pseudonymity, users may play with gender identity.[298] This research presents evidence that the Internet does not overcome the gender binary and that in cyberspace the masculine, fit, white, abled body is the natural body. This is along the lines of the recent findings according to which the behaviour of young users online show a strong attachment to gender binarity.[299]

Research showed that the 'prevalence of weight/height discrimination is (…) comparable to rates of racial discrimination';[300] linked to this is the lack of law preventing aesthetic discrimination. This article does not claim that racial discrimination is ontologically the same as aesthetic discrimination, but sometimes they are expressions of similar issues and prejudices and, in rethinking

---

[297] Allucquère Rosanne Stone, *The War of Desire and Technology at the Close of the Mechanical Age* (Cambridge: MIT Press, 1995) 181.

[298] Jouët Josiane, 'Une communauté télématique : les axiens' *Réseaux* 7, no 38 (1989): 49.

[299] Claire Balleys, 'L'incontrôlable besoin de contrôle. Les performances de la féminité par les adolescents sur YouTube' (*Genre, sexualité & société*, 1 June 2017). Available at|: www.gss.revues.org/3958, last accessed 31 October 2017.

[300] Rebecca M. Puhl, Tatiana Andreyeva and Kelly D. Brownell, 'Perceptions of Weight Discrimination: Prevalence and Comparison to Race and Gender Discrimination in America' *International Journal of Obesity* 32 (2008): 992, 999.

discrimination laws, new protected characteristics should be taken into account. Moreover, as intersectionality theory shows,[301] different forms of discrimination and exclusion are in some way connected and overlap.[302] Therefore, they cannot be understood and analysed in silos. Furthermore, the scenarios when discrimination is illegal should be broadened: there is no reason why discriminating against a disabled person as a member or guest of a private club or association is illegal but doing so in an online community where the person spends a considerable amount of their time is not.[303]

The analysis of the legals of MSM apps confirmed that users do not read them because they are too long and complicated. Obscure legals can hardly constitute the basis for the social contract of the IoB. It is proposed, however, that the data protection by design approach be interpreted jointly with transparency and accountability to encompass the design of the legals. These should be better drafted (short, clear, consistent) and should stimulate the user's attentiveness (eg through gamification, visualisation, etc.).[304] Only if the IoB providers understand that privacy is a competitive advantage, will the private ordering of privacy become fairer.

Hidden in the contractual quagmire of the legals, are provisions which are arguably unenforceable. MSM apps attempt to disclaim all liability for damages resulting from the interaction with the app or between the users, even when the app has knowledge of the illegal activity and this results in personal injury

---

[301] The theory was first presented by Kimberle Crenshaw, 'Demarginalizing the Intersection of Race and Sex: A Black Feminist Critique of Antidiscrimination Doctrine, Feminist Theory and Antiracist Politics' *University of Chicago Legal Forum* 1, no 8 (1989): 139. She believed that 'theories and strategies purporting to reflect the Black community's needs must include an analysis of sexism and patriarchy. Similarly, feminism must include an analysis of race if it hopes to express the aspirations of non-white women' (ibid 166). A more updated idea of intersectionality is presented by Patricia Hill Collins and Sirma Bilge, *Intersectionality* (Polity 2016) 2, according to whom 'people's lives and the organization of power in a given society are better understood as being shaped not by a single axis of social division, be it race or gender or class, but my many axes that work together and influence each other'. Intersectionality evolved to encompass other identities and protected characteristics; see Devon W Carbado, 'Intersectionality. Mapping the Movements of a Theory' *Du Bois Review* 10, no 2 (2013): 303. For an application related to queer people and Islam see, for instance, Fatima El-Tayeb, "Gays who cannot properly be gay': Queer Muslims in the Neoliberal European City' *European Journal of Women's Studies* 19, no 1 (2012): 79.

[302] For instance, racial discrimination is associated with increased body mass index (Gilbert C. Gee et al, 'Disentangling the Effects of Racial and Weight Discrimination on Body Mass Index and Obesity among Asian Americans' *American Journal of Public Health* 98, no 3 (2008): 493.

[303] See Paul Michaels, 'The Use of Dating Apps within a Sample of the International Deaf Gay Male Community' (IGALA9 conference, Hong Kong, May 206).

[304] Suffice to say that the first law of usability – the rules on how a website should be designed – can be summed up as 'don't make me think'. If the brain is switched off, it is unlikely the user will behave in a privacy-aware way. See Steve Krug, *Don't Make Me Think: A Common Sense Approach to Web Usability* (San Francisco: New Riders, 2nd edn, 2005).

or death.[305] While the exclusion or restriction of liability for death or personal injury resulting from negligence is obviously unenforceable under consumer protection legislation,[306] the possibility to exclude liability when the intermediary has knowledge of the illegal activities carried out in the context of the intermediation would go against the letter and the spirit of the eCommerce Directive.

This study, finally, showed the ambiguous role played by privacy (or by its rhetorical use). The traditional justification for the immunity from intermediary liability (and the related lack of general monitoring obligation) is rooted in privacy and freedom of expression. This study brought evidence of an inconsistent reference to privacy. On the one hand, MSM apps claim to want to respect their users' privacy and that, therefore, they do not monitor or have control over them. Thus, they create the preconditions for invoking immunity from intermediary liability on grounds of lack of knowledge. On the other hand, they act as the online police, allowing only certain user-generated content and only certain behaviours (eg by excluding everything which is deemed immoral). They blame it on the app store providers, who would not make their apps available if they do not comply with Apple's and Google's guidelines. However, secretly allowing the app stores providers to monitor the users of the MSM apps is in violation of these users' privacy. MSM will have decide either to actually respect their users' privacy and freedom of expression, thus placing themselves in a position to invoke immunity from intermediary liability or keep controlling and monitoring their users, in which case they will not be able to exclude liability in the event of knowledge of illegal behaviours. Arguably, if privacy were a mere smokescreen, the justification for not making the intermediary liability stricter would no longer be tenable.

To conclude, the IoB promises more efficient and interconnected bodies. However, there are a number of privacy and ethical issues that cannot be overlooked. In the IoB, we are losing control over the body for at least three reasons. First, the perception of our body is heavily influenced by our online experience (eg while using dating apps). Second, businesses are realising that the body is the most important source of personal data and they are endeavouring to extract it in ways which are often unfair and opaque. Third, smart devices not only measure our biometric parameters, but they also directly affect them (eg with implantable technologies), Now, in the *Capital*, Marx describes the labourer as nothing else than labour-power 'devoted to the self-expansion of capital'.[307] The fact that

---

[305] Grindr Terms, clauses 2, 8(3)(15) 20. On the enforceability of the most common contractual provisions in online services see Marco Loos and Joasia Luzak, 'Wanted: a Bigger Stick. On Unfair Terms in Consumer Contracts with Online Service Providers' *J Consum Policy* 39 (2016): 63.

[306] See, for instance, the Consumer Rights Act 2015, s 65.

[307] Marx, *Capital vol 1* (1867, Chicago: Charles H. Kerr, Eng tr, 1909) 291.

the time 'for free-play of his bodily and mental activity'[308] is taken away from the labourer is a major enslaving factor. The Internet of Things[309] and the circular economy[310] are leading to the death of ownership related to the loss of control over our goods;[311] with the IoB we risk being stripped of the last thing we used to own: our body. This may be the dawn of a new proletariat.

[308] Ibid 291.

[309] When one buys a car, one owns and therefore has exclusive control over the car. If one buys a smart car, one may have control over its hardware, but not on the software and service components. See Myriam Bianco, 'Take Care, Neo: The Fridge has You. A technology-aware legal review of consumer usability issues in the Internet of Things' (2016) Working paper no 1/2016. Available at: www.nexa. polito.it/nexacenterfiles/FINAL_Take%20care,%20Neo_%20the%20Fridge%20has%20you_A%20 technology-aware%20legal%20review%20of%20consumer%20usability%20issues%20in%20the%20 Internet%20of%20Things_0.pdf, last accessed 28 September 2017. There is already case law about preventing owners from using the goods they purchased because of the third parties' assertion of intellectual property rights (see *MicrobeadsAG v Vinhurst Road Markings* [1975] 1 WLR 218). These cases risk becoming commonplace when all the devices embed software or other immaterial goods protected by intellectual property rights. Cf Christopher Millard, W. Kuan Hon and Jatinder Singh, 'Internet of Things Ecosystems: Unpacking Legal Relationships and Liabilities' (2017) 2017 IEEE International Conference on Cloud Engineering 286, 288; M. Scott Boone, 'Ubiquituous Computing, Virtual Worlds, and the Displacement of Property Rights' *Journal of Law and Policy* 4, no 1 (2008): 91.

[310] The circular economy refers to 'closed production systems, ie new systems where resources are reused and kept in a loop of production and usage, allowing to generate more value and for a longer period' (Andrea Urbinati, Davide Chiaroni and Vittorio Chiesa, 'Towards a New Taxonomy of Circular Economy Business Models' *Journal of Cleaner Production* 168 (2017): 487). For the purpose of (with the excuse of) putting in place environmentally friendly policies, the circular economy justifies the retention of the ownership by the manufacturer of the device, who will look after the maintenance and, finally, reuse of the rented/leased device (this idea was suggested by Sean Thomas, 'Law, the Circular Economy, and Smart Technology' (SLS2017 conference, Dublin, September 2017). The fact that we no longer own our devices (and more generally goods), however, can have very dangerous consequences (even practical, for instance if a regime like the Directive 1999/44/EC of the European Parliament and of the Council of 25 May 1999 on certain aspects of the sale of consumer goods and associated guarantees [1994] OJ L 171 does not apply if there is no transfer of ownership).

[311] For other legal issues of Internet of Things and circular economy, in particular on the competition law implications of the 'product as a service' and of the 'predictive maintenance', see Marco Ricolfi, 'IoT and the Ages of Antitrust' (2017) Nexa Center for Internet & Society Working Paper No 4/.

3

How Machine Learning Generates Unfair Inequalities and How Data Protection Instruments May Help in Mitigating Them

LAURENS NAUDTS

Abstract

Machine learning processes have the potential to bring about both the reconstruction of society and the reconstruction of the self. Whereas machine learning's effects on societal structures appears to primarily raise questions concerning equality as a principle of justice and non-discrimination, machine learning's effects regarding the self seem mainly opposed to fundamental values such as privacy and data protection. This chapter will first present an assessment on how machine learning practices generate (unfair) inequalities, and how this affects both the group (societal) and individual level. In the second section, it will be argued that, even though the data protection framework primarily focuses on the individual data subject – and as a consequence, does not seem to set as a main goal the remediation of unfair inequalities – the GDPR might nonetheless enable societal interests, beyond individual data protection, to be taken into account. More specifically, the GDPR's risk-based approach and increased emphasis on accountability, could stimulate data controllers to consider, more broadly, the wider impact of their data operations. Rooted in the aforementioned principles, data protection impact assessments and codes of conduct in particular, could provide the necessary grounds for encouraging data controllers to reflect upon the societal effects of machine learning processes. Finally, in order to achieve 'fair machine learning', an appeal will be made towards increased multi-stakeholder involvement and dialogue. For instance, self-assessment procedures, such as the DPIA, could be further informed by academic and societal debates concerning machine learning and fairness.

Keywords

Machine learning, equality, privacy, data protection, data protection impact assessment, codes of conduct

1. Machine Learning:
Social Reconstruction and the Self

In Mind, Self and Society, George Herbert Mead contemplates that the changes humans make in the social order necessarily involves changes within themselves.[1] 'In short', Mead argues, 'social reconstruction and self or personality reconstruction are the two sides of a single process – the process of human social evolution'.[2] Mead's ideas reflect the current ethical and legal debate concerning machine learning, mainly when the latter are deployed for 'algorithmically' guided decision making and profiling purposes. In particular, Mead's words touch upon the key changes machine learning practices are thought to bring about: the reconstruction of society, and the reconstruction of self. In legal scholarship these changes correspond with the discussions concerning the potential impact of machine learning on equality and non-discrimination on the one hand, and privacy and data protection on the other.

Equality related issues arise from the idea that machine learning processes might restructure current societal strata on the basis of yet-to-be discovered parameters hidden within data sets.[3] Hence, in recent years, there has been an increased attention, both within academia and media, regarding the 'discriminatory' effects of machine learning.[4] The degree at which machine learning processes learn to differentiate between data, and as a consequence, individuals and groups of individuals, increases the risk that these forms of differentiation come into conflict with intuitive notions of equality as a principle of justice. The societal impact of Big Data analytics can also be found in the discussions concerning group privacy.[5]

---

[1] George H. Mead, *Mind Self and Society from the Standpoint of a Social Behaviorist* (Chicago: University of Chicago, 1934).

[2] See Mead, n 1 at 309.

[3] Anton Vedder and Laurens Naudts, 'Accountability for the Use of Algorithms in a Big Data Environment', *International Review of Law, Computers & Technology* 31, no. 2 (2017): 210, https://doi.org/10.1080/13600869.2017.1298547.

[4] See, inter alia, Latanya Sweeney, 'Discrimination in Online Ad Delivery', 29 January 2013. Available at: https://arxiv.org/ftp/arxiv/papers/1301/1301.6822.pdf; Toon Calders and Indrė Žliobaitė, 'Why Unbiased Computational Processes Can Lead to Discriminative Decision Procedures' in *Discrimination and Privacy in the Information Society* edited by Bart Custers, Toon Calders, Bart Schermer and Tal Zarsky (Dordecht: Springer, 2013), 43–57; Tal Zarsky, 'Understanding Discrimination in the Scored Society', *Washington Law Review*. 89, no. 4 (2014): 1375–1412; Solon Barocas and Andrew D. Selbst, 'Big Data's Disparate Impact', *California Law Review* 104 (2016): 671.

[5] Linnet Taylor, Luciano Floridi, and Bart van der Sloot, eds., *Group Privacy* (Cham: Springer International Publishing, 2017). Available at: https://doi.org/10.1007/978-3-319-46608-8.

When considering legal protection against the deployment of machine learning techniques, including profiling, there is a growing awareness that the law should look beyond the protection of the individual.

At the same time, machine learning technologies have an effect on the self and individuality, whether directly or indirectly, whether merely virtual or real. Indeed, and especially when deployed for profiling purposes, individuals are attributed certain features by (semi-) automated processes, and as such, are given a datafied double life. For an online shopping platform, an individual might be considered an avid jazz fanatic, whereas in reality he might enjoy hip hop instead. Such a reclassification of the individual on the basis of data might not have an immediate spill-over effect into reality. Yet, the consequences of automated attributions could be far more consequential, (eg in the context of credit scoring or predictive policing). In this context, a (group) profile can alter opportunities, and shape future lives.[6]

Perhaps more important, Mead's reflections hint towards the existence of an interrelationship between the reconstruction of society and the reconstruction of the self: changes that occur on the societal level, also affect society's individual constituents. In similar fashion, changes brought forth by machine learning on the societal or group level, are likely to affect individuals. The chapter will investigate this potential relationship, and the consequences it relationship might have. First, one particular form through which societal changes might occur via machine learning will be explored: the generation of unfair inequalities. In the first section, an analysis will therefore be made on how inequalities might arise through automated processes, and how they might impact both groups and individuals. Second, if such a relationship exists, then it could be further investigated whether or not the legal frameworks that correspond to these forms of reconstruction, (ie equality and data protection law, can inform one another).[7] In the second section, it will be argued that, even though the data protection framework primarily focuses on the individual – and as a consequence, does not set as a main goal the remediation of unfair inequalities – the GDPR might nonetheless enable the safeguarding of societal interests, beyond individual data protection. In particular, the GDPR's risk-based approach and increased emphasis on accountability could serve as a gateway for encouraging a broader ethical reflection amongst data controllers. Rooted within this heightened focus on self-assessment, data protection impact

---

[6] In 'nudging' or 'filter bubble' scenarios, the impact on the self might also be more hidden or gradual.

[7] The chapter does not aim to explore the characterisation or conditions under which certain inequalities are to be considered fair or unfair. For the sake of argument, it will nevertheless assume that equality and fairness are related, and that, as a consequence, the inequalities discussed within this chapter could potentially be unfair or have unfair consequences. For example, within political philosophy, theories of distributive justice provide guiding moral principles concerning the fair distribution of benefits and burdens of citizens within society. Oftentimes, these theories postulate some form of equality to ensure the fair allocation of benefits and burdens across citizens. Nevertheless, it is worth mentioning that not all theories of justice put forward equality as a critical principle in defining a just society. Other normative principles, such as self-ownership and autonomy, could be deemed more important.

assessments and codes of conduct could provide the necessary legal instruments to stimulate data controllers to better consider the societal impact of machine learning processes. In turn, unfair machine learning outcomes could be better identified and mitigated.

2. Algorithmic Inequalities

Machine learning processes inherently differentiate. Indeed, their goal is often to provide a seemingly rational and statistical, i.e. data-driven, basis upon which individuals (or groups of individuals) can be distinguished.[8] Whether they serve to categorise, classify, prioritise or filter data[9], the patterns and correlations machine learning processes find can serve as the basis to differentiate amongst individuals and groups of individuals. In turn, they allow decisions with regard to these individuals or groups of individuals to be made. Throughout the data chain, differentiation takes place on, at least, two different levels. First, the learning process will make a distinction between the data it has been fed. When a company looks to find the 'ideal' employee, the machine will have to learn, on the basis of historical data, what features constitute the 'ideal' employee, features relevant for the hiring process. The hiring decision itself, is the second instance where differentiation will take place. Whereas the former form of differentiation is inherent to the learning process itself, the latter constitutes the application of the found 'differentiation' grounds. As decision-making processes naturally imply that choices have to be made, differentiation will naturally occur. The widespread nature of machine learning in our everyday lives, as well as the scope and impact they might have, requires further investigation into the nature of these differentiation processes. Due to the increased usage of machine learning processes, the risk that these differentiation processes might result in unfair results increases too.[10] Considering these processes impact the allocation of burdens and benefits, the treatment or opportunities of the persons involved, there is an additional risk that these practices interfere with intuitive notions of equality as a principle of justice.

2.1. Contextual Dependence, Group Formation and Social Reconstruction

The machine learning debate is often dominated by a focus on the decisions humans make when developing machine learning, the prejudices of previous

---

[8] See Barocas and Selbst, 'Big Data's Disparate Impact', n 4 at 677.

[9] Nicholas Diakopoulos, 'Algorithmic Accountability: Journalistic Investigation of Computational Power Structures', *Digital Journalism* 3, no. 3 (4 May 2015): 398–415. Available at: https://doi.org/10.10 80/21670811.2014.976411.

[10] See Vedder and Naudts, 'Accountability for the Use of Algorithms in a Big Data Environment' n 3 at 218–219.

decision-makers, or the danger that machine learning reflects the biases that persist within society at large.[11] As such, the focus remains on a specific group of biases: the algorithm reproduces or reinforces unfair inequalities that are linked to 'protected' classes that exist within society. For instance, a bias against a protected class can be the result of biased training data, the non-sensitive definition of target variables or the labelling of training examples.[12] The focus on 'protected classes' is also present within the 'fair machine learning' debate. In recent years, the machine learning community has aimed to formalise fairness (ie.embed a certain notion of fairness into machine learning processes by 'design').[13] Unsurprisingly, the goal of fair machine learning is to reduce unfair machine learning outcomes. Even though various normative approaches towards the formalisation of fairness currently exist, including techniques based upon egalitarian theories,[14] envy-freeness literature and game theory,[15] in practice, fair machine learning primarily aims to avoid unfair outcomes linked to 'sensitive attributes'. These sensitive attributes however, often correspond to the protected classes found in non-discrimination law, such as gender and ethnicity.[16]

---

[11] See, for instance, Barocas and Selbst n 4.

[12] See *amongst others:* Calders and Žliobaitė, 'Why Unbiased Computational Processes Can Lead to Discriminative Decision Procedures' n 4; Barocas and Selbst n 4.

[13] See *amongst others:* Salvatore Ruggieri, Dino Pedreschi, and Franco Turini, 'Data Mining for Discrimination Discovery', *ACM Transactions on Knowledge Discovery from Data* 4, no. 2 (2010): 1–40. Available at: https://doi.org/10.1145/1754428.1754432; Binh Thanh Luong, Salvatore Ruggieri, and Franco Turini, 'K-NN as an Implementation of Situation Testing for Discrimination Discovery and Prevention' (San Francisco: ACM Press, 2011), 502. Available at: https://doi.org/10.1145/2020408.2020488; Moritz Hardt, Eric Price, and Nathan Srebro, 'Equality of Opportunity in Supervised Learning', *ArXiv:1610.02413 [Cs]*, 7 October 2016. Available at: http://arxiv.org/abs/1610.02413; Cynthia Dwork et al, 'Fairness Through Awareness', *ArXiv:1104.3913 [Cs]*, 19 April 2011. Available at: http://arxiv.org/abs/1104.3913; Muhammad Bilal Zafar et al, 'From Parity to Preference-Based Notions of Fairness in Classification', *ArXiv:1707.00010 [Cs, Stat]*, 30 June 2017. Available at: http://arxiv.org/abs/1707.00010; Muhammad Bilal Zafar et al, 'Fairness Beyond Disparate Treatment & Disparate Impact: Learning Classification without Disparate Mistreatment', *ArXiv:1610.08452 [Cs, Stat]*, 2017, 1171–80. Available at: https://doi.org/10.1145/3038912.3052660; Pratik Gajane, 'On Formalizing Fairness in Prediction with Machine Learning', *ArXiv:1710.03184 [Cs, Stat]*, 9 October 2017. Available at: http://arxiv.org/abs/1710.03184.

[14] Parity-based fair machine learning techniques have strong egalitarian roots. In these techniques, fairness has been interpreted through notions like group fairness, individual fairness or equality of opportunity. See, inter alia, Luong, Ruggieri, and Turini, 'K-NN as an Implementation of Situation Testing for Discrimination Discovery and Prevention' n 13; Dwork et al, 'Fairness Through Awareness' n 13; Hardt, Price, and Srebro, 'Equality of Opportunity in Supervised Learning' n 13; Zafar et al, 'Fairness Beyond Disparate Treatment & Disparate Impact' n 13.

[15] Preference-based fairness techniques have their roots in envy-freeness literature and game theory. Machine learning is considered fair, when "given the choice between various sets of decision treatments or outcomes, any group of users would collectively prefer its treatment or outcomes, regardless of the (dis)parity as compared to the other groups." Zafar et al, 'From Parity to Preference-Based Notions of Fairness in Classification' n 13.

[16] For instance, if one looks as the databases used within fair machine learning research, protected classes, represented through sensitive attributes, are almost always present and key to research. Sorelle A. Friedler et al, 'A Comparative Study of Fairness-Enhancing Interventions in Machine Learning', *ArXiv:1802.04422 [Cs, Stat]*, 12 February 2018. Available at: http://arxiv.org/abs/1802.04422.

Machine learning processes are contextually dependent: they interact with data, technologies, the environment in which they are ultimately deployed, etc.[17] In this regard, they not only take meaning, they also shape and create meaning.[18] As such, machine learning generates its own bias regardless of the ones that existed throughout the development process. The machine learns from examples and finds what it itself deems relevant, i.e. the machine self-generates bias. As a consequence, even if there is no inherent prejudice present within a given data set, or at least, a prejudice that seems *prima facie* unfair, unfair results could still be produced. Therefore, the inherent differentiating nature of machine learning processes, and self-generated biases, might also come into conflict with equality as a principle of justice. Such results can, but do not necessarily need to be connected to 'protected classes'.

Results found through machine learning can group together individuals or groups of individuals in seemingly random ways.[19] A wide variety of attributes could be deemed relevant by an automated decision-making system. As a consequence, and especially in a Big Data context, group profiles, or generalisations, do not necessarily represent a conglomerate of individuals bound or formed by explicit ties, such as salient traits.[20] Does person A make an 'ideal' employee? Is person B likely to default? Is person C likely to develop cancer? Even though the ultimate outcomes of machine learning processes can be tangible, e.g. is someone likely to default, the data groups that represent these outcomes do not necessarily have to be. The features that a machine learning process has found relevant for determining an outcome might be captured in simple terms. Attributes, such as age, wage, geographic location, etc., are easy enough to understand. Yet, this amalgamation of attributes can be perceived as incidental. For the persons involved, the resulting outcome might thus seem arbitrary.[21] Moreover, considering the nature of these groups, and the ease at which they can be formed through automated

---

[17] Vedder and Naudts, n 3 at 209–10.

[18] Jonathan Roberge and Louis Melançon, 'Being the King Kong of Algorithmic Culture Is a Tough Job after All: Google's Regimes of Justification and the Meanings of Glass', *Convergence: The International Journal of Research into New Media Technologies* 23, no. 3 (2017): 308. Available at: https://doi.org/10.1177/1354856515592506.

[19] It should be noted that these groupings are referred to as seemingly random. They are not random as such. Rather, they seem random as the logic behind these groupings is not always easily captured, nor is their statistical relevance apparent beforehand. The groups are random in the sense that they might be perceived as random. See Vedder and Naudts n 3. According to Kammourieh et al, machine learning can affect groups in four main ways. First, analytics can help discover new information concerning pre-existing, self-defined 'active' groups. Second, non-apparent groups can be identified on the basis of pre-defined parameters. Third, groups could be discovered through new analytical approaches, without parameters having been defined in advance. Finally, within the latter analytics processes, the risk that new groups are identified, increases as a 'step within the analytic process', without data scientist necessarily being aware thereof. Lanah Kammourieh et al, 'Group Privacy in the Age of Big Data', in *Group Privacy*, edited by Linnet Taylor, Luciano Floridi, and Bart van der Sloot (Cham: Springer International Publishing, 2017), at 41–42. Available at: https://doi.org/10.1007/978-3-319-46608-8_3.

[20] Anton Vedder, 'KDD: The Challenge to Individualism', *Ethics and Information Technology* 1, no. 4 (1999): 275–281; Taylor, Floridi, and van der Sloot n 5; and Kammourieh et al. n 19.

[21] See Vedder, n 20 at 278; Vedder and Naudts n 3 at 210.

means, it seems highly unlikely that they all can be referred back to a protected class, which traditional research has focused on.[22] Even where these groups are not linked to protected grounds, but rather are what they are, a grouping of seemingly innocuous, yet statistically relevant, attributes, they might still lead to unfair results and outcomes. On the group level, automated operations might lead to (negative) stereotyping and stigmatisation of the group involved.[23] The latter are often the root of unfair, unequal treatment within society. As such, they can restructure society in unfair ways. Even when such groups at one point served as a proxy for a protected group, if applied systemically, they could start to live a life on their own. They become dissociated with the 'protected' class they initially were a proxy of, because they are applied to all individuals covered by the group, not simply those individuals within the group that are usually considered for protection due to their relation to a protected class.

2.2. From the Group to the Individual

An unfair impact on a group, likely has an effect beyond the collective on its individual members. In essence, individual members are no longer judged on the basis of their actual merits, but they are treated on the basis of characteristics they supposedly share with their group.[24] Following such as process, an automated process might deprive an individual of an opportunity, based upon some piece of historical data that no longer corresponds with the individual's real capabilities. Taking an Aristotelian, formal notion of equality, the problem could then be redefined as follows: the individual wishes to be treated differently against the peers within the group of which he is a member.[25] In terms of the self, and regardless of whether this treatment should be considered fair or unfair, through categorisation, the individual is being ascribed characteristics which might not correspond with the individual's (perception of the) self.[26] This, in turn, can reduce the individual's claim towards self-ownership and autonomy.

Machine learning's influence on the self could also be approached via the notion of moral equality. Moral equality prescribes the treatment of individuals as equals, that is, with equal respect and dignity.[27] Delacroix finds a link to be present between pervasive profiling and moral equality through Sangiovanni's notion

---

[22] Moreover, the presence of a sensitive attribute should not necessarily be considered unfair. Quite the opposite, it might be relevant for the given decision.

[23] See also: Mireille Hildebrandt and Serge Gutwirth, eds, *Profiling the European Citizen: Cross-Disciplinary Perspectives* (New York: Springer, 2008); Daniel Keats Citron and Frank Pasquale, 'The Scored Society: Due Process for Automated Predictions', (2014) *Wash L Rev* 89, no 1; 1–33; Tal Z Zarsky, 'Understanding Discrimination in the Scored Society', (2014) *Wash L Rev* 89, no 4, 1375–1412.

[24] Vedder (n 20).

[25] See also: Zarsky, 'Understanding Discrimination in the Scored Society' n 5 at 1409.

[26] Vedder and Naudts (n 3).

[27] Ronald Dworkin, *Taking Rights Seriously* (Cambridge, MA: Harvard University Press, 1977).

of 'social cruelty'.[28] According to Sangiovanni, the recognition of an equal status amongst individuals means as much as for persons to treat another with humanity. On the opposite side, treating another as inferior is wrong, a form of cruelty.[29] Moral equality requires the rejection of such cruelty. Social cruelty then, is considered as 'the unauthorized, harmful and wrongful use of another's vulnerability to attack or obliterate one's capacity to develop and maintain an integral sense of self'. In its most systemic forms, social cruelty aims to break down a person's ability to self-present.[30] Drawing from this notion, Delacroix adds that the 'seamless adaptation of our environment on the basis of our past, machine-readable behaviour provides fertile ground for inferiorising treatment that is wrong not because it violates some norm of fairness but rather because it threatens our unique ability to develop and maintain a sense of self'.[31] The ability to develop and maintain a sense of self is dependent, however, upon an 'ability to preserve a gap between the self presented to the world and the self that is concealed'.[32] These dangers also loom within machine learning processes. Whether or not a computer representation of the self is accurate, the line between the presented and concealed self becomes blurred as one's persona is captured through data. The control an individual has over his or her representation of the self is diminished in an environment where an individual characteristics are partly attributed through automated generalisations.[33]

3. The Data Protection Toolbox: The Search for the Collective

The GDPR is primarily built around the protection of the data subject. The data subject is, however, mainly envisaged as a singular entity. Rather than considering the term 'data subject' as being capable of representing a collective of data subjects, the GDPR is mainly interpreted from the perspective of the data subject as an individual entity. Though the individuality of data protection laws might allow for adequate remedies with regard to unequal treatment on the individual level, eg the level of the data subject, the current interpretation of the GDPR does not allow for

[28] Sylvie Delacroix, 'Pervasive Data Profiling, Moral Equality and Civic Responsibility' (Data for Policy, London, 2018); Andrea Sangiovanni, *Humanity without Dignity: Moral Equality, Respect, and Human Rights*. (Cambridge, MA: Harvard University Press, 2017) as cited by Delacroix at 4–5.

[29] Ibid, Sangiovanni.

[30] Ibid, 76 and 83.

[31] Delacroix (n 28) at 5.

[32] Ibid at 5.

[33] This process moreover creates a perception gap between the individual and the machine learning process. If a decision is made vis-à-vis the individual, the individual, when considering the outcome that might affect him, will likely take into account his or her emotions, feelings, past experiences, etc (Vedder and Naudts n 3). Machine learning processes are however agnostic of this context. Rather, they take into account historical data to ascertain or predict the individual's behaviour. This 'perception' gap is not without any consequences. It muddies the expectations of the individual and affects the

an adequate mitigation of the negative impact machine learning might have with regard to the groups that are generated.[34] Moreover, it might even fail to capture the particular nature of a group's impact on the individual.

Nevertheless, there are notions present in the GDPR that already hint at a more collective approach.[35] Maybe then, and if exploited, they could allow interests, linked to group formation, to be adequately taken into account. For instance, the GDPR explicitly recognises the discriminatory risks of data processing activities in recitals 75 and 85. Similarly, the 'special categories' of data have their roots in traditional discrimination grounds and can be referred back to the protected classes found in both international human rights treaties and substantive discrimination laws. Furthermore, following recital 71, data controllers should, in the context of profiling, minimise the discriminatory effects on natural persons on the basis of racial or ethnic origin, political opinion, religion or beliefs, trade union membership, genetic or health status or sexual orientation, or that result in measures having such an effect. Nevertheless, the gap between the individual and the collective, group level does not solely depend upon the inclusion of discrimination within the text of the law.

In practice, the European Court of Justice, in its landmark *Huber* decision, also sought to bridge the gap between privacy, data protection and equality. The Court was asked whether the processing and storage of personal data within a centralised register concerning data of (and from) foreign nationals was compatible with the prohibition on discrimination on the basis of nationality, and whether such processing could be considered necessary for the performance of a task carried out in the public interest. The Court ultimately sanctioned discrimination on the basis of nationality in the processing and storage of personal data.[36] In its decision, the ECJ linked together data protection and equality concerns through the concepts of 'necessity' and 'proportionality', leaving the room for an equality sensitive interpretation of Articles 5 and 6 of the GDPR.[37] Convergence between the two frameworks therefore seems possible. Moreover, according to Gellert et al,

---

assessment of machine learning processes. The 'perception gap' problem could inform the interpretation of data protection laws. More specifically, data protection laws should allow this gap to be bridged. If one considers the much discussed 'right to an explanation', one would expect that the explanation grants the data subject information in a manner that allows him to understand the 'thinking' process of a computer.

[34] Taylor, Floridi, and van der Sloot n 5.

[35] For the collective dimension of privacy and data protection, see also: Alessandro Mantelero, 'Personal Data for Decisional Purposes in the Age of Analytics: From an Individual to a Collective Dimension of Data Protection', (2016) *Computer Law & Security Review* 32: 238–55, http://dx.doi.org/10.1016/j.clsr.2016.01.014; Alessandro Mantelero, 'From Group Privacy to Collective Privacy: Towards a New Dimension of Privacy and Data Protection in the Big Data Era', in *Group Privacy: New Challenges of Data Technologies*, ed Linnet Taylor, Luciano Floridi, and Bart van der Sloot (Cham: Springer International Publishing, 2017), 139–58, https://doi.org/10.1007/978-3-319-46608-8_8.

[36] C-524/06 *Huber v Federal Republic of Germany* (16 December 2008).

[37] Raphaël Gellert et al, 'A Comparative Analysis of Anti-Discrimination and Data Protection Legislations' in Custers et al (eds) *Discrimination and Privacy in the Information Society* (Springer, 2013), 77.

the right to data protection and non-discrimination are complementary and it seems unlikely that the articulation of non-discrimination and data protection law would lead to 'antagonistic results'.[38] Even in the case of statistical, unfair differentiation, not based on the protected grounds in discrimination law, 'unfair differentiation' could be tackled by interpreting data protection, taking into account an equality perspective.

Yet, without having to overly rely on renewed conceptual interpretations of fundamental data protection notions via the courts, through the increased focus on accountability and risk-based assessments, the GDPR equally opens up the room for data controllers to take into account the group dimensions of their data processing activities. Here, group notions of data protection, or rather equality as such, could enter the mind of data controllers without hard legal requirements.

3.1. Accountability and Risk-Based Approach as a Means to Bridge the Gap between the Individual and the Group

The heightened focus of the GDPR on accountability, and similarly, a risk-based approach, has increased the responsibility for data controllers concerning the effects of their envisaged data processing activities on the data subjects and society at large. Often perceived as a privacy and data protection enhancing principle, the notion of accountability permeates throughout the GDPR ways that go beyond the explicit obligation of data controllers to simply demonstrate compliance with data protection principles.[39,40] In simple terms, accountability requires data controllers to provide good reasons and explanations with regard to the decisions they take or the actions they perform. In this interpretation of accountability, the GDPR promotes the principle through self-assessment mechanisms, such as keeping data processing records, the performance of a data protection impact assessment and transparency requirements.[41] Indeed, these mechanisms urge data

---

[38] Ibid, 81–82.

[39] See, inter alia, Colin Bennett, 'International Privacy Standards: Can Accountability be Adequate?' *Privacy Laws and Business International* 106 (2010) 21–23; Daniel Guagnin, Leon, Hempel, eds. *Managing Privacy through Accountability* (Basingstoke: Palgrave Macmillan, 2012). Joeseph Alhadeff, Brendan van Alsenoy and Jos Dumortier. 'The Accountability Principle in Data Protection Regulation: Origin, Development and Future Directions' in *Managing Privacy through Accountability*, edited by D. Guagnin, L. Hempel, and C. Ilten (Basingstoke: Palgrave Macmillan 2012), 49–82. doi:10.1057/9781137032225; Denis Butin, Marcos Chicote and Daniel Le Métayer. 2014. 'Strong Accountability: Beyond Vague Promises' in *Reloading Data Protection*, edited by Serge Gutwirth (Dordrecht: Springer Science + Business Media) 343–369. Available at: https://doi:10.1007/978-94-007-7540-4_1; Christian Zimmermann, and Johana Cabinakova 'A Conceptualization of Accountability as a Privacy Principle' in *BIS 2015 Workshops*, edited by W. Abramowicz, (Berne: Springer International Publishing Switzerland). Available at: https://doi:10.1007/978-3-319-26762-3_23.

[40] GDPR, Art 5: The controller shall be responsible for, and be able to demonstrate compliance with the GDPR, and in particular that the controller complies with the data protection principles of lawfulness, fairness and transparency; purpose limitation; data minimisation; accuracy; storage limitation; integrity; and confidentiality.

[41] Vedder and Naudts, n 3.

controllers to self-reflect on the impact their processing activities might have, and to justify these actions if they choose to proceed with certain high risk activities. In addition, through transparency, relevant information must be conveyed to the wider public. After the data controller has gone through a process of self-reflection, the audience at large should thus be able to assess and evaluate the data controller's reasoning and data processing activities in their own right. Likewise, self-reflection is conveyed in the idea that recent data protection laws, and the GDPR in particular, are to be viewed as instruments that primarily regulate risks.[42] Within a risk-based approach, the nature, scope, context and purposes of the processing operations, and the corresponding levels of risk for data subjects, determine the protective measures that are to be taken by data controllers.[43] Gellert notes that the GDPR combines the use of risk management tools with a calibration of the data controllers' obligations according to the level of risk at stake.[44] Considering the overall importance of accountability, it is not unusual that the data controller has an additional responsibility to gauge the risks of processing operations.

As the principle of accountability and the risk-based approach primarily rely upon the data controller's self-reflection and self-assessment vis-à-vis processing operations, including machine learning, they could also encourage the data controller to take into account the impact of their data processing activities on natural persons, rather than data subjects as such, as well as random groups, beyond concerns related to the fundamental right to data protection. Even if, in themselves, these devices are built around, or stem from, an individual data protection framework, they could be envisaged as templates for more collective sensitive musings. In other words, throughout this process, other fundamental interests, such as equality, could be taken into account. Two instruments in particular seem to allow room for data controllers to think about the impact of their data processing activities on a wider scale: the data protection impact assessment and codes of conduct. The self-evaluating nature of these instruments primarily encourages an ethical reflex from controller, or in the case of a code of conduct, a group of data controllers. They do not prohibit machine learning practices altogether, but rather, they could be envisaged as a stepping block towards fair machine learning. They thus allow the market to operate within a non-constrictive regime. Indeed, 'one can hardly conceive a system, other than in the context of a totalitarian

[42] Raphaël Gellert, 'We Have Always Managed Risks in Data Protection Law: Understanding the Similarities and Differences between the Rights-Based and the Risk-Based Approaches to Data Protection', *European Data Protection Law Review (EDPL)* 2 (2016): 481–92; R. Gellert, 'Discussion On Risk, Balancing, and Data Protection: A Response to van Der Sloot', *European Data Protection Law Review* 3, no. 2 (2017): 180–86. Available at: https://doi.org/10.21552/edpl/2017/2/7.

[43] Council of the European Union, 'Note on Proposal for a Regulation of the European Parliament and of the Council on the protection of individuals with regard to the processing of personal data and on the free movement of such data (General Data Protection Regulation): 2012/0011 (COD)' 30.6.

[44] Raphaël Gellert, 'Data Protection: A Risk Regulation? Between the Risk Management of Everything and the Precautionary Alternative', *International Data Privacy Law* 5, no. 1 (1 February 2015): 13. Available at: https://doi.org/10.1093/idpl/ipu035.

regime, in which all actions which could potentially fall under anti-discrimination laws should be declared beforehand in order to confirm that they are lawful'.[45] Instruments like DPIAs and codes of conduct have, as an additional benefit, that they shift back the responsibility from the data subject to the data controller. The exercise of data subject's rights might require from the individual an unachievable level of data governance or privacy self-management.[46]

(a) *The Data Protection Impact Assessment*

According to the GDPR: 'Where a type of processing in particular using new technologies, and taking into account the nature, scope, context and purposes of the processing, is likely to result in a high risk to the rights and freedoms of natural persons, the controller shall, prior to the processing, carry out an assessment of the impact of the envisaged processing operations on the protection of personal data."[47] The Data Protection Impact Assessment (DPIA) consists of a multi-tiered analysis.[48] First, it should include a systematic description of the envisaged processing operations and the purposes of the processing, including, where applicable, the legitimate interest pursued. Second, it requires an assessment of the necessity and proportionality of the processing operations in relation to the purposes. Third, an evaluation of the risks to the rights and freedoms of data subjects the data-processing activities entail, should be made. Finally, the data controller must provide a description of the envisaged measures foreseen to address these risks. It is exactly the requirement to analyse both risks and countermeasures that encourages data controllers to consider more broadly the impact of machine learning, regardless of whether the risks ultimately materialise.

No exhaustive list of high risk activities has been provided by the GDPR.[49] It only provides for a closed list of examples. Therefore, it currently remains unclear, and thus interpretable, what a high risk exactly entails or when processing activities are likely to result in a high risk to the 'rights and freedoms of natural persons'. The Article 29 Working Party (WP) did try to provide additional guidance in the

---

[45] Daniel Le Métayer and Julien Le Clainche, 'From the Protection of Data to the Protection of Individuals: Extending the Application of Non-Discrimination Principles', in *European Data Protection: In Good Health?*, edited by Serge Gutwirth et al. (Dordrecht: Springer Netherlands, 2012), 322. Available at: https://doi.org/10.1007/978-94-007-2903-2_15.

[46] Jonathan A. Obar, 'Big Data and "The Phantom Public": Walter Lippmann and the Fallacy of Data Privacy Self-Management', *Big Data & Society* 2, no. 2 (27 December 2015). Available at: https://doi.org/10.1177/2053951715608876.

[47] GDPR Art 35, § 3.

[48] Ibid, Art 35, § 7 (a)–(d).

[49] Some examples are nonetheless listed by the GDPR. Relevant to the context of machine learning, a DPIA shall be required where a systematic evaluation of personal aspects relating to natural persons based on automated processing, including profiling, takes place, and on which decisions are based that produce legal effects concerning the natural person or similarly significantly affect the natural person. In addition, a DPIA should also be performed where processing activities cover on a large scale special categories of data.

matter through the development of a list of criteria to be taken into consideration when determining the risk of data processing.[50]

First, according to Article 29 WP, the evaluation and scoring of individuals, including profiling and prediction, is more likely to result in a high risk to the fundamental interests of natural persons. Following recitals 71 and 91 of the GDPR, a particular concern is declared with regard to the evaluation and scoring of 'aspects concerning the data subject's performance at work, economic situation, health, personal preferences or interests, reliability or behaviour, location or movements'. Second, automated-decision making with legal or significant effect should be subject to heightened scrutiny by the data controller.[51] In their guidelines on automated decision making, the Art. 29 WP has already considered that there is a significant effect on natural persons where processing may lead to the exclusion or discrimination against individuals. Interestingly enough, the Art. 29 WP departs from traditional 'discrimination' grounds to grounds that are not as easily captured, such as 'rural and barely making it', 'ethnic second-city strugglers' and 'tough start: young single parents'.[52] Third, the scale at which data are processed should also be taken into account. Here, the data controller should consider the number of data subjects concerned, the volume of data and the range of different data items processed, the duration or permanence of the data processing activity and finally, the geographical extent of the processing activity. One could argue that through the notion of scale, issues that stem from the social reconstructive nature of machine learning could enter the ambit of DPIAs. Finally, matching or combining datasets and the innovative use or the application of new technological (eg advancements in machine learning, or organisational solutions are considered to lead to higher risks as well). Taking these criteria into consideration, one could very well argue that a DPIA could serve as an instrument to reflect upon the negative consequences machine learning has with regard to equality as a principle of justice.

Even though the GDPR does not abandon its data protection roots altogether, as it still depends upon whether personal data have been processed, the legal provisions concerning the DPIA do provide room for other fundamental values to be taken into account. In this regard, the Article 29 WP states that, even though the reference within the GDPR to the rights and freedoms of data subjects primarily concerns the rights to data protection and privacy, they may also involve other fundamental rights, including the prohibition of discrimination.[53] In practice,

---

[50] Article 29 Data Protection Working Party, 'Guidelines on Data Protection Impact Assessment (DPIA) and Determining Whether Processing Is "Likely to Result in a High Risk" for the Purposes of Regulation 2016/679', 4 April 2017.] at 7–10.

[51] GDPR, Art 22, §3.

[52] Article 29 Data Protection Working Party, 'Guidelines on Automated Individual Decision-Making and Profiling for the Purposes of Regulation 2016/679' (Article 29 Data Protection Working Party, 3 October 2017), 10.

[53] Article 29 Data Protection Working Party, 'Guidelines on Data Protection Impact Assessment, n 4; Article 29 Data Protection Working Party, 'Guidelines on Automated Individual Decision-Making and Profiling for the Purposes of Regulation 2016/679' n 52.

data protection authorities (DPA) also focus their attention on impacts beyond data protection. In their DPIA guidelines, The French CNIL indicated that the feeling of natural persons that their fundamental rights, such as the right to freedom of expression and non-discrimination, would be violated, should likely be considered as a 'significant' moral impact, in the data controller's risk assessment.[54] Similarly, the UK and Belgium DPA's highlight discrimination in their guidelines for data controllers in assessing and identifying the risks of their data processing activities.[55] The broad notion 'moral impact' could include unfair inequalities in general and could stimulate (and perhaps require) data controllers to consider more widely the effects of their operations.[56] Where the DPIA would require consideration of other fundamental rights, interests and moral impact, the process of drafting a DPIA favours the acknowledgement of unfair impacts by the data controller. Indeed, the data controller would first be required to list all the potential risks involved with data processing, only after which he can esti-mate their likelihood and the counter-measures to be foreseen. Even where the risk to unfair inequalities would ultimately be negligible – and therefore might not require the introduction of safety measures – the data controller would at least be expected to consider the associated risks. Furthermore, the effects of data process-ing on equality might become more widespread where DPA's are made public.

Importantly, the DPIA provisions consider the risks of data processing activi-ties on natural persons, rather than data subjects.[57] Therefore, a DPIA should

---

[54] CNIL, 'PIA, Knowledge Bases', 2018, 4.

[55] Information Commissioner's Office, 'GDPR DPIA Guidance', 22 March 2018, https://ico.org.uk/media/about-the-ico/consultations/2258459/dpia-guidance-v08-post-comms-review-20180208.pdf; Commissie voor de Bescherming van de Persoonlijke Levenssfeer, 'Aanbeveling Uit Eigen Beweging Met Betrekking Tot de Gevensbeschermingseffectbeoordeling En Voorafgaande Raadpleging (CO-AR-2018-001)', 28 February 2018, https://www.privacycommission.be/sites/privacycommission/files/documents/aanbeveling_01_2018.pdf.

[56] See CNIL, 'PIA, Knowledge Bases' n 54 at 4–5.

[57] In addition, GDPR, Art 35(9) stipulates that 'where appropriate, data controllers shall seek the views of data subjects or their representatives on the intended processing, without prejudice to the protection of commercial or public interests or the security of processing operations'. Unfortunately, the GDPR does not further specify when such a consultation would be 'appropriate'. In addition, GDPR, Art 35(9) stipulates that 'where appropriate, data controllers shall seek the views of data subjects or their representatives on the intended processing, without prejudice to the protection of commercial or public interests or the security of processing operations'. Unfortunately, the GDPR does not further specify when such a consultation would be 'appropriate'. In their guidelines on the DPIA, the WP29 does note that, in cases where the controller is of the opinion that the views of data subjects should not be sought, the justification therefor must be documented. For instance, when such an enquiry would 'compromise the confidentiality of companies' business plans or would be disproportionate or impracticable' (Article 29 Data Protection Working Party, 'Guidelines' n 50 at 13). According to the Belgian DPA, the decision to engage with data subjects lies with the data controller. They nevertheless consider that where, taking into account the nature, scope, context and purposes of data processing, as well as the potential impact on those involved, 'sufficiently weighty reasons' to carry out a consultation are present, the views of data subjects should indeed be sought. The Belgian DPA adds that a consulta-tion might be particularly recommended where data subjects have access to essential information, or can formulate important feedback, relevant to the performance of the DPIA.; (CBPL, 'Aanbeveling Uit Eigen Beweging Met Betrekking Tot de Gegevensbeschermingseffectbeoordeling En Voorafgaande Raadpleging' (CBPL, 28 February 2018), 31–32).

measure the risk of data processing not only on the individuals whose data have been processed, but also on those persons whose data have not been processed. As such, the data controller could be expected to evaluate the risks of data exclusion or underrepresented data sets. Moreover, and unlike Article 22 of the GDPR, (ie the right not to be subject to individual decision-making solely based on auto-mated processes) the provisions concerning DPIAs do cover decision-making processes that are not 'solely' automated.[58] As such, the DPIA might not suffer from the same interpretational constraints as the right not to be subject to auto-mated decision-making.[59] In sum, the DPIA allows for a risk-assessment beyond the individual.

(b) Codes of Conduct

The GDPR encourages 'associations or other bodies representing categories of controllers or processors' to draw up codes of conduct, which should serve to facilitate its effective application.[60] They also serve more inclusive purposes. The GDPR notes that codes can take into account the 'specific characteristics of the processing carried out in certain sectors and the specific needs of micro, small and medium enterprises'.[61] As methods of self-regulation, codes of conduct could be drafted in manners that go beyond the legal state of the art, protecting interests other than privacy and data protection. They could include measures to increase fair machine learning.

Currently, the scope of codes of conduct remains unclear, nor does their adoption seem a hard obligation under the GDPR. For instance, what exactly encompasses 'associations or other bodies representing categories of controllers or processors', beyond the fact that it provides an indication that they are likely to be sector specific? Codes of conducts could nevertheless become a valuable instrument in the mitigation of the negative effects of machine learning, even at a sectoral level.[62] They could enable the clarification of data processing activities on a wider scale, mapping the particular dangers of machine learning practices in industries where these technologies are dominant. In turn, in a form of self-regulation, they could propose risk mitigation measures or guidelines towards

---

[58] Article 29 Data Protection Working Party, 'Guidelines' n 50 at 29.

[59] See, inter alia, Lee A. Bygrave, 'Automated Profiling: Minding the Machine: Article 15 of the EC Data Protection Directive and Automated Profiling', *Computer Law & Security Review* 17, no. 1 (2001): 17–24; Sandra Wachter, Brent Mittelstadt and Luciano Floridi, 'Why a Right to Explanation of Automated Decision-Making Does Not Exist in the General Data Protection Regulation', *International Data Privacy Law* 7, no. 2 (2017): 76–99; Sandra Wachter, Brent Mittelstadt, and Chris Russell, 'Counterfactual Explanations without Opening the Black Box: Automated Decisions and the GDPR', 2017.

[60] GDPR, art 40.

[61] GDPR, art 40 §2.

[62] The Art 29 WP also encourages the development of sector-specific DPIA frameworks. Article 29 Data Protection Working Party, 'Guidelines' n 50 at 16.

fair and transparent machine learning. According to Article 40, §2 of the GDPR, codes of conduct would specify *amongst others*, fair and transparent processing, the legitimate interests concerning the collection of personal data, the information that is to be provided to the public and to data subjects, etc.

In addition, codes of conduct should be sensitive towards various societal perspectives, and take into account opinions from other actors than the responsible data controllers. In this regard, the GDPR expressly notes that 'associations and other bodies representing categories of controllers or processors should consult relevant stakeholders, including data subjects where feasible, and have regard to submissions received and views expressed in response to such consultations'.[63] Such stakeholders could (and should) also include societal interests groups, like consumer protection organisations or equality bodies.[64] Through multi-stakeholder engagement, the code of conduct can become an instrument that enables a more societal bird's-eye-view to be taken into account, and could therefore be of particular interest with regard to the monitoring of large-scale machine learning, where the risk of a potentially negative impact on the societal level is greater. In their recent guidelines on automated individual decision-making, which garnered extensive interest from the machine learning community, the Article 29 WP hinted at a similar approach. As part of their 'best practices', they note that controllers should explore options such as codes of conduct for auditing processing involving machine learning, as well contacting ethical review boards to assess the potential harms and benefits to society of particular applications for profiling.[65] Though they do not directly promote a far-reaching multi-stakeholder approach, the instruments they call upon do require the data controller to look further than their own offices, and third-party engagement.

A caveat should nonetheless be made concerning sector-specific, purpose-driven approaches. The deployment of machine learning techniques could have a broad, societal impact, not limited to a given context or sector. For instance, when considering financial areas, should the code of conduct be limited to the banking services of financial institutions or their insurance activities? Moreover, should the latter then also cover private companies not linked to major financial institutions? Surely, the impact of credit scoring is likely to influence the opportunities of persons in associated, yet distinct areas of commerce. Furthermore, codes of conduct might be unable to tackle chained or cross-industry machine learning activities. Codes of conduct should therefore also be subject to periodic reviews, whereby appropriate consideration can be given to the effects that certain practices have had over time, on a wider societal level.

---

[63] GDPR, recital 99.
[64] See also n 62 (GDPR, Art 35, § 9).
[65] Article 29 Data Protection Working Party, 'Guidelines' n 50 at 32.

3.2. The Guiding Role of Data Protection Authorities

Both in the case of the Data Protection Impact Assessment and Codes of Conduct, data protection authorities (DPA) do not play a passive role. Following Article 41, §5 of the GDPR, draft codes of conducts should be submitted to the relevant supervisory authorities who shall provide an opinion on whether the code of conduct applies. Moreover, the supervisory authorities are responsible for approving the draft code if they find that it provides 'sufficient appropriate safeguards'. Upon acceptance, the authority shall register and publish the code. The interpretative function of DPAs, or the European Data Protection Board, should therefore be an active one, towards qualitative control. In the case of codes of conduct, where a supervisory authority considers insufficient feedback to have been received from societal stakeholders, such as consumer protection organisations or perhaps in this particular context, equality and anti-discrimination groups, the supervisory authority could request the code of conduct to be amended. The supervisory authorities play a similar guiding role with regard to DPIAs. Following the GDPR, they can establish and make public a list of the kind of processing operations which are subject to the requirement to draft a DPIA. They might also draft a list of those processing operations that should not be subject to an impact assessment.[66] In the case of a prior consultation, the advisory role of the supervisory authority can be even greater. Where the supervisory authority is of the opinion that the intended processing referred to would infringe the GDPR, in particular where the controller has insufficiently identified or mitigated the risk, the supervisory authority shall, within period of up to eight weeks of receipt of the request for consultation, provide written advice to the controller.

It should also be noted that DPAs are aware and already took position with regard to both the individual and collective nature of data processing activities.[67] Furthermore, their practical insight into the actual practices of data intensive industries, make them, when focusing on data protection and fundamental rights, well placed to balance arising conflicts with regard to the use of data.[68] Mantelero rightfully argues that bodies representing collective interests, such as data protection supervisory authorities, 'should not only partially exercise traditional individual rights on behalf of data subjects, but also exercise other autonomous rights relating to the collective dimension of data protection'.[69]

---

[66] GDPR, Art 35, § 4 and 5.

[67] Alessandro Mantelero, 'Personal Data for Decisional Purposes in the Age of Analytics: From an Individual to a Collective Dimension of Data Protection', *Computer Law & Security Review* 32 (2016): at 251–252. Available at: http://dx.doi.org/10.1016/j.clsr.2016.01.014.

[68] Ibid.

[69] Alessandro Mantelero, 'Personal Data for Decisional Purposes in the Age of Analytics: From an Individual to a Collective Dimension of Data Protection', (2016) *Computer Law & Security Review* 32: 238–55, http://dx.doi.org/10.1016/j.clsr.2016.01.014 at 252.

Whilst it is true that DPAs will experience an increased administrative burden due to the GDPR's arrival, it should be noted that DPAs should not be the sole party responsible for ensuring proper consideration of fair data processing activities. If other interests, beyond privacy and data protection, are indeed affected, a multi-stakeholder approach should be encouraged, whereby supervisory authorities seek engagement with data controllers, ethical bodies, societal interests groups and the machine learning community in order to map the impact of machine learning better.[70]

3.3. What About Group Rights?

The GDPR introduced the possibility for data subjects to be represented via non-profit organisations. Data subjects have the right to mandate a not-for-profit organisation to lodge a complaint on their behalf to supervisory authorities and to exercise their right to an effective judicial remedy against a supervisory authority, the data controller or processor.[71] Moreover, Member States may also provide that these organisations have the ability to act independently, regardless of data subjects' mandate.[72] Through representation, data subjects could now, in principle, launch collective data protection enforcement actions. Alternatively, if Member State law allows, non-profit organisations could act in defence of collective interests.

Collective action, or the exercise of group rights, faces its own set of difficulties however, especially when considering the particular nature of the inequalities discussed above. First, unfair inequalities might relate to groups that are not easily tangible. As a consequence, there might be little cohesion amongst individual group members. They might simply have a feeling of being arbitrarily treated against, without necessarily considering that there might have been others who were subject to similar treatment. In turn, they might not organise themselves to act collectively.[73] While each individual member might raise its own claim independently, a link between individual claims might only be found in the case of structural and blatant unfair machine learning practices, or where thorough oversight mechanisms exist. Considering the nature of the groups that are formed through machine learning, a collective action against potential unfair outcomes, is thus unlikely to arise naturally. Moreover, unfair inequalities might not necessarily have an immediate negative impact on the individual members as such, but only on the group as a whole. If reliant on individual claims, the group impact

---

[70] For multi-stakeholder involvement, see also: Mantelero n 67.

[71] GDPR, Art 80 see also, Arts 77, 78 and 79.

[72] Ibid, Art 81.

[73] See also: Anton H. Vedder (2000). 'Medical Data, New Information Technologies, and the Need for Normative Principles other than Privacy Rules' in *Law and Medicine: Current Legal Issues 2000: Volume 3* edited by M. Freeman, and A. Lewis (Oxford: Oxford University Press) 441–459 and Vedder n 20 at 278.

might remain dormant. Whilst a non-profit organisation could still pursue collective interests even where it has not been mandated, other obstacles would still need to be overcome. First, the unfair impact would have to be detected, which, and again considering the nature of groups involved, might prove to be difficult. Second, a judicial claim requires the violation of some legal right. Unfair inequalities might not always correspond with the current, substantive interpretation of non-discrimination law, nor do they necessarily entail an infringement of data protection law. Legal remedies therefore provide little guarantees in this regard. Indeed, 'unfair' inequalities are more an ethical and societal matter, rather than a legal one. Even though certain processes might be questionable from an ethical perspective, they are not necessarily illegal. Finally, it should be noted that the aforementioned provisions consider the 'data subject' only, rather than natural persons. Yet, unfair inequalities, on both the individual and group level, can occur even where the data of individual members have not been processed, or where the data subjects as such, e.g. in the case of data exclusion, remain largely unaffected.

3.4. It is Not Necessarily About Compliance

Data controllers face uncertainty regarding the implementation of the GDPR in fear of non-compliance. The proposed measures should not necessarily entail a direct extension to cover additional fundamental interests. As indicated above, many issues raised in this chapter are of an ethical and societal nature, rather than a legal one. Accountability and risk-based mechanisms are promising because, at least to a certain degree, they enable a moral or societal impact to be taken into account. Within a DPIA, controllers should consider the broader impact of the processes evaluated: they are required to list all the risks involved concerning data processing. Likewise, codes of conduct could encourage data controllers to reflect more broadly upon their activities by setting a certain standard with regard to which data processes would be fair in a given sector. As far as the burden of this 'ethical' reflection is concerned: it should not be carried solely by data controllers or DPAs. Fair machine learning can only be achieved within an 'ethically aware' data culture. As such, it requires multi-stakeholder involvement. The DPIA and Code of Conduct should not be seen as instruments that provide immediate salvation. Rather, they can become instruments to facilitate the evolutionary progress towards fair machine learning, by allowing a multi-disciplinary thinking process to take place.[74] As the public attention for data protection has increased due to

---

[74] The draft of the DPIA should not be considered as a one man endeavour. Rather, it will require the involvement from a variety of people involved in the data chain of command. For instance, not only the data protection officer, but also IT staff should be included in the process. Moreover, as certain DPA's already indicated in their DPIA guidelines, product developers should equally consider drafting accompanying DPIA's as a guidance document concerning the deployment of their tools. At the same time, codes of conducts should be drafted with due attention of societal stakeholders.

the GDPR's introduction, so could the potential impact of machine learning gain attention through an overall higher level of awareness amongst all stakeholders involved.

3.5. The Role of Theories of Justice, Fairness and Equality As a Principle of Justice

The question concerning when and why exactly certain forms of machine learning become fair or unfair cannot be addressed within this chapter. Nevertheless, further research is required with regard to the function of equality as a principle of justice for evaluating the fair nature of machine learning.[75] As Binns rightfully notes: 'Questions of discrimination, egalitarianism and justice are of significant interest to moral and political philosophers, who have expended significant efforts in formalising and defending these central concepts.' In other words, philosophical accounts of equality, as a leading principle within theories of justice, and its relationship with fairness, allow reflection on fundamental questions that arise in the context of machine learning.[76] In section 2.1, it was said that the machine learning community has already made efforts to embed fairness into the design of machine learning practices.[77] If data processing operations should occur in a fair manner, the contributions that are currently being made in the field of fair machine learning, can and should play an important role when considering the future responsibilities of data controllers. In any case, discussions concerning fairness within machine learning – both with regard to its articulation and technical formalisation – can inform the draft process of the data protection impact assessment and (sectoral) codes of conduct.[78] Moreover, they might enable a more 'egalitarian' sensitive interpretation of the GDPR in general. Viewing machine

---

[75] Laurens Naudts, 'Fair or Unfair Differentiation? Luck Egalitarianism as a Lens for Evaluating Algorithmic Decision-Making' (Data for Policy Conference, London, 2017). See also: Reuben Binns, 'Fairness in Machine Learning: Lessons from Political Philosophy', in *Proceedings of Machine Learning Research* (Conference on Fairness, Accountability and Transparency, New York City, 2018). It should be emphasised, however, that the question regarding whether or not machine learning processes are fair or unfair largely depends upon one's normative viewpoint. For example, though many theories of justice formulate egalitarian principles as moral guidance, not all theories deem equality as important. Libertarian theories, for instance, are likely to favour individual autonomy and self-ownership above equality.

[76] Reuben Binns, 'Fairness in Machine Learning: Lessons from Political Philosophy', in *Proceedings of Machine Learning Research* (Conference on Fairness, Accountability and Transparency, New York City, 2018), at 9.

[77] See section 2.1.

[78] The articulation of fair machine learning should be considered distinct from its formalisation. Before fairness can be formalised, it should first be articulated. In essence, it refers to efforts made to formulate what it means exactly for machine learning to be fair, and what a fair outcome of machine learning processes could be. Here, one could draw from theories of distributive justice to formulate an answer to the question what fair machine learning would entail. Even though no single right answer exists, an articulation of fairness can subsequently lead to the formalisation of fairness, (ie the technical integration of a given notion of fairness into the design of the machine learning process).

learning through the lenses provided by theories of justice could increase our understanding of the fair and unfair nature of these processes, and perhaps at one point, will enable a line between fair and unfair machine learning to be drawn.

4. Conclusion

Data protection laws do not have as their main function the regulation of unfair inequalities. Nevertheless, equality and data protection are fundamental values that are interlinked and as such can inform and influence one another. Without having to rely upon the conceptual reinterpretation of privacy and data protection as fundamental rights in order for more collective, equality-related, interests to be taken into account, data protection impact assessments and codes of conducts can already encourage data controllers to reflect upon the potential negative effects of machine learning more broadly. Whereas, on a micro-scale, data protection impact assessments stimulate data controllers to take into account the generation of unfair inequalities following their deployment of machine learning, codes of conduct could be a means to map the impact of machine learning on equality on a macro-scale (eg on the sectoral or societal level). Codes of conduct could further-more propose self-regulatory risk-mitigation strategies. Both instruments have as an advantage that they are mainly rooted within the GDPR's risk-based approach and its increased emphasis on accountability. Rather than focusing on the right to data protection as such, the latter principles mainly require data controllers to justify their data processing activities and reflect upon their potential impact. Given that these processes might not only come into conflict with the fundamental right to data protection, but other fundamental values as well, accountability and risk-based assessments could therefore provide the necessary soil for safeguard-ing all affected values. The progress towards fairer machine learning nevertheless relies upon multi-stakeholder involvement. In this regard, supervisory authorities, guided and informed by a variety of stakeholders, could play an important role in overseeing whether or not all relevant interests were taken into account within self-assessment procedures. At the same time, it should be gauged to what extend ethical and legal considerations that go beyond the individual nature of privacy and data protection, and also take into account the wider, social reconstruction impact of machine learning, can inform data protection laws, and the application thereof by data controllers.

Acknowledgment

This chapter was supported by the VICTORIA project which has received funding from the European Union's Horizon 2020 research and innovation programme under grant agreement No 740754, and by imec, Flanders' digital research centre and incubator.

4

'Nothing Comes between My Robot and Me': Privacy and Human-Robot Interaction in Robotised Healthcare

EDUARD FOSCH VILLARONGA, HEIKE FELZMANN,
ROBIN L. PIERCE, SILVIA DE CONCA, AVIVA DE GROOT,
AIDA PONCE DEL CASTILLO AND SCOTT ROBBINS

Errant consilia nostra, quia non habent quo derigantur;
ignoranti quem portum petat nullus suus ventus est

'If a man does not know to which port he is sailing, no
wind is favorable to him'

LXXI Seneca Lucilio Suo Salutem, *Epistulae Morales*
Ad Lucilium, L.A. Seneca.

Abstract

The integration of cyber-physical robotic systems in healthcare settings is accelerating, with robots used as diagnostic aids, mobile assistants, physical rehabilitation providers, cognitive assistants, social and cognitive skills trainers, or therapists. This chapter investigates currently still underexplored privacy and data protection issues in the use of robotic technologies in healthcare, focusing on privacy issues that are specifically related to human engagement with robots as cyber-physical systems in healthcare contexts. It addresses six relevant privacy concerns and analyses them with regard to the European context: 1. The distinctive privacy impacts of subconsciously incentivised disclosure in human-robot interaction. 2. The complexity of consent requirements, including consent for data processing as well as consent for robotic care provision, both governed by different norms and user expectations. 3. Privacy challenges and opportunities arising from conversational approaches to privacy management with robots. 4. The application of data portability requirements in the context of a person's substantive reliance on robots. 5. The privacy risks related to robot-based data collection in the workplace. 6. The need to go beyond simpler Privacy by Design approaches, which reduce privacy to data protection, towards designing robots for privacy in a wider sense. We argue that the communication and interaction with robots in healthcare contexts impacts not just data protection concerns, but wider consideration of privacy values, and that these privacy concerns pose challenges that need to be considered during robot design and their implementation in healthcare settings.

Keywords

Privacy, data protection, human-robot interaction, socially assistive robots, healthcare, consent, medical confidentiality, robots, artificial intelligence, exoskeletons, dementia

1. Introduction

The development of robots for use in healthcare settings has been accelerating significantly over the last few years and it is projected to grow by 22.1 per cent between 2017 and 2024.[1] National and international robot strategy documents highlight the importance of developing robots for use in the field of healthcare with a variety of arguments, from increased cost-effectiveness to protections for the health and safety of workers to the urgent need to address demographic challenges where increasing numbers of persons in need of care are met with declining numbers of available caregivers.[2] Japan plans to increase robot use by caregivers and care-receivers by 80 per cent across care settings.[3]

Because the adoption of robots raises substantial ethical, legal, societal[4] and regulatory issues,[5] the field of robotics is now beginning to receive attention from political and regulatory actors, and these issues are also increasingly discussed in general public discourse. Early in 2017, the European Parliament (EP) released the Resolution on Civil Law Rules on Robotics 2015/2103(INL).[6] It is a pioneering

---

[1] 'Global Medical Robots Market Forecast 2017–2024' NKWood Research, Accessed 27 February 2018. Available at: www.inkwoodresearch.com/reports/medical-robotics-market/#report-summary.

[2] 'Multi-annual Roadmap 2020', SPARC, last modified 2 February 2015. Available at: www.eu-robotics.net/cms/upload/downloads/ppp-documents/Multi-Annual_Roadmap2020_ICT-24_Rev_B_full.pdf.

[3] 'New Robot Strategy', The Headquarters for Japan's Economic Revitalization, last modified 10 February 2015. Available at: www.meti.go.jp/english/press/2015/pdf/0123_01b.pdf.

[4] Yang, Guang-Zhong, Jim Bellingham, Pierre E. Dupont, Peer Fischer, Luciano Floridi, Robert Full, Neil Jacobstein et al, 'The grand Challenges of Science Robotics.' *Science Robotics* 3, no 14 (2018): eaar7650.

[5] Leenes, Ronald, Erica Palmerini, Bert-Jaap Koops, Andrea Bertolini, Pericle Salvini, and Federica Lucivero. 'Regulatory challenges of robotics: Some guidelines for addressing legal and ethical issues.' *Law, Innovation and Technology* 9, no 1 (2017): 1–44.

[6] 'Civil Law Rules on Robotics', European Parliament resolution of 16 February 2017 with recommendations to the Commission on Civil Law Rules on Robotics (2015/2103(INL)), last modified

effort to raise legal and regulatory concerns of emerging robot technologies at the European level – including care and medical robots – but the resolution also shows some significant deficits: it lacks technical awareness and contains provisions that may be 'morally unnecessary and legally troublesome' such as the ascription of personality to synthetic persons.[7] As an all-embracing attempt to cover cyber-physical systems more generally, the resolution lacks complexity when addressing legal issues specifically concerning healthcare robots and artificial intelligence; it highlights primarily the dehumanisation of caring practices due to the insertion of care robots into the healthcare context. The European Commission (EC) agrees that legal action in the field of robotics is urgently required because 'doing otherwise would negatively affect the development and uptake of robots.'[8] While the EC acknowledges the need to revise the Machinery or the Defective Product Directive,[9] other aspects like the definition of a robot and the identification of what exactly should fall under the protected scope of such pieces of legislation are not completely clear.

In light of these uncertainties and delays that characterise the current public policy making process, industry and regulatory private actors have stepped into the breach and have begun to develop standards that regulate various robot application domains. Currently, there are already established standards addressing ethical, legal and societal issues (ELSI) of these technologies, including the British Standard (BS) 8611:2016 'Robots and robotic devices. Guide to the ethical design and application of robots and robotic systems'[10] and the IEEE Global Initiative on Ethics of Autonomous and Intelligent Systems with their document on 'Ethically Aligned Design: A Vision for Prioritising Human Well-being with Autonomous and Intelligent Systems.'[11] These contributions provide a general discussion of ethical concerns related to robotics, while specific issues relating to care robotics are covered by the ISO 13482:2014 Robots and Robotic Devices – Safety Requirements for Personal Care Robots.'[12] However, while the attention to

---

16 February 2017. Available at: www.europarl.europa.eu/sides/getDoc.do?pubRef=-//EP//NONSGML+TA+P8-TA-2017-0051+0+DOC+PDF+V0//EN.

[7] Bryson, Joanna J., Mihailis E. Diamantis, and Thomas D. Grant. 'Of, For, and By the People: The Legal Lacuna of Synthetic Persons.' *Artificial Intelligence and Law* 25, no 3 (2017): 273–291.

[8] 'Follow up to the European Parliament resolution of 16 February 2017 on civil law rules on robotics', European Commission, last modified 16 May 2017. Available at: www.globalpolicywatch.com/2017/08/what-is-a-robot-under-eu-law/.

[9] 'Evaluation and Fitness Check (FC) Roadmap' European Commission, last modified 12 September 2016. Available at: http://ec.europa.eu/smart-regulation/roadmaps/docs/2016_grow_027_evaluation_defective_products_en.pdf.

[10] 'BS 8611:2016 Robots and robotic devices. Guide to the ethical design and application of robots and robotic systems', British Standard Institute, last modified April, 2016. Available at: https://shop.bsigroup.com/ProductDetail/?pid=000000000030320089.

[11] 'Ethically Aligned Design' IEEE, last modified December, 2017. Available at: http://standards.ieee.org/develop/indconn/ec/ead_v2.pdf.

[12] 'ISO 13482:2014 Robots and Robotic Devices – Safety Requirements for Personal Care Robots', International Standard Organization, last modified February, 2014. Available at: www.iso.org/standard/53820.html.

robotics by regulatory and private sector actors is welcome, these measures have certain shortcomings. Standards only cover particular impacts, predominantly safety concerns, and offer a limited protected scope, insofar as they do not address special protected categories of users. These documents are also inadequate from a legal point of view insofar as they do not provide legally binding rules; they are not directly enforceable because they do not establish consequences (sanctions) for violations and generally lack precision.[13] Reliance on private-sector initiatives also risks the decentralisation of regulation,[14] and conveys the impression that what used to be in the remit of law is now being privatised.[15] The focus on particular private sector interests has led to a situation where legally significant impacts such as privacy and data protection, while present in the debate, have been comparatively underemphasised.[16]

In a context where multiple regulatory bodies provide patchy coverage of a field of practice due to diverging aims and interests, neither the regulator nor the addressees might be in the position to define clearly and with certainty what actions are required[17] when users' rights might be at stake. This is particularly problematic in the context of socially assistive robots (SARs) that are aimed at enhancing health and wellbeing, whether through caregiving, providing treatment, or health monitoring. The inherent vulnerability of the patient in the healthcare context pushes to the fore the need to ensure that vulnerabilities are not exacerbated through inadequate attention to relevant legal concerns.

Some of these concerns relate to privacy and data protection, which manifest themselves in a variety of ways. For instance, the processing of sensitive data in SARs to generate social reactivity, when based on models that have not been screened well enough, may have unpredictable feedback effects.[18] SARs may go beyond other Internet-of-Things (IoT) objects in obtaining intimate virtual and physical mapping of private or institutional living, due to their additional information gathering potential.[19] Although robots cannot yet reliably identify the social

---

[13] Delmas-Marty, M., *Le flou du droit* (Paris: Canopé, 1986).

[14] Guihot, Michael and Anne F. Matthew, and Nicolas Suzor, Nudging Robots: Innovative Solutions to Regulate Artificial Intelligence (28 July 2017). *Vanderbilt Journal of Entertainment & Technology Law*, Forthcoming. Available at SSRN: https://ssrn.com/abstract=3017004.

[15] Fosch-Villaronga, Eduard, and Antoni Roig. 'European Regulatory Framework for Person Carrier Robots.' *Computer Law & Security Review* 33, no 4 (2017): 502–520.

[16] Fosch Villaronga, Eduard. 'Towards a Legal and Ethical Framework for Personal Care Robots. Analysis of Person Carrier, Physical Assistant and Mobile Servant Robots.' (PhD diss., Erasmus Mundus Joint Doctorate in Law, Science and Technology Consortium, 2017).

[17] Sabel, Charles, Gary Herrigel, and Peer Hull Kristensen. 'Regulation under Uncertainty: The Coevolution of Industry and Regulation.' *Regulation & Governance* (2017).

[18] De Groot, Aviva. 'Dear Robot. The special effects of socially, assistive robots on the privacy related rights of care receivers' (LLM Diss. University of Amsterdam, 2017).

[19] van den Berg, Bibi. 'Mind the Air Gap.' In Serge Gutwirth, Ronald Leenes and Paul De Hert (eds), *Data Protection on the Move, Current Developments in ICT and Privacy/Data Protection* (Dordrecht: Springer, 2016), 1–24.

roles of actors in a care setting, such as inhabitants, personal and formal visitors, close and remote family or delivery services, they can nevertheless potentially share any information gathered on users and their environment with companies and third parties. SARs are also at risk of being hacked, exposing users to particular privacy risks.[20] Medical confidentiality issues may arise when patients confide in social robots as friends rather than agents of the care system and expect such information to remain outside the care system. Yet other issues might ensue from emotional data capture, a rapidly developing field where the reliable processing of emotions of the users and subsequent initiation of effective emotionally driven interaction might soon become feasible.[21]

For this chapter, we selected critical concerns about the use of healthcare robots that are specifically linked to the interaction between humans and robots and that have been comparatively underexplored in the literature until now, in order to highlight the complexity of data protection and privacy concerns that arise in the use of healthcare robots.

2. Healthcare Robots and Stakeholders in Robotised Healthcare

In recent years, healthcare robots, defined as 'systems able to perform coordinated mechatronic actions (force or movement exertions) on the basis of processing of information acquired through sensor technology, with the aim to support the functioning of impaired individuals, medical interventions, care and rehabilitation of patients and also to support individuals in prevention programs,'[22] have been employed in a wide range of healthcare settings.[23] Driving this phenomenon are the consequences of the demographic regression in developed countries: 'older persons are projected to exceed the number of children for the first time in 2047.'[24] These demographic developments mean that an increasing number of

---

[20] Kaminski, Margot E., Matthew Rueben, William D. Smart, and Cindy M. Grimm. 'Averting Robot Eyes.' *Maryland Law Review* 76 (2016): 983.

[21] Fosch-Villaronga, E. and J Albo-Canals. 'Robotic Therapies: Notes on Governance' Workshop on Social Robots in Therapy: Focusing on Autonomy and Ethical Challenges. *Human Robot Interaction Conference* 2018, forthcoming.

[22] 'Roadmap for Robotics for Healthcare' The European Foresight Monitoring Network, last modified November, 2008. Available at: www.foresight-platform.eu/wp-content/uploads/2011/02/EFMN-Brief-No.-157_Robotics-for-Healthcare.pdf.

[23] Garmann-Johnsen, Niels, Tobias Mettler, and Michaela Sprenger. 'Service Robotics in Healthcare: A Perspective for Information Systems Researchers?', last modified August 2014. Available at: www.researchgate.net/publication/267763443_Service_Robotics_in_Healthcare_A_Perspective_for_Information_Systems_Researcher.

[24] 'World Population Ageing 2013' United Nations, Department of Economic and Social Affairs Population Division, last modified 2013. Available at: www.un.org/en/development/desa/population/publications/pdf/ageing/WorldPopulationAgeing2013.pdf.

older persons in need of care will need to be cared for by a younger generation whose numbers have dramatically decreased.[25] Given the increase in professional care delivery, a large number of older persons can be expected to enter nursing homes and hospitals and substantially increase demand for medical care and assistance in daily living, on top of already significant levels of healthcare care needs.[26]

Robot strategies envisage that the key objectives of healthcare – to contribute to quality, safety and efficiency of care; to promote the shift to preventive and personalised care; and to support the availability of long term care for people in need[27] – will be increasingly met by robots. The robots that have been developed so far are robots that promise to relieve human staff of physical burdens, such as delivery robots, lifting robots, exoskeletons for nurses or nurses' aids; robots that provide instruction, reminders and support of healthcare-related patient activities, such as cognitive assistive robots, or physical rehabilitation robots; robots that perform or support the realisation of specialised physical skills, such as surgery robots; robots that provide support for physical functions, such as exoskeletons for patients in rehabilitation for mobility impairments; and robots that provide cognitive therapeutic activities for patients, for example social competence training for patients with autism, or reminiscence therapy for patients with neurodegenerative disorders, such as dementia (see Figure 4.1).

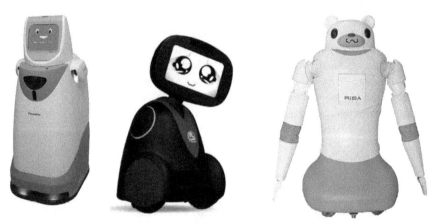

Figure 4.1 Examples of healthcare robots: from left to right Hospit(R) from Panasonic, eBuddy from Bluefrog Robotics, and RIBA from Tokai Rubber Industries

[25] 'Will a Robot Care for my Mom?' Colin Angle, TedMed, last modified 2009. Available at: www.tedmed.com/talks/show?id=7193.

[26] 'Supply and Demand Projections of the Nursing Workforce: 2014–2030' US Department of Health and Human Services, last modified 21 July 2017. Available at: https://bhw.hrsa.gov/sites/default/files/bhw/nchwa/projections/NCHWA_HRSA_Nursing_Report.pdf.

[27] See 'Roadmap for Robotics for Healthcare' n 22.

Indeed, robots help deliver care in novel ways. For instance, researchers in autism-related traditional interventions were confronted with the task to investigate the complex relationship between the acquisition of communication skills, social-emotional factors and types of transactional support that predict better outcomes for children with autism. This was greatly challenged by the fact that, although autistic children have comparable developmental difficulties, there are huge differences among them. Robots promise to optimise care delivery because they can adapt easily to each individual's needs,[28] they are predictive and repetitive, and also very engaging.[29] Furthermore, with the help of ambient intelligence technologies, information from the session can be collected for further analysis and improvement in a way that not feasible before.[30]

Concerning the efficiency of care, some hospitals have started incorporating autonomous ground vehicles (AGV) in their facilities to over internal delivery routes. An idea already debated in the nineties,[31] these robots help streamline some of the basic tasks previously performed by nurses (ie deliver food, medicines and clothes from the kitchen, pharmacy or laundry room to the patients' rooms). They may have non-biomimetic or humanoid shape, and can work steadily 24/7, only requiring maintenance.

Each of these types of robots raises particular legal and ethical concerns. However, considered from a privacy and data protection perspective some common themes emerge, relating to the collection and use of potentially sensitive data from healthcare and domestic settings with regard to patients, bystanders and healthcare staff, and with corresponding implications regarding design responsibilities of robot developers. While patient users tend to be the focus of attention in most ethical and legal discussions of healthcare robots, patient users are only one of many stakeholder groups. As this chapter illustrates, a privacy and data protection angle on the discussion is particularly helpful for exploring the complexity of the stakeholder network for healthcare robotics which may include cloud service providers, third parties, the institution as a whole, different types of users, workers interacting with the robots as well as manufacturers (see Figure 4.2).

---

[28] Barco, Alex, Jordi Albo-Canals, Carles Garriga-Berga, Xavier Vilasís-Cardona, Laura Callejón, Marc Turón, Claudia Gómez, and Anna López-Sala. 'A Drop-out Rate in a Long-term Cognitive Rehabilitation Program through Robotics aimed at Children with TBI.' In *Robot and Human Interactive Communication, 2014 RO-MAN: The 23rd IEEE International Symposium*. IEEE, 2014, 186–192.

[29] Valenzuela, Emelideth, Alex Barco, and Jordi Albo-Canals. 'Learning social skills through LEGO-based social robots for children with autism spectrum disorder at CASPAN center in Panama.' In *2015 Conference Proceedings, NewFriends*, edited by Heerink, M. and Jong, M. de (2015).(Windeshelm: Flevoland, 2015).

[30] 'Meet Hookie' Dynatech, last accessed 1 March 2018. Available at: http://hookie.dynatech2012.com/home/.

[31] 'Automated Guided Vehicles. Time Out Analysis' University of Michigan, last modified 1 July 1992. Available at: http://umich.edu/~ioe481/ioe481_past_reports/w9208.pdf.

Figure 4.2 Human-Robot Interaction stakeholder complexity

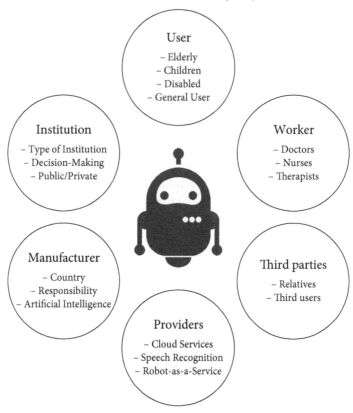

3. Six Privacy Issues for Healthcare Robots: The Distinctive Lens of Human-Robot Interaction

Having as a starting point the objectives of healthcare and the systemic issues that the sector is facing, this section shows how the complex net of relationships among the actors involved, all bearing different needs and interests can be unraveled from the perspective of privacy and data protection. We outline privacy and data protection challenges for healthcare robots for different stakeholders, using the lens of human-robot interaction (ie the way robots and humans work and function together in the healthcare context). This focus will allow us to highlight a critical element that distinguishes healthcare from other services and sectors: the care of individuals, frequently in circumstances of vulnerability.

3.1.   Confidentiality, Induced Trust and the Nudging of Disclosure

The use of social robots has been shown to influence disclosure behaviour of those who interact with them. This phenomenon has particular significance in healthcare contexts, where disclosure by patients takes place in a protected confidential setting. The core principle of medical confidentiality, a species of privacy, governs the interaction between patients and healthcare professionals, protecting knowledge of what is being said, seen, and done from outsider access. A range of contextual values, ethical norms and considerations with regard to confidential information are at play in daily health care practices. These are inevitably not fully reflected by the laws that govern these relationships. Accordingly, using social robots in these settings poses challenges with regard to the management of complex privacy related responsibilities.

Medical confidentiality legally protects any kind of information shared between the patient and their professional caregivers and stretches out to anyone professionally involved in care delivery or the processing of relevant information, like administrative personnel and technicians. Outside of that circle, information can only be shared with a patient's explicit consent and following her autonomous choices. These requirements are governed by national laws and professional self-regulation. For informational relations that fall outside of these laws' legal domains (think of exchanges with visitors, or a patient's private health care app) data protection rules on medical and health-related data are applicable. The European General Data Protection Regulation prohibits processing of these data except on the basis of a limited list of exceptional grounds, medical treatment being one of them (GDPR, Article 9). These protections support the establishment of trusted relationships in which a care receiver feels comfortable to disclose sensitive information, without fear of wider disclosure, thereby facilitating care delivery that fits her needs.[32] In that sense, there is a clear public interest, as is recognised by the World Health Organisation.[33] Confidentiality also protects a care receiver's autonomous treatment decisions by shielding the process from outside influence, including paternalistic interference by persons around the care receiver.[34]

When social robots are cast in the role of care providers or care assistants, their behaviour needs to be compliant with these demands of confidentiality. This not

---

[32] Allen, Anita, 'Compliance Limited Health Privacy Laws' in *Social Dimensions of Privacy: Interdisciplinary Perspectives* edited by Roessler, B. and D. Mokrosinska (Cambridge: Cambridge University Press 2015), 261–277.

[33] 'Human Rights and Health', World Health Organization, last modified December 2017. Available at: www.who.int/mediacentre/factsheets/fs323/en/.

[34] Dworkin, Gerald. 'Can you Trust Autonomy?' *The Hastings Center Report* 33, no 2 (2003): 42–44.

only pertains to their own interactions with patients, as they are likely to impact the relationships of patients with their human caregivers as well. Effects on patients' disclosure autonomy and on trust building, and the consequences of secret robot confidences are complications that need to be taken seriously. Relations between SARs and care recipients have distinctive characteristics. Users appear to be keen on establishing a relationship, as illustrated by a quote from a test subject about a robot, who stated 'I think I want to see him as something that is alive. He's charming.'[35] On a more subconscious level, Human Robot Interaction (HRI) research convincingly shows that anthropomorphic projections and ascriptions of purpose, even in the face of unpredictable,[36] unexplained or erroneous robot behaviour,[37] are strong and highly resistant to elimination. One study showed how users explained a robot's movements in relation to the goals that they expected it to pursue, without considering the possibility of a purely technical explanation.[38] In another study, a robot which asked a human to put an object 'up there' but gestured towards the floor was experienced as particularly likeable or playful, rather than faulty.[39]

The same unconscious projections seem to stimulate the establishment of trust in robots, which happens easily and quickly. Research has shown that people trust robots even when they have clear evidence that such trust is unjustified.[40] In a study on emergency evacuation scenarios, participants consistently followed a robot despite previously seeing the same robot navigate poorly. The robot led 26 participants into a dark room with no exits during a simulated fire, and no one thought to safely exit the way they came in rather than following the robot's instructions.[41] As will be shown next, this trust sometimes trumps that which is put in humans.

This 'natural trust' in robots has positive effects on patients' willingness to disclose, as they not only feel at ease to do so but are stimulated as well. In health

---

[35] Frennert, Susanne, Håkan Eftring, and Britt Östlund. 'Case Report: Implications of Doing Research on Socially Assistive Robots in Real Homes' *International Journal of Social Robotics* 9, no 3 (2017): 401–415.

[36] Darling, Kate 'Extending Legal Protection to Social Robots: The Effects of Anthropomorphism, Empathy, and Violent Behaviour Towards Robotic Objects' in *Robot Law* edited by Ryan Calo, Michael Froomkin, Ian Kerr (Cheltenham: Edward Elgar Publishing 2016), 213–231.

[37] See Salem, Maha, Friederike Eyssel, Katharina Rohlfing, Stefan Kopp, and Frank Joublin. 'To Err is Human (-like): Effects of Robot Gesture on Perceived Anthropomorphism and Likability' *International Journal of Social Robotics* 5, no 3 (2013): 313–323.

[38] Wortham, Robert H., Andreas Theodorou, and Joanna J. Bryson. 'Robot Transparency: Improving Understanding of Intelligent Behaviour for Designers and Users.' In *Conference Towards Autonomous Robotic Systems* (Cham: Springer, 2017), 274–289.

[39] See Salem et al, n 37.

[40] Salem, Maha, Gabriella Lakatos, Farshid Amirabdollahian, and Kerstin Dautenhahn. 'Would You Trust A (Faulty) Robot?: Effects Of Error, Task Type and Personality on Human-Robot Cooperation and Trust.' In *Proceedings of the Tenth Annual ACM/IEEE International Conference on Human-Robot Interaction,* (New York: ACM, 2015), 141–148.

[41] Robinette, Paul, Wenchen Li, Robert Allen, Ayanna M. Howard, and Alan R. Wagner. 'Overtrust of Robots in Emergency Evacuation Scenarios.' In *Human-Robot Interaction (HRI), 2016 11th ACM/IEEE International Conference* (IEEE, 2016), 101–108.

care settings, the presence of robots has been shown to help care receivers feel at ease. Paro the baby seal has been found to alleviate stress in persons with dementia, some of whom are enticed into interacting with social robots even when they refuse to respond to human interaction.[42] Care receivers with less cognitive impairment have been found to experience robots as more predictable and less demanding in interaction than humans.[43] There is extensive evidence that social robots in different practice contexts consistently stimulate their interaction partners to disclose information more readily, and with fewer inhibitions than in the context of human relationships.[44] Patients are known to disclose more to a robot than to telepresence screens or cameras, making robots potentially particularly suitable for monitoring purposes.[45]

These effects are noted by Kaminski et al, who describe the impact on the 'disclosure autonomy' function of medical confidentiality: sharing health related information according to one's own preferences.[46] Robots' framing as socially interactive entities stimulates care receivers to disclose even more, partly because disclosure of personal information is a behaviour that is generally rewarded in interactive contexts. The therapeutic trust-building phase of patients and caregivers can be speeded up when a robot enters the relationship; the initial testing of an interactions partner's trustworthiness can be shortened.[47] Calo further warns that robots might be employed to exert their 'super-human leverage.' The robot's human-like appeal is amplified in absence of the socially inhibiting, self-censoring effect that is a part of human interaction.[48] The trust building phase between patient and caregiver has merits of its own, as patients need to be able to trust their caregivers independently of robotic presence. That system of natural trust development is interfered with and can be potentially exploited by using robots. Manipulations of patients' willingness to disclose risks to erode the disclosure autonomy function of medical confidentiality.

Considering that social robots are designed to draw on these human inclinations to ensure their effective functioning, a robot's role should be carefully

---

[42] Kahl, Björn, Matthias Füller, Thomas Beer, and Sven Ziegler. 'Acceptance and Communicative Effectiveness of Different HRI Modalities for Mental Stimulation in Dementia Care' in *New Frontiers of Service Robotics for the Elderly* edited by Di Nuovo, E., F. Broz, F Cavallo, P Dario (IEEE 2014), 11–14.

[43] Bryson, Joanna J. 'Robots Should Be Slaves.' *Close Engagements with Artificial Companions: Key Social, Psychological, Ethical and Design Issues* (2010): 63–74.

[44] Thomasen, Kristen, 'Examining the Constitutionality of Robot-enhanced Interrogation' in *Robot Law* edited by Ryan Calo, Michael Froomkin, Ian Kerr (Cheltenham: Edward Elgar Publishing 2016) pp. 306–330.

[45] Sedenberg, Elaine, John Chuang, and Deirdre Mulligan. 'Designing Commercial Therapeutic Robots for Privacy Preserving Systems and Ethical Research Practices Within the Home.' *International Journal of Social Robotics* 8, no 4 (2016): 575–587.

[46] See Kaminski et al, n 20 at 983.

[47] See Thomasen n 44.

[48] Calo, M. Ryan. 'Robots and Privacy.' in *Robot Ethics: The Ethical and Social Implications of Robotics*, edited by Lin, Patrick, Keith Abney, and George A. Bekey (Cambridge, MA: MIT Press 2011).

constructed to avoid complications. Transparency with regard to a robot's function and operational capacities is especially of concern in healthcare settings. The hidden nature of information processing by robots is likely to lead to lack of awareness about the nature and extent of information processing that goes on. A robot's capabilities should be communicated to patients and other users to allow them to reflect on their engagement with the robot. Disappointment about unexpected uses of information collected by robots will harm the trust of patients in robots and the caregivers that employ them.

This means the programming of robotic behaviours needs careful consideration. Using interpersonal clues, robots can be designed to make users more comfortable, for instance by 'averting robot eyes', thereby distracting them from the fact that information is still being collected.[49] Apart from how this harms a patient's legitimate expectations, this paves the ways for abuse in the form of covert collection of, for example, sensitive images. With earlier introductions of covert recording technologies, these highly invasive privacy interferences became a pervasive problem, targeting black women disproportionately.[50] Depending on who the robot users are and in what contexts recording is taking place, covert robot recording might similarly disproportionately affect members of certain groups or include a significant level of sensitive information. This risks eroding these groups' trust in medical confidentiality, discouraging them to seek care.

But robots might also be used to enhance an established human therapeutic relationship. Pettinati et al. researched whether the robot Nao, as a 'peripheral tool', might be used to alert caregivers to norm violations in talking sessions between caregivers and care receivers, for example when patients that suffer from Parkinson's disease show a loss of expressivity and a doctor reacts negatively. As a first tested step, an attending, but not recording Nao was considered non-intrusive by test subjects, even though it was experienced as listening in on them. Human attendance on the other hand, they reported, would disturb their disclosure readiness.[51]

However, a positive difference in comfort that patients feel with robots compared to their human caregivers can cause problems of its own. If patients spend much time with a social robot, especially if this time is experienced as rewarding, they might begin to conceive of the robot as a friend rather than a healthcare aid. This might have an effect on how they perceive the norms of disclosure that the robot is likely to follow. Accordingly, they might consider information given to the robot to be confidential to the robot itself rather than to the care system within which robot the robot is deployed, and feel betrayed if such information is passed on to human caregivers. While human nurses are used to balancing conflicting demands

---

[49] Kaminski, et al, n 20 at 983.
[50] See Allen n 32 at 261–277.
[51] Pettinati, Michael J. et al, 'The Influence of a Peripheral Social Robot on Self-Disclosure' (2016) 25th IEEE International Symposium on Robot and Human Interactive Communication (RO-MAN).

for confidentiality and disclosure in the complex context of caring relationships,[52] and are able to use their discretion based on their understanding of specific patient needs and expectations, this goes beyond current capabilities of robots. The rules of transparency of robot data to the healthcare team might follow different principles and therefore pose particular challenges in terms of who has the control and authority to disclose patient information to the healthcare team. As Draper and Sorrell point out, it would, for instance, be highly problematic from an informational autonomy point of view to use robotic data recording to 'second-guess the older person's own testimonies',[53] especially if that data has been gained as a result of induced willingness to disclose in the presence of the robot.

3.2. Complexities of Consent in Healthcare Robotics

Consent is a core requirement for data processing. Consent must be voluntary and informed, with a clear explanation of what data is being collected, what the data will be used for, and how long it will be stored. However, consent to the collection and use of data by the robot also occurs within the context of healthcare which carries its own norms and requirements for consent. Accordingly, the robot operates under both data governance schemes in that, as it collects data, it must comply with Data Protection laws and, as a healthcare aid, must comply with any requirements for consent for these health activities. The multi-functional SAR operating as a caregiver sits within the regulatory domains of each of those functions. Consequently, as a matter of medical ethics, consent must meet requirements of voluntariness, competence of the patient, clear and full disclosure of relevant information accompanied by comprehension of that information.[54,55] From a legal viewpoint, consent 'should be given by a clear affirmative act establishing a freely given, specific, informed and unambiguous indication of the data subject's agreement to the processing of personal data relating to him or her.'[56] Moreover, beyond the fact that the controller shall demonstrate that the data subject has given their consent, and offers an easily accessible withdrawal possibility to the data subject; the processing of sensitive data such as health data implies that explicit consent has been given. During the consent process it should be made clear that not only is

---

[52] Nissenbaum, Helen. *Privacy in Context: Technology, Policy, and the Integrity of Social Life* (Stanford: Stanford University Press, 2009).

[53] Sorell, Tom and Heather Draper, 'Robot Carers, Ethics, and Older People', Ethics and Information Technology 16, no 3 (2014): 183–195.

[54] Faden, Ruth R., and Tom L. Beauchamp. *A History and Theory of Informed Consent*. (Oxford: Oxford University Press, 1986).

[55] Beauchamp, Tom L., James F. Childress, *Principles of Biomedical Ethics* (7th edn). (New York: Oxford University Press, 2012).

[56] Regulation (EU) 2016/679 of the European Parliament and of the Council of 27 April 2016 on the protection of natural persons with regard to the processing of personal data and on the free movement of such data, and repealing Directive 95/46/EC (General Data Protection Regulation (GDPR)).

the robot functioning as a caregiver, but also as a data processing device and both types of functions should be explicitly authorised by the care receiver or his or her surrogate. In addition to that, it should also be clarified who is a data controller and who is a data processor. As seen in Figure 4.2, the healthcare sector may involve multiple actors, including doctors, personnel, healthcare institution, providers of services, possible lessors for certain equipment or the users themselves. Based on the definitions and regimes established by Articles 4, 26, and 28 of the GDPR, this scenario requires the identification of the de facto role of each actor. This will be of greater importance for those patients using healthcare robots used at home, because, whereas the household exception (GDPR, Article 2) would exist for the users vis-à-vis their guests/domestic collaborators provided that all the conditions are met; it would not apply with regard to the companies providing the monitoring services and carrying out the processing of the data.

The importance of regard for consent in the use of healthcare robots is underscored by the fact that, due to their interactive nature, robots as cyber-physical systems are often not immediately recognised by users as data-processing devices that may require consent for their data usage. Instead, they tend to be experienced and conceptualised primarily as interactive partners, albeit as 'liminal objects' between animate and inanimate, as Turkle highlights.[57] Due to the *anthropomorphisation effect*[58],[59] humans tend to project and attribute human-like features to even very simple objects and often ascribe function on the basis of similarities to human anatomy.[60] As pointed out by de Groot, this might lead to significant misconceptions about data processing: not only might robot 'eyes' see more than human eyes, there might also be other sensors with no human equivalent, capturing large amounts of data, for example for navigation purposes or for supporting effective and safe HRI.[61] Additionally, such data might be shared with different companies for improvement purposes (eg robots often rely on externally developed speech recognition services). In those cases of further data use, the controller might not see themselves as responsible for the processor's adherence to data protection laws.[62] Data may also be processed remotely in the cloud, blurring the relationships, responsibilities and liabilities among various actors, such as users, manufacturers, and cloud service providers.[63]

---

[57] Turkle, Sherry. *Alone Together: Why We Expect More from Technology and Less from Each Other.* (London: Hachette, 2017).

[58] See Salem, et al, n 37 at 313–323.

[59] Rault, Jean-Loup. 'Pets in the Digital Age: Live, Robot, or Virtual?.' *Frontiers in Veterinary Science* 2 (2015): 11.

[60] Mead, Ross, and Maja J. Mataric. 'Robots Have Needs Too: People Adapt their Proxemic Preferences to Improve Autonomous Robot Recognition of Human Social Signals.' *New Frontiers in Human-Robot Interaction* 5, no 2 (2015): 48–68.

[61] See De Groot n 28 at 28.

[62] 'Privacy Policy' Terms of Use, ToyTalk, last modified April 11, 2017. Available at: https://toytalk.com/hellobarbie/privacy/.

[63] Fosch-Villaronga, E. and Millard, C. 'Robots, Clouds and Humans. Challenges in Regulating Complex and Dynamic Cyber-Physical Ecosystems', *SSRN* (2018), forthcoming.

Consent requirements must take into account the vulnerability of the robot user. The nature of the vulnerability that has resulted in the need for robotic assistance may compound the complexity of consent requirements. Assistive robots are strongly promoted as a way to address the care and support needs of an aging demographic; many of those robots are targeted at users with early dementia or other cognitive impairments. The consent process for care receivers with cognitive impairments is particularly demanding due to the complexity of their capacity, which may be inconsistent and fluctuating. Jurisdiction-specific capacity legislation provides the legal basis for consent for persons with cognitive impairments, with a human rights based focus on the presumption of capacity, while acknowledging that a balance needs to be struck between the patient's autonomy and informational privacy rights and the duty of beneficence. The consent process might involve additional parties that support the patient, or in the case of severely impaired capacity serve as decision-making proxies. As highlighted above, consent needs to include both the authorisation of the use of the robotic assistance for healthcare purposes as well as data protection consent, such as consent to make available user information to additional parties to ensure the provision of competent and comprehensive care.[64]

The mechanism of achieving consent for the use of robotic assistance could be tailored to enhance understanding and the exercise of autonomy by the care receiver and achieve an optimal level of transparency and accuracy. A two-phase model of consent could be conceived here: It would be initially the responsibility of the service provider to facilitate the user's consent to the use of robot as healthcare aid, including its most important data protection aspects. However, once the robot has been accepted as healthcare aid and is in use, it might be possible to have the robot initiate conversations about consent with users and provide further information and implement the ongoing consent process for any emerging changes. With the increasing availability of sophisticated conversational interfaces this options becomes increasingly attractive (see 3.3. below). Ongoing information and consent facilitation by the robot would constitute a form of dynamic consent,[65,66,67] allowing users to be kept abreast of relevant developments, but also

---

[64] Ienca, M. and Fosch-Villaronga, E. (2018) 'Privacy and Security Issues in Assistive Technologies for Dementia: The Case of Ambient Assisted Living, Wearables and Service Robotics'. In *Assistive Technologies for Dementia Care*, edited by Fabrice Jotterand, Marcello Ienca, Tenzin Wangmo, and Bernice Elger (Oxford; Oxford University Press, 2018).

[65] Kaye, Jane, Edgar A. Whitley, David Lund, Michael Morrison, Harriet Teare, and Karen Melham. 'Dynamic Consent: A Patient Interface for Twenty-first Century Research Networks' *European Journal of Human Genetics* 23, no 2 (2015): 141.

[66] Williams, Hawys, Karen Spencer, Caroline Sanders, David Lund, Edgar A. Whitley, Jane Kaye, and William G. Dixon. 'Dynamic Consent: A Possible Solution to Improve Patient Confidence and Trust in How Electronic Patient Records are used in Medical Research.' *JMIR Medical Informatics* 3, no 1 (2015).

[67] Budin-Ljøsne, Isabelle, Harriet JA Teare, Jane Kaye, Stephan Beck, Heidi Beate Bentzen, Luciana Caenazzo, Clive Collett et al 'Dynamic Consent: A Potential Solution to Some of the Challenges of Modern Biomedical Research.' *BMC Medical Ethics* 18, no 1 (2017): 4.

to manage their own privacy preferences in a time-sensitive manner – in short, enhancing their opportunities to exercise informational autonomy. However, limitations of the robot's ability to facilitate such communications need to be kept in mind, and the option to engage in ongoing consent conversations with the service provider being should always be available.

Another aspect of consent process arises as a result of the interaction of the robot with any other humans other than the care receiver who may be present. As we discuss later in this chapter, this may involve the observation and collection of information about the caregiver and other human staff who may be working in the presence of the care receiver and the robot. As we note below, SARs whether in homes or institutions will be functioning in the context of the workplace of other humans. This raises privacy considerations with regard to what extent these workers consent to the processing of data collected about them. As we argue, consent from these workers needs to be obtained if a data protection compliant workplace is to be provided. However, it remains uncertain whether workers are really free to provide consent in the full sense to the processing of data, or how this applies to purely machine-to-machine communications.[68]

3.3. Conversational Privacy Management with Robots

SARs with socially communicative capabilities can give physical and cognitive support to elderly persons, disabled persons, or many other types of users.[69] Robots that provide instructions or remind users of certain tasks, as well as those designed for cognitive therapeutic activities often deploy vocal communication capabilities together with other types of user interfaces, such as buttons or interactive screens. Personal healthcare companions like Mabu or Buddy, for instance, use a vocal notification system to remind patients when to take their medicines.[70,71] These capabilities have also been used in robots that are designed to support elderly patients and patients with dementia.[72] Robots can ask patients why they got up in the middle of the night, remind them to go to the toilet or, if they see that patients are opening the door to exit, they can talk to them or broadcast messages from family members to try and dissuade them from

---

[68] Recital 12 of the Proposal for a Regulation of the European Parliament and of the Council concerning the respect for private life and the protection of personal data in electronic communications and repealing Directive 2002/58/EC (Regulation on Privacy and Electronic Communications).

[69] Broadbent, Elizabeth, Rebecca Stafford, and Bruce MacDonald. 'Acceptance of Healthcare Robots for the Older Population: Review and Future Directions.' *International Journal of Social Robotics* 1, no 4 (2009): 319.

[70] 'Mabu', Catalia Health, last accessed 2 March 2018. Available at: www.cataliahealth.com.

[71] 'Buddy', Bluefrog Robotics, last accessed 2 March 2018. Available at: www.bluefrogrobotics.com/en/home/.

[72] 'Mario Project', Managing ACtive and Healthy Aging with the Use of Robotics, European Union, last accessed, 2 March 2018. Available at: www.mario-project.eu/portal/.

leaving.[73] Therapeutic robots for neurodevelopmental disorders such as autism spectrum disorder talk with their users to play with them, help them learn and stimulate social responses, thereby providing skills training as well as creating emotional bonds.[74]

Conversational user interfaces, although removing reliance on screens[75] and aiming towards achieving the 'ultimate human-computer interface',[76] raise the question whether users will, at some point, forget the fact that they are talking with a machine. Indeed, 'the most profound technologies are those that disappear. They weave themselves into the fabric of everyday life until they are indistinguishable from it.'[77] The close integration between users and friction-free conversational interfaces could reduce the users' awareness of the information they share with a system that may be collecting and processing information comprehensively and continuously.[78] Indeed, in order to understand the patient's interactions and reply appropriately, robots deploy natural language analysis methods that collect vast amounts of data, which in turn serve to refine its overall performance over time. The collection and processing of personal data – voice patterns, content of the conversations – that is also particularly sensitive data – health and behavioural data – creates concerns with regard to processing, profiling, and data transfers to third parties, as required for reliance on outside services such as speech recognition services. Such data would also have potential value for possible secondary uses that are not primarily related to the performance of the service, such as marketing and behavioural advertising.

While the use of vocal commands is increasingly popular, due to ease of use, comfort and potential health benefits,[79] on the other hand, the possibility that family members, neighbours or caregivers themselves can gain intimate knowledge about them due to overhearing their conversations with the robot might make users uncomfortable. Users might prefer a non-conversational interface that allows the content of their interactions to remain more private. Speech interfaces also come with additional vulnerabilities in terms of security and safety (eg the risk that other persons might be able to establish a conversation with the robot and potentially gain access to user information or change the robot's settings) but also

[73] Sharkey, Amanda, and Noel Sharkey. 'Granny and the Robots: Ethical Issues in Robot Care for the Elderly.' *Ethics and Information Technology* 14, no 1 (2012): 27–40.

[74] Diehl, Joshua J., Lauren M. Schmitt, Michael Villano, and Charles R. Crowell. 'The Clinical Use of Robots for Individuals with Autism Spectrum Disorders: A Critical Review.' *Research in Autism Spectrum Disorders* 6, no 1 (2012): 249–262.

[75] Krishna, Golden. *The Best Interface is no Interface: The Simple Path to Brilliant Technology.* (Harlow: Pearson Education, 2015).

[76] Harkous, Hamza, Kassem Fawaz, Kang G. Shin, and Karl Aberer. 'PriBots: Conversational Privacy with Chatbots.' In *WSF@ SOUPS*. 2016.

[77] Weiser, Mark. 'The Computer for the 21st Century.' *Scientific American* 265, no 3 (1991): 94–105.

[78] See Ienca and Fosch-Villaronga, n 64.

[79] Courtney, Karen L. 'Privacy and Senior Willingness to Adopt Smart Home Information Technology in Residential Care Facilities.' *Methods Inf Med*, 47, no 1 (2008): 76–81.

in terms of autonomy and free will, as it may not be clear to what extent normative behaviours should be enforced by robot and artificial intelligent healthcare technologies.

The interaction with robots with conversational capabilities may have an effect on how users perceive what counts as private. Technology shapes the way humans experience reality and operate within it. According to the theory of technological mediation, the types of relations, the points of contact, and the mutual influence between humans and technologies impact on how humans interpret and even construct reality.[80] Technology becomes a filter and, at the same time, an agent determining how individuals *see* the world.[81] If it is true that 'dialogue changes both parties, and its outcome cannot be predetermined'[82] then robot agents with conversational capabilities may affect us in ways that are potentially unpredictable. This means that, apart from other aspects,[83] designers of socially interactive robots need to be cognisant of the potential impact of seemingly innocuous technical solutions that may however change significantly the way in which the robot will be integrated into users' lives. Speech-based interaction may constitute such a substantially significant change.

As already indicated in section 3.2. conversational interfaces could be potentially suitable to enhancing privacy management, and could be specifically developed to help data subjects navigate privacy settings and policies in a more engaging and user friendly manner. The communication of privacy settings and policies is a notoriously problematic area of privacy management; the traditional approach to 'notice and consent' has long been criticised as ineffective and in need of improvement.[84] An example for such a conversational interface for privacy management is *PriBots*, a conversational bots product capable of providing support to users with regard to the privacy options of a website, product, or company.[85] Inspired by commercial bots used to provide easily and clear responses to online shoppers, *PriBots* can give explanations, answer questions, and help users to automatically change privacy settings. Such a product could potentially be used in healthcare robots. Conversational bots could deliver information to facilitate compliance with GDPR requirements, such as information concerning data processing, purposes, data transfer, the requirements of Articles 12 and 13 or Chapter III of the GDPR. Such bots might facilitate an increased level

---

[80] Verbeek, Peter-Paul. 'Toward a Theory of Technological Mediation.' *Technoscience and Postphenomenology: The Manhattan Papers* (2015): 189.

[81] Verbeek, Peter-Paul. ' Beyond Interaction: A Short Introduction to Mediation Theory.' *Interactions* 22, no 3 (2015): 26–31.

[82] Gittins, Anthony J. 'The Universal in the Local: Power, Piety, and Paradox in the Formation of Missionary Community.' *Mission and Culture: The Louis J. Luzbetak Lectures* (2012): 133–87.

[83] Gortzis, L.G. 'Designing and Redesigning Medical Telecare Services.' *Methods of Information in Medicine* 46, no 1 (2007): 27–35.

[84] Calo, Ryan. 'Against Notice Skepticism in Privacy (and Elsewhere).' *Notre Dame L. Rev.* 87 (2011): 1027.

[85] See Harkous et al, n 76.

of interactivity which could help data subjects improve their understanding of the content of the privacy policy of a given company. Such bots could also be deployed to help alert users to changes and deliver relevant information in an easily accessible and interactive way during the entire lifespan of the healthcare robot, in the manner of dynamic consent interfaces.[86] Such an approach to the provision of privacy relevant information would support the principle of transparency and privacy by design and by default. If such an approach to conversational privacy management is combined with voice recognition, it can also help foster privacy and data protection by delivering more tailored information to different subjects using the same robot, such as multiple patients, medical staff, parents or tutors.

It will be important to deploy these conversational interfaces only when it can be assured that the legal information can be presented accurately in this format, that the quality of the interaction is sufficiently high such that users receive appropriate responses to their queries or wider interactions with the system and that the interface performs at least as well as human interaction with regard to ensuring the user's understanding of the information delivered. This will require careful user studies, which should ideally be designed not just to capture comparative performance of such interfaces with privacy policies or human conversation, but also to capture qualitative differences in use and user experience, to do justice to the recent statement of the EP ascribing wider accountability of robotics engineers 'for the social, environmental and human health impacts that robotics may impose on present and future generations.'[87] A data protection impact assessment (GDPR, Article 35) could prove that the robots have been designed in the most privacy-friendly possible way. However, the consequences of technological mediation through the innovation of conversational interfaces and their impact on wider elements of privacy deserve attention in their own right.

3.4. Data Portability and the Robotised Self

The application of data protection and privacy regulation to healthcare robots needs to remain cognisant of the dual nature of robots with their constitution as cyber-physical entities: they are at the same time part of the virtual and the tangible world. This greatly affects the translation of general principles of regulations, including data protection, to these entities. The right to data portability in relation to healthcare robots is a case in point, as ensuring appropriate robot functioning might not only depend on which data is collected and processed but also, and largely, depend on its specific embodiment. The possibility to transfer data from one controller to another is unlikely to be as simple as 'copy-paste'

---

[86] See Kaye, Jane et al, n 65 at 141.
[87] See Civil Law Rules on Robotics n 6 at 20.

because different specific embodiments of the robots in question might prevent users from adequately using such data, even if they are in possession and control of their data.

Embodiment is a particularly clear problem in relation to physical assistant robots such as exoskeletons. These have been used for lower limb rehabilitation, for gait rehabilitation of stroke patients, to help the mobility of persons with disability or older persons, or to support users with functional disorders in their legs.[88,89,90] In essence, these robotic devices help users to walk, which does not just affect mobility but also has impact on other essential physiological parameters.[91] Such robots are envisaged as providing mobility support for persons that might allow them alternative forms of mobility outside of wheelchair use and also make them less dependent on human caregivers.[92]

From a data protection point of view, wearable exoskeletons are not just entities that provide physical support, but like other wearable computing devices they are 'body-borne computational and sensory devices that can collect a wide range of information from the user's body and from the user's environment.'[93] Exoskeletons are normally bulky, rigid and worn over clothing, although the latest research in soft materials and innovative textiles works towards making them more comfortable and unobtrusive.[94] They are meant to work in a 'seamless integration with the user's residual musculoskeletal system and sensory-motor control loops,'[95] in a way that robot design and human needs are intertwined. To do so, a highly complex set of data relevant for this performance needs to be used. This can be highly variable and depend on internal factors, such as age, mental state of the person, physical

[88] Zhang, Qian, Min Chen, and Limei Xu. 'Kinematics and Dynamics Modeling for Lower Limbs Rehabilitation Robot.' In *International Conference on Social Robotics* (Berlin: Springer, 2012) 641–649.

[89] Yamawaki, Kanako, Ryohei Ariyasu, Shigeki Kubota, Hiroaki Kawamoto, Yoshio Nakata, Kiyotaka Kamibayashi, Yoshiyuki Sankai, Kiyoshi Eguchi, and Naoyuki Ochiai. 'Application of Robot Suit HAL to Gait Rehabilitation of Stroke Patients: A Case Study.' In International Conference on Computers for Handicapped Persons (Springer, Berlin) 2012, 184–187.

[90] Nozawa, Masako, and Yoshiyuki Sankai. 'Control Method of Walking Speed and Step Length for Hybrid Assistive Leg.' *International Conference on Computers for Handicapped Persons* (Springer, Berlin, 2002), 220–227.

[91] 'Assistive ExoSkeleton ExoLite', Exomed, last accessed 2 March 2018. Available at: www.exomed.org/main.

[92] Rupal, B.S., A. Singla, and G.S. Virk. 'Lower Limb Exoskeletons: A Brief Review.' In Conference on Mechanical Engineering and Technology (COMET-2016), (IIT (BHU), Varanasi, India, 2016) 130–140.

[93] 'Wearable Computing', *The Encyclopedia of Human-Computer Interaction*, last accessed 2 March 2018. Available at: www.interaction-design.org/literature/book/the-encyclopedia-of-human-computer-interaction-2nd-ed.

[94] 'Soft Exosuits', Harvard BioDesign Lab, last accessed 2 March 2018. Available at: https://biodesign.seas.harvard.edu/soft-exosuits.

[95] Tucker, Michael R., Jeremy Olivier, Anna Pagel, Hannes Bleuler, Mohamed Bouri, Olivier Lambercy, José del R Millán, Robert Riener, Heike Vallery, and Roger Gassert. 'Control Strategies for Active Lower Extremity Prosthetics and Orthotics: A Review.' *Journal of Neuroengineering and Rehabilitation* 12, no 1 (2015): 1.

strength, any pathology that may be affecting the person's gait indirectly or factors that are external to the person like the quality of the surface or the lightning.[96] Similar to pre-existing maps used for autonomous cars, pre-existing gait patterns serve as reference trajectories for exoskeletons; such patterns are then combined with individual gait patterns and personalised data from the individual user in order to ensure a safe real-time performance tailored to individual needs.

The symbiotic nature of the interaction between the lower-limb exoskeleton and the individual user increases dramatically the dependence of the user on the robotic device, especially if the device facilitates the realisation of a highly valued function for the user. Such dependence could create anxiety when the device does not work, frustration when the creator decides to stop producing it, as happened for instance with the iBot project,[97] or when the user buys a new device and needs to engage in intense training once again to adapt the device to their individual movement patterns. The right to data portability enshrined in Article 20 of the GDPR might serve as an effective remedy to this problem as it could ensure that the data from a previous robot is not lost and could be implemented in a new robot. However, this requirement might imply significant changes to technical approaches to the design and development of such devices.

The right to data portability entitles data subjects to receive the personal data that they have provided to the controller in a 'structured, commonly used and machine-readable format.' The Article gives the right to users to 'transmit those data to another controller without hindrance from the controller to which the personal data have been provided.' In the case of exoskeletons, for instance, the physical embodiment of the robot might play an important role because the portability of such data will be limited by the physical characteristics and limitations of the particular devices in question. Gait pattern and other data to help configure the personal profile of the user might have to be translated to another device. The new exoskeleton might not include certain features of the previous robot or might be substantially physically different. As exoskeletons exert direct forces on the user, highly sensitive adaptation to the user's individual characteristics is required (eg for elderly or disabled users whose impairment might change over time). This means that while data portability might at first sight seem primarily a right centered on data protection, it is also highly safety relevant, insofar as the safety of the user could be compromised if this portability is not implemented properly.

This extends to the security of processing mentioned in Article 32 of the GDPR. This pushes for the implementation of resilient measures to secure the processing of data. This provision should be read together with the concept of reversibility

---

[96] Rupal, Baltej Singh, Sajid Rafique, Ashish Singla, Ekta Singla, Magnus Isaksson, and Gurvinder Singh Virk. 'Lower-limb Exoskeletons: Research Trends and Regulatory Guidelines in Medical and Non-medical Applications.' *International Journal of Advanced Robotic Systems* 14, no 6 (2017).

[97] 'iBot', Wikipedia, last accessed March 2, 2018. Available at: https://en.wikipedia.org/wiki/IBOT#Production_Ends.

mentioned in the EP Resolution 2015/2103 (INL), which states that 'a reversibility model tells the robot which actions are reversible and how to reverse them if they are. The ability to undo the last action or a sequence of actions allows users to undo undesired actions and get back to the 'good' stage of their work.'[98] Although such measures may be implemented, the inextricable connection between the data processing and the care-receiver's safety may suggest a need to revisit these provisions in the light of, for instance, a fall, as there may be no straightforward resilient/reversible measures when the care-receiver may have suffered injury.

The cyber-physical nature of robot technology will force data controllers to take into account the specificities of the embodiment of the robot when developing interoperable formats that enable data portability (GDPR, recital 68). In the development of future standardised evaluation criteria and clear effectiveness and safety evaluations, which are currently still missing,[99] the data portability requirement should be considered alongside other factors. This also suggests that, in the future, although a single-impact assessment may apply (eg the data protection impact assessment enshrined in GDPR, Article 35) it might not fully mitigate the specific data-related risks robots may cause. A multi-factored impact assessment that identifies a range of different impacts of this technology, and considers carefully the links and dependencies between different factors, such as data protection compromising safety, could thereby help produce safer technology.[100]

3.5. Privacy and Robot Data Collection in the Workplace

As indicated in Section 3.2, the interplay of healthcare robot stakeholders is very complex: it includes private or public institutions, manufacturers, robot users, cloud services, third parties and many workers, including doctors, nurses, therapists and other members such as technicians and administrative personnel. Workers may be exposed to these technologies without having been consulted and hold an attitude of suspicion towards them;[101] the privacy and data-protection rights of workers who are required to interact with robot technology during their professional duties may be compromised. Indeed, the use of robot technology opens the door to new and highly problematic privacy impacts such as new forms of surveillance or the eventual data-driven displacement of workers. Common examples of robotisation in the healthcare work sector are exoskeletons to support staff that perform taxing physical tasks, such as lifting, or social robots working alongside

---

[98] European Parliament Resolution n 6.

[99] See Tucker et al, n 99.

[100] Fosch-Villaronga, E. 'Creation of a Care Robot Impact Assessment'. *WASET, International Science Journal of Social, Behavioral, Educational, Economic and Management Engineering*, 9, no 6 (2015): 1817–1821.

[101] Kristoffersson, Annica, Silvia Coradeschi, Amy Loutfi, and Kerstin Severinson-Eklundh. 'An Exploratory Study of Health Professionals' Attitudes about Robotic Telepresence Technology.' *Journal of Technology in Human Services* 29, no 4 (2011): 263–283.

humans and patients, both increasingly supported by artificial intelligence (AI) and deep learning technologies. While exoskeletons are meant to improve the working conditions of staff, social robots may be introduced as tools to be used by practitioners or therapists.

Due to the intrinsically symbiotic nature of exoskeletons, their use introduces safety and health concerns. For instance, exoskeletons can pose hazards to workers when transferring the load from one part of the body to another. As robots may shift the worker's center of gravity, their balance may be compromised. However, they also raise privacy concerns insofar as the devices can collect large amounts of data regarding the performance of the worker, necessary to facilitate and optimise the performance of the device. However, this also entails comprehensive monitoring of the workers' activities: lifting, pushing, pulling, turning, throwing or catching. Activities that were not datafied before can now be quantified for efficiency purposes, either for developing guidance on correct posture and usage, for identifying misuse of the device, or for identification of particularly highly performing workers (eg those that adapt more quickly to the device and perform better with it). Moreover, because these robotic devices are personalised by nature, the data collected from the worker may provide a comprehensive profile of worker characteristics, including health and personal information. This means that this technology is likely to further push the boundaries of the 'transparent employee',[102] offering the possibility to monitor employee behavioural and personal data and eventually perhaps even to link it to financial incentives or penalties via the same company or through insurance companies.[103] For instance, discrimination for weight reasons is likely to arise, due to frequently fixed maximum weight requirements for such robotic devices.[104]

Robots are also increasingly combined with AI capabilities. Deep learning and AI can be used to assist health professionals by providing automated classification, detection, and image segmentation in ways humans could never do.[105] Researchers assume that, especially with regard to certain domains, such as radiology, this can help professionals to perform more efficient screening procedures, diagnosis of conditions and their development over time.[106] Although decision support systems that combine aggregated patient information have existed for a while,

[102] 'Artificial Intelligence and Robotics and Their Impact on the Workplace' IBA Global Employment Institute, last modified April, 2017. Available at: www.ibanet.org/Document/Default. aspx?DocumentUid=c06aa1a3-d355-4866-beda-9a3a8779ba6e.

[103] Evelyn Theiss, 'Get Healthy or Pay Higher Insurance Rates, Cleveland Clinic Employees are Told' Cleveland, 12 February 2012. Available at: www.cleveland.com/healthfit/index.ssf/2012/02/join_or_ pay_more_cleveland_cli.html.

[104] See Fosch Villaronga n 16.

[105] Chartrand, Gabriel, Phillip M. Cheng, Eugene Vorontsov, Michal Drozdzal, Simon Turcotte, Christopher J. Pal, Samuel Kadoury, and An Tang. 'Deep Learning: A Primer for Radiologists.' RadioGraphics 37, no 7 (2017): 2113–2131.

[106] Lee, June-Goo, Sanghoon Jun, Young-Won Cho, Hyunna Lee, Guk Bae Kim, Joon Beom Seo, and Namkug Kim. 'Deep Learning in Medical Imaging: General Overview.' Korean Journal of Radiology 18, no 4 (2017): 570–584.

progress in this domain conveys the impression that for certain tasks humans will soon be outperformed by machines. The danger is that even in the domain of healthcare which long seemed to be immune to automatisation, there is the increasing risk that professional tasks may become susceptible to computerisation or automation. Big data techniques could substitute non-routine cognitive tasks, and progress in robot dexterity could allow robots to increasingly perform manual tasks and hence lead to a deep transformation of healthcare workplaces.[107,108,109] A large quantitative study on industrial robots and human replacement shows that there is a tendency towards worker replacement in industrial environments due to the productivity effect of robots; such developments are likely to apply to healthcare workplaces as well.[110]

When it comes to the healthcare sector, however, so far there has been no comprehensive data collected on the effect of robot use on care worker replacement, most likely due to the early stages of robot use in healthcare settings. In 2015 the BBC released a software tool based on research by Carl Frey and Michael Osborne[111] that shows the likelihood of automation of several types of work.[112] Although this software was only based on one study, it gives some interesting indication regarding the likelihood of automation of several healthcare-related jobs. While medical practitioners and physiotherapists are said to run only a 2 or 2.1 percent automation risk, other professions like dental nurses, nursery nurses or assistants, nursing auxiliary assistants, care workers and home caregivers are identified as having a much higher probability of replacement (60%, 55.7%, 46.8% and 39.9% respectively). Medical radiographers and dental technicians are thought to be at 27.5 percent risk of being automated, ophthalmic opticians 13.7 percent, whereas paramedics or speech and language therapists are given lower risk ratings at 4.9 percent (or 0.5%) respectively. Other related professions also face a high risk of being automated, for instance, software healthcare practice managers and medical secretaries risk 85.1 percent, and hospital porters 57.3 percent. However, at this point, it is difficult to predict clearly what occupations and specific tasks are most likely to disappear or be replaced by machines, and how this will translate into jobs that will be lost. Hence, Frey and Osborne suggest that any such figures should be viewed with caution.

---

[107] Arntz, Melanie, Terry Gregory, and Ulrich Zierahn. 'The risk of automation for jobs in OECD countries: A comparative analysis.' *OECD Social, Employment, and Migration Working Papers* 189 (2016): 0_1.

[108] Frey, Carl Benedikt, and Michael A. Osborne. 'The Future of Employment: How Susceptible are Jobs to Computerisation?' *Technological Forecasting and Social Change* 114 (2017): 254–280.

[109] Manyika, James, Susan Lund, Michael Chui, Jacques Bughin, Jonathan Woetzel, Parul Batra, Ryan Ko, and Saurabh Sanghvi. 'Jobs Lost, Jobs Gained: Workforce Transitions in A Time of Automation.' *McKinsey Global Institute, December* (2017).

[110] Acemoglu, Daron, and Pascual Restrepo. 'Robots and Jobs: Evidence from US Labor Markets.' *SSRN* (2017).

[111] See Frey and Osborne n 111.

[112] 'Will a Robot Take Your Job?' BBC, last accessed 2 March 2018. Available at: www.bbc.co.uk/news/technology-34066941.

This raises nevertheless the question how far a 'human in the loop' will remain desirable. Although the data-protection laws refer to the 'right not to be subject to a decision based solely on automated processing [...] which produces legal effects concerning him or her' and the 'right to obtain human intervention on the part of the controller' (GDPR, Article. 22), it is uncertain whether this will (and should) be enforced. Depending on technical advances it is possible that referring to a human could endanger the rights of users, for example if humans turn out to be less safe or efficient at performing a task than the machine, or if the human referral process leads to unjustifiable delays. However, such automatisation may lead to the delegation of sensitive tasks and promote the 'de-responsibilisation' of humans vis-à-vis machines.[113]

A larger question that draws on privacy considerations but has significance for wider workers' rights and employer responsibilities relates to what responsibility a hospital or care facility has with regard to the eventual displacement of workers if the employer introduces technologies in the workplace that ultimately contribute to the automatisation of some of the employees' tasks, while potentially relying on workers' data in the process. Although this problem might have to be addressed under national legislation (GDPR, Article 88), this seems to suggest that workplaces will need to adjust and accommodate different adaptations to face the challenges of transformation due to robotic and AI innovations. This could be done in two ways:

Firstly, employers need to support their workforce by re-shaping training and introducing specific education initiatives with technological competences.[114] This entails the redefinition of the job description, roles and responsibilities, as well as a need to clarify tasks in the daily routine, work methods, and the re-identification of risks faced by workers, either young or more senior. Additionally, and before implementing any robotic or automated system, the employer will need to perform a task analysis in order to re-assess skills by occupation, identify skill trends and look at the deskilling effects.

Secondly, employers need to adapt the workplace environment, the processes and communication to accommodate human-robot interaction in a collaborative manner. Knowing that healthcare workers are in constant dialogue and communication with other healthcare professionals and patients, the technology must be introduced in a way that allows workers to positively influence the changes, determine how it will be used by them. In this new way of workplace collaboration, researchers recommend including a proactive approach by integrating

---

[113] Yang, Guang-Zhong, Jim Bellingham, Pierre E. Dupont, Peer Fischer, Luciano Floridi, Robert Full, Neil Jacobstein et al, 'The grand challenges of Science Robotics.' *Science Robotics* 3, no 14 (2018): eaar7650.

[114] Arnzt,M., T. Gregory and U. Zierhan 'The Risk of Automation for Jobs in OECD Countries: A Comparative Analysis', OECD Social, Employment and Migration Working Papers, No 189. (Paris: OECD, 2016).

(1) qualitative risk assessment; (2) adapting workplace strategies and refine requirements; (3) adopting an appropriate level of precaution; (4) ensuring global applicability; (5) promoting the ability to elicit voluntary cooperation by companies; and (6) ensuring stakeholder involvement.[115]

The insertion of robot technologies in the healthcare workplace may impact the rights of the workers. Working with robots and automated systems requires the provision of workers' consent to processes and operations that use personal data following the data protection principles. Although the GDPR is not specific about this, such cases should be legitimate and employers should explicitly and appropriately inform workers (principle of transparency) on how their private information or knowledge will be used during and for their employment relation (finality). Workers would need to previously agree to working under conditions in which the employer might invade their privacy by addressing the new individual rights under the GDPR. These issues could be dealt with in a collective agreement. If workers could be replaced by robots or AI technologies that have been fed with their data or based on their knowledge and *savoir-faire*, it appears justified to demand responsibilities to the employers. The privacy of the workers plays a meaningful role in the deployment of the AI and robotics system. As workers whose data and knowledge are informing the systems that are likely to replace them may not be in the same location or work for the same employer, a wider approach should be taken to reciprocity obligations and protections. In this respect, we claim that an international effort to tackle this problem should be promoted.[116]

3.6. Designing Privacy for Healthcare Robotics: Beyond Simple Privacy by Design

The wide range of privacy concerns discussed in the previous sections raise particular challenges for the design process. While those in charge of the technical side of robot development tend to be familiar with the general idea of 'privacy by design',[117] they often lack understanding of what types of concerns exactly the protection of privacy should entail. In particular, there tends to be little understanding among technical staff of the requirements of the GDPR beyond ensuring data security. However, understanding the values that are at stake is necessary for the prospective design and implementation of robots which realise those values in healthcare contexts.

---

[115] Murashov, Vladimir, Frank Hearl, and John Howard. 'Working Safely with Robot Workers: Recommendations for the new Workplace.' *Journal of Occupational and Environmental Hygiene* 13, no 3 (2016): D61–D71.

[116] Decker, Michael, Martin Fischer, and Ingrid Ott. 'Service Robotics and Human Labor: A First Technology Assessment of Substitution and Cooperation.' *Robotics and Autonomous Systems* 87 (2017): 348–354.

[117] Cavoukian, Ann. 'Privacy by Design [Leading Edge].' *IEEE Technology and Society Magazine* 31, no 4 (2012): 18–19.

The design of privacy-preserving healthcare robots requires an integrated approach that ensures that the many facets of privacy are understood by developers and translated adequately into technical specifications. This includes clarifying the requirements of the GDPR for healthcare robotics, as well as doing justice to wider privacy concerns that go beyond data protection. According to Friedman et al.'s 'value sensitive design'[118] approach, an integrated approach to design should include the combination of conceptual analysis of privacy concerns (also their relation to other relevant values), stakeholder perspectives on privacy in this particular field of application, and reflections on the technical realisability of such considerations.

Value-sensitive design is a methodology that tries to unearth the values at stake through a comprehensive process that starts with an analysis of who the stakeholders are and what their needs, values and concerns are with regard to a specific problem. Developing a comprehensive conceptual understanding and communicating about these needs and values with designers and helping them to understand what those values mean in practice is meant to help them translate those values into specific design requirements, although some authors contest these assumptions.[119] To illustrate such an analysis, van Wynsberghe uses the idea of a lifting robot to show that two different designs manifest a different sets of values. The first robot she discusses is a robot which has a torso, two arms, and a face. This robot can lift the patient much like a human would. The problem, according to Van Wynsberghe is that when a nurse or other hospital staff lifted the patient it helped to manifest the care values (eg of interpersonal attentiveness and reciprocity). Without a human being there, these values could not be realised. However, a different design in which the nurse wears a robotic exoskeleton solves the problem of a nurse being able to lift a patient (maximising the care value of competence) whilst also not diminishing the values of attentiveness and reciprocity[120,121,122]

With regard to the values of data protection and privacy, it is essential for designers to understand that there is not just one, but many different design possibilities due to significant case-by-case differences in technologies and application contexts. Robots are often made for use in a variety of contexts, and they come with

[118] Friedman, Batya, Peter H. Kahn, Alan Borning, and Alina Huldtgren. 'Value Sensitive Design and Information Systems.' In *Early Engagement and New Technologies: Opening Up the Laboratory*, (Dordrecht: Springer, 2013), 55–95.

[119] Koops, Bert-Jaap, and Ronald Leenes. 'Privacy Regulation cannot be Hardcoded. A Critical Comment on the 'Privacy by Design' provision in Data Protection Law' *International Review of Law, Computers & Technology* 28, no 2 (2014): 159–171.

[120] Van Wynsberghe, Aimee. Designing Robots for Care: Care-centered Value-sensitive Design.' *Science and Engineering Ethics* 19, no 2 (2013): 407–433.

[121] van Wynsberghe, Aimee. 'A Method for Integrating Ethics into the Design of Robots.' *Industrial Robot: An International Journal* 40, no 5 (2013): 433–440.

[122] Van Wynsberghe, Aimee. *Healthcare Robots: Ethics, Design and Implementation* (Abingdon: Routledge, 2016).

a variety of sensors and capabilities. In some setting, a subset of capabilities may need to be disabled to ensure realisation of important values in this context. For example, many contemporary robots are equipped with cameras and microphones for navigation and interaction, which, however, in certain healthcare contexts may invade a patient's privacy. For instance, a robot with the task of cleaning bedpans should not have a microphone which listens in on patients nor have cameras that record its environment.[123] Thinking about the tasks that the robot will or can realise during the design process may inform the value modelling and may lead to the conclusion that there are tasks that should be considered 'off-limits'. This might include tasks that interfere with important values such as privacy, or include tasks that may involve complex capabilities such as moral responsibility which robots do not currently have (but may have at some point in the future).[124]

There is an urgent need to put both technical and organisational measures in place to ensure appropriate considerations of privacy values in the design process. However, even if such measures are in place, substantive difficulties with designing and implementing for values would remain, especially with regard to foreseeing unintended consequences or possible problems in the future. Understanding whether the values of security, privacy, transparency, etc. will be diminished or enhanced in a particular context with the use of a particular robotic platform is highly complex, and such predictions are uncertain. Such assessment requires the combination and integration of a range of specialised expertise which no single profession can claim to have by themselves. It requires input from technical people who know what a robot's capabilities are, from ethicists who understand what it means to realise ethical values, and from lawyers who know which legal requirements need to be followed.[125,126] Therefore the use of multidisciplinary test beds or living labs should be regarded as a *conditio sine qua non* for the realisation of truly safe and ethical robots.[127]

4. Conclusion

Although bringing a wide range of benefits and possibilities, the growing presence of robots in our daily lives raises ethical, legal and societal concerns to experts, industry, workers and the general public. This paper focused in particular on six

---

[123] Will Knight, 'The Roomba Now Sees and Maps a Home' *MIT Technology Review*, September 16, 2015, www.technologyreview.com/s/541326/the-roomba-now-sees-and-maps-a-home/.

[124] Bryson, Joanna J., Mihailis E. Diamantis, and Thomas D. Grant. 'Of, For, and By the People: The Legal Lacuna of Synthetic persons.' *Artificial Intelligence and Law* 25, no 3 (2017): 273–291.

[125] van Gorp, Anke, and S. van der Molen. 'Parallel, Embedded or Just Part of the Team: Ethicists Cooperating within a European Security Research Project.' *Science and Engineering Ethics* 17, no 1 (2011): 31–43.

[126] Van Wynsberghe, Aimee and Scott Robbins. 'Ethicist as Designer: A Pragmatic Approach to Ethics in the Lab.' *Science and Engineering Ethics* 20, no 4 (2014): 947–961.

[127] Fosch Villaronga, n 16.

challenging areas of concern where the use of robots raises data protection and privacy issues. We argue that the insertion of robots in the healthcare sector raises particular challenging questions because, in healthcare, technological innovation, such as robots, both supports and challenges the realisation of the duty of care for vulnerable members of society. Because this element of 'care' materialises via complex relations between healthcare institutions, doctors, medical and non-medical personnel, patients and relatives, and designers this paper has identified and reflected upon some of the less explored consequences for privacy and data protection arising within this network of stakeholders.

In the chapter, we acknowledge that SARs operate both as data-processing devices, governed by data governance schemes, and as a healthcare aid, governed by professional norms. This means they will have to be compliant with both the GDPR, medical law and the medical ethics tradition. We also argue that the traditional elements of trust characterising the doctor–patient relationship are likely to undergo a shift with the insertion of robots into the care setting, as patients are often more prone to disclose information to robots, while robots are often not correctly identified as information processing devices. From the perspective of confidentiality, we highlight that it is important to carefully craft the purpose of the robot, and be transparent about its capabilities and functioning to avoid undesirable privacy impacts. Risks might also derive from the unwitting disclosure of information through overheard conversations with robots; and also from unconsented secondary uses of patient or worker data collected by the robot. In this respect, awareness mechanisms should be put in place to reduce privacy violations of those interacting socially with the robot.

Among the critical points emerging from this analysis, we give reasons to consider privacy-related aspects when designing robots that will interact with many types of user. Ensuring compliance with the GDPR, whose provisions are vague and technology-neutral, can pose a challenge for the realisation and implementation of robots that will have substantial variation of purposes, uses and embodiments. In particular, we highlight that structural differences among models and embodiments might impede full portability of the data collected. In this respect, we assert that the dual nature of robots – cyber and physical – needs to be integrated as a fundamental part of any future regulatory instrument governing robot technology, which requires going substantially beyond general data protection requirements in the regulation of robots.

In addition, we raise the question of the privacy and data protection implications of robots with conversational capabilities. We argue that conversational HRI might have unexpected consequences due to the way in which the robotic technology mediates the perception and construction of reality for patients and workers. While greater transparency and clarity can be achieved through conversational interfaces applied to privacy and data protection settings, this may affect the construction of the notion of privacy. This could, in turn, affect the correct implementation of the GDPR. We also identify additional issues with regard to workers in the healthcare sector, who may be required to cooperate and interact with robots, which may affect their privacy in various ways. Appropriate training, adjustments in the work environment, as well as appropriate guidelines in the application of the GDPR for healthcare workers appear necessary for the future.

Based on the issues identified, a comprehensive multi-impact assessment is desirable to identify not only a range of different impacts of this technology, but also the links and dependencies between different factors and stakeholders to implement the GDPR and other regulations in a way that captures these complexities. Accordingly, we suggest that the endorsement of a wider value sensitive approach to design for privacy that does justice to a wider range of privacy values is preferable to a design approach that is focused primarily on data protection concerns. To achieve such an approach, multi-disciplinary collaboration of technologists, ethicists and lawyers, among others, and the willingness to give a voice to all relevant stakeholders, especially those who will be most directly affected by the use of robots in healthcare is needed.

5

Navigating Law and Software Engineering Towards Privacy by Design

Stepping Stones for Bridging the Gap

IVO EMANUILOV,[1] KIM WUYTS,[2] DIMITRI VAN LANDUYT,[3]
NATALIE BERTELS,[4] FANNY COUDERT,[5]
PEGGY VALCKE,[6] AND WOUTER JOOSEN[7]

Abstract

Modern society is governed not only by legal rules but, to a large extent, also by computer code. From biometric access control systems, through connected smartwatches, to autonomous aircraft systems, the very fabric of social life is largely dependent on software. The continuous changes and the need for frequent adaptation disrupts social control regulatory mechanisms such as the law. The resulting gap between the open-ended and vague legal rules and the strict imperatives of computer code creates significant challenges to the fundamental rights and freedoms of individuals. An infamous example of the difficulties experienced by the law is the concept of privacy by design and its practical implementation which, despite the decades-old regulatory push, still remains largely a theoretical concept with little impact on how software is actually designed. The chapter proposes four stepping stones that will help bridge the gap between the legal implications of regulatory privacy frameworks such as the General Data Protection Regulation (GDPR) and the practice of privacy-driven software engineering. These stepping stones build upon each other starting from the establishment of a common conceptual framework of privacy and data protection terminology, to

[1] KU Leuven Centre for IT & IP Law – imec.
[2] imec-DistriNet, KU Leuven, 3001 Leuven, Belgium.
[3] imec-DistriNet, KU Leuven, 3001 Leuven, Belgium.
[4] KU Leuven Centre for IT & IP Law – imec.
[5] KU Leuven Centre for IT & IP Law – imec, EDPS.
[6] KU Leuven Centre for IT & IP Law – imec.
[7] imec-DistriNet, KU Leuven, 3001 Leuven, Belgium.

defining legal support for a data protection impact assessment, through providing decision and trade-off support for technical and organisational mitigation strategies in the software development lifecycle, to assuring legal accountability with traceability throughout software development.

Keywords:

Data protection, Privacy, Privacy by design, Requirements engineering, Software engineering, Software development lifecycle

1. Introduction

Today's society is governed by a wealth of legal and computer code. The growing complexity of the legal system is accompanied by equally growing complexity of software systems. Autonomous intelligent systems such as self-driving cars, drones, wearables and other connected devices are now capable of complex analysis of the environment, automated decision-making, self-governed behaviour and autonomous adaptation to changes. Against this backdrop, social control regulatory mechanisms, such as the law, are often pointed at as being incapable of dealing with the changes, unknowns and uncertainties brought about by technological advances. An infamous example of the difficulties experienced by the law is the concept of 'privacy by design' and its practical implementation. Despite the regulatory push over a couple of decades, the vagueness of 'privacy by design' has rendered it largely a theoretical concept with little impact on privacy engineering. The problem of how it could be practically implemented reveals the more fundamental issue of how the practice of law is to be linked with the practice of software engineering and how the gap between these two seemingly unrelated disciplines could be bridged.

2. Legal Code and Computer Code

Law exists as a formal system of rules (code) aimed at creating temporal connections and temporal relations making the uncertain and unpredictable future certain and predictable.[8] Its role is thus to ensure certainty and predictability as essential conditions to all its traditional functions (ie regulatory, symbolic, dispute resolution, and protective legality).[9]

---

[8] HLA Hart et al, eds, *The Concept of Law*, 3rd edn, Clarendon Law Series (Oxford, New York: Oxford University Press, 2012); Niklas Luhmann, *Rechtssystem und Rechtsdogmatik*. (Stuttgart: W. Kohlhammer, 1974).

[9] Erik Claes, Wouter Devroe and Bert Keirsbilck, 'The Limits of the Law', in *Facing the Limits of the Law* (Berlin: Springer, 2009), 4–11. Available at: https://doi.org/10.1007/978-3-540-79856-9_1.

Much like the 'legal code' that governs a society, computer code creates 'laws' that govern the behaviour of a computer system.[10] Both software engineers and lawyers follow certain conventions in terms of the form in which their 'code' is expressed. Researchers have already recognised that the growing complexity of technology and the diverging approaches of lawmakers to the structure and composition of laws turns legal code into a body of rules that can hardly be comprehended by a single person.[11] More importantly, unlike computer code, legal code is by definition imprecise so as to cover as wide a spectrum of cases as possible.[12] This makes the task of a software engineer entrusted with the implementation of legal requirements in a specific solution close to impossible. Although legal code and computer code share some common features, reducing the legal system to a pure collection of imperative executable instructions expressed in a natural language is simplistic at best.[13]

While software engineers are not expected to provide interpretation of the laws they are asked to implement, the way in which they construe the law plays a major role in a system's compliance.[14] Software engineers are not equipped with the tools necessary to elaborate a legal requirement sufficiently precise to be technically implemented. In order to understand a legal rule and to implement it effectively, engineers need to be aware of at least three categories of factors inherent to most jurisdictions, as described by Sacco:[15] (1) 'legal formants' (ie the elements that constitute the 'living law' of a state, including the legislation but also the links between the provisions, case law, legal doctrine and regulatory acts);[16] (2) 'cryptotypes' (ie the principles, (ethical) values and assumptions underpinning the legal norms);[17] and (3) 'synecdoche' (ie the fact that not all rules are fully articulated and that unexpressed general rules may be referred to by special rules).[18]

The challenge of considering these often dispersed, vague, value-based and open-ended factors in a system's design is further exacerbated by lawyers having little or no knowledge of requirements engineering and no understanding of the process of engineering the architecture, design and operation of software-intensive

---

[10] William Li et al, 'Law Is Code: A Software Engineering Approach to Analyzing the United States Code', *Journal of Business & Technology Law* 10, no 2 (2015): 298.

[11] Ibid at 297.

[12] Ibid at 306.

[13] G. Boella et al, 'A Critical Analysis of Legal Requirements Engineering from the Perspective of Legal Practice', in *2014 IEEE 7th International Workshop on Requirements Engineering and Law (RELAW)*, 2014, 15. Available at: https://doi.org/10.1109/RELAW.2014.6893476.

[14] D.G. Gordon and T.D. Breaux, 'The Role of Legal Expertise in Interpretation of Legal Requirements and Definitions' in *2014 IEEE 22nd International Requirements Engineering Conference (RE)*, 2014, 273. Available at: https://doi.org/10.1109/RE.2014.6912269.

[15] Rodolfo Sacco, 'Legal Formants: A Dynamic Approach to Comparative Law', *The American Journal of Comparative Law* 39, no 1 (1991): 343.

[16] Ibid at 344.

[17] Ibid at 384.

[18] Ibid at 386.

systems. As a result of this knowledge gap, software engineers tend to either over-simplify the complexity of law or ignore the legal aspects altogether. The effect is that legal considerations are in practice often either retrofitted into a system at a stage where the design and large part of the development process has finished, or completely left out as a matter to be governed by the internal policies of the system's end user.

3. Engineering Legal Requirements: The Case of Privacy by Design

The struggle of engineering legal requirements in software code is all the more evident in the domain of privacy and data protection. The rights to data protection and privacy have long been recognised as fundamental rights applicable to both the online and the offline world. Rapid developments in the field of information and communication technologies, however, have challenged the effective and efficient enforcement of these rights.[19] For decades, regulators and developers have been seeking ways to embed the values of data protection and privacy into the design process. Although a number of privacy-enhancing technologies (PETs), principles, guidelines, best practices and methods have emerged during the years, they account for only part of the solution.

The concept of privacy by design extends beyond the realm of technical solutions to cover also organisational practices and business models in a holistic way. Privacy-enhancing technologies are not in themselves sufficient. Software engineers need to know when these solutions should be used and how to pinpoint the most suitable solution to a particular problem. This process needs to begin at the design stage since retrofitting of any such technology in existing systems is unlikely to yield satisfactory results.[20] Against the background of decades-old calls for incorporating decisions about privacy early in the software development lifecycle,[21] the alignment of legal and computer code is still a challenge which, despite some recent legislative initiatives in the EU, remains largely unsolved.

Only recently has the concept of privacy by design made its way in an official legal instrument of the EU: the General Data Protection Regulation (GDPR). The principles of data protection by design and by default introduce into the legal framework the concept of privacy by design, a principle which has found growing

---

[19] ENISA, 'Privacy and Data Protection by Design – from Policy to Engineering', Report, 15 January 2015, 1, Available at: https://publications.europa.eu/en/publication-detail/-/publication/6548a14b-9863-410d-a8a6-c15a0137d281.

[20] Ibid at 2.

[21] Ann Cavoukian et al, 'Privacy by Design: The 7 Foundational Principles. Implementation and Mapping of Fair Information Practices', *Information and Privacy Commissioner of Ontario, Canada*, 2009.

recognition amongst the privacy engineering community and amongst national, European and international policy bodies since 1995.[22,23,24,25]

The objectives of EU policy makers in this regard are twofold. First, they seek to increase the implementation of the provisions of the GDPR in practice. A basic assumption of the data protection by design concept is that regulation is only one aspect of privacy and data protection. Second, building privacy into the design and the architecture of processing systems should ease compliance. It is expected that these provisions will strengthen the accountability of data controllers and processors.[26] These are required to demonstrate compliance by adopting internal policies and technical and organizational measures (eg, minimisation of the amount of personal data processed or implementation of security features).

Article 25(1) of the GDPR introduces the concept of 'data protection by design' in EU data protection law. The text provides that controllers are obliged to implement appropriate technical and organisational measures which are *designed* to implement data-protection principles in an effective manner and to integrate the necessary safeguards into the processing. Article 25(2) clarifies the meaning of 'data protection by default' by specifying that the implemented measures must ensure that, by default, only personal data which are necessary for each specific purpose of the processing are processed.

The differences between 'by default' and 'by design' have been interpreted by Lee Bygrave in the context of the references to the data protection principles in both provisions.[27] Thus, while 'data protection by design' refers to the 'data-protection principles' in general,[28] 'data protection by default' addresses the principles of data minimisation and purpose limitation only.

---

[22] Henk Van Rossum et al, *Privacy-Enhancing Technologies. Vol. 2*, Achtergrondstudies En Verkenningen (Den Haag: Registratiekamer, 1995).

[23] European Commission, 'Communication from the Commission to the European Parliament and the Council on Promoting Data Protection by Privacy Enhancing Technologies (PETs) (COM/2007/0228 Final)', 2 May 2007. Available at: http://eur-lex.europa.eu/legal-content/en/TXT/?uri=CELEX%3A52007DC0228.

[24] European Commission, 'Communication from the Commission to the European Parliament, the Council, the European Economic and Social Committee and the Committee of the Regions: A digital agenda for Europe (COM/2010/0245 Final)' 17. Available at: http://eur-lex.europa.eu/legal-content/EN/ALL/?uri=CELEX%3A52010DC0245, fn 21.

[25] Thrity-second International Conference of Data Protection and Privacy Commissioners, '32nd International Conference of Data Protection and Privacy Commissioners, Jerusalem, Israel, 27–29 October, 2010, Resolution on Privacy by Design', 27 October 2010. Available at: https://icdppc.org/wp-content/uploads/2015/02/32-Conference-Israel-resolution-on-Privacy-by-Design.pdf.

[26] EDPS, 'Opinion of the European Data Protection Supervisor on Promoting Trust in the Information Society by Fostering Data Protection and Privacy, OJ C 280/01', 2010. Available at: https://edps.europa.eu/sites/edp/files/publication/10-03-19_trust_information_society_en.pdf.

[27] Lee A Bygrave, 'Data Protection by Design and by Default : Deciphering the EU's Legislative Requirements', *Oslo Law Review* 1, no 2 (2017): 106.

[28] Arguably referring to the principles relating to processing of personal data proclaimed in Art. 5, GDPR.

The broad references to the basic principles of data protection point to the finding that the measures of data protection by design and by default are not only of a technical nature. This understanding is also reinforced by the text of recital 78 which clarifies that controllers should adopt internal policies and implement measures which meet the principles of data protection by design and data protection by default. Thus, the systematic interpretation of Article 25 (1) and (2) and recital 75 leads to the conclusion that the notion of 'data protection by design and by default' includes not only technical but also organisational measures.

The GDPR guides data controllers on when and how to implement these measures by providing both contextual and temporal clues. Thus, in determining the appropriate measures, the controller must hold account of: (1) state of the art, (2) cost of implementation, (3) nature, scope, context and purposes of processing and (4) risks of varying likelihood and severity for rights and freedoms of natural persons posed by the processing. These factors should be considered both at the time of the determination of the means for processing and at the time of the processing itself.

Generally, compliance with the principle of data protection by design comprises four steps: (1) risk analysis, (2) translation into technical requirements, (3) implementation into system design and (4) periodic review. Three main issues arise in that regard. First, in relation to the nature of the risks to be tackled, the GDPR is concerned with the risks posed by the processing of personal data performed by the data controller to individuals' rights and freedoms, including but not limited to the right to privacy. This includes risks of theft, discrimination or financial loss (recital 75). Second, in relation to the methodology used to perform the risk assessment, the GDPR only requires the controller to use objective assessment criteria (recital 76). It gives complete freedom to the data controller in the choice of the methodology. Third, in relation to the expected outcome of the risk analysis, this should enable the identification of mitigation measures that could be translated into technical and organisational requirements. These should enable the data controller to demonstrate compliance with all requirements of the GDPR.

Given the high-level approach taken by the legislator, any methodology that aims to support data controllers in the compliance of their obligations of implementing the principles of data protection by design and by default should thus be clear about the options taken about each of the three aspects. They should further enable data protection authorities to assess objectively the steps taken by the data controller to ensure compliance with the GDPR.

In the cases of processing 'likely to result in a high risk to the rights and freedoms of natural persons', the context of the processing operations will often be determined during a data protection impact assessment; this will enable controllers to select appropriate measures. This interpretation is also supported by the Article 29 Working Party's Guidelines on Data Protection Impact Assessment (DPIA) whereby controllers are advised to start a DPIA 'as early as practical in the design of the processing operation even if some of the processing operations are still unknown'.[29]

The GDPR situates the 'design' stage at the time of determination of the means.[30] According to Article 4(7), a controller is the person who 'determines the purposes and means of the processing'. Thus, as Lee Bygrave points out, it could reasonably be concluded that the 'design' stage is equated with time when a controller assumes this status.[31] However, in the software development lifecycle, the design stage follows the early stages of requirements elicitation and specification and consists of 'translating' these requirements into a 'blueprint' for constructing the software.[32] Thus, it follows that the legal and technical meaning of 'design' could differ.

The consequences of the differences in the interpretation between the legal and technical meaning of 'design' are significant. First, except for the cases of tailor-made solutions based on a controller's specifications, it is highly unlikely that a data controller would be involved in the development of an end product. Unlike controllers, according to recital 78, producers of 'products, services and applications' are only '*encouraged* to take into account the right to data protection when developing and designing such products, services and applications' (emphasis added). The GDPR further encourages them to *make sure* that controllers and processors can fulfil their data protection obligations. Besides the fact that none of these *encouragements* are binding on the producers, it is questionable how a producer of a solution could *make sure* that a data controller *is able to fulfil* their obligations, given that the concept of data protection by design and by default encompasses not only technical but also organisational measures. Thus, despite their ambitious scope, the recital's provisions can hardly be seen as anything but wishful thinking.

Furthermore, Article 25 of the GDPR has been rightly criticised for its cryptic legalese[33] which effectively defies the regulation's purpose of encouraging developers to consider the right to data protection. The regulation's complex language, the missing guidance for assessing the *appropriateness* of the implemented measures and the diverging understanding of when the 'design' stage begins are effectively stalling the conversation between the engineering and the legal community.[34] As a result, the gap between legal experts and software engineers is widening at an exponential rate, undermining the regulation's ultimate goal of ensuring a 'consistent and high level of protection' and removing the obstacles to flows of personal data (recital 10).

---

[29] Article 29 Data Protection Working Party, 'Guidelines on Data Protection Impact Assessment (DPIA) and Determining Whether Processing Is "Likely to Result in a High Risk" for the Purposes of Regulation 2016/679', 4 October 2017, 13. Available at: http://ec.europa.eu/newsroom/document.cfm?doc_id=47711.

[30] See Bygrave n 27 at 116.

[31] Ibid.

[32] Roger S Pressman and Bruce R Maxim, *Software Engineering: A Practitioner's Approach* (McGraw-Hill Education, 2014), 338.

[33] Bygrave, n 27 at 117.

[34] Ibid.

While the difficulties experienced by software engineers and legal experts alike have long been recognised, hardly any practical solutions have been offered to contribute to the bridging of this gap. Despite the emergence of various privacy engineering tools, methodologies and techniques aimed at supporting the impact assessment, currently no risk assessment techniques specifically addressing data protection exist. In addition, legal and technical risk assessment methods approach the concept of 'risk' from different angles. For example, threat modelling is a typical approach in software engineering to assess security- and/or privacy-related risks in a software system. Its main goal is to determine what can go wrong in a software system. These threats that are posed to a system always have a 'misactor' as origin. Although the misactor does not always have malicious intent in the identified threat scenarios (ie in addition to threats by actual attackers, also accidental misuse by a trustworthy user can cause threats), threats are always initiated by someone (intentionally or not). IT security and privacy risk assessment thus focus on the protection of the software system against misactors who succeed in compromising the integrity, confidentiality and authenticity of the data under attack.

In contrast, for data protection, the risks stem mainly from the data controller or processor (ie the entity with access to the data) even for legitimate purposes. The goal here is to protect the individual against any misuse of the personal data entrusted to the data controller. The only initiative which intends to bridge this gap is outlined in the recent report on privacy engineering and management systems released by the US National Institute of Standards and Technologies.[35] This report, however, only sets a roadmap to develop privacy risk assessment methodology. Also, it only addresses the US concept of privacy, not providing an answer to the new obligations created under the GDPR.

There is thus *a large gap* between the legal implications of regulatory privacy frameworks such as the GDPR and the practice of privacy-driven software engineering. To realise this overall goal, this chapter identifies and motivates four action points that need to be tackled to bridge this gap, and that therefore deserve more attention on the research agenda of both communities.

4. Stepping-Stones to Bridge the Gap

4.1. Creating a Common Conceptual Framework of Privacy and Data Protection Terminology

One of the main hurdles in bootstrapping the interdisciplinary conversation is that of conceptual and terminological mismatch between the two domains.

---

[35] Gary Stoneburner, Alice Y Goguen, and Alexis Feringa, 'Risk Management Guide for Information Technology Systems', *Special Publication (NIST SP) – 800-30*, 1 July 2002. Available at: https://doi.org/151254.

By way of example, even the term 'privacy' already has different and even competing definitions in both research domains. Software engineers often have an approach to privacy that is limited to the protection of individuals' personal space. Furthermore, they often understand 'data protection' to be limited to security measures aimed at preserving the confidentiality of information. In contrast, legal experts instrumentalise broader notions of 'privacy' and 'data protection' and situate them in the framework of fundamental rights.

In addition, the open-ended language of legal texts, rich in cross-references and domain-specific definitions of concepts, make them an extremely difficult target for software engineers.[36] For example, the GDPR consists of a considerable number of open-ended rules and principles that need to be construed depending on the context of application and in line with the binding interpretation given by courts. Software requirements, however, need solutions equally valid for all situations independent of the context. Systematically defining the key concepts is therefore essential to facilitate cross-disciplinary communication and to translate the vague legal notions into technical requirements.

Software engineers experience difficulties in understanding the ambiguous and vague legal language. The alien terminology and often naive understanding of legal concepts on the part of the engineering community reinforces a vision that aims to take the legal considerations outside the realm of the software engineering and leave them to the end users. The lack of common language between the two communities has long been recognised as a major impediment to encouraging a more open dialogue engaging both sides.

One major obstacle for the setting of such constructive dialogue is that 'frames of meaning' or discourses of each of these stakeholders are different, often specific to their profession or their position in the society. These consist of problem definitions, preferred solutions, appreciative systems (value systems that enable the normative framing of the problematic situation) and overarching theories that help make sense of the situation supplying the stakeholder with languages and repertoires to describe and interpret the situation empirically.[37]

Researchers have argued that the various elements of frames of meaning should be seen as potential objects for discourse among the stakeholders as, in a context of technology assessment, they have one important common element: the meaning each of the actors attributes to the technological artefact under scrutiny.[38] The outcome does not necessarily need to be the establishment of fully shared meanings as this could be too ambitious and often extremely difficult to reach, if not impossible, but rather to aim for 'congruent meanings'[39] on the question of 'what

---

[36] Paul N Otto and Annie I Antón, 'Managing Legal Texts in Requirements Engineering', in *Design Requirements Engineering: A Ten-Year Perspective*, Lecture Notes in Business Information Processing (Berlin, Heidelberg: Springer, 2009), 376. Available at: https://doi.org/10.1007/978-3-540-92966-6_21.

[37] John Grin and Henk van de Graaf, 'Technology Assessment as Learning', *Science, Technology, & Human Values* 21, no 1 (1 January 1996): 72–99. Available at: https://doi.org/10.1177/016224399602100104.

[38] Ibid.

[39] Ibid.

best/better really means'. Achieving such congruent meanings, however, requires a deliberate effort and appropriate conditions.

While various solutions have been proposed in literature, none of them seems to tackle the issue systematically. Suggestions range from creating a distance between the engineers and the actual legal text,[40] through explaining the values and assumptions underpinning the legal rules and relying on less formal sources of law to supply the 'missing links',[41] to encouraging engineers to become 'legal knowledge engineers' capable of explaining 'the dynamic functionalities of legal requirements and their formalisation'.[42] Each of these solutions clearly has an intrinsic value and could be a stepping stone in bridging the terminological gap between software engineers and legal experts. However, the lack of a systematic approach that has been tested, verified and validated by representatives of both communities remains a major obstacle.

A comprehensive and systematic approach to the development of a common conceptual framework needs to be rooted in principles that are equally fundamental to both domains. Two well-known methods of legal interpretation could act as basis of this framework: the systematic and the teleological method of interpretation.[43]

The systematic method of interpretation reveals the place of a legal rule or legal concept in the legal system and its interactions and links with other rules and concepts. In the language of software engineers, this method enables the identification of the (inter)dependencies (coupling) between a program's modules or routines. Just like software engineers strive to achieve as low coupling as possible, lawyers are aiming for a simpler legal system with as few 'dependencies' as possible. Through a systematic interpretation of a concept or a legal rule, engineers and lawyers can agree on a common understanding of how this rule works in a particular context and ensure that it is repeatedly and indiscriminately applied in the same manner. Furthermore, the method of systematic interpretation allows both parties to easily identify the impact of legislative changes or judicial decisions on the operation of a rule or the interpretation of a concept. By employing, for example, visual aids, such as conceptual mapping embodying the principles of legal design,[44] both communities could enhance their mutual understanding of the common concepts they work with.

---

[40] Aaron K. Massey et al, 'Evaluating Existing Security and Privacy Requirements for Legal Compliance', *Requirements Engineering* 15, no 1 (2010): 122. Available at: https://doi.org/10.1007/s00766-009-0089-5.

[41] See Boella et al, n 13 at 19.

[42] Ibid at 15.

[43] Nadzeya Kiyavitskaya, A. Krausová, and N. Zannone, 'Why Eliciting and Managing Legal Requirements Is Hard' in *2008 Requirements Engineering and Law*, 2008, 4. Available at: https://doi.org/10.1109/RELAW.2008.10.

[44] Michael Curtotti, Helena Haapio, and Stefania Passera, 'Interdisciplinary Cooperation in Legal Design and Communication', SSRN Scholarly Paper (Rochester, NY: Social Science Research Network, 26 February 2015). Available at: https://papers.ssrn.com/abstract=2630953.

To ensure the systematic interpretation yields results aligned with the legislator's intention, these results need to be linked to the purpose a rule or a concept has in the legal system. Thus, the method of teleological interpretation, which aims to discover the purpose of a rule (goal), could be employed to verify and substantiate the results of the systematic interpretation. However, there are at least two caveats which concern teleological interpretation. First, it could often depend on considerations that may lie outside the legal system and it is the legal expert's task to assess the credibility of these considerations. Second, teleological interpretation often relies on non-binding sources (eg the preparatory works of a legal instrument, and their legal effect should be equally subject to careful expert evaluation).

If applied to the context of privacy and data protection, these methods could produce interesting results. For example, they could enhance software engineers' understanding of fundamental notions such as 'proportionality' and 'necessity', which are of crucial importance in a data protection impact assessment (GDPR, Article 35(7)(b)). Equally, the engineers' perspective on notions such as 'confidentiality', 'integrity', 'availability', 'resilience', 'security measures and mechanisms' could improve a legal expert's understanding of the technological concepts underpinning the legal framework. A common, shared framework that is continuously developed and updated by both communities could further engage them in meaningful discussions crystallising into a steadily growing techno-legal 'vocabulary'.

4.2. Defining Tool Support for Legal Data Protection Impact Assessment (DPIA)

Even though developers are only *encouraged* by the GDPR to take into account the right to data protection in the design and development of products, services and applications, market demand will undoubtedly incentivise them to deliver compliant 'off-the-shelf' solutions. To meet this demand, developers will need to engage themselves in a continuous assessment of the risks to the rights and freedoms of natural persons likely to emerge as a result of the processing of personal data by their products or services. These risks can be systematically assessed using the legal tool provided by the GDPR (ie the data protection impact assessment). Even though the GDPR obliges controllers, and not developers, to carry out a DPIA for processing which is likely to result in a high risk to the rights and freedoms of natural persons, there is nothing in the regulation that prohibits software developers from carrying out an impact assessment in their own right.[45]

---

[45] Certainly, the ultimately responsible person remains the data controller who is subject to the obligations laid down in GDPR, Art 35.

Developers could be incentivised to consider data protection in the software development lifecycle if they are provided with the right tools. If a data protection impact assessment is to begin at the design stage (in the technical sense) of a product's development, the developers must be supported by adequate tools that they are comfortable working with. Much of modern software development occurs in integrated development environments which provide developers with tools enabling them to write, test and debug software. Thus, any such impact assessment support tool must necessarily be integrated naturally into their workflow.

Presently, there are many unknowns as to the precise format and structure of a DPIA. Seen primarily as a legal tool, a DPIA is, in practice, disconnected from the technical architecture of software products and also from non-technical stakeholders not involved in the software engineering process. Therefore, there is a need to define a systematic process for conducting DPIAs and documenting the outcome of the assessments. The goal is to provide systematic DPIA support which is at least partially automated and which integrates legal and technical privacy knowledge into data protection by design tools adapted to the software development lifecycle. For any such tool to be successful, it must be based on a sound methodology.

Several methodologies exist to perform general risk analyses[46] or software security risk analyses.[47] Some have been specified to consider data protection issues in specific domains, such as, for example, ISO 27018 which implements ISO 27005 to the field of cloud computing. However, all these methodologies contain only general guidelines and associated controls without linking legal to technical requirements for software design. This has given way to several attempts to design methodologies that bridge this gap both in the legal and engineering field.

Most of the initiatives carried out in the legal domain concentrate on the development of risk assessments for the performance of DPIAs.[48,49] Their objective is to identify risks to individuals' rights and freedoms and to define mitigation measures based on the criteria of the GDPR. Recommendations, however, are often too high level to be used as technical requirements. In addition, they are based on a series of legal assumptions which are not known to their recipients (engineers and other stakeholders), making it very difficult to engage in any constructive dialogue.

---

[46] For example, ISO Guide 73:2009 'Risk Management – Vocabulary', ISO 31000 'Risk Management', ISO 27005 'Information Security Risk Management'.

[47] Such as OWASP's Risk Rating Methodology. Available at: www.owasp.org/index.php/, OWASP_Risk_Rating_Methodology, Microsoft's DREAD Methodology. Available at: https://msdn.microsoft.com/en-us/library/ff648644.aspx, and NIST's Risk management guide for information technology systems, special publication 800-30, or SEI's OCTAVE. Available at: www.cert.org/octave/.

[48] Information Commissioner Office, 'Code of Conduct "Conducting Privacy Impact Assessments"', 25 February 2014. Available at: https://ico.org.uk/media/for-organisations/documents/1595/pia-code-of-practice.pdf.

[49] IAPP, 'AvePoint Privacy Impact Assessment', last accessed 29 September 2017. Available at: https://iapp.org/resources/apia/.

Initiatives in the field of engineering have attempted to bridge this gap by trying to systematise the concepts of the data protection frameworks and to ease their translation into the software engineering process[50,51,52,53,54,55,56,57,58,59,60]. While these initiatives have managed to translate legal concepts into concrete guidelines for software design, they all fail to capture the complexities of undefined legal concepts, such as proportionality, which are deliberately worded in very general terms to be able to capture the multiple contexts of uses of personal data.

A few initiatives, such as the French Data Protection Authority's Privacy Impact Assessment[61] and others[62] have tried to develop privacy risk analysis in the field of privacy by translating risk analysis methods of the IT security field to data protection. Although many of these techniques consider privacy during impact assessment, currently no risk assessment techniques specific to data protection exist. In addition, these methods assess risks from a technological perspective, and do not include the notion of legal risk. They struggle with the fact that IT security

---

[50] Marit Hansen, Meiko Jensen, and Martin Rost, 'Protection Goals for Privacy Engineering', in *2015 IEEE Security and Privacy Workshops (SPW)* (Los Alamitos, CA: IEEE Computer Society, 2015), 159–66. Available at: https://doi.org/10.1109/SPW.2015.13.

[51] PRIPARE, 'PRIPARE Handbook: Methodological Tools to Implement Privacy and Foster Compliance with the GDPR', 7 March 2016. Available at: http://pripareproject.eu/.

[52] OASIS, 'Privacy Management Reference Model and Methodology (PMRM) Version 1.0, OASIS Committee Specification 02', 17 May 2016. Available at: http://docs.oasis-open.org/pmrm/PMRM/v1.0/cs02/PMRM-v1.0-cs02.html.

[53] See ENISA, n 19.

[54] Jaap-Henk Hoepman, 'Privacy Design Strategies', in *ICT Systems Security and Privacy Protection*, IFIP Advances in Information and Communication Technology (IFIP International Information Security Conference, Berlin, Heidelberg: Springer 2014), 446–59.

[55] Carlos Jensen, 'Designing for Privacy in Interactive Systems' (Georgia Institute of Technology, 2005).

[56] Shareeful Islam, Haralambos Mouratidis, and Stefan Wagner, 'Towards a Framework to Elicit and Manage Security and Privacy Requirements from Laws and Regulations' in *Requirements Engineering: Foundation for Software Quality*, Lecture Notes in Computer Science (International Working Conference on Requirements Engineering: Foundation for Software Quality, Springer, Berlin, Heidelberg, 2010), 255–61. Available at: https://doi.org/10.1007/978-3-642-14192-8_23.

[57] A. Siena et al, 'A Meta-Model for Modelling Law-Compliant Requirements', in *2009 Second International Workshop on Requirements Engineering and Law*, 2009, 45–51. Available at: https://doi.org/10.1109/RELAW.2009.1.

[58] Travis D. Breaux, Matthew W. Vail, and Annie I. Anton, 'Towards Regulatory Compliance: Extracting Rights and Obligations to Align Requirements with Regulations', in *Proceedings of the 14th IEEE International Requirements Engineering Conference*, RE '06 (Washington, DC, USA: IEEE Computer Society, 2006), 46–55. Available at: https://doi.org/10.1109/RE.2006.68.

[59] Travis Breaux and Annie Antón, 'Analyzing Regulatory Rules for Privacy and Security Requirements', *IEEE Transactions on Software Engineering* 34, no 1 (2008): 5–20. Available at: https://doi.org/10.1109/TSE.2007.70746.

[60] Luca Compagna et al, 'How to Integrate Legal Requirements into a Requirements Engineering Methodology for the Development of Security and Privacy Patterns', *Artificial Intelligence and Law* 17, no 1 (2009): 1–30. Available at: https://doi.org/10.1007/s10506-008-9067-3.

[61] Commission Nationale Informatique et Libertés, 'Commission Nationale Informatique et Libertés, PIA Manual', 10 July 2015. Available at: www.cnil.fr/fr/node/15798.

[62] Mina Deng et al, 'A Privacy Threat Analysis Framework: Supporting the Elicitation and Fulfillment of Privacy Requirements', *Requirements Engineering* 16, no 1 (2011): 3–32. Available at: https://doi.org/10.1007/s00766-010-0115-7.

and data protection have different approaches as to who the attacker and the assets to be protected are. It was already highlighted that IT security risk assessment focuses on the protection of the IT system against outsiders who try to compromise the integrity, confidentiality and authenticity of the data under attack, while in data protection, the risks stem mainly from the data controller or processor. The goal, thus, must be to protect the individual against any misuse of the personal data entrusted to the data controller.

Finally, other initiatives have focused exclusively on accountability aspects, developing methodologies addressed to legal departments to ensure the follow-up of all processes and documents relevant for privacy compliance, such as the Privacy Management Accountability Framework of Nymity.[63] These initiatives, however, are not linked with the software development process. Traceability of design decisions is a pervasive topic in software engineering research[64,65], and the research domain of architectural knowledge management[66,67,68] focuses explicitly on how to document architectural knowledge (ie the decision process, not just its end result) but also the rationale and detailed design decisions made. However, to date, no effort has been made to verify to what extent these techniques will provide documentation that sufficiently supports data controllers in complying with their legal obligations.

Therefore, there is an urgent need for interdisciplinary research towards the development of privacy risks assessment frameworks and the implementation of the principle of data protection by design. It is no longer enough to address the challenges raised by the use of software systems to the protection of fundamental rights, in particular to the rights to privacy and data protection, solely from a legal or an engineering perspective.

Thus, currently, there is no single uniform approach to addressing data protection and privacy concerns at the level of software development where the legal requirements can be 'embedded' into the design. Despite the existence of both generic and more specific approaches for elicitation of legal requirements, none of them addresses systematically data protection concerns.

---

[63] Available at: www.nymity.com/data-privacy-resources/privacy-management-framework.aspx, last accessed 29 September 2017.

[64] Antony Tang, Yan Jin, and Jun Han, 'A Rationale-Based Architecture Model for Design Traceability and Reasoning', *Journal of System Software* 80, no 6 (2007) 918–934. Available at: https://doi.org/10.1016/j.jss.2006.08.040.

[65] Jane Cleland-Huang et al, 'Best Practices for Automated Traceability', *Computer* 40, no 6 (2007): 27–35. Available at: https://doi.org/10.1109/MC.2007.195.

[66] Kristian Kreiner, 'Tacit Knowledge Management: The Role of Artifacts', *Journal of Knowledge Management* 6, no 2 (2002): 112–23. Available at: https://doi.org/10.1108/13673270210424648.

[67] Muhammad Ali Babar et al, eds, *Software Architecture Knowledge Management* (Berlin, Heidelberg: Springer, 2009). Available at: https://doi.org/10.1007/978-3-642-02374-3.

[68] Philippe Kruchten, Patricia Lago, and Hans van Vliet, 'Building Up and Reasoning About Architectural Knowledge' in *Quality of Software Architectures*, Lecture Notes in Computer Science (International Conference on the Quality of Software Architectures, Berlin, Heidelberg: Springer, 2006), 43–58.

Existing methods include logic-based approaches to modelling regulation,[69] access control approaches to capturing privacy-related requirements of legal texts,[70] mark-up-based representations[71] and even reusable requirements catalogues.[72] However, these approaches have remained largely unemployed in the software engineering community due to 'lack of tool support'.[73] Thus, the ultimate goal of software engineers and legal experts should be the development of a tool that can easily be integrated into the developer's daily workflow to support the design of systems processing personal data. Such a tool must be based on a sound inter-disciplinary methodology holding account of the principles of privacy and data protection not only from a technical but even more so from a legal perspective.

4.3. Providing Decision and Trade-Off Support for Technical and Organisational Mitigation Strategies in the Software Development Life-Cycle

Trade-off decision making (ie finding good compromises between desired soft-ware qualities such as security and usability, but also privacy) is key to software engineering and privacy-driven software engineering practices should allow such appropriate trade-off decisions to be made. It is, however, not straightforward to identify the most suitable mitigations (be they technical, organisational or legal) for identified privacy risks. Pragmatic trade-offs will have to be made that take into account the effort (and monetary cost) of implementing the mitigating solution. These involve difficult questions (eg whether the solution introduces important functional changes, whether it impacts the performance of the system, whether it needs to be hosted on expensive powerful hardware, whether it is complex to implement and thus requiring much development efforts etc). Additional efforts to align the level of mitigation and the risk for the data subject are required (eg, more advanced privacy enhancing solutions will be required when highly sensitive personal information is being processed *en masse* than when only a small set of pseudonymised data are being collected), and regarding the impact the solution has on other software qualities (eg, a privacy solution that introduces anonymous authentication to protect the identity of the user can conflict with a security requirement that demands user accountability, and hence identifiability).

Several proposals and efforts indexing and cataloguing such privacy engi-neering knowledge into reusable *privacy knowledge bases*. These aim explicitly

---

[69] Paul N. Otto and Annie I. Anton, 'Addressing Legal Requirements in Requirements Engineering', in *15th IEEE International Requirements Engineering Conference (RE 2007)*, 2007. Available at: 7, https://doi.org/10.1109/RE.2007.65.

[70] Ibid at 9.

[71] Ibid at 10.

[72] Ibid at 11.

[73] See Kiyavitskaya, Krausová, and Zannone n 43 at 2.

at consolidating reusable software engineering knowledge to assist the trade-off decision process (eg the LINDDUN framework,[74,75] has a solid basis of privacy knowledge support to aid the analyst and software architect in the privacy assessment and mitigation process). The PriS method[76] also provides knowledge support by means of privacy-process patterns to describe privacy requirements, and a classification of implementation techniques categorised according to privacy patterns to facilitate implementation decisions. In addition, the privacy community is actively collaborating to maintain an online privacy patterns catalogue.[77] Ongoing standardisation efforts such as the ISO 27550 highlight the need for tools that implement privacy by design and the GDPR principles, systematic risk elicitation and assessment, but also stress the importance of methods and knowledge bases on privacy-driven engineering.

However, the existing knowledge base consolidates mostly software engineering knowledge yet does not include all legal concepts. There is thus a clear need to expand the existing software knowledge bases with the required legal concepts to be able to support the legal notion of data protection by design. These will need to be described in a crisp, understandable and generic fashion to allow software engineers to make technical trade-offs that take into account legal considerations.

4.4. Assuring Legal Accountability with Traceability Throughout the Software Development Lifecycle

Accountability is one of the most prominent requirements of the GDPR. One of the obligations imposed on data controllers is to be able to demonstrate that risks to the fundamental rights of natural persons have been mitigated, and that the principles of privacy by design were followed throughout the entire software development lifecycle. To address this goal, additional process-level documentation is required, not only about the process but also the actual design decisions and their rationale. In the research domain of software engineering, this is referred to as 'architectural knowledge management' (ie those practices that involve properly documenting design decisions, their rationale, the design context).

Each of the steps in the software engineering process will require suitable documentation with respect to the decisions that reflect the legal obligations. First, legal

---

[74] See Deng et al, n 62.

[75] Kim Wuyts, 'Privacy Threats in Software Architectures', 16 January 2015. Available at: https://lirias.kuleuven.be/handle/123456789/472921.

[76] Christos Kalloniatis, Evangelia Kavakli, and Stefanos Gritzalis, 'Addressing Privacy Requirements in System Design: The PriS Method', *Requir. Eng.* 13, no 3 (2008): 241–255. Available at: https://doi.org/10.1007/s00766-008-0067-3.

[77] Available at: www.privacypatterns.org and www.privacypatterns.eu, last accessed 29 September 2017.

requirements need to be translated into technical requirements. Potential conflicts with existing functional or non-functional (eg security, usability, performance) requirements need to be resolved (and properly documented). This combined set of technical requirements then needs to be instantiated in the system's architecture by introducing architectural building blocks and solutions (such as privacy and security patterns). Not only will these decisions have to be documented properly, the causal relation between decisions and requirements must also be documented and maintained for auditability purposes. In the final stages of the development lifecycle, the architecture is instantiated with a specific implementation. Documenting (and verifying) this final step will be the most challenging as it will require a profound understanding of both the legal and technical privacy requirements as well as a technical expertise in software development and privacy enhancing technologies. Tooling could be introduced to support automated verification, however, the research community on privacy-driven software engineering is at the same level as, for example, the research communities on software security; tool support for automated verification of privacy properties is close to non-existent. In fact, even for security, only limited support for automated verification (eg penetration testing tools) is available (let alone practically usable in a cost-effective fashion), thus significant parts of the verification process still require manual checks.

It will be key to examine existing privacy engineering methodologies to determine how their outputs can be extended to support liability management and argumentation throughout the development process. Furthermore, the documentation should not be written in language that is too technical so as to make sure that lawyers, data protection officers and supervisory authorities will be able to understand it.

Software is increasingly being delivered as a service (instead of well-delineated products) and trends such as agile software development, continuous adaptation/integration all involve constant change and the fast and frequent evolution of software-intensive systems. Taking this reality into account imposes the additional requirement of being able to manage different versions of software architectures and their corresponding traceability documentation over time (versioning systems), to keep this documentation synchronised with reality (the architecture must be a reflection of systems in production, not of designs that have eroded away over time, as it is often the case in practice). Furthermore, governance systems are required to reason about the (legal) impact of change, to monitor legal assurance in a continuous fashion and signal the appropriate stakeholder (eg a DPO) when significant changes occur over time. Finally, software systems increasingly will have to take legal notions into account, or at least document them in the context of production systems. Middleware and platform support for legal notions such as the legal basis for processing, the consent or level of awareness of the involved natural person, the enforcement of data storage policies (eg, retention periods for data storage), access control systems and self-service dashboards to enact the fundamental user rights (eg right to access, right to be forgotten etc) are currently still strongly lacking.

As one of the main use cases for generating and maintaining process rationale and traceability documentation is related to the ability of processors and controllers to demonstrate compliance with legal requirements (such as data protection by design), the outcome of such documentation must also be practically usable for stakeholders with a legal background. In other words, a translation step is required between technically orientated architectural decisions and legal mitigations; here, again, the need for a common conceptual framework is highlighted.

Furthermore, to allow proving that these documents were not tampered with or changed after the fact, additional countermeasures are required, for example, integration with a trusted time stamping authority (a digital notary, or the application of large-scale consensus-based technology such as blockchain).

5. Conclusions

This chapter has highlighted and discussed the need to bridge two seemingly unrelated research domains – legal research and software engineering research – to truly attain effective concretisation and implementation of legal directives such as privacy by design. In this position chapter, four stepping-stones were discussed to bridge the gap that currently exists and provide motivation as to why these can only be addressed with strong interdisciplinary research.

To attain these stepping stones, research on privacy-enhancing technology needs to embed a dialogue between legal stakeholders and more technically orientated researchers. The verification of these technologies from a legal perspective involves not just assessing whether they appropriately implement the legal requirements, but also whether they are in line with the 'legal formants', 'cryptotytes' and 'synecdoche' of the 'living law' and this endeavour cannot be accomplished by software engineers alone.

Consensus on a common and coherent conceptual framework is an essential step in bridging the gap between software engineers and legal experts. Such a framework is essential for the development of a sound interdisciplinary methodology that could lay the foundations of a new generation of decision and trade-off support tools for software engineers to assure legal compliance and traceability in the software development lifecycle. The correct implementation, testing and validation of legal requirements also requires extensive technical expertise, even more so in the domain of privacy and data protection. To successfully manage the sheer complexity of software-intensive systems, a new approach is required which yields a shared agenda between software engineers and legal experts; an agenda where the issues are discussed in a common language towards the pursuit of shared goals: a strong and coherent legal framework equally protecting the fundamental rights of citizens in the online as well as in the offline world.

Acknowledgement

This research is partially funded by the Research Fund KU Leuven and the KUL-PRiSE project.

6

R.I.P.: Rest in Privacy or Rest in (Quasi-)Property?

Personal Data Protection of Deceased Data Subjects between Theoretical Scenarios and National Solutions

GIANCLAUDIO MALGIERI

Abstract

The protection and management of personal data of deceased persons is an open issue both in practical and in theoretical terms. The fundamental right to privacy and to personal data protection (as well as secondary legislation, as GDPR) seems inadequate to cope with the data of deceased data subjects. Accordingly, data controllers might be free to process this data without any guarantee. This might have an adverse effect not only on memory and the post-mortem autonomy of the deceased, but also on living relatives.

Different theoretical solutions have been proposed: post-mortem privacy (based on post-mortem autonomy); the analogical application of copyright law or of inheritance law (data as digital assets). The concept of 'quasi-property' (from common law jurisprudence) might also prove interesting.

Some EU Member States have already provided different solutions for the data of deceased people. We will compare three examples: Estonian Data Protection Law, Italian Data Protection Law and the new French '*Loi sur la République Numérique*' and Catalan law on the '*digitals voluntats*' (which adopt an approach similar to advanced healthcare directives).

Keywords

Personal data, privacy, deceased data subjects, post-mortem privacy, quasi-property

1. Introduction: The Reasons for Research

The protection and management of personal data of deceased persons is an open issue both in practical and theoretical terms. The digital identity of data subjects persists after their biological death: the difficulty of considering this 'digital' inheritance in terms of assets that can be inherited, a commodity that can be freely processed or components of a post-mortem personality that should be protected has triggered an interesting debate.[1]

In particular, this research should be conducted for at least three reasons: (a) finding a protection for our own personal data beyond our life, considering in particular the life-transcending protection of personality that several national legal systems accept; (b) finding a protection for the bereaved (relatives, spouse, descendants or friends of the deceased person) against *adverse effects* of a free processing of personal data of the deceased persons; and (c) understanding the limits and the borderlines of privacy and personal data protection in this problematic field and how alternative theoretical paradigms (like 'quasi-privacy', 'quasi-subjects' or *demi-personnalité* and quasi-property) could help.

As shown below, the GDPR does not provide any protection for data of deceased data subjects (recital 27) but allows Member States to provide eventual forms of post-mortem data protection.

The research questions and objectives are therefore: which is the best form of protection for personal data of deceased persons (protected as property or as personality elements) looking both at theoretical possible solutions (post-mortem privacy, commodification of data, quasi-property data) and at relevant national implementations already existing (in particular four cases will be compared as four different frameworks: the Italian and Estonian data protection law and new French 'Loi pour une République Numérique' and Catalan 'voluntats digital' law).

At the same time, it is important to understand the affected interests of the bereaved persons (relatives, friends of the deceased) and how post-mortem privacy could protect them, considering the European courts jurisprudence and the US common-law concept of 'quasi-property'.

---

[1] Edina Harbinja, 'Post-mortem privacy 2.0: theory, law, and technology', *International Review of Law, Computers & Technology*, 31, no 1 (2017): 26–42; Hans Buitelaar, 'Post-mortem Privacy and Informational Self-determination', *Ethics Inf Technol*, 19, (2017): 129–142; Giuseppe Ziccardi, *Il libro digitale dei morti. Memoria, lutto, eternità e oblio nell'era dei social network*, (UTET, Milano, 2017); Lilian Edwards and Edina Harbinja, 'Protecting Post-mortem Privacy: Reconsidering the Privacy Interests of the Deceased in a Digital World', *Cardozo Arts & Entertainment Law Journal*, 32, no 1, (2013): 101–147; Irina Baraliuc, 'Law and Technology of Online Profiles After Death', *Jusletter IT*, 27 February 2012; Elaine Kasket, 'Access to the Digital Self in Life and Death: Privacy in the Context of Posthumously Persistent Facebook Profiles, *Scripted*, 10, no 1, (2013): 7–18. Carl Öhman and Luciano Floridi, 'The Political Economy of Death in the Age of Information: A Critical Approach to the Digital Afterlife Industry', *Minds & Machines* 27 (2017): 639. Available at: https://doi.org/10.1007/s11023-017-9445-2. Heather Conway and Sheena Grattan, 'The 'New' New Property: Dealing with Digital Assets on Death' in *Modern Studies in Property Law*, Volume 9 edited by Heather Conway and Robin Hickey, 1st edn, (Oxford: Hart Publishing, 2017), 99–115.

Accordingly, Section 2 will address the different possible theoretical scenarios for the management of personal data of deceased data subjects ('data freedom', 'quasi propertisation' and post-mortem privacy). Then, Section 3 will analyse legal solutions in Europe taking into account the European Charters (European Convention on Human Rights and EU Charter of Fundamental Rights) and the ECtHR jurisprudence. Section 4 reveals that secondary law is also an important reference for life-transcending personality protection. Consequently, Section 5 focuses on data protection law at national levels, comparing Italian, Estonian, French and Catalan post-mortem privacy regulations. These national solutions suggest an interesting analogy with an advance healthcare directive (where decisional privacy on vegetative body is similar to informational privacy on post-mortem personal data). This is addressed in Section 6. Section 7 deals with the common law concept of 'quasi-property'. This might be one way to protect successors, relatives, spouses and friends, whose interests are often adversely affected after the death of the data subject (eg abusive interference, online behavioural advertisements based on grief exploitation, indirect and elusive form of secondary data processing – when personal data of the deceased are used to unlawfully infer health or genetic data of the relatives).

2. The Destiny of Personal Data after the Data Subjects' Death: Three Scenarios

In principle, to understand the different possible legal solutions for post-mortem data processing it is necessary to investigate the (at least) three different possible scenarios for personal data after the death of the data subject: (a) the 'data freedom' scenario, which consists in a full commodification of these data without any protection for the deceased and for the bereaved; (b) the 'quasi-property' scenario, in which the personal data of a deceased person are 'inherited' by heirs; and (c) the post-mortem privacy scenario, where the privacy of the data subject is protected even after death, through specific measures (possibly by releasing advance directives or delegating a person to implement those directives).

Scenarios (a) and (b) are both based on the reification of personal data (commodity of the data controller or component of the estate); while scenarios (b) and (c) strongly limit the data controllers and tend to protect the interests of the data subject or of his/her successors against commercial interests of other subjects.

The following sections address these different scenarios.

2.1. 'Data Freedom' or 'Commodification'

The first theoretical scenario is the 'data freedom' scenario, according to which there might be a whole commodification of post-mortem data: when a data subjects dies, the data controller can process his/her personal data without any restriction or limitation.

He/she can also sell or transmit these data to other parties: he/she can thus economically profit from these data, use them for non-anonymized analytics purposes or publicly disclose these data.[2]

In this scenario, several interests can be adversely affected. From the perspective of the deceased person, his or her informational self-determination can be violated. Several scholars have highlighted the issue of posthumous harm to the *right to informational privacy* after death (eg a right to personal immunity from unknown, undesired or unintentional changes in one's identity).[3] This could involve the will of a data subject to delete his or her data after death; his or her will to hide some aspects of his or her life or to over-represent some other aspects of himself/herself. In other terms, what might be violated in this 'data freedom' scenario would be the right to self-representation of 'public persona'[4] after death.

Actually, in this scenario, other interests are strongly affected: we consider, in particular, the interests of the bereaved (relatives, friends, descendants of the deceased data subject).

They can be affected under at least three perspectives. First, the non-protection of data of deceased data subjects could lead to a moral harm to their grief and memory. The mere fact of receiving e-mails or communications related to the deceased relative/spouse/ascendant could be harmful for the intimate sphere of the bereaved.

Second, the personal data of deceased data subjects might be used to better 'exploit' the vulnerability of the bereaved. If we consider the case of personalized advertisements, personal data about the deceased could be freely used to perform more effective and pervasive marketing practices (eg when details of the deceased person and his/her kind of relationship with the bereaved are transposed or reflected in personalised advertisements, videos, images, etc).[5]

---

[2] See, eg, Tamlin Magee, 'What Happens To Your Data After You're Dead?', *Forbes*, 19 November 2013, Available at: www.forbes.com/sites/tamlinmagee/2013/11/19/what-happens-to-your-data-after-youre-dead/2/#62720e2d579d (last accessed: 22 May 2018). As for the afterlife personal data industry, see more generally Carl Ohman and Luciano Floridi, 'An Ethical Framework for the Digital Afterlife Industry', *Nature Human Behaviour*, 2, (2018): 318–320.

[3] See Edwards and Harbinja, n 1 at 110. Hans Buitelaar, n 1 at 129; Luciano Floridi, 'The Ontological Interpretation of Informational Privacy', *Ethics and Information Technology*, 7 (2005): 185–200.

[4] Andrei Marmor, 'What is the Right to Privacy?', *Philosophy & Public Affairs*, 43, no 1, (2015): 3–26. See also Jeremy Bentham rephrased by Ngaire Naffine, 'When Does the Legal Person Die? Jeremy Bentham and the 'Auto-Icon'', *Australian Journal of Legal Philosophy*, 25, (2000): 79–95, 90 according to whom 'Every man is his best biographer'. See also, interestingly, John Christman, 'Telling Our Own Stories: Narrative Selves and Oppressive Circumstance', in *The Philosophy of Autobiography* edited by Christopher Cowley (London: University of Chicago Press, 2015), 122–140.

[5] Ryan Calo, 'Digital Market and Manipulation', *George Washington Law Review*, 82 (2013): 995, 1029 who refers to the risk to be micro-targeted as 'bereaved' of a deceased person and receive personalised advertising that exploit their grief. See, on a different, but parallel, topic, Jeremy N. Bailenson et al., 'Facial Similarity Between Voters and Candidates Causes Influence', 72 *Pub. Opinion. Q.* (2008): 935, 935–61.

Third, personal data of the deceased data subjects could be used to infer information about their living relatives. The most emblematic examples are health or genetic data. It has been widely argued that 'secondary data subjects' (relatives) can be affected by data processing of solely 'primary data subjects' genetic data (ie individuals whose data are being processed under their consent or under another legal basis).[6] In this hypothetical 'data freedom' scenario, data controllers might be, in principle, free to use sensitive data of deceased persons to produce 'scores' or decisions on the relatives without an explicit processing of sensitive data (the only personal data of the 'secondary data subject' – the deceased's relative – might be the familial relationship with the 'primary subject' – the deceased person). In other words, data controllers could elaborate predictions or inferences through sensitive data without any of the restrictions under Article 9 of the GDPR.

It might be argued that a subject's genetic data is inherently 'personal data' of third persons (relatives).[7] However, even though these data might be 'related' to other people, such sensitive data might be turned to 'scores' or 'risk indicators' (non-sensitive data) after the death of the 'primary' data subjects to elude GDPR, Article 9 restrictions.

However, the relationship between the health data of a person ('primary data subject') and those of his or her relative ('secondary data subjects') might be weak in principle, even though in practice (through data mining and Big Data technologies) several predictions and inferences might be possible on 'secondary data subjects' using only the health data of their relatives.[8]

2.2. Post-Mortem Privacy

The opposite scenario is based on the full protection of 'post-mortem privacy'.

Under this scenario, personal data protection persists even when the data subject dies. The data subject can give anticipated dispositions for his or her post-mortem data processing or delegate someone to exercise his or her rights after death.

Post-mortem privacy has several theoretical and practical limits. In particular, we highlight the 'problem of the subject'[9] (ie the theoretical difficulty of conceiving interests that persist in the absence of an interested subject).

---

[6] Mark Taylor, *Genetic Data and the Law: A Critical Perspective on Privacy Protection*, (Cambridge University Press, Cambridge 2012), 107–112.

[7] Article 29 Working Party, working document on Genetic Data WP91, 17 March 2004, passim.

[8] On the wide and relative notion of health data in the Big Data era see Gianclaudio Malgieri and Giovanni Comandé, 'Sensitive-by-distance: Quasi-Health Data in the Algorithmic Era', *Information and Communications Technology Law*, 26 (2017): 229–249.

[9] Joel Feinberg, *The Moral Limits of the Criminal Law Volume 1: Harm to Others*, (Oxford: Oxford Scholarship Online, 1987), 34 ff.

The problem of the subject can be divided into three sub-problems: (a) the problem of the 'interest', (b) the problem of the 'harm' and (c) the problem of the 'narrator'.

The 'problem of the interest' is a procedural law issue: it refers to the fact that no interest can be harmed if there is nobody 'interested in' it.[10] A demonstration of this 'problem' is that in several legal systems '*actio personalis moritur cum persona*': it is not possible to take legal action for the protection of non-pecuniary interests of an individual after his or her death.[11]

The 'problem of the harm' refers to the fact that any injury to the privacy of the deceased would have no effect on the 'victim'. The deceased data subject cannot concretely suffer from the consequences of his/her post-mortem privacy violation, so that any 'harm' would result in a so-called 'no-effect injury'[12].

The problem of the 'narrator' is related to the need of an active will that can guide and shape a digital identity. In other words, the expression of digital persona is not static but dynamic (the data subject decides which personal data to share, correct, erase, port, even under the data protection rights guaranteed in the GDPR). Deceased persons, can no longer express their autonomy on their digital life, there is no 'narrator' who can self-regulate the processing and management of their digital identity.[13]

These three sub-problems (that are also true for other situations, such as post-mortem copyright management) are not real obstacles. As regards the problem of the 'interest', we could argue that several (even personal or 'moral') legal actions are carried out even after the persons' death. An emblematic example is the action for the restoration of non-pecuniary damages in several civil law countries: heirs can also inherit the restoration for moral harms or damages to health of the deceased.[14] Another interesting example, in several European criminal law systems, is the possibility for the bereaved (eg relatives and spouse) to bring a legal action against people who have offended the deceased.[15]

As regards the problem of the 'harm', we can argue that a violation of post-mortem privacy could result in two different harms: on the one hand, a posthumous harm can, in principle, retroactively damage the interests of ante-mortem data subjects;[16] indeed, according to several scholars the law should protect a 'life transcending integrity' of individuals. In other words, privacy as a human right is theoretically based on *autonomy* and *dignity*:[17] after the death of the

---

[10] Stephen Winter, 'Against Posthumous Rights', *Journal of Applied Philosophy*, 27, no 2, (2010): 186–199.

[11] See Edina Harbinja, n 1 at 33. See in UK case law: *Baker v Bolton*, 1808 1 Camp 493.

[12] Huw Beverley-Smith, 'The Commercial Appropriation of Personality' (Cambridge: Cambridge University Press. 2000), 124; see Winter n 10 at 186–199.

[13] See Floridi, 'The Informational Nature of Personal Identity', *Minds & Machines*, 21 (2011): 549–566.

[14] See, eg, Italian Corte di Cassazione, SS UU n 15350/2015.

[15] See, eg, Italian Criminal Code, Art. 597, comma 3.

[16] Buitelaar, n 1 at 129–142, 133; see Feinberg, n 35 at 34 ff.

[17] See Harbinja, n 1 at 30–31. See also Frederik Swennen, 'Er is leven na de dood. Persoonlijkheidsrechten na overlijden', *Tijdschrift voor Privaatrecht*, 50, no 3 (2013): 1489–1553.

individual, both these aspects should be still protected. It is argued that *dignity* is life-transcending (the respect for the memory;[18] while, at the same time, *autonomy* is projected into the future (our goals are based on the future, even on a post-mortem future).[19]

As regards the problem of the 'narrator', it has been argued that actually the lack of a narrator for the personal identity of the deceased is neither so true in theory nor unsolvable in the practice. Indeed, some scholars argue that the discursive and textual ontology we presented during our lifetime (especially on social networks) constitutes a post-mortem vicarious existence with no need of narrators,[20] even where Artificial Intelligence can substitute the narrator counter-predicting how the data subjects would have behaved *if he or she had been alive at that moment.*[21]

From a more practical perspective, however, the narrator can always delegate a new narrator (a relative, a friend), or the law can determine a vicarious narrator (the heir). The narrator could anticipate his or her narration through an advance directive.[22]

In other words, the post-mortem privacy scenario might lead to a 'quasi-data-subject' (the deceased data subject), according to the theories of the '*demi-personnalité juridique*'[23] and of different gradations of legal personhood, depending on the level of interaction that the digital persona displays.[24] These ideas find an interesting confirmation in the pre-birth legal protection of the unborn: some European Civil Codes state that the unborn can be the subject of rights (he/she can receive donations or testamentary dispositions) but these are conditional to the birth. It is a form of protection of a quasi-subject beyond life[25] that can be similar, in principle, to the protection of the deceased.

---

[18] Ronald Dworkin, *Life's Dominion: An Argument About Abortion and Euthanasia* (New York: Knopf Doubleday Publishing Group, 1993 and 2011).

[19] Buitelaar, n 1 at 139.

[20] Ibid at 138–139.

[21] See, eg, ETER9 a social network (in BETA stage) as described by Buitelaar, n 1 at 130. See also, interestingly, *NECTOME*, a new start up that offers to preserve grey matter of human brain through a vitrification process, for a life-transcending existence of individuals' consciousness through cloud services and AI, see Alex Hern, 'Startup wants to upload your brain to the cloud, but has to kill you to do it', *The Guardian*, 14 March 2018, Available at: https://amp.theguardian.com/technology/2018/mar/14/nectome-startup-upload-brain-the-cloud-kill-you?__twitter_impression=true (lasy accessed 15 March 2018). Similarly, REPLIKA (https://replika.ai) is an AI that learns from the user and can replicate his/her personality after his/her death, see Casey Newton, 'Speak, Memory. When her best friend died, she rebuilt him using Artificial Intelligence', *The Verge*, Available at; www.theverge.com/a/luka-artificial-intelligence-memorial-roman-mazurenko-bot (last accessed 15 March 2018).

[22] See the French '*Loi pour une la republique Numérique*', Art. 63, below.

[23] Buitelaar, n 1 at 139; J. Rombach, 'Prae-en postpersoonlijkheidsrechten en-plichten', *Weekblad voor Privaatrecht, Notaris-ambt en Registratie*, 94, no 4774, (1963): 297–299.

[24] Buitelaar, n 1 at 139.

[25] Art. 1, Italian Civil Code.

2.3. 'Quasi-Propertisation' or 'Personal Data Inheritance'

An intermediate scenario is the quasi-propertisation scenario. In principle, personal data are valuable 'assets',[26] that can be considered immaterial goods; at the same time it might be trade secrets for the data controller,[27] a copyrighted work,[28] or it might be protected through other Intellectual Property rights (IPRs).[29]

Accordingly, personal data could be 'inherited' as (digital) goods or as IPRs on intangibles. But as all IPRs in the European framework, even *moral rights* are protected. Therefore, a full commodification is impossible. What is possible could be a 'quasi-propertisation', as I will explain below.[30]

Interestingly, copyright law, in particular, the Berne Convention for the Protection of Literary and Artistic Works (1886 as revised in the 1979), provides a post-mortem personality protection in the form of inheritance for descendants.

Article 7(1) states that 'the term of protection [of economic rights] granted by this Convention shall be the life of the author and *fifty years after his death*'.[31] So there is a post-mortem copyright protection.

At the same time, Art. 6-bis(2) extends moral rights (ie the right to claim authorship of a work and to object to modifications to that work) after the death of the author. It provides that moral rights '*shall, after the author's death, be maintained, at least until the expiry of the economic rights, and shall be exercisable by the persons or institutions authorized by the legislation of the country where protection is claimed*'. This provision has been implemented extensively in national systems (eg in France and Italy, moral rights after death are eternal).[32]

What arises from these provisions is an (at least temporary) life-transcending protection of 'public persona', granted to heirs (or to explicitly delegated persons[33]) and with inalienable rights for a limited period.

---

[26] Gintare Surblyte, 'Data as Digital Resource', *Max Planck Institute for Innovation & Competition*, 2016, Research Paper No 16–12.

[27] Gianclaudio Malgieri, 'Trade Secrets v Personal Data, Possible solutions for balancing rights', *International Data Privacy Law*, 6, no 2, (2016): 102–116.

[28] Pamela Samuelson, 'Privacy as Intellectual Property', *Stanford Law Review*, 52 (1999): 1125. Gianclaudio Malgieri, 'User Provided Personal Content in the EU: Digital Currency Between Data Protection and Intellectual Property', *International Review of Law and Technology*, 32, no 1, (2018): 118–140.

[29] See, eg, the case of 'trademarks': Ann Bartow, 'Our Data, Ourselves: Privacy, Propertization, and Gender', *University of San Francisco Law Review*, 34 (2000): 633–704.

[30] Lauren Henry Scholz, 'Privacy as Quasi-Property', *Iowa Law Review*, 101, no 3 (2015). Available at: http://ssrn.com/abstract=2567579, 12. See also Gianclaudio Malgieri, 'Ownership" of Customer (Big) Data in the European Union: Quasi-Property as Comparative Solution?', *Journal of Internet Law*, 11 (2016): 2–12.

[31] Italics added.

[32] See Art. L121-1 of the French Code de la Propriété Intellectuelle (Loi 92-597). See also Art. 23 of the Italian Legge sul Diritto d'Autore, L. 633/1941.

[33] See, eg, Art. L121-1 and L121-2, Code de la Propriété Intellectuelle.

As we can observe, this scenario is different from the 'commodification' (or data freedom) scenario: here the deceased's data are subject to a controlled and respectful propertisation to the advantage of the deceased or of his/her heirs. In this case, propertisation is a form of protection of individual's rights and not a form of commodification.[34]

This form of limited propertisation of data inheritance can be found in the US common law concept of 'quasi-property': as it will be shown in Section 7, quasi-property is a form of protection similar to property,but based on inalienability (for the respect of moral and intangible values) and on a relational and liability-like structure. It was conceived for property on corpses, but we can easily draw an analogy with the personal data of the deceased.[35]

However, in theoretical terms, this form of protection is similar to post-mortem Intellectual Property protection.

There may be an analogy between this form of post-mortem copyright protection and the post-mortem data protection described above. Indeed, both copyrighted works and personal data are valuable intangible goods that embed the personality of the individual (author/data subject).[36]

Interestingly, it has been also argued that data are part of a 'personal domain':[37] individuals have sovereignty over a spatial zone, which is determined by their (even digital) body.[38]

It seems clear that this scenario has more in common with post-mortem privacy scenario than with the commodification scenario: here data controllers are not fully free to process data without any restrictions. Heirs (or other legitimated subjects) inherit personal data and can act on behalf of the descendants for the respect of (even) moral interests.

3. Primary Law: Constitutional Charters and the European Court's Jurisprudence

After this quick overview of the three theoretical scenarios for the destiny of personal data after the death of the data subject, we should analyse how European law regulates this phenomenon and try to understand which one of the three paradigms is best represented in the European legal system.

---

[34] Daniel R. Ortiz, 'Privacy, Autonomy, and Consent', *Harvard Journal of Law and Policy*, 12, (1988): 91–97, 92; Nadezhda Purtova, 'The Illusion of Personal Data as No One's Property', *Law, Innovation, and Technology*, 7, no 1, (2015): 83–111.

[35] See Shyamkrishna Balganesh, 'Quasi-Property: Like, but not Quite Property', *University of Pennsylvania Law Rev*iew 160 (2012): 1891. *Hackett v Hackett*, 26 A. 42, 43-44 (R.I. 1893); *Gardner v Swan Point Cemetery*, 40 A 871 (RI 1898). Scholz, n 30 at 12.

[36] See, eg, Samuelson, n 28 at 1125.

[37] Joel Feinberg, 'Autonomy, Sovereignty, and Privacy: Moral Ideals in the Constitution?', *The Notre Dame Law Review*, 58 (1983): 445–492.

[38] Hans Buitelaar, n 1 at 134.

We will first address primary law (the European Convention on Human Rights and the EU Charter of Fundamental Rights), then secondary law (national systems in general and data protection law).

As regards, primary law, the European Convention on Human Rights (ECHR) does not explicitly protect post-mortem privacy. Article 8(1) provides that 'everyone has the right to respect for his private and family life, his home and his correspondence' and there is no explicit reference to privacy protection after death.

Analogously, Articles 7 and 8 of the EU Charter of Fundamental Rights (CFR) does not explicitly address privacy or data protection beyond the life of individuals: they both refer to 'everyone' as the subjects of rights, but the reasonable interpretation of these texts is generally limited to a living natural person.

To better understand the impact of ECHR (and indirectly of the EU CFR) on post-mortem privacy, it would be useful to analyse the European courts' jurisprudence.

The European Court of Human Rights (ECtHR) has addressed the issue of private life protection in the case of deceased people in several cases.

In principle, for some human rights protected within the ECtHR, it has explicitly recognized a post-mortem protection, in particular Article 2 (right to life), Article 3 (prohibition of torture) and Article 6 (right to fair trial).[39] Actually, in these cases what is at stake is a violation (of the right to life, of the prohibition of torture, of the right to a fair trial) which has occurred during the life of the individual, whose restoration is requested in a legal action (which persists even) after the death of the data subject.

Apart from these situations, we should now analyse ECtHR jurisprudence under Article 8 of the ECHR.

The first case is *Pannullo and Forte v France* (2002).[40] According to the Court, a delay in burial procedures is a violation of private life (not of the deceased person) but of the parents of a deceased baby.[41] In other words, the Court recognises a private life protection under Article 8(1) in case of deceased people, but such protection covers only the living relatives, not the deceased.

A second case that has addressed the issue of private and family life under Article 8 of the ECHR is *Znamenskaya v Russia* (2005).[42] In this case, the Court admits that the refusal to establish the paternity of a woman of a stillborn child and to change his name accordingly is considered a violation *of the mother's private life*.[43] Although the dispute is about the parenthood and the surname of the deceased person, what is at stake is not the private life of the deceased child, but the protection of the family life of the mother.

---

[39] As recognised in ECtHR, Decision as to the admissibility of Application no 1338/03 by the Estate of Kresten Filtenborg Mortensen v Denmark, 15 May 2006.

[40] ECtHR, *Pannullo and Forte v France*, Application no 37794/97, 30 January 2002.

[41] Ibid, §§ 31–40.

[42] ECtHR, *Znamenskaya v Russia*, Application no 77785/01, 2 June 2005.

[43] Ibid, § 30.

A third relevant case is the Court's decision on the admissibility of an application. In *Estate of Kresten v Denmark* (2006):[44] after the death of Mr Kresten, his estate (represented by his legitimate son) alleged a violation of Article 8, when the Danish court accepted the request of two people to carry out a genetic test on his corpse to determine whether he was their biological father. The ECtHR admits that 'the concept of 'private life' is a broad term not susceptible to exhaustive definition. It covers the 'physical and psychological integrity of a person'. In addition, the Court acknowledges that 'it was settled case-law that *an individual had rights under the Convention even after death*',[45] but it adds that 'it would stretch the reasoning developed in this case-law too far to hold in a case like the present one that DNA testing on a corpse constituted interference with the Article 8 rights of the deceased's estate'.[46]

In other terms, ECtHR does not exclude, in principle, the entitlement of human rights to deceased persons (as in the case of rights at ECHR, Articles 2, 3 and 6) but the Court jurisprudence has never addressed a case in which 'private and family life' of a deceased person can be protected after his/her death.

There is one early case in which the European Commission of Human Rights had recognised some forms of post-mortem private life protection. In *Application No 8741/79*,[47] the Commission admitted that the applicant's wish to have his ashes spread out over his own land 'was so closely connected to private life that it fell within the sphere of Art. 8'. However, the Commission found, that *not every regulation on burials constituted an interference with the exercise of that right.*[48]

Accordingly, the post-mortem respect for 'burial directives' might be compatible with the respect for private life under Article 8. This is a form of life-transcending decisional privacy.[49]

Interestingly, while for Articles 2, 3 and 6 of the ECHR the post-mortem protection refers to violations (of the right to life, of the prohibition of torture, of the right to a fair trial) *during the life* of the individual, whose restoration is discussed after his death, for this last case on Article 8, the respect of 'burial wills' is nothing but a *post-mortem respect* for the autonomy and dignity of the deceased person.

As that case is an isolated decision, from Strasbourg jurisprudence we can conclude that some form of non-patrimonial will can be protected within a post-mortem 'private life' concept, but this protection is just sectorial (on a case-by-case basis).

---

[44] See n 39.
[45] Italics added.
[46] See n 39.
[47] European Commission on Human Rights, Application N° 8741/79, déc. 10.3.81, D.R. 24, pp. 140–143.
[48] Ibid.
[49] The notion of decisional privacy is well developed in Bart van der Sloot, 'Decisional Privacy 2.0: The Procedural Requirements Implicit in Article 8 ECHR and its Potential Impact on Profiling', *International Data Privacy Law*, 7, no 3, (2017): 190–201.

What really emerges from the ECtHR jurisprudence is the protection of the bereaved (descendants, spouses, relatives, heirs). As we have argued, the academic debate often ignores their interests, but they are very relevant under several perspectives: the moral protection of grief and memory (the right to be left alone with or to respect their grief); the commercial protection from elusive forms of sensitive data processing (using sensitive data to 'score' relatives without processing their sensitive data);[50] the protection from exploitation of grief through personalized advertisements (ie based on neuromarketing) representing images or videos that reminds them of the deceased person or the experience of the bereavement.[51]

4. Secondary Law: Post Mortem Personality Protection in National Laws

After this overview of the post-mortem protection under primary law, it would be interesting to address how secondary law (national or derivative law in the EU) addresses the issue of post-mortem privacy and see how such existing legal solutions adopt one or more paradigms among the three scenarios.

We will first address some non-exhaustive examples in national legislation; in the next section we will focus on data protection law (at both EU and national level).

As regards some forms of post-mortem personality protection in national legal systems, we should first mention legal actions for the restoration of moral damages after death.[52] In several legal systems, heirs can inherit the restoration for damages to health of a deceased person; at the same time non-pecuniary losses (even emotional distress, or violation of his/her image or his/her privacy) can be restored post-mortem.[53] In other words, life interests (even 'moral' life interests) of individuals can be protected even after death; in general, the heirs can 'represent' the deceased and receive a restoration on their behalf.

Is this is a moral or a pecuniary protection of the deceased person or a pecuniary protection of the estate (and so a protection of the heirs)?

The ambiguous nature of moral damage restoration (an economic restoration for a moral injury) is even more problematic when it is 'inherited'. Since this restoration is *iure hereditatis* (on behalf of the deceased) we can exclude that this is a direct protection of the heirs' moral interests. What is protected is the

---

[50] See Taylor, n 6 at 111.

[51] See Calo n 5 at 1029.

[52] See, in general, Mauro Tescaro, 'La tutela postmortale della personalità morale e specialmente dell'identità personale', *Jus Civile. It*, 2014. Available at: www.juscivile.it/contributi/2014/17_Tescaro.pdf (last accessed 8 March 2018).

[53] See the emblematic example of Italian Corte di Cassazione, Sezioni Unite, sent. N. 15350/2015 which has accepted the inheritance of the right to be restored from 'danno biologico' (damage to health) and moral damages.

non-pecuniary interest of the deceased (health, emotional wellbeing, privacy, etc.) '*in the form*' of a pecuniary interest (the estate) of the heirs.

Another post-mortem 'personality' protection of the deceased is copyright law. Articles 7 and 6-bis of the Berne Convention[54] state that economic rights of the author should persist for 50 years after death. Legitimate descendants can exercise even moral rights on behalf of the deceased author for the same period.

In this case we can more easily identify the protected interests: post-mortem economic rights do not protect the deceased but eventually his or her heirs (or legitimate owners of these rights) who can materially profit from these rights. However, post-mortem moral rights are probably the clearest form of life-transcending protection of the 'public persona'[55] The right (of an heir) to claim the authorship of a work or to object to some modifications on behalf of the deceased is an evident expression of the life-transcending right not to be falsely represented and in general of a post-mortem right to informational self-determination.[56]

However, the moral protection of the deceased can also indirectly protect the bereaved: post-mortem moral rights can protect their grief and memory against external abuse of the image of the deceased relative/spouse/ascendant.

Another example of the life-transcending respect of personal autonomy and dignity is the binding value of non-pecuniary testamentary clauses in several legal systems (eg in several civil law countries).[57]

It has been argued that even pecuniary testamentary clauses are a post-mortem protection for the personality[58] or the autonomy of the deceased testator.[59]

An example of legally binding moral wills can be found in Strasbourg Case Appl. 8741/79, where the respect for burial directives of the deceased are considered necessary to respect his or her private life under Article 8 of the ECHR.

A similar form of post-mortem autonomy protection can be found in European legislation about interference (eg examinations and transplantation) with corpses. An emblematic example is section 16(1) of the Danish Act on Coroner's Inquest, post-mortem examinations and transplantation that states: 'Interference with a corpse, may take place only if the deceased person, having turned 18 years old, gave his or her consent in writing.'

---

[54] Berne Convention for the Protection of Literary and Artistic Works (as amended 28 September 1979).

[55] See Feinberg, n 35 at 34 ff.

[56] See, eg, Edwards and Harbinja n 1 at 83–129.

[57] See, eg, Italian Civil Code, Art. 587.

[58] Jean C. Sonnekus, 'Freedom of Testation and the Aging Testator', in *Exploring the Law of Succession: Studies National, Historical and Comparative*, edited by Kenneth Reid, Marius de Waal, and Reinhard Zimmermann, (Edinburgh: Edinburgh University Press, 2007), 78–99, 79 who argues that the freedom of testation is an inner aspect of the testator's personality rights and as such it cannot be detached from an individual, delegated or transferred from another person. See also Harbinja, n 1 at 33.

[59] Similarly, Marius J. De Waal, 'A Comparative Overview', in *Exploring the Law of Succession: Studies National, Historical and Comparative*, edited by Kenneth Reid, Marius de Waal, and Reinhard Zimmermann, (Edinburgh: Edinburgh University Press, 2007), 169 and Laurence M. Friedman, 'The Law of the Living, the Law of the Dead: Property, Succession and Society', *Wisconsin Law Review*, 29 (1966): 340–378, 355 qualify the freedom of testation as the manifestation of *autonomy*, having a considerable effect on the emancipation of the individual.

Even in this case, dignity and autonomy persist after the death of the interested person. The anticipated regulation of corpses is particularly interesting for our discussion: personal data have been often defined as the 'digital body' of individuals.[60] The analogy between the human body and personal data can be seen even in a post-mortem scenario: if national legislations guarantee a post-mortem protection of corpses (the deceased's body) they might also well protect personal data (the deceased's *digital* body). Such an analogy between the post-mortem regulation of the corpses and the deceased's personal data will be addressed in Section 6.

5. Secondary Law: EU and National Data Protection Law

If we look at data protection law, Directive 95/46/EC did not mention deceased data subjects. Member States were thus free to regulate the processing of personal data of deceased data subjects.

Several Member States (Bulgaria, Czech Republic, Denmark, Estonia, France, Italy, Latvia, Lithuania, Portugal, Slovakia, Slovenia and Spain[61]) have provided a regulation for post-mortem data protection in different forms, while few Member States explicitly exclude this protection.[62] In the next section, Italy, Estonia, France and Cataluña will be analysed as three emblematic models of three different frameworks.

The General Data Protection Regulation (GDPR) does not explicitly regulate post-mortem data protection. Recital 27 of the GDPR states as follows: 'this Regulation does not apply to the personal data of deceased persons. Member States may provide for rules regarding the processing of personal data of deceased persons.'

It is now necessary to investigate how national legislations can eventually implement these rules.

5.1. Estonian Data Protection Act: The IP-like (or Quasi-Propertisation) Model

A first emblematic example is the Estonian Data Protection Act (which has implemented Directive 95/46/EC).

---

[60] Stefano Rodotà, 'Trasformazioni del corpo', *Politica del diritto*, vol 1, marzo (2006): 3–24. See also Giusella Finocchiaro, 'Corpo digitale e informazioni nella sanità elettronica', 2017, *Salute e Società*, vol. 2, 32–41.

[61] Damian McCallig, 'Data Protection and the Deceased in the EU', Paper presented at the CPDP, Brussels, 24 January 2004.

[62] It is the case in Cyprus, Ireland, Sweden and the United Kingdom. See McCallig, n 61.

Section 13 regulates the 'processing of personal data after death of data subject' and states as follows:

> 'after the death of a data subject, processing of personal data relating to the data subject is permitted only with the written consent of the successor, spouse, descendant or ascendant, brother or sister of the data subject, except if consent is not required for processing of the personal data or if thirty years have passed from the death of the data subject. If there are more than one successor or other persons specified in this subsection, processing of the data subject's personal data is permitted with the consent of any of them but each of the successors has the right to withdraw the consent'.

The main elements of this provision are: the written consent of successors (if required as a legitimate basis) for the further processing of post-mortem data; a limited period of 30 years for this protection; a dispute resolution clause in a case of conflicting interests (if there are more successors they unanimously need to give the consent, but each of them can withdraw a previous consent).

Interestingly, what is regulated here is only the legitimate basis for the processing (consent), there is no reference to the exercise of data protection rights after the death of the data subject. In other words, in case of deceased data subjects the data controllers just need to ask for the written consent of the successors to continue to process those data (unless there are other legitimate bases – performance of a contract, public interest, legal obligation, legitimate interest, etc).

At the same time, it is not necessary a merely *unambiguous* consent (as provided in Article 7(a) of the Data Protection Directive for the general processing of personal data) or an *explicit* consent (as provided at Art. 8(2)(a) for the processing of special categories of data) but a *written* consent.

In other words, there is an over-protection of the deceased's personal data, since a stronger manifestation of consent (written) for processing such data is required than for processing sensitive data.

Another interesting aspect is the temporary nature of this protection: just 30 years. This is similar to copyright post-mortem protection (where economic rights are protected at least for 50 years after the death of the author).

The dispute resolution clause is similar to copyright law: successors must unanimously give their written consent for the processing of personal data, but at the same time each of them can withdraw consent.[63] Written consent is required as it is difficult to prove the unanimous consent of all successors in any other form.

The bereaved are not protected here unless they are legal successors of the deceased.

At the same time, the data subject has no binding tools for his/her post-mortem data protection (eg he/she cannot release any anticipated directives or delegate someone to manage his/her personal data after death).

---

[63] See, eg, the Italian case, Art. 10, co. 3, legge sul diritto d'autore: for works of joint authorship all authors can defend moral rights *autonomously*, but the work publication is permitted only *with the consent of all the authors.*

If we look at the three scenarios described above, the Estonian legal solution is probably more similar to quasi-propertisation: its deep analogies with IPRs; the protection of solely legal successors who can 'inherit' the management of personal data (and withdraw consent) and no specific value to the post-mortem autonomy of the data subject can exclude both a post-mortem privacy and a commodification scenario.

5.2. Italian Personal Data Protection Code: The Kantian Hybrid Model

Another emblematic example is the Italian Data Protection Code[64] (which has implemented Directive 95/46/EC). Article 9(3) states that the data subject's rights (right to access, right to rectification, right to object, right to erasure) 'where related to the personal data concerning a deceased, *may be exercised by any entity that is interested* therein or else acts to protect a data subject or for *family-related reasons* deserving protection'.

Thus, data protection rights can be exercised even after the death of the data subject by anyone that is interested.[65] This wide approach can be defined a 'Kantian' model. Indeed, Immanuel Kant stated that everyone is entitled to adopt the defence of the *bona fama defuncti* of the deceased and that this should be regarded as part of the 'Recht der Menschheit'.[66]

Interestingly, this wide approach can be found in burial cases in common law systems.[67]

The 'problem of the subject' (in particular, the problem of the interest) is thus 'solved' here by extending the group of legitimated subjects. In addition, it states that whoever is interested can act either 'to protect [the deceased] data subject [rights] or for family-related reasons deserving protection'. It means that the interests protected here are twofold: (a) the privacy interests of the deceased; and (b) any other family-related interests of the bereaved.

In other words, the Italian solutions can be a 'weak' example of post-mortem privacy protection (scenario 2 above) because the data subject cannot preventatively express his directives for the processing of his/her personal data after death.

---

[64] Codice in materia di protezione dei dati personali, d.lgs. 196/2003.

[65] Actually this wide approach has been implemented in practical terms in a narrow (estate-related) sense, see eg, Provvedimento del Garante per la Protezione dei Dati del 18 maggio 2017, Available at: www.garanteprivacy.it/web/guest/home/docweb/-/docweb-display/docweb/6623316 (last accessed 8 March 2018).

[66] Immanuel Kant, *Die Metaphysik der Sitten. Das Privatrecht*, (Frankfurt am Main, 1977; Erstdruck: Königsberg (Nicolovius) 1797), S. 388-406, 3. Available at: www.zeno.org/Philosophie/M/Kant,+Immanuel/Die+Metaphysik+der+Sitten/Erster+Teil.+Metaphysische+Anfangsgründe+der+Rechtslehre/1.+Teil.+Das+Privatrecht+vom+äußeren+Mein+und+Dein+überhaupt (last accessed 9 March 2018). See also Buitelaar, n 1 at 135.

[67] See the US Case, *Pierce v Proprietors of Swan Point Cemetery*, 10 RI 227, 235–44 (1872).

It is also an example of the quasi-propertisation model (scenario 3): family-related interests can perhaps also be economic interests related to the estate. In the Italian model, data protection rights are 'inherited' and they can thus be considered a (limited) form of management of digital assets (personal data of the deceased).

However, this model does not help if there is conflict between different 'interested' subjects.[68] At the same time, the will of the data subject has no value: he/she cannot release anticipated directive on the management of his/her personal data after death and cannot delegate a person to make decisions on his/her behalf.

5.3. Full Post-Mortem Privacy Solutions

(a) French Legislation: General or Specific Directives

The final and most interesting example is the new French law: 'Loi pour une République numérique'.[69]

Unlike the Estonian and Italian provisions, the French law is GDPR-compliant (or at least GDPR-aware). The protection of data of deceased data subjects is deeply regulated. Article 63(2) provides as follows:

'I. The rights in this section [data protection rights] end with the death of the data subject. However, they can be temporarily maintained in accordance with the following II and III.

II. Anyone can set directives for preservation, deletion and disclosure of his personal data after death. These directives are general or specific.

The directives concern all personal data relating to the data subject and may be registered with a digitally trusted third party certified by the CNIL [the French Data Protection Authority].

The general directives and the trusted third party where they are registered are recorded in a single register, whose terms and access are set by a decree of the Council of State.

The specific directives concern the processing of personal data explicitly mentioned in them. They are registered with data controllers. There must be a specific consent of the data subject and it can not result from the mere approval of general terms and conditions.

The general and specific directives define how the person intends that the rights mentioned in this section be exercised after his/her death. The respect of these directives is without prejudice to the provisions applicable to public records containing personal data.

---

[68] E. Kasket, Access to the Digital Self in Life and Death: Privacy in the Context of Posthumously Persistent Facebook Profiles, (2013), Scripted, 10(1), 7–18, 10 highlights how in the era of social networks, more people can be in conflict for our post-mortem privacy management (eg the heir, a friend, etc.).

[69] LOI n° 2016-1321 du 7 octobre 2016 pour une République numérique.

When the directives provide the communication of data which also contain personal data relating to third parties, this communication must be in accordance with this Act.

The data subject may amend or revoke its directives at any time.

The directives mentioned in the first paragraph of this II may designate a person responsible for their execution. When the data subject dies this designated person is entitled to acknowledge these directives and ask data controllers to execute them.

If no person has been designated or if the designated person dies (unless other alternatives are expressed in the directives), the heirs of the deceased data subject are entitled to acknowledge these directives and ask data controllers to execute these directives.

Terms of uses or services that contravene to these directives shall not apply.

In the absence of directives or otherwise mentioned in those directives, the heirs of the data subject can exercise after his/her death the rights mentioned in this section to the extent necessary:

– to the organisation and settlement of the deceased's estate. As such, the heirs can access the personal data processed to identify and obtain communication of relevant information for the liquidation and distribution of the estate. They may also receive communication of digital goods or data amounting to family memories, transmissible to the heirs;
– to communicate to the data controller that the data subject has died. As such, the heirs can close the accounts of deceased users, object to the continuation of personal data processing or ask for an update of these data.

The data controller must justify, upon request of the heirs and at no cost for them, that he/she has been compliant with the provisions of this section.

The disagreements between heirs on the exercise of rights under this paragraph are brought before the competent high court.'

This provision is probably one of the most advanced forms of personal data protection of deceased data subjects in Europe. It is certainly the most effective representation of scenario 3 (ie post-mortem privacy).

Here the 'problem of the subject' (ie the problem of the interest, the harm and the narrator)[70] is solved through advance directives through which the data subject can preventively express his/her decisions on the post-mortem processing of his/her personal data. At the same time, he/she can delegate a person that can actively exercise data protection rights (respecting the general or specific directives) on behalf of the deceased. In other words, there is a *preventive narration* through directives and a *post-mortem delegated executor of that narration*.[71]

Interestingly, the French solution provides also subsidiary details where the data subject does not set any directive; if he/she does not designate a specific person (or that person dies); and if there is no agreement among the successors.

---

[70] See, eg, Feinberg, n 35 at 34 ff. See also Section 2.2.
[71] See Floridi, n 13 at 549–566. Buitelaar, n 1 at 137.

Another interesting feature is the division between personal data and 'digital goods'. If the designated person can exercise data protection rights on behalf of the data subject (according to his/her directives), the heirs can 'receive communication of *digital goods* or data amounting to family memories, transmissible to the heirs', unless there is a directive that states otherwise.

Obviously, there is not a strict division between personal data and digital goods,[72] but the deceased can decide not only on his/her personal data but also on digital goods (heirs can have access to digital goods if there are no different directives from the deceased). It means that in the conflict between economic interests and personality interests around data, personality interests always prevail under French Law.

This is an absolute form of 'post-mortem privacy' scenario, where the protection of 'digital estate' is conditional to the will of the deceased person.

Actually, copyright law still applies: the heirs can exercise economic and moral rights for works authored by the deceased (including digital works).[73] Actually, the deceased can also indicate different people to exercise these rights.[74] Therefore, we should understand if the post-mortem privacy directives could be considered a valid form of testament for the transmission of IPRs. Another interpretative problem would be how to reconcile post-mortem privacy directives (eg where the deceased has delegated one person to manage 'digital goods' – valuable data also in terms of Intellectual Property) with a conflicting testament that regulates the transmission of the economic and/or moral rights of the author.

However, one may argue that just as for the succession of material goods, for digital goods, the freedom to testate should be limited to the protection of 'legitimate heirs'.[75] Actually, when 'goods' are inherently linked to the personality of the deceased person, freedom to testate is considered unlimited. This is the case in copyright law and post-mortem privacy protection.[76]

Lastly, we notice the role of 'terms of services' (ToS). In the lack of specific legal provisions, ToS were the only source for the regulation of data of deceased persons.[77] French law explicitly states that ToS cannot be considered a 'directive' (post-mortem directives need explicit consent); in case of conflict between ToS and directives, the directives always prevail.

---

[72] On the overlap between, eg, personal data and trade secrets see Malgieri, n 27 at 102–116.

[73] See Art. L121-1, Code de la Propriété Intellectuelle (Loi 92-597).

[74] See, eg, Art. L121-1 and L121-2, Code de la Propriété Intellectuelle: 'L'exercice peut être conféré à un tiers en vertu de dispositions testamentaires'.

[75] See, eg, Miriam Anderson; Esther Arroyo i Amayuelas (eds), *The Law of Succession: Testamentary Freedom: European Perspectives* (Groningen: Europa Law, 2011).

[76] See, eg, Arts L121-1 and L121-2, Code de la Propriété Intellectuelle and Art. 63(2), Loi sur la République Numérique.

[77] Harbinja, n 1 at 26–42.

(b) *The Catalan Legislation: The Case of Digital Testament*

In Cataluña a similar law has been approved for the regulation of post-mortem privacy (Llei 10/2017).[78]

This law, which has amended the Catalan Civil Code in the section dedicated to testaments and successions, is similar to Article 63 of the French Law but has several differences.

It is based on '*voluntats digitals*' (ie *digital 'wills'*) the equivalent of *directives* in French law.

Here, there is no distinction between general and specific digital wills. They should primarily contain the name of the 'executor',[79] but can also contain directives concerning the erasure of data, right to access, etc.

These 'voluntats digitals' are revocable at any time and can be released in a testament or registered in an Electronic Register, supervised by the public administration.

Where the person has not written any 'voluntats digitals' (neither in a testament nor in the Electronic Register) the ToS or contractual clauses between the data controller (eg Social Network Service) and the data subject apply: the heirs can exercise the right to access, erase and withdraw the consent, according to the ToS subscribed by the deceased. If the 'voluntats digitals' does not explicitly mention the right of the executor to access his or her personal data after his/her death, the executor (or the heir) needs judicial authorisation to access such data.

Unlike the French solution, testaments and digital wills are never in conflict: digital wills can be expressed in testaments. In addition, it is explicitly stipulated that if there is a valid testament, the 'voluntats digitals' previously registered in the Electronic Register have no value. In other words, here there is no possible conflict between the testamentary 'economic' transmission of digital goods and post-mortem privacy protection: the same source (the testament) should regulate both elements.[80]

Unlike the French law, the Catalan law explicitly recognises a binding value for ToS: if no 'voluntats digitals' have been released, all actions by the heirs must be respectful of the ToS.

A last element should be highlighted here: the 'voluntats digitals' is applicable not only when the person dies, but also when the person loses his or her mental capacity and mental autonomy due to a persistent illness or deficiency.[81] This last element can lead us to a comparison between 'digital directives' and the 'advance healthcare directive' which is discussed below.

---

[78] Llei 10/2017, del 27 de juny, de les voluntats digitals i de modificació dels llibres segon i quart del Codi civil de Catalunya.
[79] Art. 411-10, par. 1, Codi civil de Catalunya.
[80] Art. 411-10, Codi civil de Catalunya.
[81] Art. 222-2, Codi civil de Catalunya.

6. Exploiting the French (and Catalan) Case: Data as Digital Body

6.1. Advance Healthcare Directives Model

The post-mortem privacy model proposed by the French law and also the Catalan reference to persons without mental autonomy leads us to consider the analogy between digital directives and 'advance healthcare directives'.

Indeed, like post-mortem privacy directives and 'advance healthcare directives' are based on revocable and non-pecuniary anticipated wills, recorded in a national register. Both designate specific persons who should execute such directives.[82] In addition, they both regulate the 'body' of non-autonomous subjects (ie the physical body of a vegetative person[83] or the *digital body* of a deceased person).[84]

Indeed, (both decisional and information) privacy is based on three elements:

- an *autonomous will* that takes
- *decisions* on a
- *personal domain.*

Personal domain is a physical space (the body) or digital space (personal data) where human is sovereign.[85]

When a person dies, his/her personal domain persists online, but there is no more autonomous will, so no decisions can be taken.

Similarly, when a person loses his/her mental capacity or autonomy, her personal domain persists (eg her body, but also her personal data) but there is no more autonomous will and so no decisions can be taken.

The legal solution that is used for protecting decisional privacy of persons without mental capacity was the advance directives based on two elements: an anticipated expression of will and the designation of an 'executor'.[86] Interestingly, this model is adopted also for post-mortem privacy protection (see, eg, French Law).

6.2. Personal Data of Deceased Data-Subjects as Quasi-Property

The analogy between data of deceased persons and corpses can be found also in the US jurisprudence on 'quasi-property'.

---

[82] Roberto Andorno; Nikola Biller-Andorno and Susanne Brauer, 'Advance Health Care Directives: Towards a Coordinated European Policy?', *European Journal of Health Law*, 16, no 3 (2009): 207–227.

[83] For the similarity between vegetative persons and deceased data subjects see Buitelaar, n 1 at 137. See also Rodotà, n 60.

[84] See, similarly, Edwards and Harbinja, n 1 at 123 on the case of organ donation.

[85] See Feinberg, n 37 at 445–492. Buitelaar, n 1 at 134.

[86] See Andorno et al n 82 at 207–227.

As already mentioned, personal data inheritance is a limited form of (pecuniary and moral) transmission of personal data of the deceased person. How can this limited form of inheritance be regulated? Is it necessary to conceive a new legal concept? Perhaps, the US legal concept of 'quasi-property' may help.

Quasi-property is a hybrid concept elaborated in common law legal systems for a heterogeneous group of 'goods'. In particular, quasi-property is a form of 'relational', 'contextual' and 'liability-like' proprietary protection elaborated by the US jurisprudence to protect corpses, journalistic information, trade secrets, etc. In more specific terms, quasi-property is not an absolute right on goods, but a contextual protection against the illegitimate misappropriations of special categories of goods (intangible goods or non-commercial goods).[87]

Quasi-property was a concept originally conceived for corpses (eg in the state of Rhode Island)[88] and was recently proposed for privacy protection.[89] If we look at the jurisprudential reasoning about quasi-property on corpses we can find interesting reflections also for our discussion on the protection of the bereaved (spouse, descendants, friends) of the deceased data subjects.[90]

It has been argued that to the common law courts, corpses seemed deserving of some protection against mutilation to protect '*the emotional interests of the family and the next of kin*'. The very reason for protection was 'not treating corpses as ordinary ownable resources'.[91]

In more technical terms, quasi-property has thus emerged as the American common law term 'for the possessory or custodial interest that members of a deceased's family had over the deceased's mortal remains for purposes of disposal'.[92] The use of the term, and the development of a liability regime, were motivated by the impetus to protect the 'personal feelings' or 'sentiment and propriety' of the next of kin in having the corpse buried.[93]

It enabled relatives to recover *damages upon commercial and non-commercial interferences* and located the middle-level principle motivating this right in the idea of possessing the corpse.[94] Therefore, quasi-property is a right to protect bereaved/heirs/relatives acting in their own interests (eg against 'commercial interferences' (such as commercial exploitation of grief).

---

[87] See Balganesh, n 35 at 1891.

[88] Ibid. See, eg, the Supreme Court of Rhode Island cases, *Hackett v Hackett*, 26 A 42, 43-44 (RI 1893); *Gardner v Swan Point Cemetery*, 40 A 871 (RI 1898).

[89] Scholz, n 30 at 12.

[90] See eg Elizabeth Searcy, 'The Dead Belong to the Living: Disinterment and Custody of Dead Bodies in Nineteenth-Century America', *Journal of Social History*, 48, no 1, (2014): 112–134.

[91] See W.L. Prosser et al (eds), *Prosser and Keeton on the Law of Torts*, 5th edn (Michigan: West Group, 1984), § 12, at 63: '[T]he courts have talked of a somewhat dubious "property right" to the body, usually in the next of kin, which ... cannot be conveyed, can be used only for the one purpose of burial, and not only has no pecuniary value but is a source of liability for funeral expenses.'

[92] Balganesh, n 35 at 1891.

[93] *Hackett v Hackett*, 26 A 42, 43-44 (RI 1893). See also Balganesh, n 35 at 1891.

[94] See Balganesh, n 35 at 1891.

Interestingly, quasi-property has been considered useful also for protecting privacy[95] and personal data, as an alternative to commodification of data.[96] So, quasi-property can be easily used in the case of post-mortem data protection. Successors, heirs and relatives can inherit a (limited) property right on the deceased's personal data. Since these inherited goods are similar to a digital 'corpse' and represent the personality and identity of the deceased, it might not be possible for a full commodification of these data, while a 'quasi-propertisation' would be a good option.

In other words, quasi-property might be a good conceptual tool for protecting the interests of the bereaved *iure proprio* and not *iure successionis*.

As we have already said, quasi-property protection of the bereaved is consistent with the third scenario and there are interesting analogies with copyright law. At the same time, the analysis of the European Courts' jurisprudence has revealed that under the ECHR what is primarily protected is the interesst of the bereaved, more than the interests of the deceased. In other words, each national system should provide at least a form of protection for the bereaved (this can also be an indirect protection for the dignity and privacy of the deceased person, eg through a form of limited quasi-propertisation or personal data inheritance).

7. Conclusion

The protection of information privacy of deceased persons is an open issue both in practical and theoretical terms. The digital identity of data subjects persists after their biological death.

In principle, Section 2 describes the three different scenarios for the management of personal data of the deceased: (a) no protection; (b) a limited inheritance of such data in the form of quasi-propertisation; and (c) full post-mortem privacy.

The GDPR does not protect the data of deceased data subjects, but Sections 3 and 4 have revealed that in Europe, both in primary law and in secondary law there are unambiguous references to the post-mortem protection of personality (eg life-transcending copyright, inheritance of damages restoration, non-pecuniary testamentary clauses, etc). If we focus on data protection law, we can find heterogeneous examples.

Section 5 has conducted a comparison between different national post-mortem privacy solutions:

(1) the commodification or data freedom scenario is a reality in most EU countries, where there is no reference to personal data protection after death.

---

[95] Scholz, n 30 at 12.
[96] Malgieri, n 30 at 2–12.

If no protection is provided, data controllers might be free to process these data, thus violating not only the life-transcending informational self determination of the data subject, but also the interests of the bereaved, like their grief and memory (eg they might be the object of marketing grief exploitation or elusive data processing based on the genetic or health data of their deceased relatives).

(2) the quasi-propertisation or Intellectual Property-like scenario is based on a limited protection of data as inheritable good is a reality mostly in Estonia and Italy (addressed in Sections 5.1 and 5.2), where the protection is mostly based on successors. The European Court jurisprudence seems to reveal the importance of protecting the interests of the bereaved, as Section 3 reveals.

(3) The post-mortem privacy scenario is a reality in France and Cataluña (see Section 5.3) where each data subject can release some advance directives and delegate a trusted person to manage his or her post-mortem data processing.

Scenario 2 can find interesting examples in the common law debate around 'quasi-property', addressed in Section 7, a liability-like form of property on corpses (or on personal data). It would be the best protection for the bereaved interests.

At the same time, Scenario 3 can be implemented in practice through the model of Advance Healthcare directives, as explained in Section 6. Indeed, the 'problem of the subject' for post-mortem privacy can be solved through anticipated directives of the deceased subject and a designated person who will act on behalf of the deceased data subject.

In conclusion, an adequate way to cope with post-mortem privacy risks might be a combination of moral protection and limited economic protection: anticipated directives for the processing of personal data after death (protecting the deceased autonomy and dignity). If there are no pecuniary indications in the directive or if no directive has been released, a quasi-propertisation of such data should be to the advantage of the successors (thus protecting the interests of the bereaved).

This combination of scenarios can also encourage positive afterlife personal data transmission: if data commodification is prevented, but a controlled transmission is permitted, it would be also possible to enhance 'data philanthropy' or 'medical data donation' for research purposes, respecting both the will of the deceased person and his/her heirs (eg organ donations).[97]

Acknowledgement

The author is grateful to Edina Harbinja, Gianmarco Gori, Paul De Hert, Giovanni Comandé and the reviewers of this book and of Bileta 2018 for the insightful

---

[97] See the proposal of Jenny Krutzinna, Mariarosaria Taddeo and Luciano Floridi, 'Enabling Posthumous Medical Data Donation: A Plea for the Ethical Utilisation of Personal Health Data' (1 April 2018). Available at: https://ssrn.com/abstract=3177989.

comments on this draft chapter. The author is also grateful to the researchers who took part at the TILT Seminar in Tilburg dedicated to the draft of this chapter, in particular Bart van der Sloot, Silvia De Conca, Emre Bayamlioglu, Raphael Gellert, Tommaso Crepax, Aviva de Groot. The author is also grateful to the PhD students of the PhD Programme in Data Science at Scuola Normale Superiore di Pisa, where this chapter was also presented as a paper.

7

Massive Facial Databases and the GDPR
The New Data Protection Rules Applicable to Research

CATHERINE JASSERAND

Abstract

Several large-scale facial databases have been set up outside the EU for research purposes. They contain photographs crawled from the Internet or existing photo platforms. One of them, MegaFace, is of particular interest. Set up by a research team in the United States, the database contains 1 million faces of about 700,000 individuals. It has been released by the University of Washington to enhance the performance of face recognition algorithms. Researchers in Europe claimed that under the Data Protection Directive, they could not set up similar databases as they had to obtain individuals' consent to process their biometric data. With the application of the GDPR, they wonder whether they will be able to set up massive databases like MegaFace, and on which legal grounds they could rely. To address their concerns, the chapter uses MegaFace as a case study to determine the characteristics of similar databases. It analyses the nature of facial images extracted from an existing platform to be stored in a very large database. Based on the classification of facial images, the chapter investigates the different legal grounds under which researchers in the EU could process facial images for research purposes as well as the implementation of safeguards that are imposed to the processing for research purposes (GDPR, Article 89(1)). In conclusion, the chapter establishes that the GDPR does not require individuals' consent to process their facial images. However, the other grounds on which they could try to rely, 'legitimate interest' and 'public task' might not be so easily met. Last, researchers processing the images for research purposes are subject to the adoption of safeguards, which could be challenging to implement in practice.

Keywords

GDPR, personal data, biometric data, consent, facial image, facial recognition, scientific research exception, sensitive data

1. Introduction

At various conferences in the field of biometrics, several scientists claimed that under their national data protection regime, based on the previous Data Protection Directive, they were not able to process biometric data without obtaining the consent of individuals to whom the data relate.[1] Yet, they also raised awareness about the existence of large-scale face databases set up outside the EU, obviously without individuals' consent. This is the case of the MegaFace database set up by the University of Washington,[2] the Casia WebFace constituted by the Chinese Academy of Sciences,[3] or the Labeled Faces in the Wild (LFW) database created by the University of Massachusetts. MegaFace is different from the other databases as, to date, it is the largest public face database to use photographs of 'ordinary' individuals, (ie, not public figures or celebrities). The database is composed of 1 million photos originating from 690.000 individuals.[4] By comparison, Casia WebFace and LFW contain a relatively low number of individuals (called 'identities') and are limited to photos of celebrities. As noted by Nech and others, the pictures of celebrities might bias the performance of matching algorithms as they are most likely taken by professional photographers and are of very high quality.[5]

This chapter attempts to address the concerns expressed by scientists, in particular whether they can set up databases similar to MegaFace under the rules of the General Data Protection Regulation (GDPR).[6] The possible application of the GDPR to MegaFace or any other foreign face database falls outside the scope of this chapter. Following this introduction, Section I presents the characteristics of MegaFace and briefly describes the notion of 'research'. Section II analyses the

[1] Discussions held with scientists at the EAB (European Association of Biometrics) Research Project Conference of 2017 and the IBM Conference of 2017 on Preserving Privacy in an age of increased surveillance – A Biometrics Perspective.

[2] Ira Kemelmacher-Schilzerman et al., 'The MegaFace Benchmark: 1 Million Faces for Recognition at Scale', IEEE Conference on Computer Vision and Pattern Recognition (CVPR) (2016).

[3] Gary B. Huang et al. 'Labeled Faces in the Wild: A Database for Studying Face Recognition in Unconstrained Environments'. Available at: http://vis-www.cs.umass.edu/lfw/lfw.pdf' [all weblinks were last accessed on 15 May 2018].

[4] Private databases such as DeepFace (Facebook) or FaceNet (Google) contain photographs of several million individuals (more than 10 million individuals for FaceNet); however, those databases are not open for research.

[5] Aaron Nech et al., 'Level Playing Field for Million Scale of Face Recognition' (2017): 2. Available at https://arxiv.org/abs/1705.00393.

[6] European Parliament and Council Regulation 2016/679 of 27 April 2016 on the protection of individuals with regard to the processing of personal data and of the free movement of such data and repealing Directive 95/46/EC (General Data Protection Regulation) [2016] OJ L119/1.

legal nature of a facial image and assesses whether and when it constitutes a type of sensitive data. Section III addresses the issue of the legal grounds under which the processing of facial images for research purposes is permitted. Finally, Section IV focuses on the implementation of the safeguards required to process personal data for research purposes and questions the feasibility of pseudonymising facial images.

2. Background

This section presents the characteristics of the database of reference as well as the research purposes for which the facial images are processed.

2.1. Facial Images Crawled from an Existing Database

The facial images contained in MegaFace have not been crawled from the Internet but from an existing photo database set up by Yahoo: the Yahoo! Flickr images database, (the YFCC100 M Dataset).[7] The Yahoo database is a public database of photos and videos. It is composed of a majority of photos, 99.2 million, which do not all portray individuals. Each picture is associated with a 'Flickr identifier', which contains metadata about the photo including the Flickr user who created the file. To assemble MegaFace, researchers have extracted the photos from the Yahoo! Database and matched them, as much as possible, with Flickr accounts.[8] Then based on the photos collected, they have created 690 000 'unique identities', also called 'unique subjects'.[9] All the photos included in MegaFace have been released under a Creative Commons licence, which depending on its terms of use, allows or not to re-use the images under the condition that their author is credited. The issue of the re-use of a photograph portraying an individual is not only a copyright issue (linked to the authorship of the photograph), but also a major data protection issue. The authorisation given by the photographer to re-use the photos he or she uploaded should not be interpreted as the consent given by the individuals portrayed in the photos to re-use their images. This issue will be briefly discussed later in the chapter.[10]

The facial images available on Flickr are valuable for face recognition research: most of them have been taken with 'unconstrained pose, expression, lighting and posture'.[11] They are of different qualities (amateur or professional) and

---

[7] 'Yahoo Flickr Creative Commons 100 Million Dataset', as cited in Bart Thomee et al., ' YFCC100M: the New Data in Multimedia Research', Communications of the ACM, 59, no 2 (2016).

[8] And the understanding of the author of this chapter.

[9] The term 'unique identities' is used in Kemelmacher-Schilzerman, 'The MegaFace Benchmark'; although not defined, it relates to 'single individual'.

[10] Although an exhaustive discussion on the relationship between copyright rules and data protection issues goes beyond the scope of this chapter.

[11] Kemelmacher-Schlizerman, n 2 at 2.

different resolutions (scanned, digital). They also represent faces from different angles (face, profile), and individuals of different origins (such as different skin colours), portrayed with various accessories (glasses, hats, etc.) and in different environments (including group photos).[12]

The purpose of the MegaFace dataset is to allow researchers to train the performance of their identification and verification algorithms with a very large set of images. To test the matching algorithms, researchers compare facial images contained in MegaFace (called 'gallery') with other images contained in two different existing databases (called 'probe sets'): the FG-NET dataset (face-ageing database) and the FaceScrub dataset (celebrity face database).[13] Face verification algorithms establish whether a given pair of facial images belongs to the same person; whereas face identification algorithms match a given probe photo (from FaceScrub or FG-NET) with another image of the same person in the gallery (ie, MegaFace). As a consequence, the identification or verification of an individual results from the output of the algorithms (ie, from the comparison processing between two or several sets of facial images). This clarification is useful to discuss the regulatory definition of 'biometric data' in the next section.

According to the first results shared by the research team, algorithms that have performed very well on a small scale (eg, 95%, have dropped to 35% with the MegaFace dataset).[14] The benefits of a database like MegaFace from a scientific research perspective are obvious. However, as it will be discussed in the following sections, it might not be that simple for EU researchers to set up a similar database under the GDPR regime.

2.2. Facial Images Processed for Research Purposes Only

The MegaFace dataset has been constituted and can only be used for non-commercial research and educational purposes. Its scope of use is more limited than the notion of 'scientific research' under the GDPR.

As described in the GDPR, the notion is broad enough to include research pursued by universities and institutes in the field of face recognition as well as commercial research.[15] Recital 159 of the GDPR specifies, in particular, the following:

> (...) For the purposes of this Regulation, the processing of personal data for scientific research purposes should be interpreted in a broad manner including, for example,

---

[12] See examples of pictures at: http://megaface.cs.washington.edu/dataset/subset.html.

[13] Kemelmacher-Schlizerman, n 2 at 2.

[14] The example given is based on the algorithms used in the 'Labeled Faces in the Wild' database, which contains 13,000 images of 5,000 individuals), see Kemelmacher-Schlizerman, n 2 at 2.

[15] On the breadth of the definition of research and the research exemption applicable to sensitive data in the GDPR, see Kärt Pormeister, 'Genetic Data and the Research Exemption: Is the GDPR Going Too Far?' *International Data Privacy Law*, 7, no 2 (2017): 138.

technological development and demonstration, fundamental research, applied research and privately funded research.

As will be addressed in the other sections of the chapter, specific data protection processing rules apply to research purposes, which thus includes commercial research.

3. Classification of Facial Images

A facial image is the image of an individual's face, which is static (a photograph) or moving (video).[16] A face contains distinctive characteristics, which allows the recognition of an individual. From a biometric perspective, recognition is either the (biometric) identification or the verification of an individual.[17] The two processes consist of comparing two or more facial images together, either to establish who an individual is (identification) or confirm his or her identity (verification).[18] The processing of facial images measures the most salient features of a face to establish similarities or differences between at least two sets of facial images (or templates).[19]

In the context of the training of a face database such as MegaFace, identification means 'determining the identity of a face image';[20] whereas verification consists in 'verifying if two images of faces are the same person'.[21]

With the introduction of a definition of biometric data in the GDPR, there is a need to question the status of facial images as personal data as well as biometric data.

3.1. Facial Image as Personal Data?

To qualify as personal data, a facial image must relate to 'an identified or identifiable individual'.[22] In Opinion 02/2012, the Article 29 Working Party

---

[16] For a detailed definition, see Els Kindt, *Privacy and Data Protection Issues of Biometric Applications: A Comparative Legal Analysis* (Dordrecht: Springer, 2013), 156.

[17] From a scientific perspective, recognition covers identification and verification, see ISO/IEC 2387-37 on the harmonized biometric vocabulary, definition of 'biometric recognition', under term 37-01-03; the definition given by the A29WP is inaccurate as according to the A29WP, face recognition also covers the categorisation function (i.e., the use of biometric data for age, gender classification) see A29WP, 'Opinion 02/2012 on facial recognition in online and mobile services', 00727/12/EN WP 192 (2012): 2.

[18] For further details on facial recognition, see Anil Jain et al., 'Chapter 1, Introduction' in *Introduction to Biometrics*, edited by Anil Jain et al. (New York: Springer, 2011), 10–12; Patrick Grother et al., 'Face Recognition Standards', in *Encyclopedia of Biometrics*, edited by Stan Z Li (Dordrecht: Springer, 2015), 468.

[19] For further details on facial recognition, see Anil Jain et al., 'Chapter 3, Face Recognition' n 18.

[20] Aaron Nech et al., 'Level Playing Field for Million Scale of Face Recognition' (2017): 1. Available at: https://arxiv.org/abs/1705.00393.

[21] Ibid at 1.

[22] GDPR, Art 4(1).

(the A29WP)[23] stated that when an image used for facial recognition 'contains an individual's face which is visible and allows for that individual to be identified it would be considered personal data'.[24] However, the identification of an individual depends 'on the quality of the image or the particular viewpoint'. The A29WP considered that images with individuals too far away or with blurred faces would most likely not be regarded as personal data.[25] The classification of facial images as personal data is no longer a matter for debate.[26] More interesting is the discussion on the nature of facial images as biometric data or sensitive data.

3.2. Facial Images as Biometric Data?

In the GDPR, biometric data are defined as:

> personal data resulting from specific technical processing relating to the physical, physiological or behavioural characteristics of a natural person, which allow or confirm the unique identification of that natural person, such as facial images or dactyloscopic data (Article 4(14)).

(a) Characteristics of Biometric Personal Data

The definition is composed of four elements. To qualify as 'biometric data', the data at stake first need to be personal data (ie, relate to an identifiable or identified individual).[27] Thus, the data cannot be biometric data without first reaching the threshold of identifiability.

Second, they result from a 'specific technical processing.' The GDPR does not specify the meaning of this processing, but one could imagine that it encompasses the different technical phases of biometric recognition: from the acquisition of a biometric image to its transformation into a biometric template and its comparison with another or several set(s) of biometric data.[28] As long as they comply with the criteria of the definition, both a biometric image and a biometric template could fall under the definition of biometric data.

Third, the definition refers to the biometric characteristics, 'physical, physiological or behavioural', which are transformed during the process into data.

---

[23] The Article 29 Data Protection Working Party is an independent body advising the European Commission on data protection matters; replaced by the European Data Protection Board set up by the GDPR; however the opinions of Art 29 on the interpretation of the Data Protection Directive are still relevant.

[24] A29WP, 'Opinion 02/2012': 4.

[25] Ibid.

[26] For more details on the establishment of facial images as personal data, see analysis made by Kindt, n 16 at 160–162.

[27] GDPR, Art 4(1).

[28] See, eg, A29WP, 'Opinion 02/2012': 2.

The last criterion 'allow or confirm the unique identification' is ambiguous on two counts. First, it is not clear to what it refers: to the results of the technical processing? To the quality of the biometric characteristics? To the function of biometric data? The structure of the sentence does not shed light on these issues.[29] However, following recital 51 of the GDPR, photographs need to be '*processed*' to qualify as biometric data.[30] Second, there is significant uncertainty concerning the meaning of 'unique identification.'

(b) Meaning(s) of 'Unique Identification'

From the wording of recital 51, one understands that facial images processed for either biometric identification purposes (referred to as 'unique identification') or for verification (referred to as 'authentication') are biometric data.[31] But this reading is inconsistent with Article 4(14) of the GDPR. In that provision, the two functions are defined as 'allowing the unique identification' and 'confirming the unique identification'. Thus, logically, in that definition, 'unique identification' cannot refer to biometric identification. Instead, it is suggested to approach the notion from a data protection perspective. As such, it would not replace the biometric identification function, but refer instead to the highest threshold of identification, where individuals are identified (i.e. singled out) thanks to their 'unique' biometric attributes.

Under the previous data protection regime, Kotschy made a similar analysis. She considered that 'biometric data (photos, fingerprints, DNA) or personal identification numbers (PINs) ... would achieve truly *unique identification*.'[32] To confirm this interpretation, one could observe that the phrase 'unique identification' is not only found in the definition of 'biometric data', it is also used in relation to health data, which includes 'a number, symbol or particular assigned to a natural person to *uniquely identify* the natural person for health purposes'.[33] Besides, in Opinion 4/2007 on the concept of personal data, A29WP analysed the particular nature of biometric data and observed their 'unique link' to an individual to allow his or her identification.[34]

Following this analysis, 'unique identification' might not refer to biometric identification, but to an individual's identity instead. As such, the processing of

---

[29] As interpreted by Els Kindt, 'Having Yes, Using No? About the New Legal Regime for Biometric Data', *Computer Law and Security Review* (2018): 1–16.

[30] GDPR, recital 51 reads as follows: 'The processing of photographs should not systematically be considered to be processing of special categories of personal data as <u>they are covered by the definition of biometric data only when processed through a specific means allowing the unique identification or authentication of a natural personal</u>' [emphasis added].

[31] It is quite common to use authentication as a synonym of verification, even if the biometric community does not support such a use; see ISO/IEC 2382-37, term 37.01.03.

[32] Waltraut Kotschy, 'Article 8, Directive 95/46/EC' in *Concise European IT Law*, edited by Alfred Bullesbach et al. (Netherlands: Kluwer Law International 2010) 35.

[33] GDPR, recital 35 (emphasis added).

[34] A29WP, 'Opinion 4/2007 on the concept of personal data', WP 136 (2012): 8–9.

biometric data would allow either the establishment of an individual's identity (described as 'allowing the unique identification') or the confirmation of his or her identity (described as 'confirming the unique identification').

(c) Biometric Sensitive Data?

Such an interpretation also has an impact on the biometric data that fall within the scope of sensitive data. According to Article 9(1) of the GDPR, the processing of '*biometric data for the purpose of uniquely identifying a natural person*' is sensitive processing. As analysed by Kindt, only the 'comparison processing' of biometric data might fall within the scope of biometric sensitive data.[35] An individual is identified – either for biometric identification or verification purposes – when his or her biometric data are positively matched with previously recorded biometric data. This results from the output of a biometric recognition algorithm that measures similarities or dissimilarities between sets of data. Thus, it is the comparison between biometric data that establishes or confirms an individual's identity. It seems that Article 9(1) of the GDPR is quite restrictive and would not apply to the extraction of biometric data from a platform or to their storage in a facial database. However, if the facial images stored in the database reveal sensitive information, they could still fall into the category of sensitive data. For instance, depending on the background of a picture (eg specific location, specific event), accessories (eg headscarves, kippah), a facial image could reveal 'religious beliefs', 'political opinions', 'ethnic origin', 'health' condition or 'sexual orientation'. All these pieces of information constitute sensitive data.[36]

Based on this analysis, the next section analyses the rules applicable to the processing of personal and sensitive data.

4. Legal Grounds for Lawful Processing

EU researchers are concerned that they will be required to obtain individuals' consent to set up face databases for research purposes. This would prevent them from creating databases on the same scale as MegaFace. Which other legal grounds could they invoke?

4.1. Initial or Further Processing?

First of all, what is the nature of the processing at stake? Is crawling an existing platform an initial collection of personal data or further processing of those data? The answer is crucial to determine the rules applicable to the processing.

---

[35] See Kindt, n 29 at 1–16.
[36] GDPR, Art 9(1).

How is the notion of 'further processing' approached in the GDPR? From the data controller's perspective? Or from the data subject's perspective? In the first case, the researchers are not the initial data controllers as they did not collect the personal data first hand. However, from their perspective, the use of personal data is an initial collection. By contrast, in the second case, the re-use of his or her personal data either by the initial data controller or a secondary controller constitutes further processing. These two different views conflict. Does the GDPR shed light on this issue?

The GDPR does not define 'collection' or 'further processing'. But Article 5(1)(b) of the GDPR sets out the principle of purpose limitation. It requires personal data to be collected for a specific purpose, and not to be further used in a way that is incompatible with that purpose. It also specifies that further processing for scientific research purposes is presumed compatible with the initial purpose of collection. In that regard, the GDPR does not determine whether this rule applies to the initial data controller or a subsequent one.

The interpretation of the A29WP on the principle of purpose limitation brings some insights. In Opinion 03/2013 published under the previous data protection regime, the Working Party analysed a series of cases to assess the compatibility between purposes. Several of these relate to further processing carried out by subsequent controllers. In particular, the Working Party investigated scenarios where personal data had been transferred to third parties to be further used for unrelated purposes.[37] It also analysed the situation where an Internet crawler application had extracted some information from a website to create a database. In these different scenarios, the A29WP did not approach the processing from the data controller's perspective, but from the data subject's one. It indeed considered these processing operations as 'further processing' of the personal data initially collected for a different purpose.

Following the A29WP's reasoning, this chapter argues that crawling a platform to collect facial images and store them in a face database is further processing.

4.2. Legal Grounds Applicable to Facial Images as Personal Data

It is assumed that the facial images selected for the research face database allow the individuals to be identified. Without this characteristic, the face database has no value. That being said, facial images are a particular type of personal data. A facial image contains the identifying features necessary to identify (i.e. distinguish or single out)[38] an individual. The image does not need to be linked to an individual's record, file or civil identity.

---

[37] A29WP, 'Opinion 03/2013 on purpose limitation', WP 2013 (2013): 1–70; see the example of smart meter data collected by energy companies and used by tax authorities or law enforcement authorities for unrelated purposes, example 20, 69.

[38] A29WP, 'Opinion 4/2007'; GDPR, recital 26.

As analysed, the extraction of facial images from an existing platform and their storage are further processing operations. As such, rules on further processing should apply. According to Article 6(4) of the GDPR, further processing of personal information can be based on the data subject's consent or on European Union or national law, which is necessary and proportionate to safeguard various public interests.[39] Alternatively, if the further processing is deemed compatible with the original purpose of collection, it can be based on the same legal basis as the initial processing.[40]

(a) Consent?

Apparently, the facial images in the scenario under review are processed without individuals' consent: millions of facial images have been crawled from an existing platform. However, in the case of MegaFace, the researchers acknowledged having only re-used photographs that were released under a Creative Commons licence. Those allow the *copyright owners* of protected works (such as photographs) to decide how others can re-use their work. On this specific issue, one can observe that first, the US researchers have not disclosed the type of licences under which the photographs processed have been released.[41] In fact, there are six types of Creative Commons licences. Some are very permissive and allow re-use for any purposes; whereas others are very restrictive and do not allow any further use.[42] Second and this is a crucial point, an agreement to re-use the photographs from an intellectual property perspective does not (necessarily) mean consent from a data protection perspective. In particular, the individuals who have consented to the re-use of the photos might not be those portrayed in the photos. The database most likely contains selfies, but there are no means to verify whether the copyright holders are the individuals represented in the photos. Thus, relying on Creative Commons licences to re-use photographs does not seem to be the appropriate approach from a data protection perspective.[43]

(b) Compatible Further Processing for Research Purposes?

According to Article 5(1)(b) of the GDPR, further processing for specific purposes (including scientific research purposes) should not be considered incompatible with the initial purpose of collection, provided that the data controller implements

---

[39] GDPR, Art 23.

[40] Ibid, recital 50; Article 6(4)(a)–(e) describing different factors to take into account to perform a 'test of compatibility' between the purposes of processing.

[41] Kemelmacher-Schlizerman, n 2.

[42] See https://creativecommons.org/licenses/.

[43] But further research on the notion of consent from both an intellectual property perspective and a data protection perspective would need to be done to draw more specific conclusions, in particular in the case of 'selfies' (ie, self-portraits where the photographer and the data subject are the same individual).

some safeguards, as defined in Article 89(1) of the GDPR.[44] The purpose of these safeguards is to compensate for the change of purposes.[45] As specified in Recital 50 of the GDPR, further processing of personal data does not need a separate legal basis. It should rely on the legal ground of the initial data collection.

But what happens when the (legal) basis under which personal data have been initially collected is unknown or is not based on an EU or Member State law? This question is not rhetorical. In the case under consideration, facial images are extracted from an existing photo platform set up by a foreign entity (ie, Yahoo) incorporated in the United States. Article 3(2) of the GDPR provides that foreign entity can be subject to the GDPR rules through their establishment within the EU or if they offer products or services to data subjects there.[46] But, the issue at stake is not the application of the GDPR to a foreign entity, but the identification of the initial ground for data collection.

In such a case, should the further processing not be considered initial processing under EU law? If so, the legal grounds for lawful processing, as set out in Article 6(1) of the GDPR should be addressed.[47] Besides individuals' consent,[48] Article 6(1) offers five legal grounds. Among them, the legitimate interests of the data controller and the performance of a public task might constitute alternative grounds to consent.[49]

(c) Based on Legitimate Interests?

Following Article 6(1)(f) of the GDPR, the processing which 'is necessary for the purposes of the legitimate interests pursued by the controller or by a third party' to whom the data are disclosed is lawful, provided that the fundamental rights or interests of the data subjects are not overridden.

As analysed by the A29WP under the previous data protection regime, the assessment is based on a case-by-case analysis.[50] The test is composed of three elements.

---

[44] GDPR, Art 5(1)(b) reads as follows: 'Further processing for archiving purposes in the public interest, scientific or historical research purposes or statistical purposes shall, following Article 89(1), not be considered to be incompatible with the initial purposes.'

[45] See A29WP, 'Opinion 03/2013 on purpose limitation' (2013), 00569/13/EN XP 203: 27.

[46] As well as if they monitor data subjects in the EU (such as profiling).

[47] The first sentence of the provision reads as follows: '[p]rocessing shall be lawful only if and to the extent that at least one of the following applies' [then follows the list of legal grounds]; the six legal grounds for processing are: the individual's consent; the necessity to process the personal data for the performance of a contract; the necessity to comply with a legal obligation to which the controller is subject; the necessity to protect the vital interests of an individual; the necessity to perform a task carried out in the public interest; and the necessity to process the personal data for the legitimate interests of either the controller or a third-party.

[48] GDPR, Art 6(1)(a).

[49] Respectively GDPR, Arts 6(1)(f) and 6(1)(e).

[50] A29WP, 'Opinion 06/2014 on the notion of legitimate interests of the data controller under Article 7 of Directive 95/46/EC', 844/14/EN WP 217 (2014); GDPR, recital 47.

The first relates to the existence of a legitimate interest. There is no list of such interests in the GDPR, but several recitals illustrate what a 'legitimate interest' might be: the prevention of fraud, direct marketing, network and info security, or reporting of possible criminal acts.[51] Scientific research is not mentioned. However, the A29WP found that the 'interest of carrying out scientific research' was one of the 'interests [that] may be compelling and beneficial to society at large' and could constitute a 'legitimate interest'.[52] In the case at stake, the question is whether the training of biometric recognition algorithms on facial images crawled from a platform is in the interest of society at large. There is an argument to support innovation and the competitiveness of European researchers. But, the two other components of the test need also to be satisfied.

Second, is the purpose of the processing necessary? The processing also needs to be proportionate and adequate to its purpose (i.e. there should be no 'less invasive means' available).[53] In the case at stake, researchers need millions of faces to test their algorithms. If they train them with fewer images – obtained with individuals' consent – the performance of the algorithm is affected. As witnessed by the creators of MegaFace, algorithms that performed well on a small scale performed very badly at a very large scale.[54] Obtaining as many facial images as possible seems to be the only option to do research on the algorithms themselves.

Third, the interests of the researchers need to be balanced against individuals' rights and freedoms. The objective of this last element is to determine the impact of the processing on data subjects. Following Recital 47 of the GDPR, the test should take into account 'the expectations of data subjects based on their relationship with the controller'. The test is based on the expectations of a reasonable person, not of a specific individual.[55] Thus, would a reasonable individual expect his or her pictures published on a photo platform to be subsequently used for research on facial recognition? Would a reasonable individual object to such processing? The answers to these questions depend on several elements. One could argue that, even if the terms and conditions of the photo platform provide that the pictures might be shared with third parties, individuals would not expect their photos to be re-used for research purposes.[56] It could also be claimed that among the users of the photo platform, some have agreed to share their pictures for any further use.[57] Those individuals could, therefore, expect any re-use to include research purposes. An essential element to take into account is the source of the data. As found by the European Court of Justice (ECJ) in the *Rigas* case,

---

[51] Several examples can be found in recitals 47, 48, 49 and 50 of the Regulation.

[52] A29WP, 'Opinion 06/2014': 24.

[53] Ibid at 29.

[54] As explained in Section 1, see n 14.

[55] A29WP, 'Opinion 06/2014': 33.

[56] Besides the issue of the validity of such terms and conditions.

[57] As observed earlier, some pictures might have been released under a very permissive Creative Commons licence; however, there is no certainty that the account user giving permission to re-use content is the individual portrayed in the pictures.

'the seriousness of the infringement of the data subject's fundamental right result-ing from the processing can vary depending on the possibility of accessing the data at issue in public sources'.[58] The facial images at stake in the scenario under review are crawled from a platform or a website. Does it make them publicly available? This is less than certain.

Last but not least, researchers carrying out research for a public university may not be able to invoke the 'legitimate interest' ground.[59] Public authorities 'in the performance of their tasks' are indeed excluded from the scope of Article 6(1)(f) of the GDPR. Their exclusion is not based on their nature (a public body) but on the 'nature of their task'.[60] A discussion can ensue on the task of research performed by public universities. Is it considered a public task? The answer is left at the national level. Some universities might also have a hybrid status, depending on the func-tions they perform. For instance, teaching could be considered as a public task, whereas promotion would be viewed as a commercial task. Thus, the situation will vary from one Member State to another.

(d) Based on the Performance of a Task Carried Out in the Public Interest?

Another ground may be available to the researchers, under the condition that the processing is 'necessary for the performance of a task in the public interest'.[61] The definition of the task is not defined in the GDPR but should set out in law at national level.[62] As described above, the issue revolves around the classification of research as a public function. The processing also needs to meet the conditions of the test of necessity.[63] As noted by the A29WP, this legal ground 'has potentially a very broad scope of application, which pleads for a strict interpretation and a clear identification, on a case by case basis, of the public interest at stake and the official authority justifying the processing'.[64]

Again, the application of this legal ground depends on its implementation at national level. In the United Kingdom, for instance, the Information

---

[58] Case C-13/16 *Valsts policijas Rīgas regiona pārvaldes Kārtības policijas pārvalde* v *Rīgas pašvaldības SIA 'Rīgas satiksme*, ECLI:EU:C:2017:336, para 32.

[59] See Art 6(1)(f), as well as recital 47 which provides the following: 'given that it is for the legislator to provide by law for the legal basis for public authorities to process personal data, that legal basis should not apply to the processing by public authorities in the performance of their tasks.'

[60] As analysed by ICO, Guide to the General Data Protection Regulation, section 'What is the 'legitimate interests' basis?'. Available at: https://ico.org.uk/for-organisations/guide-to-the-general-data-protection-regulation-gdpr/lawful-basis-for-processing/legitimate-interests/.

[61] 'or in the exercise of official authority vested in the controller', as provided by Art 6(1)(e).

[62] The ECJ specified the notion of 'task in the public interest' in *Puskar* v *Finance Directorate of the Slovak Republic*, Case C-73/16, ECLI:EU:C:2017:725, paras 106–108.

[63] Interpreted as a test of proportionality, see Case C-73/16, paras 111–113.

[64] Article 29 Data Protection Working Party, 'Opinion 06/2014 on the notion of legitimate interests of the data controller under Art 7 of Directive 95/46/EC', WP 217 (2014): 22.

Commissioner's Office is in favour of including universities in the list of public authorities and considering their 'research and teaching functions' as public tasks.[65] But the issue is not yet settled.[66]

4.3. Legal Grounds Applicable to the Processing of Facial Images as Sensitive Data

Following the analysis made in Section 2, the facial images stored in the database are not processed for 'the purpose of uniquely identifying an individual'.[67] As a consequence, they are not classified as biometric sensitive data. Among these images, those that still reveal sensitive information must be processed according to Article 9(1) of the GDPR.

(a) Compatible Further Processing for Research Purposes?

Based on Article 5(1)(b) of the GDPR, sensitive data further processed for scientific research purposes benefit from a presumption of compatibility between purposes. Their further processing is thus permitted, provided however that the safeguards defined in Article 89(1) of the GDPR, are in place. As a consequence, no separate legal ground should be necessary.[68] However, as already analysed, the legal basis under which the facial images were initially collected is most likely not known or based on foreign law. It is difficult to conclude that the initial processing was carried out under a lawful ground. Instead, it is suggested to rely on the legal grounds defined for the processing of sensitive data.

(b) Processing of Sensitive Data

Following Article 9(1) of the GDPR, the processing of sensitive data is prohibited unless an exception applies. Those exceptions are restrictively enumerated in Article 9(2). The first exception is the explicit consent of individuals, which is excluded. Obtaining the consent of hundreds of thousands of individuals portrayed in photographs is an impossible and impractical task.

---

[65] See debates on the UK Data Protection Bill. Available at: https://publications.parliament.uk/pa/cm201719/cmpublic/DataProtection/PBC153_Combiened_1-2_13_03_2018.pdf.

[66] Even if some universities recommend that their researchers process personal data for research purposes under the 'public task' ground (GDPR, Art 6(1)(e)) and sensitive data under the 'research exemption' (GDPR, Art 9(1)(j)). Available at: www.information-compliance.admin.cam.ac.uk/files/gdpr_preliminary_guidance_on_academic_research_final.pdf.

[67] They are processed to 'uniquely identify' individuals only when the recognition algorithms are run: their output leads to a match (or non-match) between two sets or several sets of facial images. It is through that matching processing that individuals are identified. See Section 2.

[68] GDPR, recital 50.

The second exception that could be invoked allows the processing of sensitive data that have been 'manifestly made public by the data subject.'[69] As the sensitive data at stake have been published by the data subject himself or herself, they do not deserve the same level of protection as other sensitive data. However, as observed by Kotschy in her interpretation of the previous regime, *'making information public* requires a deliberate act by the data subject, disclosing the data to the public.'[70] Of course, it could be objected that the data subjects themselves have not released all the photos themselves and that the photographers might have released some instead. Still, the question would deserve some attention as the database contains a variety of photos. Those include pictures taken by others, 'selfies' (i.e. self-portraits)[71] as well as pictures taken without the knowledge of portrayed individuals (such as a group photo). The researchers are reprocessing pictures contained in the database and may not be able to distinguish those that have been made available by the data subjects themselves from the other ones. As assessed by the A29WP, the notion 'has to be interpreted to imply that the data subject was aware that the respective data will be publicly available which means to everyone … In case of doubt, a narrow interpretation should be applied, as the assumption is that the data subject has voluntarily given up the special protection for sensitive data by making them available to the public …'[72] It is therefore doubtful that the EU researchers could rely on this legal ground.

Finally, the best option left to researchers is the research exception described in Article 9(2)(j) of the GDPR. The processing of sensitive data for research purposes is allowed, provided that:

> [It] is necessary for archiving purposes in the public interest, scientific or historical research purposes or statistical purposes in accordance with Article 89(1) based on Union or Member State law which shall be proportionate to the aim pursued, respect the essence of the right to data protection and provide for a suitable and specific measures to safeguard the fundamental rights and the interests of the data subject.

This provision calls for several remarks. The research exception is subject to the implementation of safeguards (Article 89(1) GDPR) and a legal basis (complying with the specific requirements of proportionality, respect of the essence of the rights, suitable and specific measures). Second, the research exception applies without individuals' consent. The 'explicit consent' exception and the research exception are both listed as exemptions from the prohibition to process sensitive data. However, Article 9(4)of the GDPR provides that Member States can adopt stricter requirements for the processing of specific types of sensitive personal data.

---

[69] GDPR, Art 9(2)(e).

[70] See analysis made by Kotschy under the Data Protection Directive, n 32 at 62.

[71] Kemelmacher-Schilzerman, n 1.

[72] A29WP, Opinion on some key issues of the Law Enforcement Directive (EU 2016/680), 29 November 2017, WP 258, 10.

Those data are genetic data, biometric data, and health-related data.[73] As analysed by Portmeister, Member States could rely on this provision to require individuals' explicit consent to process their sensitive data. And this requirement could apply to the processing of any type of biometric data as the provision is broadly worded and does not refer to biometric data processed to 'uniquely identify individuals'. In conclusion, it is not excluded that some Member States would introduce the obligation to obtain individuals' explicit consent to process their biometric data, such as their facial images for a facial research database.[74] This would echo the concerns expressed by scientists.[75]

Finally, if facial images are processed for research purposes, the safeguards defined in Article 89(1) of the GDPR must also be implemented.

5. Safeguards Imposed to Research Purposes

This section describes Article 89(1) of the GDPR and analyses more specifically the pseudonymisation of facial images.[76] It explores the feasibility of pseudonymising facial images while preserving their data utility for biometric recognition purposes.

5.1. Article 89(1) of the GDPR

Article 89(1) applies to the initial and further processing of personal and sensitive data for research purposes. The compliance with this obligation is expressly reiterated in the context of the further processing of personal data[77] and in the application of the research exception for the processing of sensitive data.[78] But this provision imposes a general obligation to adopt safeguards when personal data are processed (and *a fortiori* further processed) for research purposes.

The safeguards described in Article 89(1) of the GDPR should 'ensure that technical and organisational measures are in place'. Among the examples of measures that could be adopted by data controllers, the provision mentions the

---

[73] GDPR, Art 9(4) provides that 'Member States may maintain or introduce further conditions, including limitations, with regard to the processing of genetic data, biometric data or data concerning health.'

[74] Depending on the interpretation of the notion of 'biometric data'.

[75] This chapter results from discussions held with computer scientists at two different conferences on biometrics (the EAB Research Project Conference in 2017 as well as the IBM Conference of 2017 on Preserving Privacy in an age of increased surveillance – A Biometrics Perspective).

[76] Following GDPR, Art 89(1), other types of safeguards could be implemented for the processing of facial images. Those measures could include organisational and operational measures (data protection by design), data minimisation, encryption, etc.

[77] GDPR, Art 5(1)(b).

[78] Ibid, Art 9(2)(j).

pseudonymisation of personal data. In the context of an initial data collection, pseudonymisation is not required but strongly encouraged.[79] By contrast, in case of further processing, personal data should at least be pseudonymised, whenever feasible.[80] This suggests that personal data used for research could also be anonymised. Recital 156 specifies that, before being able to further use personal data for research, the data controller needs to assess whether he or she can de-identify the personal data at stake.[81]

Pseudonymised data are a new category of personal data introduced in the GDPR. Their processing ensures that 'personal data can no longer be attributed to an individual' because the identifying information is kept separately.[82] This means that the pseudonymised data are 'not attributed to an identified or identifiable individual'.[83] However, the process is not irreversible. Recital 26 of the GDPR clarifies that 'personal data which have undergone pseudonymisation, which could be attributed to a natural person by the use of additional information should be considered to be information on an identifiable natural person'. Anonymised or anonymous data, by contrast, are not personal data. They are described as 'information which does not relate to an identified or identifiable natural person or to personal data rendered anonymous in such a manner that the data subject is not or no longer identifiable'.[84]

5.2. Pseudonymisation of Facial Images?

In the case of facial images used for scientific purposes, the requirement of de-identification or pseudonymisation seems challenging to implement. As established, facial images do not need additional information to single out an individual. Thus, pseudonymisation, as applied to facial images, does not mean 'delinking' an image from its associated data. Instead, it means hiding, altering or removing the content of a facial image. But this aim conflicts with that of biometric recognition. Any face database needs to rely on the identifiability of individuals to be

---

[79] Ibid, Art 89(1) states: 'Those measures [i.e., technical and organisational measures] *may* include pseudonymisation provided that those purposes can be fulfilled in that manner.' (emphasis added)

[80] GDPR, Art 89(1) states: 'Where those purposes [i.e., scientific research purposes] can be fulfilled by further processing which does not permit or no longer permits the identification of data subjects, those purposes shall be fulfilled in that manner', to be read together with Recital 156 which provides that: 'the further processing of personal data for archiving purposes in the public interest, scientific or historical research purposes or statistical purposes is to be carried out when the controller has assessed the feasibility to fulfil those purposes by processing data which do not permit or no longer permit the identification of data subjects, provided that appropriate safeguards exist (such as, pseudonymisation of the data.'

[81] GDPR, recital 156 states that the further use of personal data 'is to be carried out when the controller has assessed the feasibility to fulfil those purposes by processing data which do not permit or no longer permit the identification of data subjects, provided that appropriate safeguards exist (such as, pseudonymisation of the data).'

[82] Ibid, Art 4(5).

[83] Ibid.

[84] Ibid, recital 26.

usable. Otherwise, facial recognition algorithms cannot be tested. So, is it possible to de-identify (or pseudonymise) a facial image from a data protection perspective while preserving the utility of the de-identified photos for biometric recognition purposes?

From a data protection perspective, one could consider the technique of face blurring or face pixelisation. This technique is commonly used for images extracted from CCTV. If such altered photos seem satisfactory from a data protection perspective, they are most likely unusable for a face recognition research purpose. As rightly assessed by Othman and Ross, previous research on face de-identification has proven its utility from a privacy perspective but has not permitted to keep its utility for face recognition because of the quality of the images obtained.[85]

Other researchers have introduced different methods to 'de-identify' facial images.[86] For example, Bitouk et al. have introduced a 'face swapping method' by replacing the face of an individual with another one close in appearance and extracted from a very large-scale face library based on Internet images.[87] Othman and Ross have also proposed a method based on the decomposition of a facial image into two different facial images.[88] The initial image can only be recomposed when the two separate facial images are reunited. In their illustration of the technique, the authors show the photo of an individual, who after the acquisition of his biometric features, is split into separate images of two other individuals. In the example at stake, the photo is decomposed into a picture of the actors Will Smith and Denzel Washington. It is true that, in the absence of a combination of the two images, no one can guess the identity of the third person. But if the method preserves the biometric features for biometric recognition, it does not offer the solution required by the GDPR. The two photos produced when the biometric data are stored relate to two identifiable individuals. The method developed only provides a solution for storing or sharing the facial images.

From a data protection perspective, the scientific solutions proposed by Bitouk as well as Othman and Ross do not pseudonymise the facial images. Both methods might be useful to store biometric data by obfuscating the real identity of the individuals. However, both methods use different facial images to replace the original ones. It can be argued that the facial images used in replacement (Bitouk) or decomposition (Othman and Ross) still relate to (other) identifiable individuals. One could wonder whether the requirement to pseudonymise personal data for scientific research (ie, removing any identifying information while preserving

---

[85] Asem Othman and Arun Ross, 'De-Identifying Biometric Images by Decomposition and Mixing', in *Biometric Security*, edited by David Check Ling Ngo, Andrew Beng Jin Teoh and Jiankun Hu (Newcastle -upon-Tyne: Cambridge Scholars Publishing, 2015).

[86] The author of this chapter does not have exhaustive knowledge about research conducted in face recognition but uses scientific literature for illustration purposes.

[87] Dmitri Bitouk et al, 'Face Swapping: Automatically Replacing Faces in Photographs', *ACM Transactions on Graphics*, 27, no 3, Art 39 (2008): 3.

[88] Othman and Ross, n 85 at 170.

data utility) is reachable. The review of the scientific literature is far from being exhaustive, but there is no quick answer to the question. Research must be carried out, from both data protection and a technological perspective, to determine whether a threshold of identifiability or de-identification exists.

6. Conclusion

Analysing the creation of a massive face database, such as MegaFace, this chapter has shed lights on several issues relating to the processing of facial images for research purposes within the EU.

The chapter discussed the specific nature of facial images and the conditions under which they could fall within the category of biometric data. Contrary to other types of personal data, facial images contain identifying information that is sufficient in itself to identify – single out – an individual. As analysed in this chapter, facial images become biometric data when they are processed for biometric identification or verification purposes. Yet the creation of a face database based on an existing platform does not qualify as such. The facial images stored in the face database are regarded as ordinary personal data, or sensitive data only if they reveal sensitive information about individuals.

The classification of facial images in different categories of personal data has an impact on the legal grounds for processing. A database similar to MegaFace would crawl facial images from an existing platform or the Internet. The facial images are thus processed for a purpose different than their original purpose of collection. As such, rules on further processing should apply. Following Article 5(1)(b) of the GDPR, further processing of personal data for research purposes should be deemed compatible with the initial purpose of processing and falls under the same legal basis as the initial processing. But what happens if this initial (legal) basis is unknown or based on foreign law? Should the further processing be viewed as initial processing under the GDPR to process personal data under a specific legal ground? If so, a distinction needs to be made between the facial images qualifying as personal data and the facial images qualifying as sensitive data.

In the first case, besides consent, researchers could try to rely on the 'legitimate interests' ground as scientific research might be a justification for processing. As for public Universities, they should be excluded from the scope of 'legitimate interests', depending on the nature of their functions. Instead, they could try to rely on the 'performance of a task in the public interest' ground, under the condition that their research activities are set out as such in a national law.

In the second case, where facial images qualify as sensitive data, the most promising ground for researchers is the research exception introduced in Article 9(2)(j) of the GDPR. However, there might be drawbacks. The research exception imposes several requirements on the controllers, including the adoption of safeguards. One of the measures suggested is the pseudonymisation of personal data before their use for research purposes. In the case of facial images, it is the content of the image that needs to be pseudonymised to prevent identification and not its link to metadata. Yet pseudonymising a facial image while keeping the usability of the image for facial recognition purposes might prove challenging. The issue cannot be solely approached from a data protection perspective. It calls for a technological solution that will satisfy both the legal and technical requirements.

8

Europol Regulation, US and Data Protection

JOANNA KULESZA

Abstract

The chapter covers key privacy and data protection challenges affecting the area of freedom, security and justice (AFSJ), in particular the 2016 Europol Regulation. It focuses on the privacy impact of the agency's strategic and operational agreements with third parties. The author argues that the comprehensive European privacy regulations, including the GDPR, continuously fail to address crucial threats to personal data protection resulting from the ineffective safeguards installed in Europol's third-party agreements.

Keywords

ACFJ Europol, data transfers, police cooperation, third parties

1. Introduction

Criminal policy making and law enforcement have always been the exclusive competence of states. This has remained the case regardless of the enhanced, comprehensive economic and social cooperation within the EU throughout its development. Any single EU agency or institution with a comprehensive investigative or enforcement authority would in its essence contradict fundamental principles of sovereignty with regard to criminal law authority of EU members. This remains to be the case also after the 2009 Lisbon Treaty and the departure from the concept of the three pillars of the European Union. Yet the international war on terrorism, terrorist uses of the Internet and cybercrime as well as globalised, organised international crime combined with forever new technologies supporting investigative efforts of law enforcement result in the urging need to enhance coordination of criminal investigations. Responding to this challenge the EU established a system of 'multilevel governance' aimed at providing effective coordination in criminal law matters among Member States.[1]

2. Police Cooperation within the Area of Freedom, Security and Justice (AFSJ)

Europol, the largest EU agency supporting law enforcement since late 1990s, is a key element of this system. While it holds no own authority to investigate, it has been designated to support national authorities in combating serious transnational crime. This support is offered to EU Member States through a network of contact points, usually located within national police agencies. It is also offered to third countries, on reciprocal bases, following on individual cooperation agreements. These agreements are separate from any other contracts concluded by the EU for the purposes of economic, political or social cooperation. They target fighting serious transnational crimes, with cooperation performed through a network of contact points appointed by third parties. Third parties involved in Europol's activities include: (a) European states with a well-established EU cooperation, such as Switzerland or Liechtenstein; (b) eastern and central EU candidate or partner countries, including Moldova and Serbia; and (c) non-European states, such as the United States or Canada.[2] Some of Europol's cooperation agreements refer to personal data exchanges directly, usually detailing categories of shared data and cooperation mechanisms, limiting the scope of individuals authorised to access these particular categories of information and other measures necessary to ensure privacy protection. They usually indicate national laws as specific privacy protection frameworks. Both these contracting models: those that include specific personal data provisions (operational agreements) and those that don't (strategic agreements) suffer from significant human rights deficiencies. Failing to identify specific personal data protection provisions in the operational agreements makes the cooperating parties and individuals concerned rely only on national laws, which may be significantly different from European standards, difficult to enforce from outside state territory or simply ineffective. Although the contracts themselves provide for framework privacy provisions, they heavily rely on national privacy protection laws and regulations, which are not subject to the usual adequacy decision within the EU and as such likely to fall short of EU's data protection standards. While third-party cooperation has been subject to debate and critique, the 2016 Europol Regulation together with the GDPR were perceived

---

[1] Cristina Blasi Casagran, *Global Data Protection* in the *Field of Law Enforcement*: An *EU Perspective* Routledge research in *EU Law* (Abingdon: Routledge, 2017), 9–10.

[2] For a complete list of Europol's third-party agreements see: www.europol.europa.eu/partners-agreements, last accessed February 2018.

as a mean to amend the existing faults. Unfortunately, they fail to meet this goal, as the data protection provisions in third-party agreements have not been addressed or amended by new EU regulations.

3. Europol's New Data Protection Framework

The new Europol Regulation, adopted by the European Parliament on 11 May 2016, came into force in all Member States on 1 May 2017.[3] It substantially reformed Europol's powers, while preserving its key role in supporting Member States with 'preventing and combating serious crime, terrorism and forms of crime which affect a common interest subject to Union policy'.[4] Several of Europol's tasks involved the processing of personal data. It is particularly vital when the agency collects, stores, processes, analyses and shares information, including criminal intelligence information or provides information and analytical support to member states in connection with major international events. Data processing is also of an issue when the Europol prepares threat assessments, strategic and operational analyses and general situation reports or supports member states' cross-border information exchange activities, operations and investigations, including through joint investigation teams, by providing operational, technical and financial support. Europol also supports Member States in preventing and combating particular categories of crimes facilitated, promoted or committed using the Internet.[5] In particular, Europol works together with Member States by making referrals of internet content, by which such crimes are facilitated, promoted or committed. Such referrals are made directly to online service providers and are expected to result in their 'voluntary consideration of the compatibility of the referred internet content with their own terms and conditions'.[6] This last category of activities raises significant privacy and freedom of expression concerns, discussed in detail below. Europol is also entitled to process information provided by member states, EU bodies and private parties. The agency can retrieve and process information, including personal data, which are publicly available, including on the internet.[7] This last provision implicitly includes data that was disclosed in violation of applicable privacy laws for Europol processing and was not attended to despite the original suggestion from the EDPS.[8]

---

[3] Regulation (EU) 2016/794 of the European Parliament and of the Council of 11 May 2016 on the European Union Agency for Law Enforcement Cooperation (Europol) and replacing and repealing Council Decisions 2009/371/JHA, 2009/934/JHA, 2009/935/JHA, 2009/936/JHA and 2009/968/JHA (Europol Regulation).

[4] Ibid, Art 3.

[5] An inclusive list of such crimes is attached to the Regulation in Annex I.

[6] See n 3, Art 4.

[7] Ibid, Art 17.

[8] Opinion of the European Data Protection Supervisor on the Proposal for a Regulation of the European Parliament and of the Council on the European Union Agency for Law enforcement

Europol can process personal data for purposes of:

(a) cross-checking aimed at identifying connections or other relevant links between information related to persons who are suspected of having committed or taken part in a criminal offence in respect of which Europol is competent, or who have been convicted of such an offence or regarding whom there are factual indications or reasonable grounds to believe that they will commit criminal offences in respect of which Europol is competent;
(b) analyses of a strategic or thematic nature;
(c) operational analyses; and
(d) facilitating the exchange of information between Member States, Europol, other EU bodies, third countries and international organisations.

Data processing for operational analysis is subjected to specific safeguards that include identifying the purpose of processing, detailing categories of personal data and of data subjects, processing participants, the duration of storage and conditions for access, transfer and use of the data concerned as well as the need to inform Europol's Management Board and the EDPS. Also, personal data may only be collected and processed for a specified operational analysis within a particular project. If the same personal data may be relevant for another operational analysis project, further processing of that personal data is only permitted insofar as such further processing is necessary and proportionate. Any processing of personal data must be duly documented; the documentation needs to be made available upon request to the EDPS and the appointed data protection officer.[9]

Data collected to meet Europol's tasks includes personal details, economic and financial information, identification means (including biometrics) as well as behavioural data, enabling subject profiling.[10] In addition, Europol may transfer, under specific restrictions, personal data to EU bodies, as long as those are necessary for the performance of the agency's own tasks or those of the recipient EU body.[11] The agency can also transfer data to non-member countries and international organisations, under additional safeguards and specific agreements or a decision of the Commission.[12] Personal data in Europol's disposition can also be exchanged with private parties, yet the introduced limitations to such transfers are comprehensive and likely to be effective. Data may only be exchanged given that it is received via a Europol national contact point, in accordance with national law or through a contact point of a third country or an international organisation with which Europol has concluded a cooperation agreement allowing for the exchange of personal data. Alternatively, data can be provided through the authority of a third country or an international organisation which is the subject of an adequacy

Cooperation and Training (Europol) and repealing Decisions 2009/371/JHA and 2005/681/JHA. Available at: https://edps.europa.eu/sites/edp/files/publication/13-05-31_europol_en.pdf, para. 119, p. 25.
  [9] See n 3, Art 18.
  [10] Ibid, Annex II.
  [11] Ibid, Art 24.
  [12] Ibid, Art 25.

decision by the Commission. In cases where Europol receives personal data directly from private parties and where the national unit, contact point or authority concerned cannot be identified, Europol may process those personal data, but only to identify the relevant authority or body. Subsequently, personal data kept by Europol is to be forwarded immediately to the national unit, contact point or authority concerned and deleted unless the unit, point or authority resubmits it in accordance with Europol procedures within four months of the transfer. Europol is to ensure by technical means that, during that period, the data in question is not accessible for processing for any other purpose. Also, when Europol takes part in a joint investigation team,[13] it may receive personal data directly from a private party which declares it is legally allowed to transmit in accordance with the applicable law.[14] There is no other mechanism to ensure the legality of such data nor is Europol obliged to act with due diligence when accepting it. These provisions implicitly allow Europol to deal with data that might have been obtained or shared contrary to applicable laws and frees it from any obligation to verify the legality of processed data.

4. Third-Party Data Transfers – Still Looking for a 'Safe Harbour'

As indicated above, Europol regulatory framework allows for enhanced cooperation with third states – countries outside the European Union – based on cooperation agreements. While most of those agreements suffer from similar faults – remote and likely ineffective domestic data protection mechanism, practical difficulties with access to justice by non-resident data subjects, long or unlimited data retention periods – it is the Europol cooperation with the United States of America that has been subject to most enhanced critique, reflective of the persisting, fundamentally different approaches to privacy and personal data protection on both sides of the Atlantic.[15]

The Europol–US cooperation is based on two documents: the more recent US–Europol Supplemental Agreement on the Exchange of Personal Data and Related Information (20 December 2002) (Supplemental Agreement) and the original Agreement between the United States of America and Europol (6 December 2001) (2001 Agreement). The Supplemental Agreement, despite dating back over 15 years, is the most recent development in the long-lasting European cooperation on criminal matters with the US. The fundamental rights challenges posed by the Supplemental Agreement are a direct consequence of divergent approaches to privacy and personal data protection in the two respective countries.

---

[13] Ibid, Art 5.
[14] Ibid, Art 26.
[15] For a detailed discussion on Europol–US cooperation see: Saskia Hufnagel and Carole McCartney, *Trust in International Police and Justice Cooperation* (London: Bloomsbury Publishing, 2017) 145 ff.

The original 2001 Agreement set the threshold for personal data protection at the level identified in the original Data Protection Convention and the relevant Recommendation on the use of personal data in the police sector now both replaced by the Europol Regulation of 2016.[16] The main concern with the Europol–US personal data exchange, just as with the majority of third parties cooperating with the agency based on international agreements, is a significantly different level of protection that has not been verified by the Commission as adequate.[17] The legal framework in question remains unchanged despite the departure from the inefficient Safe Harbour Agreement and despite the persisting critique of its successor – the Privacy Shield compromise. The concerns, originated by different approaches to privacy and personal protection, are enhanced by the lack of transparency on data being exchanged and in issues with enforcing European privacy guarantees beyond EU borders. Particular concerns refer to:

- data access;
- access to justice and due process in enforcing data subject rights;
- purpose limitation (data shared with the US agencies can be processed for the purposes for which it was requested, not those for which it was originally collected); and
- data retention (period and effective supervision).

The Supplemental Agreement complements the provision of the original Europol-US strategic agreement of 2001. They both target the cooperation between the parties on:

(a)   unlawful drug trafficking;
(b)   trafficking in nuclear and radioactive substances;
(c)   illegal immigrant smuggling;
(d)   trade in human beings;
(e)   motor vehicle crime;
(f)   crimes committed or likely to be committed in the course of terrorist activities against life, limb, personal freedom or property; and
(g)   forgery of money and means of payment,

as well as to illegal money laundering activities in connection with these forms of crime or specific manifestations thereof and related criminal offences.[18] These all provide for a legitimate aim for limiting individual rights and liberties. Although the restrictions on privacy are introduced in the Supplemental Agreement and thus pass the test of being provided for by law and foreseeable ('accessible to the

---

[16] P. De Hert and B. De Schutter, 'International Transfers of Data in the Field of JHA: The Lessons of Europol, PNR and Swift' in *Justice, Liberty, Security, New Challenges for EU external Relations*, edited by B. Martenczuk and S. Van Thiel (Brussels: VUB Press, 2008) 319–320.

[17] See, eg, Celine Cocq and Francesca Galli, 'Europol's Relations with External Actors including States and Organisations' in *Trust in International Police and Justice Cooperation*, n 15 at 147.

[18] See n 3, Art 1.

person concerned and foreseeable as to [their] effects'),[19] the scope and period of data access, data retention, purpose limitation and due process call into question the extent to which this is so.

As per the 2001 agreement all data that 'relate' to criminal offences listed above are subject to exchange and cooperation, but the details of such 'related' offences are not described within specific cooperation agreements, leaving room for interpretation by both: Europol agents and national points-of-contact. Interpretation of the 'relationship' between the crime and the data is left to no supervision or granted any institutional support (such as that from the EDPS) and is left to Europol's discretion. Consequentially its interpretation can lead to extensive data sharing and result in disproportionate privacy intrusions. If a genuine assessment of the US level of data protection was to be performed, the existing legal instruments would need to be amended in order to effectively comply with European data protection principles.[20] For the Supplemental Agreement such assessment would likely imply a thorough evaluation of the US data protection framework and a legitimate adequacy decision resulting in a legal framework that the existing 'Privacy Shield' arrangement still fails to provide. While such thorough analysis is still lacking, the reference to the very wording of the reviewed documents, if only in the section cited above,[21] relies upon individual interpretation of the 'relation' between the data and the offence. As observed by Casagran, the Supplemental Agreement 'does not correspond with the majority of operational agreements later adopted by Europol'.[22] Effectively, the purpose limitation principle can be circumvented by a prior consent from the providing party, enabling for a further transmission of information. Also, there is no clear time limit for the data retention period, while individuals have no right to correct or delete their data.[23] Furthermore, the provisions of the Supplemental Agreement fail to show compliance with Articles 7 and 8 of the Charter of the Fundamental Rights of the EU where they fail to specify the details of transferring personal data to the United States – derogations may not be applicable to systematic, massive or structural transfers. The provisions of the Supplemental Agreement also fail to show compliance with Directive 2016/680 Article 4, paragraph 1, lit. B which states that:

> 'further processing of personal data shall be limited to the purposes for which the information was communicated which is indifferent with the purpose for which the information was collected.[24]

---

[19] *Rotaru v Romania*, 28341/95, para 52. Available at: https://hudoc.echr.coe.int/eng#{%22itemid%22:[%22001-58586%22].

[20] See: E. De Busser 'The Adequacy of EU-US Partnership' in *European Data Protection: In Good Health?* edited by Serge Gutwirth, Ronald Leenes, Paul de Hert and Yves Poullet (Dordrecht: Springer 2012) 199.

[21] See n 3, Art 1.

[22] See Casagran, n 1 at 152.

[23] Ibid.

[24] Directive (EU) 2016/680 of the European Parliament and of the Council of 27 April 2016 on the protection of natural persons with regard to the processing of personal data by competent authorities

The treaty fails to reflect the distinction between the purpose for which the data was collected and one for which it was communicated.

The Supplemental Agreement does not contain provisions establishing the scope and/or extent for the retention of data, while also lacking any independent review of its implementation. This fails to meet the prerequisite identified in *MM v the United Kingdom*, 13 November 2012, 24029/07, paragraph 206, where the ECtHR highlighted 'the absence of a clear legislative framework for the collection and storage of data, and the lack of clarity as to the scope, extent and restrictions of the common-law powers of the police to retain and disclose caution data' as ground to violation of the fundamental rights guarantees enshrined in the ECHR. It further referred to the absence of any mechanism for independent review of a decision to retain or disclose data as complimentary to that violation. By failing to identify the maximum time limit for the implementation of the agreement, failing to set the maximum timeframe for processing data, the Supplemental Agreement also fails to meet the principle referred to in ECtHR case *MK v France* judgment of 18 April 2013, 19522/09, paragraph 45, where the Court noted that 'while the retention of information stored was limited in time, it extended to 25 years and emphasised that 'the chances of deletion requests succeeding are at best hypothetical' since an expensively long period of retention (25 years in the given case) was in practice 'tantamount to indefinite retention'.

The Supplemental Agreement provides for a broad scope of data processing and transfer, failing to identify the detailed personal scope of subjects targeted by the agreement, geographical scope and material scope, relying only on the definition of personal data, defined as all 'data relating to an identified or identifiable natural person, whereas an identifiable person is one who can be identified, directly or indirectly, in particular by reference to an identification number or to one or more factors specific to his physical, physiological, mental, economic, cultural or social identity'.[25] The agreement fails to refer to supervision or additional safeguards in case of data transfer. It simply states that transmitted data shall be limited to the purposes for which they were communicated, which does not mean that they are limited to the purpose for which they were collected. It also lacks a clear geographical scope for its implementation, again implicitly indicating the relevance of all personal data in disposition of either party. It lacks a review mechanism of the agreement, stipulating only termination of the treaty by the mutual consent of both parties. With all the faults discussed above the Europol–US bilateral cooperation follows suit of all the well-known shortcomings in the EU–US privacy and personal data protection policies.

---

for the purposes of the prevention, investigation, detection or prosecution of criminal offences or the execution of criminal penalties, and on the free movement of such data, and repealing Council Framework Decision 2008/977/JHA; OJ L 119, 4.5.2016, p. 89–131.

[25] Art 2, Supplemental Agreement.

5. Fundamental Rights Assessment of the Europol Third-Party Data Protection Standards

While overall the Europol Regulation reflects EU standards of personal data protection quite well, its new comprehensive procedure, based on one central-ised database, poses a direct threat to the individual right to privacy, primarily due to the vast scope of collected data and the broad mandate to process them in various ways, including sharing with third parties. Threat posed directly by this broad mandate and the broad scope of collected data reflects concerns confirmed (eg in CJEU case law) where the court confirmed in that any processing or stor-ing of personal data should per se be perceived as a potential illegitimate invasion of privacy.[26] The very volume of data collected, stored and processed by Europol, can be viewed as a potential privacy threat, enhanced by the variety and flexibility of processing purposes and operations, just to mention data storing, analysing, profiling as well as allowing for non-EU transfers with regard to all data, including sensitive ones. Such a broad mandate, giving ground to a rich variety of poten-tial privacy intrusions, calls for a detailed and well-justified measures explaining the necessity and proportionality of such restriction put on individual rights.[27] Meeting the prerequisite of proportionality means the need to set clear and precise rules for protecting the collected data from 'risk of abuse' and the threat of 'unlaw-ful access to and use of that data.'[28] Europol has been requested to compile data previously managed within separate databases, allowing it to operate based on one set of authorised purposes for their processing, which has been subject to academic critique as based on purely technical, rather than legal prerequisites.[29] Coudert argues that this 'silo-based approach' aims to make profiling easier, quite against the GDPR policy line and 'in direct contradiction with the normative goals of purpose limitation'. She rightfully argues that this comprehensive database and the rules for its operation would call for a Privacy Impact Assessment and suggests the use of use of metadata to provide for sufficient privacy protection.[30] She also rightfully notes that the purposes for Europol's use of data as stated in

---

[26] *Michael Schwarz v Stadt Bochum*, CJEU, case C-291/12, paras 24–25; *Digital Rights Ireland*, CJEU, joined cases C-293/12 and C-594/12, paras 29–30; *Leander v Sweden*.

[27] The criteria of 'necessity and proportionality' are well established in CJEU case law. See *Digital Rights Ireland*, n 26, para 38, referring to CFREU, Arts 7, 8 and 52 (1), where the court confirmed that 'any limitation on the exercise of the rights and freedoms laid down by the Charter must be provided for by law, respect their essence and, subject to the principle of proportionality, limitations may be made to those rights and freedoms only if they are necessary and genuinely meet objectives of general interest recognised by the Union or the need to protect the rights and freedoms of others'.

[28] See *Schwarz* n 26 at para 46.

[29] Fanny Coudert, *The Europol Regulation and Purpose Limitation: From the "Silo-Based Approach" to ... What Exactly?(Part II)*, KU Leueven Centre for IT & IP Law. Available at: www.law.kuleuven.be/citip/blog/the-europol-regulation-and-purpose-limitation-from-the-silo-based-approach-to-what-exactly-part-ii/.

[30] Ibid.

Article 18 of the Regulation, are too broad to meet the criteria of a legitimate limitation of individual privacy. Moreover, Article 19 fails to identify the purpose or criteria for allowing data to be used for other purposes, failing to meet the principles of necessity and proportionality. This vast category of purposes impacts also the compliance with other principles regarding the quality of data such as data minimisation and data accuracy.[31]

Other issues that raise concern include:

- *Collection and preservation of electronic evidence*[32]
  Europol supports Member States in preventing and combating crimes carried out using internet, including the referral of internet content to the service providers to verify the compliance with terms and conditions; it fails to set criteria for disabling access to such content or, more significantly, deletion by the service provider, provoking threats to both: individual privacy of those whose data is being processed and then deleted as well as freedom of expression of those whose content is being deleted, but also to due process in cases concerning such 'flagged' data, threatening the loss of crucial evidence hastily deleted by the service provider, 'informed' by Europol.

- *Exchange of personal data with private parties*
  Europol may receive personal data from private parties and is obliged to process them only to identify the competent authorities and to delete them within four months. Moreover it can receive personal data from private party in order to process such data for the collection of electronic evidence.[33] Europol may also transfer personal data to private parties when the transfer of personal data which are publicly available is strictly necessary for the collection of electronic evidence and the transfer concerns an individual and specific case and 'no fundamental rights and freedoms of the data subjects concerned override the public interest necessitating the transfer in the case at hand'.[34] All those exchanges fail to fall under any judicial supervision and may therefore serve as grounds for processing personal data without legitimate legal aim.

- *Effective supervision of Europol activities by European Parliament and Member States*[35]
  Article 51 of the Europol Regulation introduces the joint parliamentary scrutiny over the agency's tasks. The scrutiny of Europol's activities shall be carried out by the European Parliament together with national parliaments. This constitutes a specialised Joint Parliamentary Scrutiny Group (JPSG) established together by the national parliaments and the competent committee of the European Parliament. The EDPS has been authorised to supervise the

---

[31] Ibid.
[32] See n 3, Art 4, para 1(m).
[33] Ibid.
[34] Ibid, Art 26.
[35] Ibid, Arts 51 and 52.

EDPS, but the JPSG in its present form fails to provide any state supervision over the actions performed by the agency.

Also, the exchange of personal data with private parties[36] in connection with the collection of electronic evidence[37] raises significant privacy concerns. As already observed, Europol can receive publicly available personal data from private parties directly, without the help of national police or reference to national law, as was the case with the previous Europol regime. Under the Regulation a company must declare that it is legally allowed to transfer that data and the transfer 'concerns an individual and specific case', while 'no fundamental rights and freedoms of the data subjects concerned override the public interest necessitating the transfer'.[38]

Not only is content being removed at the discretion of the service provider, but it is also depriving the potential victims of the right to have evidence in their case properly stored and assessed with due regard to applicable law. The Regulation introduces specific obligations for Europol's EU Internet Referral Unit (IRU), which is designated to identify and report content 'incompatible' with the terms of service of 'online service providers'.[39] Upon identification of such content IRU signals it to the service provider for its 'voluntary consideration'.[40]

Electronic evidence of potential crimes is not preserved (rather promptly removed by private parties – internet service providers), but it also causes an undesired chilling effect: Europol's 'information sharing' results in potentially criminal content being removed without any legal consequence to its originator or propagator. Moreover, the legal basis for such removal or disabling access is uncertain – if the activity constitutes a criminal act according to national law, national law enforcement should preserve it as evidence for further prosecution. If it is indeed not illegal, it should neither be of interest to Interpol nor subject to content removal. As such, it fails to meet the test of legality of any restriction upon one's right to free speech.[41] Provisions of Article 4 fail to address the need to ensure due process for implementing restrictions on free speech. They also fail to ensure security of evidence collected in a potentially criminal case, instead resulting in potentially criminal content being taken offline without any liability or responsibility for its authors, publishers or propagators. The collection and preservation of electronic evidence also fails to address the issue of personal data, disregarding

---

[36] Ibid Art 26.

[37] Ibid Art 4(1)m.

[38] Ibid, Art 26. For a detailed discussion see: J. McNamee, M. Fernández Pérez, Fundamental Rights and Digital Platforms in the European Union: A Suggested Way Forward in: *Platform Regulations: How Platforms Are Regulated and How They Regulate Us* edited by L. Belli, N. Zingales (FGV Direito: Rio, 2017), 99–115.

[39] Ibid.

[40] Europol (2016) 'Europol Internet Referral Unit One Year On'.26 July 2016. Available at: www. europol.europa.eu/newsroom/news/europol-internet-referral-unit-one-year.

[41] See also: EDRI (2016), Europol: Non-transparent Cooperation with IT Companies, 18 May 2016. Available at: https://edri.org/europol-non-transparent-cooperation-with-it-companies.

the fact that some of the tagged content might in fact be personal data, failing to meet the proportionality principles as it instigates private parties' interference with the right to free speech and communication. It is therefore possible to imagine that data hastily removed by the service provider, prompted by Europol, is in fact personal data that was shared in violation of national/EU laws, yet the prompt removal will make it impossible to conduct any investigation, resulting in a failure to provide due process to those concerned.

The Regulation introduces specific obligations for Europol, having become an EU agency following the Lisbon Treaty, subject to scrutiny by the European Court and EDPS. While the European Court is authorised to review individual complaints, the EDPS general supervision targets data protection procedures, with tools ranging from recommendations to ban on data transfers. Yet the political oversight, granted to the European Parliament over Europol actions, is in its design vague and deemed to be ineffective. The Joint Parliamentary Scrutiny Group (JPSG) has been called upon to examine Europol actions' impacts on fundamental rights and freedoms of natural persons.[42] Should the EP find issues with fundamental rights protection, it may resort to offering 'summary conclusions' to national parliaments. This mechanism fails to meet the provision of Article 88(2), sentence 3 of the Treaty on the Functioning of the European Union, which provides national Parliaments with the right to scrutinise the action of EU agencies, including Europol. The JPSG is to participate in meetings of the Management Board only upon Europol's invitation, with MPs and MEPs granted the status of non-voting observers. They also hold no power in deciding upon the Executive Director of Europol, with only non-binding opinions upon the selection. Also, no right to access information on Europol's operation have been granted. As noted by Sabine Gless and Thomas Wahl, the practical application if this oversight mechanism is unclear, as it represents a new approach to accountability at the time of 'European criminal law enforcement'.[43] They emphasise, however, that the 'political' oversight excludes supervision of day-to-day operations, one that is of crucial significance to the practical implementation of the new rules.

The Europol–US cooperation raises serious concerns with regard to the right of privacy and free speech (right to communication) as well as the right to a fair trial. Due process concerns are raised by the fact that as per Article 4, paragraph 1(m) of the Supplemental Agreement potentially criminal content is to be removed at the discretion of a service provider rather than subjected to a police investigation

[42] M. Monroy, EDRI (2016) 'Oversight of the New Europol Regulation Likely to Remain Superficial.' 12 July 2016. Available at: https://edri.org/oversight-new-europol-regulation-likely-remain-superficial/

[43] S. Gless and T. Wahl, 'A Comparison of the Evolution and Pace of Police and Judicial Cooperation in Criminal Matters: A Race between Europol and Eurojust?':in *The Needed Balances in EU Criminal Law: Past, Present and Future* edited by Ch. Brière and A. Weyembergh (London: Bloomsbury Publishing, 2017) 352.

within the respective jurisdiction. If such content constitutes personal data, a potential violation of a privacy right is also at stake by the fact that one's personal data is being processed without due process. The second major concern is the lack of effective national supervision from the JSPB, designated as complimentary to the EDPS, raises concerns as to the effective supervision over the enforcement of the Regulation.

6. Recommendations

The 2016 Europol Regulation introduced a detailed privacy framework for the agency to operate with its local contact points. Yet it failed to reflect the suggestions on data limitation, transparency and effective access rights as well as a reliable review of judicial cooperation, one remaining outside the scope of existing data protection regimes.[44] The new system consistently lacks effective and comprehensive supervision over Europol's data exchanges, in particular with third countries, with general oversight granted to EDPS and much discretional authority on what data to share and by which means left at the agency's hands.[45] While the suggestions to attend to this state of affairs remain valid, it is to be expected that also the outdated bilateral treaties, in particular the Europol–US agreement, will be up for review. Such a review should result in an updated bilateral treaty, subject to effective and transparent supervision by the EDPS as well as national authorities, as well as ensuring effective legal redress for individuals whose data is at stake.

7. Conclusion

Europol activities reflect the age-long debate on the need to balance security and liberty, trying to weight in individual privacy rights and collective well-being. While this equilibrium is never easy to find, EU has a rich body of work to rely on when making policy decision and implementing their results, enshrined in law. The standards of necessity and proportionality, fundamental to European privacy protection, have not been properly reflected in current regulations, as explained above. These shortcomings might be attended to by surrendering Europol to a

---

[44] See, eg, European Parliament, 'Towards a New EU Legal Framework for Data Protection and Privacy Challenges, Principles and the Role of the European Parliament. Available at: http://www.euro-parl.europa.eu/RegData/etudes/etudes/join/2011/453216/IPOL-LIBE_ET(2011)453216_EN.pdf, p. 9.

[45] For a thorough analysis of the needed changes see: F. Boehm, *Information Sharing and Data Protection in the Area of Freedom, Security and Justice: Towards Harmonised Data Protection Principles for Information Exchange at EU-level'* (Dordrecht: Springer, 2011) 393–398.

scrupulous and effective EDPS supervision as well as its active and effective engagement with other stakeholders: civil society and service operators, with the agency acting not so much as a strict law enforcer, but rather a friendly neighbourhood policeman, seeking the root of local problems and amicable ways of settling them. Active participation in community standard setting, especially with regard to ISPs as well as a patient ear to the demands of the users would help strike the correct balance between the competing values, ones acceptable to all involved.

9

Rethinking Trust
in the Internet of Things

GEORGY ISHMAEV

Abstract

This chapter argues that the choice of trust conceptualisations in the context of consumer Internet of Things (IoT) can have a significant impact on the understanding and implementations of a user's private data protection. Narrow instrumental interpretations of trust as a mere precondition for technology acceptance may obscure important moral issues such as malleability of user's privacy decisions, and power imbalances between suppliers and consumers of technology. A shift of focus in policy proposals from trust to the trustworthiness of technology can be the first step on the way to addressing these moral concerns. It is argued that complexity of IoT systems, comprised of technological artefacts and institutional data-collecting entities, warrants the moral value of distrust as a prima facie assumption for technological design and regulatory measures. Such a conceptual perspective highlights importance of technological measures that can minimise reliance on trust in consumer IoTs and regulatory measures aimed to improve transparency of IoT architectures.

Keywords

IoT, privacy, moral trust, trustworthiness

1. Introduction

Trust is often hailed as the key component of successful Internet of Things (IoT) developments, from technological research papers to policy recommendations and corporate business strategies. Needless to say, different conceptions of trust in technology have had a fair share of use in practical studies on the social acceptance of new technologies such as Genetically Modified Organisms, Nanotechnology and others. Indeed, as Åm suggests, trust as a conceptual tool can be used for the purposes of social studies such as enquiries into whether the general public possesses sufficient understanding of new technologies.[1] It can also be incorporated to assess future perspectives of technology adoption in society, or as a crucial element of risk perception assessment by the various stakeholders. Many studies on public trust in the IoT operationalise trust in a similar fashion.

Some of the key considerations of the EU commission staff working document 'Advancing the Internet of Things in Europe'[2] are informed by the IERC position paper 'IoT governance, privacy and security issues'.[3] This paper points out that to make a positive impact on people's life, technology must be trusted and accepted. Thus, citizens' distrust in IoT technology-based systems and services can be a serious obstacle in the reaping of technological benefits. The report 'Europe's Policy Options for a Dynamic and Trustworthy Developments of the Internet of Things' suggests that a proper implementation of ethical tools such as informed consent can ensure trust in the systems and thus social acceptance of the technology.[4] Opinion report 'Digitisation of Industry Policy Recommendations' suggests that public trust in the IoT is a key factor determining speed of adoption, and refers to a number of surveys highlighting trust and a perception of risks by the users.[5]

Indeed, trust can be said to be a crucial element of a functioning modern society. Interpersonal and institutional types of trust are essential as they provide the possibility of cooperation and enable the functioning of many mundane aspects of everyday life.[6,7] Furthermore, one of the key aspects of trust is a capacity to reduce complexity, to represent social reality with simplified symbols and provide generalised expectations for actions.[8] However, such simplifications can also be irrational or unwarranted. Trust, therefore, is not something that is

---

[1] Åm, Trond Grønli. 'Trust in Nanotechnology? On Trust as Analytical Tool in Social Research on Emerging Technologies', *NanoEthics* 5, no 1 (2011): 15–28.

[2] EC (European Comission). 'Comission Staff Working Document. Advancing the Internet of Things in Europe', 19 April 2016. Available at: https://ec.europa.eu/digital-single-market/en/news/staff-working-document-advancing-internet-things-europe.

[3] IERC (European Research Cluster on the Internet of Things). 'Internet of Things IoT Governance, Privacy and Security Issues'. European Communities, January 2015. Available at: www.internet-of-things-research.eu/pdf/IERC_Position_Paper_IoT_Governance_Privacy_Security_Final.pdf.

[4] Schindler, Hélène Rebecca, Jonathan Cave, Neil Robinson, Veronika Horvath, Petal Hackett, Salil Gunashekar, Maarten Botterman, et al *Europe's Policy Options for a Dynamic and Trustworthy Development of the Internet of Things*. (Luxembourg: Publications Office, 2013). Available at: http://dx.publications.europa.eu/10.2759/22004.

[5] AIOTI (Alliance for Internet of Things Innovation). 'AIOTI Digitisation of Industry Policy Recommendations', November 2016. Available at: https://aioti.eu/wp-content/uploads/2017/03/AIOTI-Digitisation-of-Ind-policy-doc-Nov-2016.pdf.

[6] Hardin, Russell. *Trust and Trustworthiness* (New York: Russell Sage Foundation, 2002).

[7] Govier, Trudy. *Social Trust and Human Communities* (Ontario/Quebec: McGill-Queen's Press-MQUP, 1997).

[8] Luhmann, Niklas. *Trust and Power: Two Works*. (Ann Arbor: UMI Books on Demand, 1979).

univocally good, or something that should be universally desired in all contexts. [9,10] As Govier points out, while it is tempting to think that we can improve our social world by introducing 'more trust', it is not necessarily always the case.[11] The other side of trust is represented by the vulnerabilities and risks that a trustor embraces when he or she acts on trust.[12] Thus, even outright distrust can be morally justified in specific contexts, and this observation invites us to consider the real value of trust in the IoT.

Arguably, such an investigation is not a task for a single research paper, since the multitude of meanings and concepts involving trust in the IoT technology are further extended in turn by the broad definition of IoT. Still, it is possible to highlight the most pressing ethical concerns by looking at the key regulatory proposals in this area. A number of expert opinions, research papers and policy advisory reports highlight risks of IoT applications for the privacy of their users as a key issue in the future developments and implementations of these technologies.[13,14,15,16] This narrows down the research scope to user's trust regarding private data protection in consumer IoT applications. Consumer applications here refer to the systems falling into the categories of specific IoT developments aimed at individual consumers: Wearable Computing, Quantified Self and domotics, in contrast to business-to-business applications and infrastructure solutions.[17]

While ambiguity of the IoT definition is understandable in the context of emerging technology, vagueness of the 'trust' concept itself may come as surprise to some. Yet within a range of disciplines, trust remains a 'fuzzy' concept, in stark contrast to the everyday intuitive understanding of this word.[18] Furthermore, as McKnight and Chervany argue, measurements of trust often outstrip meaningful conceptualisations, which seems to be the case in the context of IoT trust as well.[19] This is not merely a matter of scholarly debate, considering that the choice of

---

[9] Baier, Annette. 'Trust and Antitrust', *Ethics* 96, no 2 (1986): 231–60.

[10] Gambetta, Diego. 'Can We Trust Trust.' in *Trust: Making and Breaking Cooperative Relations*, edited by Diego Gambetta (Oxford: Basil Blackwell Ltd, 1988), 213–37.

[11] See Govier, n 7.

[12] See Baier, n 9.

[13] Aggarwal, Charu C, Naveen Ashish, and Amit Sheth. 'The Internet of Things: A Survey from the Data-Centric Perspective' in *Managing and Mining Sensor Data* (Dordrecht: Springer, 2013) 383–428.

[14] Miorandi, Daniele, Sabrina Sicari, Francesco De Pellegrini, and Imrich Chlamtac. 'Internet of Things: Vision, Applications and Research Challenges', *Ad Hoc Networks* 10, no 7 (2012): 1497–1516.

[15] Sicari, Sabrina, Alessandra Rizzardi, Luigi Alfredo Grieco, and Alberto Coen-Porisini. 'Security, Privacy and Trust in Internet of Things: The Road Ahead', *Computer Networks* 76 (2015): 146–64.

[16] Pagallo, Ugo, Massimo Durante, and Shara Monteleone. 'What Is New with the Internet of Things in Privacy and Data Protection? Four Legal Challenges on Sharing and Control in IoT' in *Data Protection and Privacy: (In) Visibilities and Infrastructures* (Dordrecht: Springer, 2017) 59–78.

[17] WP29 (Article 29 Data Protection Working Party). 'Opinion 8/2014 on the on Recent Developments on the IoT', EU Data Protection Working Party' 16 September 2014. Available at: http://ec.europa.eu/justice/data-protection/article-29/documentation/opinion-recommendation/files/2014/wp223_en.pdf.

[18] McKnight, D. Harrison, and Norman L. Chervany. 'Trust and Distrust Definitions: One Bite at a Time' in *Trust in Cyber-Societies*, edited by Rino Falcone, Munindar Singh, and Yao-Hua Tan, (Berlin Heidelberg: Springer, 2001) 27–54.

[19] Ibid.

trust conceptualisation in policy proposals and technological designs can have very direct ethical consequences, as demonstrated for instance by the example of 'Trusted Computing'.[20,21] As a starting point of investigation this paper considers the widely adopted analytic definition of trust as a tripartite relation between trustor A trusting B (human or system) in regard to C.[22,23,24] This formulation can be used to define a user's (A) trust in the family of technical systems, unified by the consumer IoT label (B) to keep the user's private data protected (C).

More specific conceptualisations can highlight different aspects of this multi-faceted phenomenon, and the choice of an appropriate definition may either put associated moral issues in the spotlight or gloss over them. To address the question of trust value, section 2 of this chapter considers different definitions of trust such as *psychological trust, rational trust* and *trust in technology*. Addressing these distinctions highlights shortcomings of trust conceptualisations used in opinion surveys and policy recommendations which operationalise trust in the narrow instrumental fashion as a mere precondition for cooperation. It is argued that such conceptualisations tend to neglect the distinction between justified trust and trust as mere psychological disposition, ignoring the issue of trustor's vulnerability highlighted in moral philosophy. A shortcoming which is exaggerated by the observed malleability of dispositional attitudes of trust in the context of privacy related behaviour.[25,26] These findings urge us to consider rather *trustworthiness* of IoT systems as a focal point of concerns, which is a foundation of rational trust.

Section 3 defines objects of trust in IoT using reference models and highlights distinctive issues apparent from this analysis. Rational trust can be valuable insofar as it helps individuals choose optimal strategies of interaction with complex systems.[27,28] However, IoT systems represent a case of trust in hybrid part technical and part social system, where establishment of *system trustworthiness* is a non-trivial task.[29] This task can become almost impossible for the individual users

---

[20] Anderson, Ross. 'Cryptography and Competition Policy – Issues with "Trusted Computing"' in *Economics of Information Security* edited by L. Jean Camp and Stephen Lewis (Boston, MA: Springer, 2004) 35–52. Available at: https://doi.org/10.1007/1-4020-8090-5_3.

[21] Monti, Andrea. 'Trust in the Shell', *Knowledge, Technology & Policy* 23, no 3–4 (2010): 507–17. Available at: https://doi.org/10.1007/s12130-010-9131-7.

[22] Baier, n 9

[23] See Hardin, n 6.

[24] Taddeo, Mariarosaria. 'Modelling Trust in Artificial Agents, A First Step Toward the Analysis of e-Trust', *Minds and Machines* 20, no 2 (2010): 243–57. Available at: https://doi.org/10.1007/s11023-010-9201-3.

[25] Acquisti, Alessandro, Laura Brandimarte, and George Loewenstein. 'Privacy and Human Behavior in the Age of Information', *Science* 347, no 6221 (2015): 509–14.

[26] Adjerid, Idris, Eyal Peer, and Alessandro Acquisti. 'Beyond the Privacy Paradox: Objective versus Relative Risk in Privacy Decision Making', *MIS Quarterly* 42, no 2 (2018): 465–88. Available at: https://doi.org/10.25300/MISQ/2018/14316.

[27] See Luhmann n 8.

[28] See Taddeo n 24.

[29] Nickel, Philip J, Maarten Franssen, and Peter Kroes. 'Can We Make Sense of the Notion of Trustworthy Technology?' *Knowledge, Technology & Policy* 23, no 3–4 (2010): 429–44.

considering information asymmetries and power disparities between suppliers and consumers of IoT systems.[30,31,32] Analysis of current IoT reference models also shows a tendency to conflate issues of data security and private data protection. While both these issues are closely intertwined, they refer to distinctive concerns both in empirical and conceptual senses, pointing to the difference between trust in data protection and trust in the security of data.

I argue that these concerns compel us to embrace a Humean appreciation of distrust as a starting premise for the design of social institutions. Inspired by this approach, Section 4 considers technological and regulatory solutions that can be used to enhance trustworthiness of IoT systems and at least partially remove the burden of trust justification from the users of the technology.

2. Conceptualisations of Trust

2.1. Trust as an Instrumental Value

The concept of trust can have a crucial role in measurements of public attitudes towards a new technology. Expressions of trusting attitude or lack of it can serve as indicators of the social acceptance for a new technology. However, we should be wary not to slip into descriptive reductionism, conflating acceptance with moral acceptability of technology, as happens too often with private data collection tools. I argue that while existing policy proposals highlight some of the ethical concerns regarding unwarranted trust in consumer IoT systems, our understanding of trust in this context should be significantly extended to include other crucial issues. Granted, interpretations of 'trust' can vary dramatically throughout different areas of discourse and such descriptive pluralism, of course, is not itself problematic, as other contested concepts demonstrate.

The issue here lies rather with the fact that the concept of trust in policy proposals and opinion reports is often treated in a rather particular, normatively laden sense. More specifically, the value of trust in the IoT is usually interpreted in a narrow instrumental fashion, where users' trust is considered a pathway to acceptance that can enable all positive developments of the technology,[33,34,35]

---

[30] Stajano, Frank. 'Security for Whom? The Shifting Security Assumptions of Pervasive Computing' in *Software Security – Theories and Systems Mext-NSF-JSPS International Symposium, ISSS 2002 Tokyo, Japan, November 8–10, 2002 Revised Papers*, edited by Mitsuhiro Okada, Benjamin C Pierce, Andre Scedrov, Hideyuki Tokuda, and Akinori Yonezawa (Berlin: Heidelberg: Springer-Verlag, 2003) 16–27.

[31] Andrejevic, Mark. 'Big Data, Big Questions| the Big Data Divide', *International Journal of Communication* 8 (2014): 17.

[32] Christl, Wolfie, and Sarah Spiekermann. *Networks of Control: A Report on Corporate Surveillance, Digital Tracking, Big Data & Privacy* (Wien: Facultas, 2016).

[33] See AIOTI n 5.

[34] See Sicari et al n 15.

[35] Yan, Zheng, Peng Zhang, and Athanasios V. Vasilakos. 'A Survey on Trust Management for Internet of Things', *Journal of Network and Computer Applications* 42 (2014): 120–34. Available at: https://doi.org/10.1016/j.jnca.2014.01.014.

and even as a remedy to the moral dilemma of choice between privacy risks and technological benefits.[36] There is a concern that such studies using methods of focus groups and surveys may lack explanatory depth when applied in the context of emerging technologies. Indeed, apprehensions about surveys aimed to reveal public attitudes towards the IoT, are reminiscent of earlier concerns towards the validity of such methods in assessments of public perception of nanotechnologies highlighted by Åm.[37]

Some limitations of such surveys come from misplaced assumptions that it is possible to have unified responses or attitudes towards early technologies that are not yet fully presented at the markets.[38,39] This point of critique may well be justified in the context of IoT technology surveys. While some applications classified as the IoT can already be found on the market, they are fragmented in separate categories such as fitness wearables or smart home systems and thus are not necessarily perceived as a single technology.[40,41,42,43] Furthermore, it is safe to say that full implementations of interconnected sensor systems utilising all aspects of envisioned IoT architectures are still not present in consumer markets in a meaningful sense.[44] Thus, conceptualisation of generalised trust in some broad family of technological artefacts can at best serve as a reflection on attitudes of general optimism towards the idea of technological advancement.

Another, arguably more problematic shortcoming of trust conceptualisations used in reports and opinion surveys is highlighted by Davies et al.[45] When benefits of technology acceptance are framed in economic terms with little examination of the relation between promised benefits and wider social values, conceptualisations of trust tend to slip into the so called 'deficit model'. In such a model, trust in technology is treated as a scarce resource, and deficit of understanding/trust is seen as something that should be compensated to advance adoption of the technology. The main problem with such a conceptual approach where trust is treated as a scarce economic resource, is that it often fails to distinguish between cases of desirable and misplaced trust.[46] The IoT public opinion surveys indeed are mainly

---

[36] See Schindler et al n 4.

[37] See Åm n 1.

[38] Ibid.

[39] Davies, Sarah, Matthew B Kearnes, and M Macnaghten. 'Nanotechnology and Public Engagement: A New Kind of (Social) Science?' *Pan Stanford*, (2010): 473–99.

[40] Uckelmann, Dieter, Mark Harrison, and Florian Michahelles. 'An Architectural Approach towards the Future Internet of Things' in *Architecting the Internet of Things* (Dordrecht: Springer, 2011) 1–24.

[41] See Miorandi et al n 14.

[42] Gubbi, Jayavardhana, Rajkumar Buyya, Slaven Marusic, and Marimuthu Palaniswami. 'Internet of Things (IoT): A Vision, Architectural Elements, and Future Directions', *Future Generation Computer Systems* 29, no 7 (2013): 1645–60.

[43] Sicari et al, n 15.

[44] Pagallo et al, n 16.

[45] Davies. Sarah R, Matthew Kearnes, Phil MacNagh 'Nanotechnology and Public Engagement: A New Kind of (Social) Science?' in K L Kjollberg and F Wickson (eds), *Nano goes Macro. Social Perspectives on Nano Sciences and Technologies* (Stanford: Pan 2010) 405–422.

[46] See Gambetta n 10.

framed in economic terms where trust is construed as an attitude of technology's users which should be elicited to guarantee successful developments of the IoT based business models.[47]

2.2. Psychological Attitude of Trust

The shortcoming of the 'trust deficit' theoretical framework is even more pronounced in the context of trust in private data protection, as highlighted in empirical studies on privacy related behaviour of technology users. Acquisti et al. address the so called 'privacy paradox' – an observed discrepancy between privacy preferences reported by the technology users in surveys and actual decisions regarding protection of their privacy.[48] The gap between expressed preferences and the actual behaviour can be quite significant as individuals' privacy decisions are not only highly contextually dependent, but can also be influenced by a number of external factors. To understand this phenomenon, it is helpful to introduce a conceptualisation of trust referring to *psychological attitude*, which can be defined as an expectancy held by an individual that the word, promise or statement of another individual or group can be relied upon.[49]

Such an attitude or expectancy can be elicited by mere signalling – an *imitation of trustworthiness*, such as the presence of data collector's written privacy policy, which has no real impact on the actual data sharing practice.[50] Brandimarte et al. also find that mere increase in a perceived control over access to private data online, brings about an increased likelihood of sensitive, risky disclosures.[51] These observations render base default assumptions present in the 'deficit model' highly problematic. Namely, the premise that the users of technology rationally justify their trust in providers based on all available knowledge about benefits and costs of technology in the fashion of fair contractual relations. Empirical studies show this couldn't be farther from the truth, as privacy decisions and trust attitudes of technology users are subject to biases, habits and manipulations.

Of particular interest here is the experiment by Oulasvirta et al. on the privacy perception of in home surveillance by means of integrated multiple

---

[47] Some interpretation of trust in more technical papers on IoT are also reminiscent of this model. However, in this context it is crucial to be aware that interpretations of users' trust can be mixed up with technical problems of 'trust management' and 'trusted system', which have a very specific meaning in the context of cybersecurity. As Yan et al. n 35 acknowledge, little work in technical research on the IoT pays specific attention to the human-computer trust. Considering that the concept of trust in computer sciences should be seen as a motivating concept underlying many problems and contexts rather than a precise idea, some inevitable conceptual blurring should be expected. This issue is partially addressed in section 3 of this chapter.

[48] See Acquisti et al, n 25.

[49] See McKnight and Chervany n 18.

[50] Hoofnagle, Chris Jay, and Jennifer M Urban. 'Alan Westin's Privacy Homo Economicus' *Wake Forest L. Rev.* 49 (2014): 261.

[51] Brandimarte, Laura, Alessandro Acquisti, and George Loewenstein. 'Misplaced Confidences: Privacy and the Control Paradox' *Social Psychological and Personality Science* 4, no 3 (2013): 340–47.

sensor systems.[52] One of the key findings of the experiment was suppression of privacy-seeking behaviour when it came into a conflict with convenience associated with being at home. After three months, most participants started tolerating home surveillance as a feature of everyday life. At the same time, Oulasvirta et al. found that the acceptance of surveillance did not eliminate feelings of anxiety and discomfort associated with the invasive data collection, characterising new behaviour routines as fragile, and easily challenged by new events. This observation aptly demonstrates differences between rational behaviour and acceptance of technology, often misrepresented by data collectors, as a manifestation of a legitimate user's trust.

Such acceptance is closely intertwined with what Luhmann calls a routinised, thoughtless trust based on familiarity.[53] Kim found in an experimental study that anthropomorphic features in IoT appliances such as individualised voice control interfaces, can elicit more positive attitudes towards appliances, including an increase in the perceived trustworthiness of the appliance.[54] This, argues Kim, is explained by the fact that human responses to computers tend to be not only social, but also mindless, occurring because of reduced attention caused by the predominant reliance on the previously established social rules and categories. Such apprehensions about the malleability of users' trust cause significant concerns, as more IoT application such as 'Amazon Echo' and 'Google Home' use natural language processing and other technologies imitating human-like interactions.

These findings present special concerns with regards to Internet-connected children's toys that not only present a significant threat to privacy, but are also specifically designed to elicit trust attitudes from a child.[55] As Luhmann points out, rational trust is a processing of experience that takes a lot of energy and attention and requires auxiliary mechanisms such as learning, symbolising, controlling, and sanctioning.[56] As studies above demonstrate, even adult users of technology faced with the increasing complexity resort to less than optimal strategies of trusting behaviour, being unable to assess the actual *trustworthiness* of IoT systems on their own. This type of behaviour falls short of delivering the benefits of reduced complexity, whilst retaining all the risks of trust.

These observations suggest that the instrumental focus on trust in studies regarding acceptance of the IoT technology characterised by the 'deficit model', can present significant shortcomings. Such a narrow instrumental interpretation

---

[52] Oulasvirta, Antti, Aurora Pihlajamaa, Jukka Perkiö, Debarshi Ray, Taneli Vähäkangas, Tero Hasu, Niklas Vainio, and Petri Myllymäki. 'Long-Term Effects of Ubiquitous Surveillance in the Home' (ACM, 2012) 41–50.

[53] Luhmann n 8.

[54] Kim, Ki Joon. 'Interacting Socially with the Internet of Things (IoT): Effects of Source Attribution and Specialization in Human–IoT Interaction.' *Journal of Computer-Mediated Communication* 21, no 6 (2016): 420–35.

[55] Taylor, Emmeline, and Katina Michael. 'Smart Toys That Are the Stuff of Nightmares.' *IEEE Technology and Society Magazine* 35, no 1 (2016): 8–10.

[56] Luhmann n 8.

of trust stems from what Hardin calls a 'conceptual slippage', the reductionist notion of trust as a mere epistemological primitive, and not a subject of analysis.[57] Indeed, if trust is reduced to a univocally desirable attitude towards technology, and distrust as a mere obstacle to the realisation of benefits promised by technology, then the issue of users' trust in technology risks being reduced to the question of how to elicit such an attitude. These are worrisome prospects, considering that incorporation of perceptual cues eliciting psychological attitudes of trust in users is becoming an explicit subject of consumer technology design.[58]

2.3. Trustworthiness

To appreciate these concerns, we can focus on the notion of *rational trust*, which tackles issues of trust and trustworthiness from rather different perspectives than psychological accounts. Taddeo suggests the following definition of trust based on a general relational account: trustor (A) chooses to rely on a certain party, or trustee (B), to perform a certain action (C); and this choice rests on the assessment of the trustee's trustworthiness.[59] Trustworthiness here is understood as a measure (for the trustor) which indicates the likelihood of benefitting from the trustee's performance, and conversely, the risk that the trustee will not act as expected. This definition of trust focuses on one crucial aspect of such relation – reduction of complexity valuable to the trustor in Luhmann's sense.[60]

Taddeo argues that such an interpretation of trust can also be extended to explain instances of depersonalised relations, mediated by the technology. Such *e-trust* can occur in the context of a digital environment where social and moral pressure effects, playing crucial role in physical environments, are perceived differently. However, considering the ever-blurring boundary between 'offline' and 'online', distinguishing e-trust from trust becomes a more difficult task. This is even more so the case in the context of IoT solutions that effectively blur this distinction to the point where it is no longer meaningful. Thus, speaking of trust involving communication technology such as IoT, we effectively consider e-trust as well. E-trust, argues Taddeo, has same valuable property of reducing complexity for the trustor, which makes it as fundamentally important as trust in persons and social systems, as highlighted by. This approach focusing on the value of trust for the trustor, is distinct from the interpretation of trust value found in the 'deficit model'.

There are moral reasons for this focus deriving from the fact that trustor (A), giving discretion to act on one's interest, is subject to the risk that trustee (B) will

---

[57] Hardin, n 6 at 55

[58] Nickel, Philip J. 'Design for the Value of TrustTrust.' In *Handbook of Ethics, Values, and Technological Design*, edited by Jeroen van den Hoven, Pieter E. Vermaas, and Ibo van de Poel, (Dordrecht: Springer Netherlands, 2015) 551–67. Available at: https://doi.org/10.1007/978-94-007-6970-0_21.

[59] Taddeo n 24.

[60] Luhmann n 8 at 29.

abuse this discretion.[61] Indeed, if that was not the case, we would speak of predictability or control, rather than trust. Trust is also different from mere reliance, exposing the trustor to different types of vulnerabilities.[62] There is a distinction between being disappointed by the poor performance of a trustee or being betrayed and harmed by the trustee's actions. It is also suggested that the presence of so called 'reactive attitudes', or availability of moral judgments on the trustee's actions as being praiseworthy or blameworthy, characterises such moral aspects of trust. Nickel suggests that same distinction is applicable as well in the situation where the object of trust is not a person, but a technological artefact or technological system.[63] He defines *trust in technology* simply as the voluntary disposition towards reliance under condition of uncertainty, involving the attitude that technology should promote or protect the interests of a trustor.

The presence of such reactive attitudes in itself does not necessarily warrant moral concerns. After all, being angry with a TV does not necessarily make it an instance of betrayed trust. Tavani suggest an approach to the trust in technology which considers vulnerability of a trustor as a key factor of moral concerns.[64] That is, if a human engages in a direct interaction with the technological system based on expected functionality, and such interaction makes him vulnerable to risks, then this type of relation presupposes strong trust. Strong here means that such morally robust relation warrant a set of moral considerations similar (albeit not fully equivalent) to issues regarding trust between human agents. In the context of trust in private data protection, these vulnerabilities can be quite significant, involving information-based harm, informational inequality, informational injustice and undermined autonomy.[65] From that perspective smart TVs, which secretly share its owner's private data with different third parties, do seem to fall into the category of betrayed trust.

However, moral aspects of trust are not exhausted by the simple distinction between warranted and unwarranted trust. As Taddeo notices, emergence of rational trust in real life contexts involving human agents depends upon complex and shifting conditions, making it difficult to assess benefits of trust a priori.[66] Indeed, if the distinction between morally acceptable and unacceptable instances of trust relations could be reduced to the idealised notion of rational trust, then data collection practices based on the 'choice and notice' model would be rendered largely unproblematic. However, malleability of individual behaviour regarding disclosure of private information in the context of interactions with technology,[67]

---

[61] Hardin, n 6 at 12.

[62] Baier n 9.

[63] See Nickel n 58.

[64] Tavani, Herman T. 'Levels of Trust in the Context of Machine Ethics.' *Philosophy & Technology* 28, no 1 (March 2015): 75–90. Available at: https://doi.org/10.1007/s13347-014-0165-8.

[65] Van den Hoven, Jeroen. 'Information Technology, Privacy and the Protection of Personal Data.' In *Information Technology and Moral Philosophy*, edited by Jeroen Van den Hoven and John Weckert (New York: Cambridge University Press, 2008).

[66] Taddeo n 24.

[67] See Brandimarte et al, n 51.

highlights two key moral issues: distribution of power and conflicting interests in trust relations.

The first is more than just an issue of power imbalance characterised by the uneven distribution of risk and benefits, which generally occurs in any trust relation.[68] Baier highlights a significant distinction between the cooperative trust occurring between equally distrusting peers standing in approximately balanced positions of power, and trust between parties who had uneven power distribution beforehand.[69] If a trustor's standing beforehand was disadvantageous then it can be further undermined by the incurred risks of trust relations. Thus, in cases where the trustee has a significant advantage over the trustor, such an arrangement should at the very least be treated cautiously. Furthermore, if such an asymmetric trust relation takes place on the background of conflicting interests, we simply cannot speak of any rational trust at all.

It seems that both these concerns are present in the case of user trust in the IoT. The increasing complexity of data-collecting technology coupled with users' lack of technical expertise, prevent said users from properly assessing the risks and benefits.[70,71] In this sense, power imbalance manifests as information asymmetry between suppliers of the technology and the individuals affected by it, whom are often oblivious to its true capacity, or even of its presence. What is arguably even more problematic is that economic incentives seem to drive interests of the consumer IoT suppliers further away from the interests of individual users with regard to private data protection, echoing the paradigm of moral failures which characterise the online advertising industry.[72]

Given this analysis of the value of trust, it becomes apparent that the problem of trust in the IoT is not a descriptive question of why the users do or do not trust in technology. Showing that people trust in technological design does not imply that it is trustworthy, nor the other way around.[73] It is first and foremost an ethical question of whether individuals can rationally trust in IoT technology, which in turn hinges upon whether IoT technology can be made trustworthy in respect to private data protection. Only after an affirmative answer to that question it is possible to start addressing the issue of how the scrutiny of trustworthiness can be made available to the users of technology, the second condition necessary for the emergence of a rational trust. Trustworthiness of the IoT technology can be considered a viable concept insofar as we can speak of trustworthy technology at all. It is not immediately clear though whether we should consider

---

[68] Indeed, generally, a trustor delegating certain actions to the trustee prior to the promised benefits thus carries immediate risks. A trustee, however, defaulting on the obligation, receives immediate benefits, while carrying only the probability of future risks such as sanctions, reputation damage, lack of future cooperation etc.

[69] Baier n 9.

[70] See Stajano n 30.

[71] See Andrejevic n 31.

[72] See Christl and Spiekermann n 32.

[73] Nickel n 58.

trustworthiness of smart devices, networks, technology suppliers or service providers. Thus, the next necessary step is to address the question of the objects of trust in the IoT.

3. Objects of Trust in the IoT

3.1. Reference Models and Architectures

The term IoT is, firstly, an encompassing label which designates a technological model for a wide range of emerging products and services, thus making it hard to identify immediately specific objects of trust. This issue is apparent in light of the observation that 'IoT' being an umbrella term includes a great multitude of technologies such as various wireless communication protocols, sensor technologies, encryption protocols and many others. Neither is it possible at present to identify exemplary flagship products representative of the whole range of consumer IoT designs.[74] One way to tackle this ambiguity is to define IoT as any system fitting into a certain design paradigm. The EU Commission staff working document on 'Advancing the Internet of Things in Europe' characterises the first stage of IoT development as an ecosystem where all objects and people can be interconnected through communication networks in and across private, public and industrial spaces, and report their status and/or about the status of the surrounding environment.[75]

From the system-level perspective the IoT then can be defined as a highly dynamic and radically distributed networked system, composed of numerous smart objects that produce and consume information.[76] Architectures of IoT can have different levels of decentralisation depending upon the scale and complexity.[77,78] This also means that some entities in such a model may be comprised of networks including multiple actors, having various roles in distributions of data flows. The way to provide a more specific conceptualisation is to consider the IoT reference model with a particular architecture and system logic, present in most products and services employing smart objects. Gubbi et al. define key enabling components of the IoT: (1) Hardware – including sensors, actuators and embedded

---

[74] Pagallo et al, n 16.

[75] EC (European Comission). 'Commission Staff Working Document. Advancing the Internet of Things in Europe' Communication from the Commission to the European Parliament, the Council, the European Economic and Social Committee and the Committee of the Regions. (Brussels: 19 April 2016).

[76] Miorandi et al, n 14.

[77] Ibid.

[78] Mashal, Ibrahim, Osama Alsaryrah, Tein-Yaw Chung, Cheng-Zen Yang, Wen-Hsing Kuo, and Dharma P Agrawal. 'Choices for Interaction with Things on Internet and Underlying Issues', *Ad Hoc Networks* 28 (2015): 68–90.

communication hardware; (2) Middleware – on demand storage and computing tools for data analytics; and (3) Presentation – interfaces, easy to understand visualisation and interpretation tools and applications.[79] Conceptual similarity to this tripartite scheme is also suggested in the three-layer model of IoT, which often serves as a generic reference model.[80]

The first layer is the sensory layer (perception) which includes different sensors and actuators, the function of which is to identify objects, collect information and perform actions to exert control. This essentially comprises hardware, including RFIDs, MEMs, cameras, GPS, WI-FI modules, Bluetooth modules and so on. Second is the network layer which includes a variety of communication channels, interfaces, gateways and information management of the network. This is comprised naturally of the Internet itself but also of all other types of mobile networks, ad hoc networks and closed-circuit networks. The network layer in this model also includes data coding, extraction, restructuring, mining and aggregation. Third is the application layer which provides applications and services to the IoT end users and is essentially an interface offering diverse functionalities. These interfaces can be embedded in smart objects, be implemented in the form of smartphone apps or web-based applications.

Using the conceptualisation provided by the reference model, we can attempt to make sense of a notion of a trustworthy IoT system. Here it is helpful to reflect on the meaning of *trustworthiness* in a technological context. In the most general sense in computer security, a trustworthy technical component or technical system is the one which performs according to a precise set of rules, and which will not deviate from these rules.[81] Artz and Gil characterise this interpretation as a 'hard security' approach which views trustworthiness as a status that should be established using traditional security techniques such as authentication, access control, encryption, etc.[82] This view essentially equates trustworthiness with a threshold of predictability, classifying something as trustworthy if its behaviour is predictable.[83] In the context of purely technological artefacts, indeed there is

---

[79] Gubbi et al, 'Internet of Things (IoT).'

[80] Some other layered models of IoT expand this conceptual structure to five or more layers, expanding data processing or data management into separate categories such as middleware layer comprised of a software. Here I agree with Pagallo et al, n 16, who argue that in the context of policy analysis, the three-layer model provides sufficient explanatory depth and has a further advantage of complementing the basic architectural levels of IoT.

[81] Although 'Trustworthy' and 'trusted' can be used interchangeably, sometimes a distinction is drawn. In the information security, a 'trusted' system or component is one whose failure can break the security policy, while a 'trustworthy' system or component is the one that will not fail (see Anderson n 20). A trusted entity here is taken in a narrow descriptive sense as being entrusted with information, without including reasons why the entity is entrusted with it. This chapter follows Anderson's distinction, treating 'trusted' as a descriptive term, and 'trustworthy' as a normative. To add to the confusion, the widely-used term 'trusted computing' is more of a marketing term referring to a family of security solutions.

[82] Artz, Donovan, and Yolanda Gil. 'A Survey of Trust in Computer Science and the Semantic Web', *Web Semantics: Science, Services and Agents on the World Wide Web* 5, no 2 (2007): 58–71.

[83] Proudler, Graeme, Liqun Chen, and Chris Dalton. *Trusted Computing Platforms TPM2.0 in Context.* (Cham: Springer International Publishing, 2015).

little sense to speak of trustworthiness in the interpersonal sense. Still, trustworthiness of a technological artefact rarely an absolute notion. Nickel et al argue that the concept of trustworthiness applied to technology can also be understood as a degree notion in the sense of reliability.[84] The more reliable artefact can be considered more trustworthy than an unreliable one.

Here it is also important to draw a distinction between trustworthiness in terms of data security and trustworthiness in terms of private data protection. It is helpful to keep in mind that in computer sciences, the problem of trust generally refers to the two main issues: securely exchanging data and securely identifying communication peers. Fundamentally, security requirements of confidentiality (preventing unauthorised reads), integrity (preventing unauthorised writes), and availability (ensuring access for authorised users), all rest on a distinction between authorised and unauthorised users.[85] Accordingly, satisfaction of trustworthiness requirements (usually shortened to 'trust requirements') is strictly related to identity management and access control issues. From the security perspective then, a trustworthy system is the one that reliably prevents unauthorised entities from accessing private data, satisfying the condition of confidentiality. However, a component or a system can be considered trustworthy in regard to privacy, if it reliably collects, stores and shares private data strictly in accordance with users' privacy preferences.[86]

As Fernandes et al point out, most of the analysis of privacy issues in current consumer IoT such as 'smart home' appliances is centred around security of devices and protocols.[87] Often, the issue of privacy in the context of IoT architectures is even conflated with the issue of data security,[88,89] and accordingly, the trust in data protection is sometimes considered as synonymous to the trust in the security of users' data.[90,91] There is little denying that the security of private data in consumer IoT systems is a cornerstone of data protection guarantees for users, especially considering how poorly designed some of such systems can be.[92] However, the

---

[84] See Nickel et al n 29.

[85] Stajano n 30.

[86] In fact, the security of a system can be completely divorced from the issue of users' privacy or even contradict it. For instance, if a trustworthy status for a user's endpoint is earned by revealing a certain number and type of credentials, and privacy of credential information is lost as the credentials are revealed, then there is a trade-off between privacy and earning of trust in the sense of security (see Artz and Gil n 82).

[87] Fernandes, Earlence, Jaeyeon Jung, and Atul Prakash. 'Security Analysis of Emerging Smart Home Applications', IEEE, 2016, 636–54.

[88] Ziegeldorf, Jan Henrik, Oscar Garcia Morchon, and Klaus Wehrle. 'Privacy in the Internet of Things: Threats and Challenges', *Security and Communication Networks* 7, no 12 (2014): 2728–42.

[89] Malina, Lukas, Jan Hajny, Radek Fujdiak, and Jiri Hosek. 'On Perspective of Security and Privacy-Preserving Solutions in the Internet of Things,' *Computer Networks* 102 (2016): 83–95.

[90] Sicari et al, n 15.

[91] Tragos, Elias Z, Jorge Bernal Bernabe, Ralf C Staudemeyer, J Luis, H Ramos, A Fragkiadakis, A Skarmeta, M Nati, and A Gluhak. 'Trusted IoT in the Complex Landscape of Governance, Security, Privacy, Availability and Safety'. *Digitising the Industry-Internet of Things Connecting the Physical, Digital and Virtual Worlds. River Publishers Series in Communications*, 2016, 210–39.

[92] Apthorpe, Noah, Danny Y. Huang, Gunes Acar, Frank Li, Arvind Narayanan, and Nick Feamster. 'Announcing IoT Inspector: Studying Smart Home IoT Device Behavior'. *Freedom to Tinker* (blog),

confidence in the reliability of security protocols does not encompass the whole spectrum of trust in the protection of private data.

The distinction between trust in security of data and trust in data protection can be elaborated through the example borrowed from interpersonal trust. Baier, arguing on the scope of trust, provides an illustration of a Greek mailman in a small village who is trusted to deliver the mail and not to tamper with it.[93] However, in a certain scenario it may be appropriate for him to read the content of the mail in order to deliver it (e.g. when it has certain urgency and recipient's address has changed). The mailman is trusted to use his discretionary power competently, non-maliciously, and transparently, making intelligent decisions about the best interests of the mail owner. Analytically, trust in the safety of the mail, confidence that it will not be stolen from the mailman by a thief, does not encompass the full spectrum of the mailman's capacity to abuse trust. It does not matter if only authorised entity has access to private data, insofar as this entity has a capacity to undermine users' privacy. As Stajano points out it makes little sense to address questions of security and authorisation if we do not ask more fundamental questions: 'authorised by whom?' and 'for those benefits?'[94]

Achievement of trustworthiness even in the minimal sense of security of data is a non-trivial task in the context of IoT. Heterogeneity of components in any given IoT system means that achieving trustworthiness of a single component does not translate into trustworthiness of a system. Furthermore, as Yan et al. argue, even ensuring trustworthiness of the whole IoT layer does not imply that the justified trust in whole system can be achieved, and any satisfactory privacy-preserving solution should address private data flows through all layers of the IoT.[95] Realisation of such a solution is a notoriously difficult task, even in the case of a system comprised only of technical artefacts. Achievement of trustworthiness in the sense of private data protection in a system which involves multiple human operators is a problem of a different scale. The more operators in such systems, the less coordinated their actions and considerations are with regard to users' interests.[96]

3.2. Data Collectors and Trustworthiness

Consumer IoT systems indeed fall into the category that Nickel et al characterise as hybrid systems, partially technical and partially social.[97] Data handling entities

---

23 April 2018. Available at: https://freedom-to-tinker.com/2018/04/23/announcing-iot-inspector-a-tool-to-study-smart-home-iot-device-behavior/.

[93] Baier n 9.

[94] Stajano n 30.

[95] Yan et al, 'A Survey on Trust Management for Internet of Things.'

[96] Nickel et al, n 29.

[97] Ibid.

in IoT architectures include not only users of technology, device manufacturers, cloud service providers and platform providers, but also all entities that collect, store and process private data. Even in the case of single smart device data collection, processing and presentation can be performed by third parties which may lead to serious privacy issues, as in case of Samsung's 'Smart TV', which shared voice recordings of users with third parties.[98] These practices are partly explained by objective factors, since the development of data processing algorithms is a costly and time-consuming task, and is often performed by specialised companies, separate from the hardware manufacturers.

However very often, the presence of data collecting entities in the IoT architecture has nothing to do with the functionality of smart devices. Christl and Spiekerman reveal an intricate ecosystem of private data markets involving data brokers of different calibre ranging from Alphabet and Facebook to lesser-known companies, actively engaging in the collection of user data from device manufacturers and suppliers of consumer IoT services.[99] One such example is the sale of household interior map data to third parties by the manufacturer of the smart home-cleaning appliance 'Roomba'.[100] Most recently, Samsung's 'smart TV' was again in the spotlight when it was discovered that simply powering up the 'smart TV' initiates communication with Google Play, Double Click, Netflix, FandangoNOW, Spotify, CBS, MSNBC, NFL, Deezer, and Facebook, even if the user does not have accounts with any of these parties.[101]

Thus, we must keep in mind that in the context of IoT architecture, these systems are not mere collections of interconnected technical artefacts. Rather, they should be seen as a complex and dynamic socio-technical system comprised of different entities, whose interests in regard to the collection of private data may be diametrically opposed to those of the technology consumers. Furthermore, the architecture of these systems can be highly dynamic, threatening reliability in terms of data protection.[102] Changes in the data flow architecture can happen almost instantly, as in the case of 'Amazon Echo' which was turned into a telephone-like device with a single software update from the manufacturer. 'Echo' users found that contact lists from connected smartphones were used to connect 'Echo' devices into a kind of social network, without any regard for the privacy preferences of the 'Echo' users.[103] One more recent example

---

[98] EPIC. 'Complaint, Request for Investigation, Injunction, and Other Relief Submitted by The Electronic Privacy Information Center', 24 February 2015. Available at: https://epic.org/privacy/internet/ftc/Samsung/EPIC-FTC-Samsung.pdf.

[99] Christl and Spiekermann n 32.

[100] Jones, Rhett. 'Roomba's Next Big Step Is Selling Maps of Your Home to the Highest Bidder.' *Gizmodo*, 24 July 2017. Available at: https://gizmodo.com/roombas-next-big-step-is-selling-maps-of-your-home-to-t-1797187829.

[101] See Apthorpe et al, n 92.

[102] A very basic notion of reliability in engineering implies performance of required functions in the given time interval.

[103] Oras, Elise. 'Alexa Calling Has a Major Privacy Flaw.' *Medium* (blog), 12 May 2017. Available at: https://medium.com/@elise81/alexa-calling-has-a-major-privacy-flaw-7ee42ddcb493.

of 'Echo' malfunctioning occurred when a conversation was recorded and shared with a random person without the device owner's knowledge.[104]

From the user's perspective, assessment of IoT device trustworthiness is a highly-complicated task, inevitably requiring certain levels of technical knowledge, an issue that was already apparent some time ago.[105] There are even fewer reliable strategies that could help a user assess trustworthiness of an entire IoT system. It is essentially an issue of epistemic impairment for users, stemming from a very limited ability to acquire evidence about all aspects of the IoT system. As Pagallo et al. point out, identification of data-collecting entities is the first challenge for private data protection in the context of IoT architectures.[106] To be trustworthy, an entity must be known to the user, a requirement which is not easily satisfiable in the context of a complex IoT architecture.

To assess the reliability of a smart device in terms of private data sharing with other entities within current IoT systems, one would have to perform a network traffic analysis as in Apthorpe et al.[107] However, such a tool is not necessarily available to an average consumer. Furthermore, this assessment may easily become obsolete in a short time as demonstrated by the example of the 'Echo'. It is sometimes suggested that from the user's perspective, trustworthiness of an IoT system can be guaranteed by the trustworthiness of a system manufacturer or service supplier.[108] However, it is clear from the above-mentioned examples that this suggestion is not feasible with the current models. Even if we could conceive an IoT system where all data flows are fully controlled by one entity, such as the smart device manufacturer, rational trust in such an entity would be highly problematic for several reasons.

One reason is the issue of conflicting interests, which renders any trust relation inherently suspicious. Indeed, manufacturers of sensor-equipped smart devices very often have direct economic interests in private data collection. This is not a problem of isolated anecdotal examples like the 'Rumba', but already an industry-wide issue.[109] Contrary to the intuitive idea of consumer IoT in which end users are the paying customers generating revenue for the suppliers with payments for products and services, actual business models lean towards the information marketplaces.[110] In that respect, the Internet of Things is reproducing the successful business models of 'traditional' Internet, dominated by data brokers and revenues from private data monetisation.

---

[104] Machkovech, Sam. 'Amazon Confirms That Echo Device Secretly Shared User's Private Audio.' *Arstechnica*, 24 May 2018. Available at: https://arstechnica.com/gadgets/2018/05/amazon-confirms-that-echo-device-secretly-shared-users-private-audio/.

[105] Stajano n 30.

[106] Pagallo et al, n 16.

[107] Apthorpe et al, n 92.

[108] AIOTI n 5.

[109] Christl and Spiekermann n 32.

[110] Nicolescu, Razvan, Michael Huth, Petar Radanliev, and David De Roure. 'Mapping the Values of IoT', *Journal of Information Technology*, 26 March 2018. Available at: https://doi.org/10.1057/s41265-018-0054-1.

Secondly, we see that the problem of skewed economic incentive is also closely intertwined with the implementation of proprietary software embedded in smart devices. Even when consumers purchase IoT hardware, they do not actually acquire property rights to the embedded proprietary software in any meaningful sense.[111] In fact, consumers merely rent such software, often without rights to alter it and without guarantees that it will retain same functionality. Not only does such approach make it difficult to scrutinise the actual private data collection protocols of sensory device, but it also provides much greater field of deliberation with regard to private data collection for the device manufacturers. The combination of skewed economic incentives and opaque embedded software creates situations when hardware products are shipped to the consumers with preinstalled malware, as in the infamous case of 'Lenovo'.[112] Furthermore, it becomes harder and harder to draw a line between privacy breaches happening because of poor implementation and malicious intent.[113] This reality, as Monti argues, creates a very distorted concept of trust in the hardware and service providers, where trust is degraded from ethical commitment to a marketing 'buzzword' used to obfuscate risks for the user.[114]

Finally, even if we could consider a sensor hardware supplier as trustworthy, it does not provide much of an evidence about trustworthiness of third parties with whom data could be shared with. This issue becomes apparent from an observation that transitivity of trust is a highly demanding property dependent on the possibility of delegation – empowering someone to extend your trust indirectly. Furthermore, if the scope of trust involves a trustee's capacity to harm a trustor's privacy, then justification of such extended trust is much more difficult to achieve.[115] By definition, if Alice trusts Bob with private information, any of his attempts to share it with a third party undermines such trust. To justifiably trust the chain of entities to handle her message containing private information, Alice must first identify all involved entities, and second, assess their trustworthiness independently from one another. This means assessing each entity's capacity to provide reliable information about its data handling practices and evidence that these practices will not be changed unilaterally.

The pessimistic conclusion here could be that, from a moral perspective, IoT systems will never be trustworthy with regards to its users' private data protection.

---

[111] Fairfield, Joshua AT. *Owned: Property, Privacy, and the New Digital Serfdom* (Cambridge: Cambridge University Press, 2017).

[112] Schneier, Bruce. 'Man-in-the-Middle Attacks on Lenovo Computers.' *Schneier on Security* (blog), 20 February 2015. Available at: www.schneier.com/blog/archives/2015/02/man-in-the-midd_7.html.

[113] The recent finding that android smartphones from well-known manufacturers were shipped to consumers with malware preinstalled at the firmware level, is both highly disturbing and yet unsurprising. Bocek, Vojtech, and Nikolaos Chrysaidos. 'Android Devices Ship with Pre-Installed Malware.' *Avast Blog* (blog), 24 May 2018. Available at: https://blog.avast.com/android-devices-ship-with-pre-installed-malware.

[114] Monti. 'Trust in the Shell,' n 21.

[115] Ibid.

However, that would be a premature resolution. The main issue here is a need for the conceptual reconsideration of trust value. Understood as a deficit good that should be elicited from the users by all means, not only does 'trust' become a buzzword as Monti warns,[116] but it also turns into a dangerous instrument of coercion. This overly exposes users to vulnerabilities which are exaggerated by the power imbalance between trustor and trustee in such relations. This does not suggest that we should abandon the benefits of IoT technology altogether. Rather, such concerns invite us to reconsider whether trust is the best instrument to reap these benefits.

Luhmann, somewhat paradoxically, suggests that a system of a higher complexity requires more trust but at the same time also needs more distrust.[117] However, this is a valid point, once we consider that distrust can also be a rational strategy aimed at eliminating a range of possible scenarios. Furthermore, distrusting someone or something does not preclude development of trust in future, given new evidence.[118] Counterintuitively then, acting on distrust to achieve justifiable trust can be a viable strategy, especially in the context of strong power imbalances or information asymmetry between trusting parties. Thus, distrust should also be considered with an end in mind, as a prima facie that can be discarded once a sufficient level of trustworthiness is demonstrably achieved. This is very much an approach in the spirit of Humean suggestion that with contriving institutional arrangements such as governments, we should start from the premise of distrust, an assumption that such institutions will be staffed by knaves.[119]

4. Building on the Distrust in the IoT

4.1. Minimising Reliance on Trust

Arguing from the Humean approach, Hardin points out that systems of checks and balances in the design of institutions in fact increase trustworthiness of the system as a whole.[120] It is reasonable, then, to embrace this approach in the design of IoT applications as socio-technical systems and try to derive some practical principles from it. One such principle is the minimisation of reliance on trust in the IoT systems. As Gambetta argues, trust is closely related to the agent's degree of freedom to disappoint a trustor's expectations.[121] Thus, when the trustee's actions

---

[116] Ibid.

[117] Luhmann n 8 at 71. Luhmannn, of course, refers to social systems, but this principle can be true of social parts in socio-technical systems.

[118] Govier, n 7 at 50.

[119] Hume, David. *Essays, Moral, Political, and Literary.* Edited by Eugene F. Miller, 1987. Available at: www.econlib.org/library/LFBooks/Hume/hmMPL6.html.

[120] Hardin, n 6 at 108.

[121] See Gambetta n 10.

are heavily constrained, the role of trust in such a relation is proportionately smaller. The same can be said of the data collecting entities in IoT architecture. The lesser freedoms an entity has with regard to private data, the less trust a user has to place in this entity.

Essentially every type of technological solution that can minimise users' reliance on trust in the system can be considered morally desirable. Edge computing as an approach might be one such solution, a technological design paradigm suggesting that as much data as possible should be aggregated and processed at the user's end (the edge of a network). Another very promising solution to the protection of private data on the IoT systems might come with the development of blockchain technologies. The latter is of particular interest in the context of this chapter since blockchain-based solutions are sometimes branded as 'trustless'[122] or even 'trust-free'.[123]

To elaborate on this point, it might be helpful to consider very briefly some of the proposed blockchain-based IoT solutions. Considering that blockchain protocol is a general purpose technology, it has a wide transformative potential for many aspects of IoT which cannot be covered in a single study.[124] Given this limitation, it makes sense to highlight some possibilities and potential limits of these technological solutions in the context of IoT consumer's trust, without going into details of particular projects. Blockchain in its most general sense can be seen as a distributed transaction database, which solves the key problem for any distributed data base – that is, the issue of record synchronisation between the nodes of the network. A key novelty of blockchain comes from the fact that this problem is solved without the need for a centralised trusted authority.

Such transaction database or more specifically a distributed ledger, is based on cryptographic hashes which provides several interesting properties. First, this is an append-only ledger which means that new records can only be added but not deleted (immutability). This also means that any new records must be generated in a specific 'block' format, containing the hash of the preceding one (resulting in a chain of blocks, and hence the name). The generation of such blocks is computationally demanding, and nodes taking part in it ('miners') are rewarded for successful generation of a valid block on a competitive basis.[125] Second, it is relatively easy to verify consistency of a new block with previous ones for any node holding a copy of the ledger (verifiability). This ingenious solution does solve the problem of trust in a very specific sense, guaranteeing that all nodes behave in a

---

[122] Christidis Konstantinos, and Michael Devetsikiotis. 'Blockchains and Smart Contracts for the Internet of Things', *IEEE Access* 4 (2016): 2292–2303. Available at: https://doi.org/10.1109/ACCESS.2016.2566339.

[123] Beck, Roman, Jacob Stenum Czepluch, Nikolaj Lollike, and Simon Malone. 'Blockchain-the Gateway to Trust-Free Cryptographic Transactions' (2016). Available at: http://elibrary.aisnet.org/Default.aspx?url=http://aisel.aisnet.org/cgi/viewcontent.cgi?article=1145&context=ecis2016_rp.

[124] Swan, Melanie. *Blockchain: Blueprint for a New Economy* (Sebastopol, CA: O'Reilly Media, 2015).

[125] This approach is rather straightforward in cryptocurrencies, where nodes generating blocks get fees for the processing of transactions in the same currency.

predictable way. It does not matter if a miner is trustworthy since malicious behaviour is costly in terms of time and computation, and easy to identify by the rest of the network.

This general scheme had found its first successful implementation in cryptocurrencies which use a relatively constrained set of rules in their protocols. Blockchain protocols, capable of encoding complex sets of rules, allow not only ledger keeping, but also distributed computation, prototypically implemented as 'Smart contracts'.[126] Smart contracts are general purpose, distributed applications that can be executed on the blockchain with code and state stored in the ledger. It is fair to say that most IoT related solutions using blockchain technology are built around smart contracts in one way or the other. Such proposed solutions can have numerous applications such as providing identity layers for network nodes, access control layers, providing secure track records of data flows, and many others.[127,128] This is a radical departure from existing client-server models where all data streams from the consumer's end point are usually aggregated and stored in the cloud provided by the hardware manufacturer, or some other entity acting as a gatekeeper for private data.[129]

Such solutions might not only increase transparency of data flows, but also provide users with better controls over their private data. For instance, providing management mechanisms for secure and transparent transfers of private data from consumer to services, such as health analytics, diagnostic services for personal car or any other remote applications, based on smart contracts. Christidis and Devetsikiotis characterise such layers as 'trustless environments', where entities on the network do not need to rely on trust in their interactions, since actions for entities are not only predictable but guaranteed by the network protocol.[130] However, as Buterin points out, blockchain systems in themselves are not 'trustless', despite being sometimes labelled this way.[131] First of all, only public (sometimes called 'permissionless') blockchains have the above-mentioned properties.[132] Second, trust solutions that work in the (relatively) narrow context of cryptocurrencies do

---

[126] See Christidis and Devetsikiotis n 122.

[127] Atzori, Marcella. 'Blockchain-Based Architectures for the Internet of Things: A Survey (2016).' Available at: *SSRN 2846810*, n.d.

[128] Dorri, Ali, Salil S Kanhere, and Raja Jurdak. 'Blockchain in Internet of Things: Challenges and Solutions', *ArXiv Preprint ArXiv:1608.05187*, 2016.

[129] It is necessary to point out that implementing blockchain solutions for the control-access layer is currently is the preferred solution for IoT applications. Storage of private data on public blockchain itself is extremely problematic from the privacy perspective and should not even be considered for any application.

[130] Christidis and Devetsikiotisn 122.

[131] Buterin, Vitalik. 'Visions, Part 2: The Problem of Trust', 27 April 2017. Available at: https://blog.ethereum.org/2015/04/27/visions-part-2-the-problem-of-trust/.

[132] Decentralisation is arguably most interesting property of blockchain technology, which is absent in so called 'private' or 'permissioned' blockchains, where instead one entity (company) decides who can become a node. This is not very different from a distributed database where trustworthiness of nodes is decided by centralised authority.

not translate easily to other domains. Even the implementation of a single smart contract which can be considered 'trustless' in meaningful sense is contingent upon the set of a very specific conditions. Strictly speaking, a more appropriate term here is a 'trust-minimised' system, since smart contracts can allow interaction between parties without reliance on trust only in a very specific context of a transaction enabled by it.

It would thus be very misleading to treat all blockchain-based solutions as 'trustless systems' and simply wrong to label them as 'trust free'. In this respect, it seems understanding of trust in blockchain implementation is not immune from Hardin's 'conceptual slippage' as well.[133] Blockchain based solutions can minimise reliance on trust in private data protection for some components of IoT architecture, but not eliminate it completely. When systems involving human operators are made more reliable through automation, users' trust is not eliminated but rather shifted from operators to the designers of the system.[134] Consider an idealised example of a technological artefact with highly predictable functionality. Such a device, say a flash drive with built in hardware encryption, still relies on distributed trust. Apart from trusting the reliability of the artefact itself, at the very least a user has also to trust the manufacturer to properly implement the encryption, the authors of that encryption protocol, and the testers who did their best to find vulnerabilities in the protocol.

Even with the radical increase of predictability of IoT components, on the larger scale, information asymmetries persist, and we inevitably run into issues of trust in developers, trust in code reviewers/auditors and trust in institutional arrangements. These issues are partially mitigated in large cryptocurrency projects like Bitcoin, which greatly benefits from a transparent and decentralised developer community. This effect essentially amounts to the distribution of trust between independent entities. However, it is much less clear how the trust problem will be solved when IoT blockchain solutions are developed and offered by commercial companies. This is not necessarily an issue of trust in commercial entities but also a problem stemming from the variety of implementations allowed by blockchain technology and the different interpretations of transparency.[135] It would also be very disappointing and disturbing to see the emergence of a new marketing buzzwords such as 'trust free', used to lure consumers into a false sense of security.

---

[133] Again, some of this confusion can be attributed to the overlap of concepts, since one can define a 'trustless' system in the same sense as the narrow interpretation of 'trustworthy', that is, the one that is fully predictable. Buterin even suggests that 'trustless' and 'trustful' systems refer essentially to the same resulting state of a predictable system, achieved through different means. Thus, the choice of the 'trustless' descriptor here highlights the point that predictability is achieved in the absence of trusted third parties.

[134] Nickel et al, n 29.

[135] For instance, IOTA, which brands its product as an alternative to IoT blockchain solutions, was found threatening researchers with legal action to prevent disclosure of vulnerabilities. See http://blockchain.cs.ucl.ac.uk/2018/04/update-partnership-iota-foundation/.

4.2. Mediating Trust

Following our discussion, it can be argued that technological solutions aimed at the minimisation of trust in the IoT should be complemented with instruments that Hardin characterises as trust intermediaries.[136] Existing solutions to the problem of impersonal trust extension via intermediaries are reputation systems. These essentially combine two functions of a trust intermediary: proof of identity for potential trustees and proof of goodwill and good sense in the form of reputational evidence. According to Simpson, a reputation system is a truthful, comprehensive and accessible record about a person (or entity) that can be used to assess one's trustworthiness.[137] Such evidence should also be impossible or very difficult to fake and be subjectively available to trustor. A reputation system then may carry two functions of a trust intermediary – providing knowledge of data collecting entities and evidence of trustworthiness for identifiable entities.

The question is whether such a system can provide sufficient incentives to data collectors not to default on trust obligations. I argue that a reputation system can act as this deterrent due to the peculiar nature of trust epistemology – a vulnerability of trust to a counter-evidence. While the evidence of past goodwill behaviour is crucial for the assessment of trustworthiness, it does not guarantee it, especially in the case of institutional trust. As Gambetta notes, past evidence does not fully eliminate the risk of future deviance. In that respect, he argues trust predicates not only on the evidence of benevolent behaviour, but also on the absence of counter-evidence.[138] This is a peculiar property of trust as an epistemic constraint: one cannot believe B to do P, if one possesses overwhelming evidence that B will not do P. The same kind of overwhelming counter-evidence can simplify an issue of an organisational reliability assessment, which is highlighted by Hardin.[139]

It is apparent that not any kind of counter-evidence is sufficient for such a role. As practice shows, data collecting companies often having an appalling record of privacy violations tainted by court decisions and public scandals, still stick to their malpractices.[140] This occurs largely because media coverage is not a reputation system, but rather a playing field where PR efforts of companies can effectively mitigate reputational damage. In Simpson's terms, such information is neither comprehensive nor subjectively available to the trustor. Thus, an effective reputation system capable of fulfilling all three roles of trust intermediary must be a standardised system, providing necessary competence, quality reputational evidence and accessibility.

---

[136] Hardin, n 6 at 140.
[137] Simpson, Thomas W. 'E-Trust and Reputation', *Ethics and Information Technology* 13, no 1 (2011): 29–38. Available at: https://doi.org/10.1007/s10676-010-9259-x.
[138] Gambetta n 10.
[139] Hardin, n 6 at 152.
[140] Christl and Spiekermann n 32.

Such systems can certainly be implemented using technological solutions, and blockchain technologies may present interesting opportunities in that respect.[141] It is, however, important to keep in mind that complete infrastructure solutions are still far away from the commercial implementation. There is also no guarantee that these solutions will disrupt current business models of private data monetisation in the consumer IoT sector, purely based on free market mechanisms. It is reasonable thus to consider possibilities of institutional arrangements, and avenues to remedy issues of trustworthiness for already existing consumer IoT products and services.

Certain interest in that respect presents an idea of 'trust labels' or 'privacy seals' which has been suggested in different contexts as a tool to establish reputation of a service provider or a product.[142,143] Some 'trust label' solutions applied specifically to the problem of privacy in the context of IoT can be found in the EU commission staff working document "Advancing the internet of things in Europe".[144] One of the ideas proposed here is the 'Trusted IoT' label that would help consumers assess end products as being compliant with the aforementioned principles. This suggestion is a part of the package together with the proposal on standardisation and liability clarifications which are considered crucial for future technological developments. Implementation of a 'Trusted IoT' label scheme is seen as a measure that would complement the upcoming GDPR regulation to help consumers with the problem of trust in the new technology. Existing proposals on a 'Trusted IoT' label largely focus on cybersecurity requirements, although promising applications of this scheme could also be extended to cover the wider issue of private data protection.

Granted, existing privacy seals developed as industry self-regulatory measures have been criticised before for the lack of standardisation and effective enforcement, and these are indeed valid concerns.[145] However, these concerns do not preclude development of institutional schemes that can offer a reputation system with truthful, comprehensive and accessible records about private data collectors (and processors) as suggested by Simpson.[146] In that respect, 'trust label'

---

[141] Pouwelse, Johan, André de Kok, Joost Fleuren, Peter Hoogendoorn, Raynor Vliegendhart, and Martijn de Vos. 'Laws for Creating Trust in the Blockchain Age', *European Property Law Journal* 6, no 3 (2017). Available at: https://doi.org/10.1515/eplj-2017-0022.

[142] De Hert, Paul, Vagelis Papakonstantinou, Rowena Rodrigues, David Barnard-Wills, David Wright, Luca Remoti, Tonia Damvakeraki, European Commission, Joint Research Centre, and Institute for the Protection and the Security of the Citizen. *EU Privacy Seals Project: Challenges and Possible Scope of an EU Privacy Seal Scheme: Final Report Study Deliverable 3.4.* Edited by Laurent Beslay and Nicolas Dubois. (Luxembourg: Publications Office, 2014). Available at: http://dx.publications.europa.eu/10.2788/85717.

[143] Rodrigues, R., D. Wright, and K. Wadhwa. 'Developing a Privacy Seal Scheme (That Works).' *International Data Privacy Law* 3, no 2 (1 May 2013): 100–116. Available at: https://doi.org/10.1093/idpl/ips037.

[144] EC (European Comission). 'Commission Staff Working Document. Advancing the Internet of Things in Europe'.

[145] See Rodrigues et al n 143.

[146] See Simpson n 137.

should be understood first and foremost not as a mere 'label' but as a certification scheme aimed at guaranteeing trustworthiness of a service or entity through the introduction of checks and balances.[147] To the large extent many failures of previous 'trust labels' stem from the fact that in the absence of underlying robust certification schemes, they are reduced to just another marketing gimmick.[148] This again shifts the focus from the trustworthiness of services in terms of data protection, to consumers' attitudes of trust.

From that perspective, any self-regulation certification is not going to deliver intended results. De Hert et al. suggest that credible certification can be achieved in the absence of conflicting interests between certifying bodies and service providers, arguing in favour of industry-independent expert bodies.[149] Such institutional arrangements can effectively decrease power imbalances between consumers and providers of IoT services. Rodrigues et al. list a number of options for the implementation of data protection certification enabled by GDPR regime for certification and seals.[150] The existence of independent certification bodies can provide consumers with the capacity to distribute trust among different institutional entities: experts, accreditation agencies and data protection authorities.[151] Furthermore, an absence of such certification would indicate that neither the device nor the device provider could be considered trustworthy with regards to data protection standards, serving as counter-evidence to trust.

Another point of consideration here is an aspect of certification which should satisfy criteria of comprehensiveness (or sufficient scope). De Hert et al. provide several examples of certification schemes in different technological contexts, highlighting key points of consideration.[152] They argue that in certain contexts (such as biometric systems), the main beneficiary of a certification scheme should be the party with the least effective power and influence over construction of the system. This principle is applicable in the context of consumer IoT as well. Of course, considering diversity of IoT products and services, as well as the dynamic nature of architectures, standardised certification is hardly feasible. Nonetheless it is reasonable to aim for a minimum standard of transparency for IoT services and processes, and not just hardware elements. It is also crucial that certification is performed on a dynamic basis, similar to vulnerability scans, rather than as a one-time assessment.

---

[147] Besides, 'trusted' may not be the best name for the scheme, considering past controversies around the brand of 'trusted computing'.

[148] It is quite telling that many 'privacy seals' emphasise marketing advantages granted by the certification (Rodrigues et al, 2013).

[149] De Hert et al n 142.

[150] Rodrigues, Rowena, David Barnard-Wills, Paul De Hert, and Vagelis Papakonstantinou. 'The Future of Privacy Certification in Europe: An Exploration of Options under Article 42 of the GDPR.' *International Review of Law, Computers & Technology* 30, no 3 (September 2016): 248–70. Available at: https://doi.org/10.1080/13600869.2016.1189737.

[151] Many elements of certification schemes such as registries could be implemented on the basis of blockchain solutions.

[152] De Hert et al n 42.

At the very least, certified IoT solutions should by default conform to the principle of minimal data collection necessary for basic functionality, and strict opt-in for any extended data sharing. Granted, it may not always be trivial to define precisely basic functionality in many smart products and services. This problem however it not a technical issue, but the intentional design of products employing advertising revenue models. Key criteria here is that consumers should always have a choice between products and services which function with or without personal data monetisation. This brings about another requirement: an availability of transparency tools in certified devices. This means that consumers should always be able to get truthful dynamic information about data which is collected in the process of service use, about all entities that have access to the data, and the tools that can be used to modify data flow in accordance with their preferences. These tools may either be integrated into a smart device itself or be available through a hub device (e.g. an app on a smartphone).

Finally, such a certification scheme should satisfy criteria of accessibility to consumers, dealing specifically with the 'label' part itself. Given the miniaturisation of sensor equipment and diversity of hardware formats, there is, once again, no 'silver bullet' solution in terms of label format. However, given ever increasing connectivity of IoT components it is reasonable to assume that most flexibility can be achieved with the implementation of digital labels. Given that all smart devices by definition have extended connectivity it is reasonable to aim for the implementation of labels in digital format.

Some interesting solutions which may serve as a basis for such labels can be found in the research on standards for digital identifiers.[153] Such identifier is essentially a cryptographically signed digital document, which allows for the reliable verification of its authenticity and contains references to additional information resources. Using a standardised format, it is possible to ensure that all necessary information (IoT certificate, links to certification body registry, links to transparency tools), even for most the most miniature device can be authenticated and accessed through a smartphone or any other smart device with connectivity module and graphic interface. In general, institutional arrangements and technological solutions should be seen as complementary tools aimed at the same goal – trustworthy IoT.

5. Conclusion

The complex nature of IoT architectures contributes significantly to privacy risks for users of such systems. In this context, the capacity of trust to reduce complexity, can indeed make the implementation of such systems more viable.

---

[153] See research by Web Cryptography Working Group. Available at: https://w3c-ccg.github.io/did-spec/.

However, it is crucial for policies and technological solutions to focus on the trustworthiness of systems and not just the psychological trust attitudes of users. If the latter becomes a goal framed in the model of 'trust deficit', instead of the promised benefits, consumer IoT systems can bring about the dystopian vision of a ubiquitous surveillance economy. Even in the absence of intentional nudging towards sharing of private data (malicious interface design) and psychological bias, the complexity of existing and future IoT systems simply does not provide technology consumers with much opportunity for balanced and rational decision making. The position of epistemic impairment significantly constrains the amount of available evidence to the users of technology which could be employed to justify trust in the system.

Another factor limiting such capacity is the non-transitive nature of trust in the protection of private data, which is particularly relevant in the context of structural data sharing. While it is possible to extend trust through the chains of data-collecting entities, to justify trustworthiness of the system as a whole, such extensions cannot be realistically achieved in the context of power imbalances. This means that justified trust in IoT systems and services can never be encompassed by trust in a single technological artefact or a single entity such as the provider of the system. To be trustworthy, the system as a whole should include both technical and institutional tools aimed at amending information asymmetries and power imbalances. Thus, based on a Humean vision of institutional design, the moral value of distrust could be used as a premise defining design requirement in IoT implementations, comprised of technical and social elements. Rephrasing Hume – without this, we shall find, in the end, that we have no security for our liberties or data, except the good-will of data collectors; that is, we shall have no security and privacy at all.[154]

This approach gives rise to a key guiding principle of minimisation of trust with all means available. Too much reliance on trust can be a burden and a serious failure of the system design, especially when the burden of establishing evidence to justify trust is placed on the trustor – the user of technology. Even in the absence of other complications, it is difficult to provide moral justification for trust relations in the context of significant information asymmetry. Consumer IoT systems can make this task next to impossible, taking into consideration economic and power imbalances between consumers and providers of technology, where interests of the latter often align with interests of data collectors. Thus, minimisation of trust here should be considered a moral imperative, a means to reduce dependence of users on the benevolence of multiple data collecting entities.

This is followed by another guiding principle which suggests a necessity to distribute trust wherever it is impossible to avoid it completely. In the context of IoT architectures, this means that users should not be left to their own devices in the process of making privacy relevant decisions, dealing with a single entity

---

[154] See Hume n 119.

such as hardware manufacturer or service provider. This can be achieved with the introduction of trust intermediaries, providing functions of expertise, tracking of data collecting entities and some means of redress in the cases of trust abuse. Such arrangements can take forms of independent certification bodies combined with technological solutions that can increase transparency of data-collecting practices. While these requirements are sometimes presented as excessively demanding, they are in fact necessary minimal measures that should be implemented to avoid paying the price of eroded privacy in exchange for the benefits of IoT.

10

Fines under the GDPR

PAUL NEMITZ

Abstract

The introduction of substantial fines for infringements in Article 83 of the GDPR constitutes an important development of European data protection law. This chapter discusses the innovation in comparison to the previous Data Protection Directive (95/46/EC), with a special emphasis on the inspiration the EU rules and practice of fining in competition law contain for fines under GDPR. It first sets out thoughts on the purpose of fines and the structure of Article 83 of the GDPR. Next, it demonstrates how competition law is inspiring the fining rules under GDPR and why DPAs are under a general duty to impose fines. It then discusses considerations on the amounts of fines and the special case of cumulation of infringements, as well as the notion of 'the undertaking', which are important both in competition law and the GDPR. As a reminder of past incoherence rather than as a starting point for future fining practices, the chapter closes by reviewing the diversity of fines under the previous directive and ends with a call on the European Data Protection Board to quickly establish a publicly accessible database on fines imposed by DPAs, in order to create the transparency necessary to ensure a coherent application of the GDPR across the European Union. In the conclusion, this chapter calls on DPAs to learn from competition law and to acquire the skills necessary for rigorous fining to bring about the necessary deterrent effect.

Keywords

Fine, Article 83 GDPR, competition law, undertaking, proportionality, DPA, powers

1. Introduction

Imposing fines will often have a higher disciplinary function than other remedies. Fines serve to discourage further infringements. Article 83 of the GDPR serves both special prevention and general prevention, since high fines for misconduct are attracting widespread attention, especially in the case of controllers or processors known in the market and to the general public. They ensure that efforts of compliance are undertaken in addition to pure profitability investments and a fortiori that the economic advantage that controllers or processors derive from infringements of the GDPR, if any, do not remain with them (see GDPR, Art. 83(2)(k)). The fines, if high enough, can reduce the incentives of non-compliance. In view of the potentially substantial fines, it is to be expected that, under Article 83 GDPR, the fine for the relevant players will provide the greatest, if not the decisive, incentive to act lawfully and thus to respect the rights of the data subject in the processing of their personal data and to make the system of the GDPR as a trust framework for personal data processing work in Europe and beyond.

Against the background of the digital economy, which is steadily increasing in importance, the GDPR thus ensures that the market continues to serve the interests of individuals and the general public. Entrepreneurial for-profit activity shall not deprive individuals of their fundamental right to data protection. The market regards any data more and more as a tradable standardised commodity ('data is the new oil', 'data is the currency of the future'). The financial burden associated with fines under Article 83 GDPR ensures that the market is encouraged to respect the specific fundamental rights positions which are inherent in personal data, which legally cannot be treated and traded in Europe like the commodities oil and currency.

Whether Article 83 can fulfil its function in practice will depend crucially on its implementation by the data protection authorities: It will be essential that the supervisory authorities are adequately resourced in terms of infrastructure, personnel and finances in order to be able to fulfil their role, also vis-à-vis internationally and globally active companies, thus enabling the GDPR to be implemented and applied effectively. The experience of competition law shows that most decisions on the imposition of fines are contested in law by the parties concerned up to the last instance. In this respect too, the supervisory authorities should ensure that they are adequately qualified and sufficiently staffed for lengthy legal disputes.

Article 83 GDPR provides for a differentiated and flexible system of fines, which allows and obliges the supervisory authorities to sanction violations with appropriate fines to deter future infringements. Article 83, paragraph 1 sets the standards for the entire sanction system in the GDPR, to which concrete measures must adhere. Paragraph 2 lays down specific criteria to be taken into account when determining the amount of a fine in a specific case. Paragraph 3 regulates cases of cumulation of data protection infringements and sets the maximum amount of the fine for them. Paragraphs 4 and 5 qualify violations of the provisions of the GDPR depending on their significance in simple or qualified violations, which accordingly result in lower or higher fines. Paragraph 6 provides for a further increase in the fine for violations of prior orders from supervisory authorities. Paragraph 7 contains a limited opening for Member States, which can exempt the public sector from fines to a limited extent. Paragraph 8 clarifies that the fines procedure and the ensuing judicial proceedings must comply with the requirements of the Union and Member State law. Finally, paragraph 9 contains special rules for Denmark and Estonia whose legal systems do not provide for the power of authorities to impose fines (see GDPR, recital 151).

2. The Inspiration from Competition Law for fines under the GDPR

Concretisations relating to Article 83 GDPR can be found in recitals 148, 150, 151, 152 and 153. Special attention should also be paid, to the fining practice of the Commission and the national authorities on competition law, to the Guidelines of 3 October 2017 of the Article 29 Working Party (the Guidelines)[1] under Article 70(1)(k) GDPR. They are intended to ensure the uniform application of Article 83.

These guidelines are, for good reasons, not so detailed that controllers and processors can insert fines into their economic calculation ex ante as part of an illegal business model. This would allow them to set prices accordingly to cover the risk of the fines calculated in advance, and thus deprive the fines of any deterrent effect, contrary to what the regulation provides. The Article 29 Working Party announced in its Guidelines under Chapter III after footnote 10 in a bracketed sentence that 'detailed calculation work would be the focus of a potential subsequent stage of this guideline'. It can only be hoped that wisdom guides this work so as to prevent controllers and processors from calculating fines in advance, which 'would devalue their effectiveness as a tool' (see Guidelines II.1. after footnote 6).

The GDPR in its fining system is inspired by the system of fines in European competition law and uses its methodology in large part. In particular, the determination of fines in terms of a percentage of overall turnover and a cap of fines determined by a set percentage of turnover of the undertaking concerned (4% in GDPR, Art. 83), is inspired by the same methodology in the Commission Guidelines on the method of setting fines imposed pursuant to Article 23(2)(a) of Regulation No 1/2003, which provides in Paragraph 32:

> The final amount of the fine shall not, in any event, exceed 10 % of the total turnover in the preceding business year of the undertaking or association of undertakings participating in the infringement, as laid down in Article 23(2) of Regulation No 1/2003.[2]

---

[1] Guidelines on the application and setting of administrative fines for the purpose of the Regulation 2016/679, Article 29 Data Protection Working Party, 17 / EN WP 253 of 3 October 2017.
[2] Guidelines on the method of setting fines according to Article 23, para 2, pt. A VO (EC) no 1/2003, OJ. 2006 C 210, 2.

Also, the Merger Regulation, in Article 14,[3] follows such a methodology of fine calculation based on turnover. A case of its application relevant to data protection, the Facebook/WhatsApp case, is discussed further below.

It is thus not surprising that recital 150 of the GDPR explicitly refers to Articles 101 and 102 TFEU, the basic provisions in the Treaty on competition law, for the definition of an undertaking on which a fine is imposed and in relation to which turnover must be calculated, to be used also in the GDPR for this purpose. In the Guidelines of 3 October 2017, the Art. 29 Working Party also refers in footnote 4 to specific ECJ jurisprudence in the area of competition law.[4]

Both data protection and competition law fall within the category of special economic administrative law. In these fields of law, infringements are often a matter of cost reducing intention or negligence, motivated by the pursuit of profit. There are costs related to compliance and in some cases high financial incentives for both competition and data protection breaches. In both areas of law, directly or indirectly, natural persons, as consumers and citizens concerned, are the victims of these infringements, either by economic disadvantage or by a deterioration of fundamental rights positions or both.

The European experience in competition law shows that the public enforcement, based on ex-officio actions and complaints, is the main driver of compliance. Private enforcement and actions for damages, even where special legislation for that purpose exists,[5] play a smaller role, with the later often being efficient only as a follow on of public enforcement findings of illegality.[6] A fortiori the private enforcement or damages claims in data protection law have so far in practice played no significant role in Europe. It is likely that, as in competition law, public enforcement will be the main compliance driver in data protection. The complexity and non-transparency of the processing of personal data led the primary legislator to foresee strong and independent data protection authorities in Article 16(2) of TFEU and Article 8 of the Charter of Fundamental Rights. This is also the key argument in favour of strong public enforcement, now that the regulation provides the DPAs the tools for this purpose. In addition, the usual enormous asymmetry of economic power and information between the individual and the

---

[3] Council Regulation (EC) No 139/2004 of 20 January 2004 on the control of concentrations between undertakings, OJ. L 24 of 29.1.2004.

[4] Generally, on the relationship between privacy and competition law see Francisco Costa-Cabral, Orla Lynskey, 'Family Ties: The Intersection between Data Protection and Competition in EU Law', *Common Market Law Review*,. 54, no 1 (2017): 11–50 at 11; on the relationship between data protection law and consumer protection law Natali Helberger and Zuiderveen Borgesius, Frederik and Reyna Agustin, 'The Perfect Match? A Closer Look at the Relationship between EU Consumer Law and Data Protection Law' Common Market Law Review, 54, no 5, (2017). Available at: https://ssrn.com/abstract=3048844.

[5] Directive 2014/104/EU adopting certain provisions on damages actions under national law for infringements of competition regulations of the Member States and the European Union, OJ. 2014 L 349, 1.

[6] See for details Jürgen Basedow, Jörg Philipp Terhechte, Lubos Tichý (eds), *Private Enforcement of Competition Law* (Verlagsgesellschaft: Nomos, 2011).

controllers and processors in the digital economy is a key argument for strong public enforcement: the individual simply cannot be left alone in this asymmetry. The creation of ever more individual rights has only a small positive compliance effect on controllers and processors if it is not accompanied by strong public enforcement.

This reality must have an impact on the application of Article 83 of the GDPR in individual cases. In many cases, its interpretation and application will be inspired by similar considerations such as those in competition law (eg Article 14 on fines in the Merger Regulation). It provides that the Commission may impose fines not exceeding 1 per cent of the aggregate turnover of the undertaking or association of undertakings concerned where, intentionally or negligently, they supply incorrect or misleading information in a submission, certification, notification or supplement thereto, in the context of merger investigations.[7]

This provision was recently applied in a case concerning personal data and data protection questions, namely profiling, in Commission Decision of 18 May 2017 imposing fines under Article 14(1) of Council Regulation (EC) No 139/2004 for the supply by an undertaking of incorrect or misleading information.[8] In this case, the European Commission imposed a fine of €110 million because, despite the availability of automated matching solutions between Facebook and WhatsApp, Facebook had stated in the investigation relating to the Merger of WhatsApp and Facebook that user matching would either have to be done manually by users, (and would therefore be insufficient and unreliable) or require Facebook to significantly re-engineer the app's code.

This case is important as it demonstrates the risk – or one might call it the temptation – to lie when it comes to describing facts on processing of personal data to the regulator, maybe in the hope that the regulator will not master the technical complexities involved. It will be important, for gaining the necessary respect and cooperation in the increasingly complex maze of processing of personal data, that DPAs rigorously increase fines at the slightest sign of negligent or intentional misleading statements when it comes to establishing facts relevant for their decisions. At the core of the unconditional duty to cooperate with the DPAs of controllers and processors as well as Data Protection Officers (see GDPR, Arts 31 and 39(1)(d)) is the duty to state the truth and DPAs need to ensure respect for this through a rigorous fining practice, following the example set by the European Commission.

The fact that in the initial phase of the interpretation and application of the GDPR comparable rules in competition law will often provide orientation does not rule out that data protection law will later develop into an independent

---

[7] See Council Regulation (EC) No 139/2004 n 3.
[8] European Commission – DG Competition, Case M.8228 – Facebook/WhatsApp (Art. 14(1) proc.), notified under document number C(2017)3192). Available at: https://publications.europa.eu/en/publication-detail/-/publication/f0da1066-8d12-11e7-b5c6-01aa75ed71a1/language-en/format-PDFA1A.

practice. However, this practice should always seek coherence of the legal system as a whole, including the relationship between fines in both competition and data protection law. In addition, it obviously must pursue consistency between the actions of data protection authorities across all Member States. With the entry into force of the Regulation, data protection authorities must be prepared to sanction infringements as consistently as possible to obtain a strong deterrent against non-compliance, as competition authorities have done for a long time in competition law infringements.

It would not be in line with the basic legal protection obligation of data protection authorities and the principle of coherence of the legal system if DPAs leave it to the, admittedly for the time being far better-equipped, competition authorities and their stringent enforcement tradition to sanction breaches of the GDPR (eg if committed by dominant companies). The investigation and then preliminary assessment of the Federal German Cartel Office, the German competition authority, in the Facebook procedure touched on data protection law and in its preliminary statement of 19 December 2017 came to the conclusion that the collection and exploitation of data from third-party sources outside the Facebook website is abusive.[9] This case and the Commission decision in Facebook/WhatsApp cited above, demonstrates the close relationship between competition and data protection enforcement. They open the door to far more intense cooperation and mutual learning between EU competition authorities (the Commission and Member States' competition authorities) and EU data protection authorities which can only be beneficial for both and to the coherence of the legal system overall.

In the US, while in substance the system of protection of personal data and the rules on privacy are different from those of the EU, the fact that the FTC has functions relating to both the protection of competition and of privacy has certainly been an advantage in terms of transferring learnings, in particular as to the rigour of investigation and how to produce enforcement decisions which withstand judicial scrutiny, from the area of competition law with a longer enforcement history to the relatively younger area of privacy law. A similar situation is possible in Europe, where competition law also has a longer and more intense history of fining than data protection law. Competition authorities thus have accumulated knowledge on the general preventive effect of fines as well as on how to withstand judicial scrutiny which is very useful for data protection authorities. It is therefore to be hoped that DPAs and competition authorities will develop intense relationships of mutual inspiration, learning and cooperation. They will after all also often be dealing with the same 'clients' in their investigation and enforcement activities.

---

[9] See www.bundeskartellamt.de/SharedDocs/Publikation/EN/Pressemitteilungen/2017/19_12_2017_Facebook.html?nn=3591568.

3. The Duty of DPAs to Impose a Fine

According to Article 83(1) GDPR, the decision of the supervisory authorities to impose fines must be guided by the principles of effectiveness, proportionality and the objective of dissuasion. The concepts of effectiveness and dissuasion merge. Article 83(1) GDPR sets out the clear objective that the fine alone must be sufficient to ensure effective sanctioning of data protection breaches with a sufficient dissuasive effect. The supervisory authorities are therefore prohibited from making the determination of the amount of the fine dependent on any claims for compensation under Article 82. It is also prohibited to them to systematically refrain from a fine. The DPAs can only abstain from a fine in the two cases under recital 148 GDPR, namely in case of a '*minor infringement or if the fine likely to be imposed would constitute a disproportionate burden to a natural person*'. Under the wording of Article 83(2), the supervisory authority has the discretion to impose a fine '*in addition to, or instead of*' of another supervisory measure under Article 58 (2)(a)–(h). This decision must be based on the principle of effectiveness and deterrence. It must always be the goal to give controllers and processors an effective incentive to act lawfully. As a rule, it will not be enough to limit the action in case of non-compliance to another supervisory measure or a fine alone. The apodictic wording of Article 83(2)(1) ('*Fines … shall be imposed*'), as well as the wording of recital 148, S. 1, make this clear. Recital 148 S. 1 GDPR allows for the *a contrario* argument because it only mentions two specific situations in which the DPA can abstain from fining, thus obliging to conclude that if these situations are not present, a fine must be imposed. In its Guidelines, the Art. 29 Working Party even states, to be absolutely clear, that:

> Recital 148 GDPR does not contain an obligation for the supervisory authority to always replace a fine by a reprimand in the case of a minor infringement ('a reprimand may be issued instead of a fine'), but rather a possibility that is at hand, following a concrete assessment of all the circumstances of the case.

So, while there is zero discretion in terms of a legal obligation to impose a fine in all cases not falling under the two exceptions in recital 148 of the GDPR, this is not the case when they fall under one of these exceptions. In those cases, depending on circumstances, the DPA can impose a fine. The indirect and wavering language of the Guidelines here reflects the previous sanctioning traditions of data protection authorities in different Member States. However, the whole purpose of the GDPR being harmonisation and following the general rules of interpretation of EU law, these previously different traditions cannot play a role anymore in the interpretation of the Regulation nor in the practice of application by the DPAs.

Article 83 GDPR however grants the supervisory authorities limited discretion in some respects. These include, in particular, the weighting of the criteria set out in paragraph 2 and the determination of the amount of the fine in accordance with paragraphs 4 and 5. However, according to the case law of the ECJ on competition law in the imposition of fines, the supervisory authorities do not have unlimited discretion.[10] On the contrary, they must comply with the general principles of law of the European Union and of its Member States, in particular, with the principle of equal treatment. As a result, DPAs have a duty to develop an administrative practice for imposing fines to deal with similar cases in a similar way. In that regard, particular importance should be attached to the Guidelines of the Article 29 Working Party/the European Data Protection Board under Article 7(1)(k) GDPR. These guidelines, similar to the Commission's Guidelines on the procedure for fines in competition law, gain quasi-normative meaning, so that deviations from the guidelines will be judiciable. This will be the case for all other Guidelines of the European Data Protection Board, given the jurisprudence on the application of Commission Guidelines. In these guidelines, the Commission sets out its future practice on competition law or state aid law in a formally non-binding act. However, based on the principle of equal treatment, the Court has considered such acts to have a self-binding effect.[11]

According to Article 83(8) and recital 148 GDPR '*reasonable procedural guarantees*' of EU and national law must be respected. In essence, this means that before the decision to impose a fine, the person concerned must be heard ('due process'). In addition, the right to judicial protection must be granted. Its design is the responsibility of the Member States' procedural law. Whether paragraph 8 also lays down the limitation period for infringements relating to the imposition of fines is more than doubtful given the predominantly substantive nature of the limitation period.

The general principles of law of the EU require that fines are motivated and justified on the basis of the method of calculation used, in such a way as to allow the addressee to comply and if necessary to seek judicial remedy.[12] The statement of reasons must mention the aspects relevant to the determination of the amount on which the supervisory authority bases its assessment of the infringement of the GDPR. However, that does not compel the DPA to give figures as to the way in which the fine is calculated, or even to exercise its discretion solely by the use of mathematical formulae.[13]

Article 83(2)(2) GDPR obliges the supervisory authorities in each individual case to fully investigate the matter: For this purpose, the supervisory bodies have at their disposal all the instruments of Article 58 GDPR. In particular, supervisors can and should, under Article 58(1)(a), oblige the controllers and processors to provide all the information needed to perform their duties. What has been said above on the duty to cooperate and to speak the truth applies a fortiori in this context.

---

[10] ECJ 28.4.2010-T-446/05, ECLI: EU: T: 2010: 165 para 140, 142 ff. *Amann & sons* and *Cousin Filterie/Commission*.
[11] ECJ 5.4.2006-T-279/02, ECLI: EU: T: 2006: 103 para 82 *Degussa/Commission*.
[12] See Amann & Sons n 10.
[13] Ibid.

The amount of the fine must be significantly higher than any profit derived from the violation of the GDPR. In particular, because a claim for damages under Article 82 GDPR will never fully apprehend all profits generated, a fine only slightly above the profits will not be enough to provide an effective deterrent. This is so also because the deterrent effect results from the likelihood of an infringement being detected multiplied by the likely size of the fine. Since the likelihood of an infringement being detected remains rather low in the present situation, given the lack of resources available for enforcement, the fines must be substantially higher in the few cases of non-compliance being detected than in a situation in which the likelihood of infringements being detected were higher.

In fact, the fines are a tool to deter non-compliance. The deterrent effect of the fines under GDPR is a factor of the likelihood of the detection of non-compliance multiplied by the size of the fine. If fines can be calculated in advance of decisions of DPAs, thus allowing business to include them in their business plans, or if the fines are simply generally too low, they cannot deter non-compliance. If DPAs were substantially better equipped with staff and technical resources to detect non-compliance, the fines could be lower. This is so because a better resourcing of DPAs would increase the likelihood of detection of non-compliance, provided additional resources are used by DPAs for detecting and investigating it. Governments and parliaments of Member States decide on the resources available for DPAs. It is thus in their hands to equip their DPAs in such a way that the likelihood of detecting non-compliance increases if they would like to see low fines applied in individual fining decisions. Unless the number of fining decisions on non-compliance increases substantially, the fines must remain high to ensure they act as a deterrent.

The poor economic situation of the controller or processor, according to recital 148 S. 2 of the GDPR, is irrelevant to the amount of the fine, as long as the fine is not imposed on a natural person. This is based on the consideration that otherwise a controller or processor in economic difficulties could gain illegal and unjustified competitive advantages from illegal behaviour. Recital 150 sentence 4 also must be read in this way.[14]

Economic concerns can never be justification for disregarding provisions of the GDPR which serve to protect positions of fundamental rights.

4. Considerations on the Amounts of the Fine

In all cases, the amount of the fine must be based on the principle of proportionality. The criteria for this purpose as set out in Article 83(2) GDPR are further detailed by the Guidelines,[15] in alphabetical order.

---

[14] See also ECJ, 06.29.2006 – C-308/04 P, ECLI: EU: C: 2006: 433 and ECJ 28.4.2010 – T-446/05, ECLI: EU: T: 2010: 165 para 198 ff.

[15] See Art 29 WP 17/EN WP 253 n 1.

Letter (a) lays down certain legal and factual criteria as the basis for determining the amount of the fine, which the supervisory authority must take into account in each individual case. Due to the conceptual breadth of these criteria and given the existence of the 'catch-all clause' in point (k), the '*nature*' and '*seriousness*' of the infringement cannot be conclusively defined. The '*severity*' of the infringement may depend on the effect or consequences of the infringement on the person concerned (ie whether an injury resulted, for example, in a particular exposure of the data subject in a narrower group of people or even the public, and whether the violation can be reversed or not). With regard to the purpose of the processing, for example, the question may arise as to whether the cause or purpose of the processing was lawful or unlawful. In this regard, the Guidelines refer to the Guidelines on purpose limitation of 2 April 2013.[16]

According to these Guidelines (WP253), the number of data subjects concerned may be an important indicator of systemic errors and a lack of proper data protection routines. The fine does not depend on proof of a causal link between the infringement and the damage, but the amount of the damage and the duration of the infringement are criteria to be taken into account.

The wording of Article 82(2) 2 GDPR ('*due regard*'), does not require either intent or negligence to be established to impose a fine. However, letter (b), which refers to the '*intentional or negligent character of the infringement*', makes it possible to take account of the degree of fault on the part of the controller or processor. In that regard, the question arises as to which fault of which person should be assigned to a legal person. The GDPR does not require the attribution of a fault within the meaning of the law of damages. The right standard is rather an administrative law *sui generis* standard. To require an organ fault (i.e. of the board or the CEO) is not necessary according to the wording. The deliberate or negligent conduct of a manager, a person responsible for processing or even the person entrusted with the specific processing operation will also have to be taken into account, depending on the circumstances of the specific case. However, the allegation against the controller or processor becomes all the more serious and thus the higher the fine, the more signs of organizational negligence (and a fortiori of intent) can be found and the more this degree of fault can be attributed to senior directors of the company or high managers, rather than merely the possibly unforeseeable or unavoidable misconduct of a middle-ranking individual. The instruction of an organ for unlawful processing is regularly regarded as intent under the Guidelines. Given the principle that the business man must know the law and must thus take measures to ensure compliance with the law in the company, and given the now numerous actions for awareness raising and offers to ensure compliance with the GDPR in the markets, it is hard to imagine a constellation with repeated infringements of the GDPR without at least negligence present.

---

[16] Guidelines on purpose limitation of 2 April 2013. Available at: http://ec.europa.eu/justice/data-protection/article-29/documentation/opinion-recommendation/files/ 2013 / wp203_en.pdf.

If controllers or processors have doubts about the legality of processing, they need to remove these doubts or stop processing until the doubts are removed. Not taking any action in such a situation constitutes deliberate acceptance of potentially breaking the GDPR and thus certainly gross negligence, if not intent. According to the Guidelines, the scarcity of funds in the implementation of the rules cannot excuse non-compliance. Signs of intent are unlawful processing despite previous notices by data protection officers or contrary to existing data protection rules adopted within the company. Examples included in the guideline are acquiring data from employees of a competitor to discredit it; modification of data in order to claim goal fulfilment, such as related to waiting periods in hospitals; trading data asserting that they would consent without regard to data subjects' statements about how their data should be used.

Negligence shall be considered under the Guidelines if existing data protection policies of the Company have not been read or followed or no data protection rules have been adopted by the Company in the first place (this can also amount to intent in terms of deliberate acceptance of the possibility of non-compliance with the GDPR). Equally, the disclosure of data without checking the absence of personal data indicates negligence according to the Guidelines, as do deficient or late technical updates of programmes or processes. It is fair to say that the Guidelines qualify as negligence a number of constellations which under national administrative or even criminal law would be qualified as intent, in particular under the category of deliberately accepting that it is possible that the law is broken.

Article (83)(2)(c) of the GDPR sets an incentive for controllers and processors to stop infringements committed as soon as possible, immediately reverse the practice and make up for any damages. In this case, the concept of damage is not exclusively related to a financial loss. A controller or processor must also strive to make up for impairments of a non-financial nature in order to benefit. Although not explicitly mentioned in the wording, the supervisory authority will conversely have to take into account that no efforts were made to make amends.

The timely and intensive efforts of the controller for 'repairs' should, according to the Guidelines, play a role in the determination of the fine, as well as the fact that other involved persons or processors were informed and thus further damage was prevented.

A leniency rule for those admitting an illegal behaviour first, as it exists in competition law, is not contained in the Guidelines so far. In view of the diverse modern constellations of co-controllers or processors in the digital economy, it could be very useful, however. This is so because leniency, if well applied, facilitates and intensifies enforcement and thus increases the general preventive effect of fines, which are a factor of likelihood of noncompliance being detected times amount of the fines. This presupposes, of course, that leniency is only granted if an actor who accuses itself will also provide substantial information allowing to pursue successfully another or even better more than one other actors who have committed infringements[17] of the GDPR. This will often be possible in constellations of cooperation between processors and controllers or co-controllers, constellations which are increasingly common in the world of the cloud and complex divisions of labour relating to the treatment of personal data.

Letter (d) provides that '*the degree of responsibility of the controller or processor taking into account technical and organisational measures implemented by them pursuant to Articles 25 and 32*' shall be taken account of in the calculation of the fine. Its regulatory content is partly reflected in letter (b), since the determination of the degree of fault will in most cases correspond to the '*degree of responsibility*'. Letter (d) gains own significance in addition to letter (b) insofar as it refers to the special provisions for data protection through technology design and privacy-friendly default settings and data security, namely Articles 25 and 32 GDPR. The technical–organizational relevance of these rules goes beyond the simple legal category of intent and negligence. Only by incorporating these provisions into the sanctioning catalogue, a real economic incentive to invest in privacy by design and by default is created, as serious and comprehensive investment in this area can significantly reduce the fine. The Guidelines also include in this context the application of organizational measures by the management referred to in Article 24 GDPR. Relevant industry standards and codes of conduct (Art. 40 GDPR) serve to determine best practice.

Letter (e) makes '*relevant previous infringements by the controller or processor*' an aggravating circumstance and thus adds an additional incentive to lawful behaviour. The pedagogical, future-orientated approach of the GDPR is particularly evident here. Moreover, criterion (e) should also be taken into account when a controller selects a processor, although if previous breaches of the GDPR are known or should have been known to the controller, for example because they have already co-operated or the previous breaches are public knowledge. This also results from Article 28(1) GDPR, which provides that '*the controller shall use only processors providing sufficient guarantees to implement appropriate technical and organisational measures in such a manner that processing will meet the requirements of this Regulation and ensure the protection of the rights of the data subject.*' Intention or negligence in disregard of this statutory duty of care and scrutiny when selecting a processor should clearly be an aggravating circumstance leading to higher fines for the controller.

According to the Guidelines, the question to be considered is whether the controller or processor has previously committed the same infringement or infringements in a similar manner, for example due to inadequate risk assessment, ignorance of the necessary procedures, negligence in dealing with data subjects, etc. By repetition the breaches referred to in paragraph 4 (2% of the world turnover of the undertaking concerned) are moved to the higher category (4% of world turnover of the undertaking concerned) in accordance with paragraph 6, and the

---

[17] See http://ec.europa.eu/competition/cartels/leniency/leniency.html.

guidelines expressly state this.[18] The Guidelines also state in Footnote 10 that DPAs should observe national rules of limitation. However, where this would put into question the coherent application of the GDPR as EU law, according to the principles of primacy and effectiveness of EU law, the DPAs will have to disregard such rules.

The Guidelines are silent on the question whether only violations within the EU or violations outside the EU can be taken as a basis for determining whether a repetition of a previous non-compliance is present. In any case, if an infringement took place outside the EU, but in a context in which EU law was applicable (eg pursuant to an adequacy decision such as the EU–US Privacy Shield or due to the large geographic applicability of the Regulation) such violations are to be included as aggravating circumstance. Proceeding this way serves the protective purpose if the prior infringement was found by a non-EU authority. Likewise, the principle of equal treatment of companies established within and outside the EU, which is within the territorial scope of the Regulation (Article 3, GDPR), supports this interpretation, since it entails the equal treatment of conduct within and outside the EU, as far as it falls under the regulation.

Letter (f) includes the degree of compliance with the obligation of the controllers and processors to cooperate with the supervisory authorities both to remedy the infringement and to mitigate any adverse effects in calculating the amount of the fine. For the calculation of the fine itself, knowledge about the turnover of the company, as well as its organization and affiliation to other companies, is absolutely necessary.

The Guidelines also clarify that co-operation under a legal obligation, such as granting access by the company to the supervisory authority, cannot be taken into account as mitigation in the discretionary assessment of the fine. Only cooperation beyond legal obligation can lead to a reduction of the fine.

Letter (g) gives special consideration, as to the level of the fine, to the '*categories of personal data affected by the infringement.*' These are the categories referred to in Articles 8–10 GDPR, thus data concerning children and sensitive data. In addition, the Guidelines cite, as discretionary criteria, the direct or indirect identification of persons; data whose dissemination directly causes harm or suffering to individuals without falling under Articles 9 or 10; and whether data was under protection, such as encryption of data.

Article 33(1) GDPR requires the responsible persons to notify the supervisory authority of any reported violations of the GDPR without delay. If this is not done, this will have a negative effect on the calculation of the fine under Article 83(2)(h). 'Without delay' in this context will have to be interpreted as the first occasion the violation has become known to the responsible person. A strict interpretation is necessary, given the high public interest in such immediate reporting.

The early co-operation of a controller and processor with a DPA beyond what the law requires could give rise to leniency, as it does in competition law

---

[18] Point III (a), in fn 9 of the Guidelines.

according to the Commission leniency notice.[19] Also under the scope of the GDPR, such a practice of rewarding whistleblowing and early cooperation could lead to increased degrees of compliance. In this context future Guidelines should provide specific assessment criteria and procedures in accordance with Article 70(1)(k). The present Guidelines make it clear that compliance with the legal obligation alone will not lead to a reduction in the fine, and that negligent, incomplete or late notification can indeed lead to a higher fine and cannot be considered minor. This problem is at issue in an investigation concerning the US Transportation Company Uber,[20] on which the Working Party 29 set up a working group on 29 November 2017.[21]

Letter (i) requires earlier instructions by a DPA to have been given to the controller or processor in relation to the same case. The Regulation sanctions in this provision the failure to comply with these earlier instructions. Contrary to letter (e), the Guidelines make it clear that this is only a question of the measures of the acting supervisory authority.

Again, letter (j) is self-explanatory. It forces controllers and processors to adhere to approved codes of conduct and approved certification procedures or conditions of certification under Articles 24(3), 28(5) and 32(3) of the GDPR. The Guidelines clarify that although codes of conduct under Article 40(4) GDPR must provide for monitoring procedures, the tasks and powers of the supervisory authorities remain unaffected (see also Articles 41(2) (c) and 42(4), GDPR). According to the Guidelines, non-compliance with the codes of conduct or certification procedures may also demonstrate intent or negligence.

As already explained, point (k) is a fall back which allows the supervisory authority to fully exercise its discretion, thus to take due account of all the circumstances of the individual case. The exemplary financial benefit of a violation will have to correspond to a mathematical value, which, in turn, must be related to a specific personal date. As an example of a possible way to calculate the value of a record about a person (eg in a social network) the company value is divided by the number of members of that network. The Guidelines make it clear that profits from violations in any case give rise to a fine.

5. Cumulation of infringements and the determination of 'The Undertaking'

If a controller or processor has committed a number of different infringements in the same processing operation or, in the case of 'linked processing operations',

---

[19] Communication from the Commission concerning the adoption and reduction of fines in cartel cases, OJ 2006 C 298, 17; see also http://ec.europa.eu/competition/cartels/leniency/leniency.html.

[20] ECJ 20.12.2017 Case C-434/15 ECLI:EU:C:2017:981 *Asociación Profesional Elite Taxi v Uber Systems Spain SL.*

[21] See http://ec.europa.eu/newsroom/just/item-detail.cfm?item_id=50083.

to several provisions of the GDPR, the total amount of the fine is limited to the amount for the most serious infringement. The purpose of this rule is also to clarify that the quantitatively increased disregard for the provisions of the GDPR is particularly in need of sanction.[22] In practical terms, this means that the fine must be increased, but cannot exceed 4 per cent (para 5).

The term *'linked processing operations'* is neither legally defined nor is it used elsewhere in the GDPR. However, according to the purpose of paragraph 3, the term must be interpreted strictly, otherwise the deterrent effect of Article 83 would be undermined. Furthermore, a narrow interpretation of the *'linked processing operations'* supports the narrow interpretation of the 'same' processing operations. If these relate to the identical processing operation, this cannot be undermined by an endless interpretation of the connected processing operations. A combination of processing operations is conceivable through several criteria, namely the identity of the data subject, the identity of the purpose of the processing, the nature of the processing operations themselves and the temporal proximity of various processing operations. In order to substantiate a connection within the meaning of paragraph 3, it is not sufficient for just one of these criteria to be met. At the very least, the identity of the data subject and the purpose of the processing must normally be available to affirm a relationship. An example of this is a social network that creates secret profiles based on personal characteristics and resells sections of this profile to an insurance broker or a company from another sector. Here the processing operations concern different purposes, so that a connection within the meaning of paragraph 3 would not exist. Otherwise, the profit of the social network from all sales transactions could be so high that a single fine within the meaning of paragraph 3 would no longer have a deterrent effect.

Despite the cap in paragraph 3, when calculating the total amount, each individual infringement and the amount of each fine under paragraph 2 (a) must be taken into account. The GDPR has been infringed on several occasions in such a case. Therefore, the total amount of the fine will in any event be higher than if only a single infringement had been committed.

Decisive in determining the amounts of the fines will be the delineation of the 'undertaking' within the meaning of Article 83(4) and (5) GDPR.

On the one hand, Article 4 No 18 should be taken into consideration. According to this, an *'enterprise'* is *'a natural or legal person engaged in an economic activity, regardless of its legal form, including partnerships or associations regularly engaged in economic activity'.* On the other hand, recital 150, sentence 3, specifically for the imposition of fines, relies on the concept of Articles 101 and 102 TFEU. According to the functional concept of enterprise governed by competition law, an undertaking is any entity engaged in an economic activity, regardless of its legal form and type of financing. In this respect, the economic unit is decisive, irrespective of

---

[22] See *Amann & Sons and Cousin Filterie/Commission*, n 10 at para 160.

whether it consists of several natural or legal persons.[23] According to the case law of the European Court of Justice, this leads to liability of the parent company for misconduct of its subsidiaries, if they 'essentially' follow their instructions due to economic, legal and organisational links.[24] In this respect, a determining factor is that it is suspected in any case if the parent company holds all the shares of the subsidiary.[25] Moreover, according to the concept of competition law, a natural person can also be an undertaking, namely if he or she is conducting a commercial business.

6. Fines until the entry into force of the GDPR

To close these reflections, let us look back at the fining practices before the entry into force of the GDPR. This is not to suggest that this should in any way be a baseline for future practice. On the contrary, practice based on the GDPR needs to rather align with competition law, not with past practice. Therefore, this is a warning on diversity and an encouragement to install a rigorous and coherent practice of fining from the outset.

The highest individual fines imposed in Europe in data protection matters have been those of the Italian Data Protection Authority with a maximum of €5.88 million.[26] This is followed by the former Financial Services Authority in London, which oversees compliance with privacy rules by banks and insurance companies. It has fined more than £2 million on several occasions.[27] The highest fine in Germany so far imposed on data protection amounted to €1.5 million.[28] In terms of the number of individual fining decisions, the data protection authorities most active in recent years, have been those of Spain, the United Kingdom and France.[29] The US FTC fines companies for failing to comply with EU Safe Harbour

---

[23] ECJ 10.9.2009 – C-97/08 P, ECLI: EU: C: 2009: 536 = ECR 2009, 816 para 55 *Akzo Nobel Commission.*

[24] Ibid at para 55.

[25] Ibid at para 60f.

[26] See www.garanteprivacy.it/web/guest/home/docweb/-/docweb-display/docweb/6009876. For context see www.garanteprivacy.it/web/guest/home/docweb/-/docweb-display/docweb/6072330 and https://iapp.org/news/a/garante-issues-highest-eu-sanction-on-record/.

[27] See, eg, the fines totalling £3 million against companies of the HSBC Group on 17 July 2009. Available at: www.fca.org.uk/publication/final-notices/hsbc_actuaris0709.pdf; https://www.fca.org.uk/publication/final-notices/hsbc_inuk0907.pdf; and www.fca.org.uk/publication/final-notices/hsbc_ins0709.pdf; See £2,275 million fines against Zurich Insurance on 19 August 2010. Available at: www.fca.org.uk/publication/final-notices/zurich_plc.pdf.

[28] The fine was against supermarket chain Lidl and led to the dismissal of the German boss of the company. See press release of the Interior Ministry of Baden-Wuerttemberg 11 July 2008. 'Data protection supervisory authorities impose heavy fines on Lidl distribution companies for serious data breaches'. Available at: www.sueddeutsche.de/wirtschaft/lidl-muss-zahlen-millionen-strafe-fuer-die-schnueffler-1.709085; see also: www.faz.net/aktuell/wirtschaft/unternehmen/datenschutz-affaere-lidl-delaulter-germany-chef-1783052.html.

[29] See www.cnil.fr/fr/les-sanctions-prononcees-par-la-cnil; and www.cnil.fr/fr/recherche/sanctions.

and other public assurances to protect customer privacy, sometimes in excess of $20 million.[30]

In Spain, the highest fine in data protection has so far amounted to €1.2 million.[31] The Spanish Data Protection Authority has in the three years 2015-17 imposed fines in 1,702 cases, resulting in a cumulated amount of €44,894,956.[32] The data protection authority of Spain reports in detail about the Fining practice.[33]

In the UK, the highest fine ever imposed by the DPA was £400,000.[34] Fines under the jurisdiction of the Financial Services Authority (now the Financial Conduct Authority) quickly exceed the 1 million mark, when it comes to protecting personal (financial) data in the jurisdiction of that authority.[35]

In comparison, fines in competition law reach billions, for example €2,42 billion in the recent Google case.[36] The legal basis in competition law allows maximum fines of up to 10 per cent of world turnover,[37] the GDPR only 4 per cent of world turnover of the undertaking concerned. Within this important difference, there should be a relative approximation of fines between the two legal bases, in line with the overall principle of coherence in the law, in particular against the background of the common purpose of general and special prevention of both legal bases and the high primary law position of data protection as a fundamental right in the digital world.

It is to be hoped that starting from Article 70(1)(y) GDPR, the European Data Protection Board will set up a register not just of cases dealt with by the European Data Protection Board, but of all decisions with fines imposed on the basis of the Regulation, very soon after it enters into force, to bring about the transparency necessary in the rule of law and for the coherent application of the Regulation, in particular Articles 58 and 83 GDPR. Until then, there is nothing left to do to gain transparency but to consult individual data protection authorities or use private overview tools, such as the PWC Privacy and Security Enforcement Tracker.[38] An official common database of decisions under the GDPR is just as indispensable

---

[30] Google paid a total of $22.5 million to the FTC following a December 2012 agreement. Available at: https://www.ftc.gov/news-events/press-releases/2012/08/google-will-pay-225 -million-settle-ftc-charges-it-misrepresented.

[31] PS/0082/2017th Facebook Inc from 21 August 2017. Available at: www.agpd.es/portalwebAGPD/resoluciones/procedimientos_sancionadores/ps_2017/common/pdfs/PS-00082-2017_Resolucion-de-fecha-21-08-2017_Art-ii-culo-4-5-6-7- LOPD.pdf.

[32] Letter to the author by the Spanish DPA.

[33] See www.agpd.es/portalwebAGPD/LaAgencia/informacion_institucional/memorias-ides-idphp.php.

[34] See details at: https://ico.org.uk/action-weve-taken/enforcement/?facet_type=Monetary+penalties&facet_sector=&facet_date=&date_from=&date_to=.

[35] See www.fca.org.uk/news/news-stories/2014-fines.

[36] Google decision of the European Commission of 27 June 2017. Available at: http://ec.europa.eu/competition/elojade/isef/case_details.cfm?proc_code=1_39740.

[37] Article 23(2) of Council Regulation (EC) No 1/2003 of 16 December 2002 implementing the competition rules set out in Arts 81 and 82 of the Treaty.

[38] PWC Privacy and Security Enforcement Tracker 2016. Available at: www.pwc.co.uk/services/legal-services/ services / cyber-security / privacy-and-security-enforcement-tracker.html.

for specific and general prevention and coherent application as is good public relations work, communicating fining decisions and their motivation in the daily press, trade press and social services.[39]

7. Conclusion

With the GDPR, data protection not only moves from a directive to a regulation but also from low (or no) fines to high fines. Seen together, the change of the legal form of the instrument, the setting up of a European Data Protection Board with the power to take binding decisions and the introduction of high fines for non-compliance, clearly expresses the will of the legislator to make sure that the rules of the GDPR are fully and coherently applied across Europe in this new age of digitalisation and pervasive personal data processing. The DPAs are entrusted with the duty to ensure this and have obtained substantial new powers for this purpose, comparable to those of competition authorities. The competition authorities have long experience in rigorous enforcement against non-compliance. The experience in competition law is that high fines are necessary to better compliance, as these bring about the necessary deterrents against non-compliance. DPAs have much to learn from this history of enforcement and fining in competition law. Much of the jurisprudence on competition law fines will mutatis mutandis be applied to data protection by the ECJ. It is now time for Data Protection Authorities to acquire the resolve necessary to stand through complex investigations, impose high fines with a strong deterrent effect and to stand through protracted judicial review battles. This requires the skills of leadership and staff competence found today in competition authorities and public prosecutors' offices. The DPAs can acquire these skills from there, by systematic cooperation and training, and by systematic recruitment of staff with experience in legal investigations subject to judicial review.

---

[39] See the last good example of ICO's intense press work in the UK on the £400,000 fine in the Carphone Warehouse case. Available at: https://ico.org.uk/about-the-ico/news-and-events/news-and- blogs/2018/01/carphone-warehouse-fined-400-000-after-serious-failures-placed-customer-and-employee-data-at-risk/.

11

Data Analytics and the GDPR: Friends or Foes?

A Call for a Dynamic Approach to Data Protection Law

SOPHIE STALLA-BOURDILLON AND ALISON KNIGHT

Abstract

In this chapter, we aim to help overcome a perceived paradox (and attendant tensions) between the two objectives of innovation and privacy/data protection, in relation to data scenarios where organisations are open to personal data they control to be reused (internally within their corporate group, or externally via a third party) for innovative purposes. We argue that to do this requires better defining key notions in data protection law, acknowledging the interdependence of data protection requirements or principles, and relying on ongoing data management processes to control complex data environments. These are the pillars of a dynamic approach to data protection law.

We start our demonstration by suggesting that the conceptualisation of data analytics by policy makers has not helped to produce clear guidance for practices going beyond the mere production of statistics. On the contrary, by drawing a distinction between the production of statistics and the rest, this approach has indirectly formed the seedbed for the view that EU data protection law, in particular the GDPR, is antithetic to data analytics. We then revisit this critique of EU data protection law to show its limits and build the argument that a more constructive interpretation of the GDPR is possible, based on a dynamic approach to data protection law. Finally, we unfold the main tenets of such a dynamic approach and ultimately suggest that the GDPR does not undermine the logic of data analytics as a form of 'data-driven general analysis', which implies a re-purposing or secondary processing of data legitimately hold by a data controller over a limited period of time and with no consequences defined prior to the analysis, although consequences could be attached in the future but only once a second impact assessment has been undertaken.

Keywords

Data analytics, legal basis, data minimisation, purpose limitation, legitimate interest, data governance

1. Introduction

'There's no doubt the huge potential that creative use of data could have ... but the price of innovation does not need to be the erosion of fundamental privacy rights.' These are the words of Elizabeth Denham, the head of the UK's Data Protection Authority – the Information Commissioner's Office (ICO) – speaking in 2017 about the benefits for patient care and clinical improvements that could result from data innovation. Her comments were made in respect of the arrangement whereby the Royal Free NHS Foundation Trust provided 1.6 million patient details to Google DeepMind for automated analytics processing as part of a trial to test an alert, diagnosis and detection system for acute kidney injury.[1] Despite its optimistic tone, however, the primary purpose of Denham's statement was, in fact, to announce a decision by the ICO finding the Trust liable for a failure in this arrangement to comply with data protection law.

Decisions such as these illustrate how striking a trade-off between enabling data innovation to flourish and, respecting privacy and related rights in ways that are lawful and aligned with the reasonable expectations of individuals, is not always an easy task. While data science provides opportunities to improve society, it also poses challenges precisely because of the ever-increasing volume and availability of data relating to persons being shared, the growing reliance on automated algorithmic processes to re-analyse them, combined with the gradual reduction of human involvement and oversight of such processes. Such challenges clearly need to be addressed to enable data science innovation to flourish in a sustainable manner.

In this chapter, we aim to help overcome a perceived paradox (and attendant tensions) between the two objectives of innovation and privacy/data protection, in particular in relation to data scenarios where organisations are open to personal data they control to be reused (internally within their corporate group, or externally via a third party) for innovative purposes. We argue that to do this requires better defining key notions in data protection law, acknowledging the interdependence of data protection requirements or principles, and, adopting a dynamic approach to data protection law relying upon ongoing data management processes.

---

[1] ICO, News and Blog, Royal Free – Google DeepMind trial failed to comply with data protection law, 3 July 2017. Available at: https://ico.org.uk/about-the-ico/news-and-events/news-and-blogs/2017/07/royal-free-google-deepmind-trial-failed-to-comply-with-data-protection-law (last accessed 3 March 2018).

Not to be misleading, data analytics practices are not always applied upon personal data. To use the trilogy of data types referred to by the UK Anonymisation Decision-Making Framework,[2] two other types of data should also be mentioned: anonymised data and apersonal data. These two types of data are clearly distinguished. 'Apersonal data' are data that are not to do with people at all (eg information concerning a mineral is not personal data and its processing is not caught by data protection rules). However, 'anonymised data' refers to information to do with people that was originally personal data, but that has been subject to a process of anonymisation such that it becomes non-personal data.

The ICO also acknowledges this reality when it states that 'many instances of big data analytics do not involve personal data at all'.[3] The European Data Protection Supervisor (EDPS) also recognises that information processed by big data applications is not always personal,[4] as does the EU Article 29 Data Protection Working Party (Article 29 WP). The latter body, while recognising that '*big data processing operations do not always involve personal data*', immediately goes on to urge caution in relation to data environments whereby '[p]atterns relating to specific individuals may be identified' including 'by means of the increased availability of computer processing power and data mining capabilities'.[5]

Whereas traditionally European Union (hereafter, EU) data protection has been approached in ways reliant upon static binary assumptions about privacy and utility acting as opposing forces at a single point of time (and, thereafter, referring back to this static 'position' in subsequent time periods), we argue that a dynamic approach indicative of a new era of data protection ushered in under the new EU General Data Protection Regulation 2016/679 (hereafter, GDPR)[6] does three things:

(1) First, it makes clear that absolute terms are problematic (in particular, terms suggesting that the two objectives are pitted against one another *in statis*).

---

[2] M Elliot, Mackey, E, O'Hara, K and Tudor, C 2016, *The Anonymisation Decision Making Framework*. UKAN, Manchester.

[3] The ICO adds, 'Examples of non-personal big data include world climate and weather data; using geospatial data from GPS-equipped buses to predict arrival times; astronomical data from radio telescopes in the Square Kilometre Array; and data from sensors on containers carried on ships.' While these examples are in the main good illustrations, this statement is slightly misleading in that it is only when context is assessed and, in particular, when it has been ascertained that the purpose of the processing is not to learn anything from individuals, that it is possible to definitely exclude the data from the category of personal data. In other words, when the data in these examples are in turn associated with people, they may relate to them (even if the data is not of a type that is directly about people).

[4] EDPS Opinion 7/2015 Meeting the challenges of big data: A call for transparency, user control, data protection by design and accountability, p. 7.

[5] Art 29 WP, WP 221, Statement on Statement of the WP29 on the impact of the development of big data on the protection of individuals with regard to the processing of their personal data in the EU, 2014, p. 3.

[6] Regulation (EU) 2016/679 of the European Parliament and of the Council of 27 April 2016 on the protection of natural persons with regard to the processing of personal data and on the free movement of such data, and repealing Directive 95/46/EC (General Data Protection Regulation) OJ L 119, 4.5.2016, pp. 1–88.

(2) Second, conceptual definitions require accommodation of, not just risk-based perspectives (focusing on the 'what' of data in terms of its content and 'why' it is to be processed, as well as the 'who' and 'how' of access-related considerations), but also risk mitigation obligations that need to be assessed and managed in context over consecutive time periods. In this sense, compliance with the GDPR should entail the setting up of a governance structure relying upon three key principles: dynamic purpose preservation, dynamic protection adaptation, and data quality assurance.

(3) Third, data protection mitigatory (also known as privacy-preserving) measures should be seen as utility beneficial, in that they can be used proactively not just defensively to facilitate data innovation. Specifically, applying pseudonymisation processes to personal data is a valuable tool for mitigating re-identification risks by those who would repurpose it for innovative ends. However, viewed dynamically – pseudonymisation process can be conceived in ways that enable organisations to adopt 'controller linkability' protective measures[7] that minimise the risk level to individuals of their personal processing operations only to the extent necessary (using available mitigations) in light of the intended benefits to be achieved.

In this chapter, we illustrate these three points through a mechanism already embedded into data protection law that has been reformulated slightly under the GDPR: the 'legitimate interests' legal basis for processing personal data. By looking at key provisions as set out in its predecessor, the EU Data Protection Directive 95/46/EC (DPD), and the latter's interpretation by EU and UK regulators and the EU courts, alongside the changes introduced by the GDPR, we draw out what applying a dynamic approach to data protection law actually means and requires for data controllers intending to engage into data analytics practices. We suggest that the choice of the legal basis should have an impact upon the effect of other key data protection principles, such as purpose limitation and data minimisation, in the same way as it has an impact upon data subject rights. Ultimately, we make the argument that the GDPR does not undermine the logic of data analytics as a form of 'data-driven general analysis', which implies a re-purposing or secondary processing of data legitimately hold by a data controller over a limited period of time and with no consequences defined prior to the analysis,[8] although

---

[7] For an overview of practical applications of 'Controlled Linkable Data' see Mike Hintze and Gary LaFever, Meeting Upcoming GDPR Requirements While Maximizing the Full Value of Data Analytics – Balancing the Interests of Regulators, Data Controllers and Data Subjects, White Paper January 2017, Available at: http://files8.design-editor.com/93/9339158/UploadedFiles/1B4F2EF8-BC8D-A12D-C9B1-7DF644A29C1F.pdf (last accessed 3 March 2018). See also H. Hu, S. Stalla-Bourdillon, M. Yang, V. Schiavo, and V. Sassone, 2017, Bridging Policy, Regulation and Practice? A Techno-legal Analysis of Three Types of Data in the GDPR. In R. Leenes, R. van Brakel, S. Gutwirth, and P. De Hert (Eds), *Data Protection and Privacy: the Age of Intelligent Machines* (Computers, Privacy and Data Protection; Vol. 10). (Oxford: Hart, 2017). The authors stress the importance of contextual controls for GDPR compliance purposes.

[8] The fact that the data would be collected especially for a data analytics purpose does not change the analysis.

consequences could be attached in the future but only once a second impact assessment has been undertaken. Therefore, we hold the view that surmising (big) data analytics as the collection and/or retention of as much data as possible in the hope that the data become useful is misleading. To quote Clarke '[t]he "big data" movement is largely a marketing phenomenon. Much of the academic literature has been cavalier in its adoption and reticulation of vague assertions by salespeople. As a result, definitions of sufficient clarity to assist in analysis are in short supply.'[9]

To introduce this discussion, we turn first to how data analytics creating innovation have been defined by those responsible for regulating data protection in the EU and UK, and the concerns they can engender when they involve data relating to persons. We highlight the limits of the analysis produced by policy makers, which is based upon an oversimplifying binary dichotomy 'production of statistics/creation of user profiles'. The limits of this analysis could explain in part the relative 'success' of the critique of EU data protection law, in particular the GDPR, which is presented as being an obstacle to innovation. We suggest, however, that it is possible to overcome these criticisms. In order to do so we then go back to the main tenets of the critique (ie the apparent zones of tension between the practice of data analytics and some foundational pillars of data protection law, such as the principles of purpose limitation, data minimisation, and data protection by design and by default).[10] Subsequently, by unfolding the implications of a dynamic approach to data protection law we aim to demonstrate that the GDPR is able to usefully accompany data analytics practices and provides for some tools to restrict data analytics practices when it is not possible to mitigate the high risks posed to individual rights and freedoms. The two pillars of a dynamic approach, as we conceive it, are: the interdependence of data protection principles, which should help determine their effects in context; as well as the necessity to monitor processing activities to ensure data quality, preserve processing purposes, and adapt protection over time.

2. The Limits of the Analysis Produced by Policy Makers

At a high level, data analytics is – as the name suggests – the extensive analysis of data using algorithms to discover meaningful patterns in data, whereby the more voluminous the data made available for analysis and the more automated the processes of analysis, the larger the possibilities for new innovation.

---

[9] See Roger Clarke, 'Guidelines for the Responsible Application of Data Analytics', *Computer Law and Security Review* 34 (2018): 467, 468.

[10] For a recent expression of this standpoint see Tal Z. Zarsky, *Incompatible: The GDPR in the Age of Big Data, Seton Law Review* 44 (2017): 995. See, also, Ira S. Rubinstein, Big Data: The End of Privacy or a New Beginning? *Int'l Data Privacy Law* 3 (2013): 74–78 at 74 and Bert-Jaap Koops, 'The Trouble with European Data Protection Law', *International Data Privacy Law*, 4, no 4 (2014): 8.

Data analytics therefore potentially covers a wide range of processing activities for different overall objectives – from commercial purposes aimed at inducing consumers to buy more goods and services, to public interest purposes aimed at protecting the public good. Both types of objectives may also be pursued in a purely research context, for example, to produce statistical information from data to create new knowledge upon communication, which may or may not be applied in later decision-making. In effect, the innovatory 'outcome' so highly prized lies in the uncovering of value hidden in data in ways surpassing human capabilities to create something novel. That novelty may then be used to tap new supply and demand possibilities creating something of economic or social value.

Within that spectrum of possibilities, from which a myriad of different data analysis models can be used, narrower purposes may be discerned. It is necessary to consider how these have been described by those formally responsible for interpreting data protection law and its regulation in the EU where the data being processed relates to persons to assess whether useful guidance has been produced or, whether a more granular and in-depth analysis is still needed to understand how EU data protection, in particular the GDPR, can adequately accompany data analytics practices as well as act as a stopper on occasion.

First, the Article 29 WP produces influential, albeit non-binding opinions and other documents interpreting key areas of data protection law. It initially touched on the issue of analytics in the context of considering web analytic tools. In its opinion on Cookie Consent Exemption ('WP194', adopted on 7 June 2012),[11] for example, the Article 29 WP describes analytics as:

> [S]tatistical audience measuring tools for websites, which often rely on cookies. These tools are notably used by website owners to estimate the number of unique visitors, to detect the most preeminent search engine keywords that lead to a webpage or to track down website navigation issues.[12]

At the same time, a key distinction is then drawn out in the opinion between such 'tools' by virtue of which different degrees of data protection risks may be discerned. The Article 29 WP describes 'a first-party analytic system' (based on 'first party' cookies) as posing 'limited privacy risks, provided reasonable safeguards are in place, including adequate information, the ability to opt-out [by the web-user of their usage in respect of their online activities] and comprehensive anonymisation mechanisms.'[13] In contrast, it describes 'third party analytics' 'which use a common third party cookie to collect navigation information related to users across distinct websites, and which pose a substantially greater risk to privacy'.[14]

---

[11] Art 29 WP, WP 194, Opinion 04/2012 on Cookie Consent Exemption, 2012. Cookies are a type of tracking technology involving the storing of data in a user's computer by a website being visited.
[12] Ibid, p. 10
[13] Ibid, p. 11.
[14] Ibid.

Setting aside for one moment the distinction between 'first-party analytics' and 'third-party analytics', which is clearly of importance and explains in part the need to transform the ePrivacy Directive[15] into an ePrivacy Regulation,[16] the Article 29 WP therefore distinguishes between the (pure) production of statistics and other types of analytics. However, while the process leading to the production of statistics is still covered by data protection law, the characterisation of 'low risks' in this context is not surprising. The real challenge lies in assessing the risks creating by other types of analytics, of which the purpose is not (or not 'purely') the production of statistics.

In a more recent opinion,[17] the Article 29 WP makes a similar distinction between web-user related analytics as either: 'usage analytics' necessary 'for the analysis of the performance of the service requested by the user';[18] or, 'user analytics' referring to 'the analysis of the behaviour of identifiable users of a website, app or device'.[19] This is to make sure the concept of 'web audience measurement' does not cover processing amounting to profiling. Once again, it is therefore admitted that the pure production of statistics is acceptable while all other types of analytics are excluded and no specific guidance is offered to comprehend them. Incidentally, even if the distinction between 'usage analytics' and user profiling makes sense in order to distinguish between low risk behaviour and other types of behaviour, this conceptual distinction raises a separate question of importance. That is whether the purpose of carrying out the 'performance of the service requested by the user'[20] is specific enough to rely upon if consent was being sought from them in such terms to justify personal data processing activities of a usage analytics type (so described) under the GDPR? In 2018, in its Guidelines on transparency under Regulation 2016/679,[21] the Article 29 WP, interpreting the new obligation of transparency, confirms:

> The following phrases are not sufficiently clear as to the purposes of processing: 'We may use your personal data to develop new services' (as it is unclear what the services are or how the data will help develop them); ... 'We may use your personal data to offer personalised services' (as it is unclear what the personalisation entails.[22]

---

[15] Directive 2002/58/EC of the European Parliament and of the Council of 12 July 2002 concerning the processing of personal data and the protection of privacy in the electronic communications sector (Directive on privacy and electronic communications) OJ L 201, 31.7.2002, p. 37 as amended by Directive 2006/24/EC of the European Parliament and of the Council of 15 March 2006 and Directive 2009/136/EC of the European Parliament and of the Council of 25 November 2009 and corrected by Corrigendum, OJ L 241, 10.9.2013, p. 9 (2009/136).

[16] Proposal for a Regulation of the European Parliament and of the Council concerning the respect for private life and the protection of personal data in electronic communications and repealing Directive 2002/58/EC (Regulation on Privacy and Electronic Communications) COM/2017/010 final – 2017/03 (COD).

[17] Art 29 WP, WP 247, Opinion on the Proposed Regulation for the ePrivacy Regulation, 2017.

[18] Ibid, p. 18.

[19] Ibid.

[20] Ibid.

[21] Art 29 WP, WP 260, Guidelines on transparency under Regulation 2016/679, Adopted on 29 November 2017, as last Revised and Adopted on 11 April 2018 (WP 260).

[22] Ibid, p. 9

The Article 29 WP has also approached the issue of defining analytics from a non-Web perspective focused exclusively on data-analysis centric concerns that link to the extent of privacy/data protection risks posed when utilised. In its opinion on purpose limitation of 2013,[23] for example, it includes a lengthy discussion of 'intrusive data analytic tools' that can be used to create so-called 'automated profiles' against the backdrop of change introduced by 'big data':

> Big data can be used to identify more general trends and correlations but it can also be processed in order to directly affect individuals. With all its potential for innovation, big data may also pose significant risks for the protection of personal data and the right to privacy ... For example, in the field of marketing and advertisement, big data can be used to analyse or predict the personal preferences, behaviour and attitudes of individual customers and subsequently inform 'measures or decisions' that are taken with regard to those customers such as personalised discounts, special offers and targeted advertisements based on the customer's profile.[24]

Thus, despite recognition of big data's potential for innovation, the Article 29 WP flags the significant risks to the protection of personal data and the right to privacy it can raise at an applied level. To this end, it distinguishes between two different scenarios. In the first one, organisations processing data relating to persons want to detect trends and correlations in the information. In a re-use context, for example, a public-sector body might release datasets to third parties, which, in turn, want to analyse them to create statistics.

In the second scenario, organisations specifically want to analyse the personal preferences, behaviour and attitudes of individuals. Again, this motivation may be manifested at a secondary usage level, such that data collected for one purpose in a retail context, for example, may be reused with the intention to harvest findings and make predictions that can subsequently be used to inform decisions taken regarding customers.

These two scenarios thus mirror the dichotomy used by the Article 29 WP in a Web context: production of statistics and, other types of analytics, which arguably would require a certain degree of profiling for which more specific guidance would be needed.

---

[23] Art 29 WP, WP 203, Opinion on purpose limitation, 2013 (WP 203).

[24] Ibid, Annex 2 (in full): 'Big data' refers to the exponential growth in availability and automated use of information: it refers to gigantic digital datasets held by corporations, governments and other large organisations, which are then extensively analysed using computer algorithms. Big data relies on the increasing ability of technology to support the collection and storage of large amounts of data, but also to analyse, understand and take advantage of the full value of data (in particular using analytics applications). The expectation from big data is that it may ultimately lead to better and more informed decisions. There are numerous applications of big data in various sectors, including healthcare, mobile communications, smart grid, traffic management, fraud detection, marketing and retail, both on and offline. Big data can be used to identify general trends and correlations but its processing can also directly affect individuals. For example, in the field of marketing and advertisement, big data can be used to analyse or predict the personal preferences, behaviour and attitudes of individual customers and subsequently inform 'measures or decisions' that are taken with regard to those customers such as personalised discounts, special offers and targeted advertisements based on the customer's profile.'

It is true that guidance on profiling has been produced at different levels. While at the international level the Council of Europe foresaw the transformation brought by big data analytics, its Guidelines on the protection of individuals about the processing of personal data in a world of Big Data[25] released in 2017 remain very high level. Its Recommendation on the protection of individuals about automatic processing of personal data in the context of profiling adopted in 2010[26] is, however, more interesting, although arguably it remains of little interest when it comes to interpreting what is in the GDPR.[27]

Anticipating the GDPR, the Article 29 WP released its Guidelines on Automated individual decision-making and Profiling for the purposes of Regulation 2016/679.[28] Under Article 4(4) of the GDPR, 'profiling' means 'any form of automated processing of personal data consisting of the use of personal data to evaluate certain personal aspects relating to a natural person, in particular to analyse or predict aspects concerning that natural person's performance at work, economic situation, health, personal preferences, interests, reliability, behaviour, location or movements.' Reading the Article 29 WP Guidelines on Automated individual decision-making and Profiling, it appears clear that the Article 29 WP envisages that the secondary data analytics stage, ie analysis to identify correlations in personal datasets after collection, would in most cases be covered by this GDPR definition of profiling. This will not be the case when the purpose of the analytics is to produce statistics and 'acquire an aggregated overview of its clients without making any predictions or drawing any conclusion about an individual.'[29] What is the Article 29 WP exactly referring to? Does it make a difference whether the data kept at the individual level is used to answer generic questions about the marketing strategy of an organisation (eg should company X produce B on

[25] Council of Europe, Guidelines on the protection of individuals with regard to the processing of personal data in a world of Big Data, T- PD(2017)01, 23 January 2017. Available at: https://rm.coe. int/16806ebe7a (last accessed 3 March 2017). This is how Big Data is defined in these guidelines: 'Big Data: there are many definitions of Big Data, which differ depending on the specific discipline. Most of them focus on the growing technological ability to collect process and extract new and predictive knowledge from great volume, velocity, and variety of data. In terms of data protection, the main issues do not only concern the volume, velocity, and variety of processed data, but also the analysis of the data using software to extract new and predictive knowledge for decision-making purposes regarding individuals and groups. For the purposes of these Guidelines, the definition of Big Data therefore encompasses both Big Data and Big Data analytics.'

[26] Council of Europe. The protection of individuals with regard to automatic processing of personal data in the context of profiling. Recommendation CM/Rec(2010)13 and explanatory memorandum. Council of Europe, 23 November 2010. Available at: www.coe.int/t/dghl/standardsetting/cdcj/CDCJ%20 Recommendations/CMRec(2010)13E_Profiling.pdf (last accessed 3 March 2018).

[27] See, eg, para 3.5: 'The collection and processing of personal data in the context of profiling of persons who cannot express on their own behalf their free, specific and informed consent should be forbidden except when this is in the legitimate interest of the data subject or if there is an overriding public interest, on the condition that appropriate safeguards are provided for by law.'

[28] Art 29 WP, Guidelines on Automated individual decision-making and Profiling for the purposes of Regulation 2016/679, WP 251, Adopted on 3 October 2017, as last revised and adopted on 6 February 2018 (WP 251).

[29] Ibid, p. 7.

top of A?)? Assuming an *a contrario* argument could then be formulated, each time the purpose is to make prediction or draw conclusion about any individual, profiling should be characterised, irrespective of the type of data-sharing environment at stake. As a result, the key distinction seems to remain between the pure production of statistics and other types of data analytics, which should as a matter of principle involve profiling. Yet, a great variety of data-sharing environment can be encountered in practice, in particular, when there is a need to outsource skill and expertise. What about a data holder wanting to share a dataset of customer data containing real addresses and synthetic names to find a reliable method to clean the dataset and eliminate duplicates for example, knowing that the data holder will then at a later stage use this technique on its own complete dataset containing real names? As it will be argued below, the characteristics of the data-sharing environment is of primary importance to identify relevant risks and thereby should have an impact upon the characterisation of the processing activity at stake.

This duality of benefits versus risks inherent in big data's potential is also acknowledged by national regulators, including the UK ICO, which has previously written about it in its 2017 report on big data and data protection (revised from an earlier version released in 2014).[30] In particular, big data concerns have been raised about the following risks associated with the usage of analytics on application:

- data combination from disparate sources on a massive scale permitting tracking and profiling of individuals with potentially very granular personal details being linked, inferred, and shared;

- non-secure data;

- non-transparent decision-making (opaque algorithms);

- the consequences of automated decision-making, including inaccuracies, discrimination, and social exclusion (and, ultimately, the creation or entrenchment of) economic imbalance;[31] and

- increased possibilities of government surveillance.[32]

---

[30] Information Commissioner, Big data, artificial intelligence, machine learning and data protection (v 2,2, 4 September 2017). Available at: https://ico.org.uk/media/for-organisations/documents/2013559/big-data-ai-ml-and-data-protection.pdf (last accessed 3 March 2018) (the ICO Big Data Report).

[31] Compare, WP 203 n 23 at 45: 'In particular, an algorithm might spot a correlation, and then draw a statistical inference that is, when applied to inform marketing or other decisions, unfair and discriminatory. This may perpetuate existing prejudices and stereotypes, and aggravate the problems of social exclusion and stratification. Further, and more broadly, the availability of large datasets and sophisticated analytics tools used to examine these datasets may also increase the economic imbalance between large corporations on one hand and consumers on the other. This economic imbalance may lead to unfair price discrimination with regard to the products and services offered, as well as highly intrusive, disruptive, and personalised targeted advertisements and offers. It could also result in other significant adverse impacts on individuals, for example, with regard to employment opportunities, bank loans, or health insurance options.'

[32] Per the Advocate General of the Court of Justice of the EU (hereafter, CJEU) in 2014 (in Joined Cases C-293/12 and 594/12, *Digital Rights Ireland Ltd v Minister for Communication*, Opinion of

However, the UK ICO analysis remains high level and it is difficult to derive any concrete guidelines for those data analytics practices that are not intended to merely produce statistics.

Returning to these two general scenarios of big data analytics usage as they emerge from the opinions of the Article 29 WP, that distinction nonetheless remains useful in identifying what safeguards might be needed to mitigate the likelihood of such risks arising, including measures related to anonymisation and pseudonymisation introduced below.

In the second scenario, the issues are more complex. In such context, anonymisation processes applied to personal data to protect individuals' privacy are less effectual than when applied in the first scenario (albeit that it has been acknowledged that anonymisation remains both desirable, as well as possible).[33] The risks associated with the potential for harm to flow to such individuals are not easily mitigated using technology. In fact, even if re-identification of data subjects is never achieved, this does not mean that data protection risks have been appropriately mitigated as data protection harm can arise even in the absence of re-identification (eg in case of discriminatory treatments of individuals subjects to automated decision-making).[34] For this reason, it is crucial to decide what data may be made available for reuse, assess its quality, and decide what – technological, organisational, and legal measures – to apply to such data prior to the sharing of such data for reuse. Even then, data protection law can be assumed to continue to apply in such contexts with respect to any recipients' secondary activities: this will be the case when the data remain personal data by purpose.[35]

The difficulty in determining how EU data protection law should be applied in scenario 2 has led some to argue that EU data protection law and the GDPR were not fit for purpose as being too restrictive and irreconcilable with the very logic of data analytics. As will be explained in the next sections, it should be possible to overcome these criticisms by adopting a dynamic approach to data protection law, which can only be contextual in nature.

AG Villavón, para 74), analytics applied to carry out bulk surveillance of online users metadata makes it possible 'to create a both faithful and exhaustive map of a large portion of a person's conduct strictly forming part of his private life, or even a complete and accurate picture of his private identity.'

[33] For instance, the ICO Anonymisation Code of Practice remarks that the effective anonymisation of personal data is both possible and desirable (p.7), '… and can help society to make rich data resources available whilst protecting individuals' privacy'. Information Commissioner, Anonymisation: Managing data protection risk code of practice, 2012, Available at: https://ico.org.uk/media/1061/anonymisation-code.pdf (last accessed 3 March 2018).

[34] GDPR Art 22 is particularly relevant here. Sub-section (1) states: '[t]he data subject shall have the right not to be subject to a decision based solely on automated processing, including profiling, which produces legal effects concerning him or her or similarly significantly affects him or her'.

[35] For this distinction see Art 29 WP, Opinion on the definition of personal data, 2007, WP136. The CJEU expressly referred to the threefold test of the 'relate to' criterion in Case C-434/16 *Peter Nowak v Data Protection Commissioner*, 20 December 2017, EU:C:2017:994, para 35.

3. The Critique of EU Data Protection Law

Data analytics has often been described as being 'antithetic' to the logic of data protection law,[36] at least as traditionally conceived (ie as a regime applicable from the stage of data collection) irrespective of the nature of the use following the collection. This has led some commentators to criticise the (re)introduction and on occasion the strengthening of so-called 'out-dated' data protection principles in the GDPR, such as the principles of purpose limitation, data minimisation and privacy by design and by default. The main arguments of the critique are thus reviewed to highlight their limits and make the case that a 'constructive' interpretation of the GDPR, which relies upon a dynamic approach to data protection law, is possible.[37]

3.1. Purpose Limitation and Consent are Ill-Adapted to Frame Data Analytics Practices

The GDPR, and its predecessor the DPD (together with domestic implementations, such as the UK Data Protection Act 1998),[38] require those subject to its rules acting in the role of data controllers to both:

- have a legal basis for processing personal data (GDPR, Article 6(1)). There is a general prohibition on processing personal data unless a particular 'legal basis' exists as a prerequisite to lawful processing. A possible six of such bases (hereafter 'conditions') are available under the GDPR. These include the most recognised condition of obtaining the data subject's consent for the processing, as well as five less well-recognised – but equally important – conditions, including the 'legitimate interests' legal basis at Article 6(1)(f).[39]

- Collect personal data only for specified, explicit, and legitimate purposes (GDPR, Article 5(1)(b)).

---

[36] See eg Omer Tene and Jules Polonetsky, 'Big Data for All: Privacy and User Control in the Age of Analytics' Northwestern Journal of Technology and Intellectual Property 11 (2013): 239 at 242 ('These principles [data minimization and purpose limitation] are antithetical to big data, which is premised on data maximization – a theory that posits that the more data processed, the finer the conclusions – and seeks to uncover surprising, unanticipated correlations'); Alessandro Mantelero, 'The future of consumer data protection in the E.U. Re-thinking the "notice and consent" paradigm in the new era of predictive analytics', *Computer Law and Security Review* 30 (2014): 643 at 651–652 ('the traditional data protection framework defined in the 1990s goes into crisis, since the new technological and economic contexts (i.e. market concentration, social and technological lock-ins) undermined its fundamental pillars: the purpose specification principle, the use limitation principle, and the "notice and consent" model').

[37] This is not to say that no refinement or improvement is needed in particular when the GDPR is not applicable. See, eg, Dennis Broeders, Erik Schrijvers, Bart van der Sloot, Rosamunde van Brakel, Josta de Hoog, Ernst Hirsch Ballin, 'Big Data and Security Policies: Towards a Framework for Regulating the Phases of Analytics and Use of Big Data', *Computer Law and Security Review* (2017): 33, 309.

[38] The UK Data Protection Act 1998 has now been replaced by the Data Protection Act 2018.

[39] Under the DPD (Art 7(f), there is also a 'legitimate interests' condition described in similar, but not equivalent, terms to how it is described in the GDPR. DPD Art 7(f)) describes the condition as

While these conditions are not the only ones to be met by data controllers, they are certainly the first hurdles to overcome. Let us start with purpose limitation. The value of having a purpose limitation principle may be questioned when it comes to analytics applied to personal data for secondary reuse purposes aimed at innovating from such data for at least two reasons.

One reason links to the difficulty of knowing the exact nature of the innovative reuse 'purpose' sought at a later time period (precisely because it is innovative) at the original time of the data being collected/generated or just prior to the start of the analysis. Hence, the criticism that purpose limitation as a condition is unfit.

It is, however, possible to first reduce the relevance of this criticism by noting that data analytics practices are more varied than is usually assumed. As Torra and Navarro-Arribas point out, the different types of data-analytic challenges that a third party may want to address include:

- *Data-driven or general purpose.* In this case, we have no knowledge on the type of analysis to be performed by a third party. This is the usual case in which data is published through a server for future use. It also includes the case that data is transferred to a data miner or a data scientist for its analysis as we usually do not know which algorithm will be applied to the data. For this purpose, anonymization methods, also known as masking methods have been developed. ['type 1']

- *Computation-driven or specific purpose.* In this case, we know the exact analysis the third party (or third parties) wants to apply to the data. For example, we know that the data scientist wants to find the parameters of a regression model. This can be seen as the computation of a function or as solving a query for a database without disclosing the database. When a single database is considered and we formulate the problem as answering a query, differential privacy is a suitable privacy model. In the case that multiple databases are considered, the privacy model is based on secure multiparty computation and cryptographic protocols are used for this purpose. ['type 2']

- *Result-driven.* In this case, the analysis (a given data mining algorithm) is also known. The difference with computation-driven approaches is that here we are not worried on the protection of the database per se, but on the protection of some of the outcomes of the algorithm. For example, we know that data scientists will apply association rule mining, and we want to avoid that they infer that people buying diapers also buy beers. Similarly, as in computation driven analysis, prevention of disclosure for this type of analysis is specific to the given computation producing the specific results. In this case, however, the

available when 'processing is necessary for the purposes of the legitimate interests pursued by the controller or by the third party or parties to whom the data are disclosed, except where such interests are overridden by the interests for fundamental rights and freedoms of the data subject which require protection under Article 1(1)'.

focus is on the knowledge inferred from the data instead of the actual data.[40] ['type 3']

Clarke also categorises analytics practices according to the purpose for which analysis is performed.[41] He distinguishes two broad categories of purposes (according to whether the analysis is aiming to deliver insights into populations, or about individuals) within which distinctly different types of problems can be tackled using different analytic techniques. These are under 'population focus' – hypothesis testing, populating inferencing, and, construction of profiles; and, under 'individual focus' – discovery of outliers, discovery of anomalies, and application of profiles. The construction and the application of profiles are therefore conceived as two distinct practices, which should not be too easily conflated, if one is driven by a risk-based approach.

Going back to the tripartite distinction drawn by Torra and Navarro-Arribas it thus appears that only data analytics type 1 would appear at first glance problematic from a purpose limitation standpoint.

A second reason explaining the questioning of the principle of purpose limitation relates to traditional reliance upon the condition of consent to legitimise personal data processing throughout its several data processing iterations: if consent is a valid legal basis, the argument goes, purpose limitation should be adapted.

This is because in the face of tighter rules surrounding consent under the GDPR,[42] many organisations will find obtaining GDPR-satisfactory (ie 'informed') consent for innovative reuse from data subjects impractical. Indeed, data subjects must be provided with a clear indication that they consent to secondary use aimed at a specific purpose, as well as being able to understand how their data will be reused, whereas the complexity of the processing operation is no defence to meeting these requirements.[43]

---

[40] V. Torra, and G. Navarro-Arribas. 'Big Data Privacy and Anonymization' in *Privacy and Identity Management. Facing Up to Next Steps*, (Dordrecht: Springer International Publishing, 2016) 15–26 at 17.

[41] Roger Clarke, August. Big Data Prophylactics. In *Privacy and Identity Management. Facing up to Next Steps* (Dordrecht: Springer International Publishing, 2016) 3–14 at 4.

[42] GDPR Art 4(11) defines the meaning of consent as 'any freely given, specific, informed and unambiguous indication of the data subject's wishes by which he or she, by a statement or by a clear affirmative action, signifies agreement to the processing of personal data relating to him or her', whereas Art 7 sets out the conditions for consent that must be demonstrated for it to be claimed satisfactorily as a legal basis for personal data processing. See also recitals 42–43.

[43] The ICO Big Data Report makes it clear that just because big data is complex, this is not an excuse for failing to obtain consent where it is required. In particular (at p. 31), organisations must 'find the point at which to explain the benefits of the analytics and present users with a meaningful choice – and then respect that choice when they are processing their personal data'. Moreover, consent may also be easily withdrawable.

See also Art29 WP, WP 202, Opinion 02/2013 on apps on smart devices, adopted on 27 February 2013 (at p. 22): '[w]ith regard to the purpose(s), end users must be adequately informed which data are collected about them and why. Users should also be made aware in clear and plain language whether the data may be reused by other parties, and if so, for what purposes. Elastic purposes such as 'product innovation' are inadequate to inform users. It should be plainly stated if users will be

Reading both Article 6(4) of the GDPR and the latest version (at the time of writing) of the Article 29 WP Guidelines on Consent[44] in conjunction, it appears that if the initial legal basis relied upon to justify personal data processing is consent, the only way to comply with the principle of lawfulness at the second stage (the data analytics stage) is to seek consent again. To repeat the exact words of the Article 29 WP: '[i]f a controller processes data based on consent and wishes to process the data for a new purpose, the controller needs to seek a new consent from the data subject for the new processing purpose.'[45] Yet, one could argue, consent is doomed in a data analytics context because the purpose simply cannot be specific. The Article 29 WP would thus be both too restrictive and illogical in this context.

Assuming informed consent is the legal basis of election, the challenge is thus to identify and formulate (for transparency reasons) a specific purpose. At this stage, it is crucial to understand that the principles of purpose limitation and transparency are intimately related. The Article 29 WP holds the view that both the scope and the consequences of the processing should be communicated to data subjects.[46] Yet, again as explained by Torra and Navarro-Arribas at least in one situation,[47] that of 'data-driven or general purpose', the purpose of the processing cannot be said to be specific.

This criticism loses its strength once it is acknowledged that consent is only one option. What if a different legal basis (from informed consent) had been chosen or was to be chosen? Organisations have at least two other options: either to rely upon the doctrine of compatibility of purposes as per Article 6(4) of the GDPR if consent was not the original legal basis or, as aforementioned to turn to finding a legal basis for secondary data usage analytics via the satisfaction of a condition other than consent such as the legitimate interests of the data controller or third parties.[48] It is true that in both cases the principle of purpose limitation is still fully relevant and applicable.

Under the doctrine of compatibility of purposes as reformulated by the GDPR, if the new purpose is compatible (ie *not in*compatible) with the original purpose for which personal data was collected/generated no new legal basis is

---

asked to consent to data sharing with third parties for advertising and/or analytics purposes. There is an important responsibility … to ensure that this information is available and easily accessible' (WP 202).

[44] Art 29 WP, WP 259, Guidelines on consent under Regulation 2016/679, Adopted on 28 November 2017, as last Revised and Adopted on 10 April 2018 (WP 259).

[45] Ibid, p. 12.

[46] See WP 260 n 21 at p. 8.

[47] To argue that the principle of purpose limitation would bar all instances of data analytics is too strong a statement.

[48] Indeed, regulators go to great lengths to publicise this message. See the ICO's blog, 16 August 2018, Available at: https://iconewsblog.org.uk/2017/08/16/consent-is-not-the-silver-bullet-for-gdpr-compliance/ (last accessed 3 March 2018). The ICO Big Data Report also makes it clear that the purpose limitation principle does not bar the repurposing of personal data as a matter of principle (p. 37).

required to justify the new processing activity.[49] This doctrine applies in situations where the initial processing is not based on the data subject's consent.

The GDPR provides some guidance (in Article 6(4)) on the criteria that data controllers must take into account when ascertaining whether a purpose of further processing is compatible with the (initial) one for which the data was originally collected. Also available are relevant opinions published by the Article 29 WP.[50] However, arguably, even if the doctrine of compatibility of purposes applies, the principle of purpose limitation still retains its grip, just like the principle of transparency as per Articles 13 and 14.

Recital 33 of the GDPR does suggest that, for scientific research purposes, the principle of purpose limitation should be relaxed because:

> It is often not possible to fully identify the purpose of personal data processing for scientific research purposes at the time of data collection. Therefore, data subjects should be allowed to give their consent to certain areas of scientific research when in keeping with recognised ethical standards for scientific research. Data subjects should have the opportunity to give their consent only to certain areas of research or parts of research projects to the extent allowed by the intended purpose.

Although the GDPR seems to adopt a broad definition of scientific research, which covers 'technological development and demonstration, fundamental research, applied research and privately funded research' (as per recital 159), this relaxation as a matter of definition only applies to scientific research. Data analytics practices are not necessarily tantamount to scientific research, as recital 159 seems to imply that publication or disclosure of research data could be expected and recital 33 refers to 'ethical standards for scientific research'. In other words, the carrying out of many data analytics practices are not necessarily tantamount to scientific research activities in the traditional sense that research ethics approval is required before it can go ahead. This would be true when it comes to data analytics practices conducted for marketing purposes or 'marketing research'. Similarly, data analytic practices do not necessarily involve scientific research carried out under the public task lawful basis (such as carried out by universities) at all.[51]

As regards the second option (ie opting for reliance upon a second legal basis to support or justify the repurposing of the personal data), given the difficulty

---

[49] See in particular GDPR, recital 50 on this point, which states: '[t]he processing of personal data for purposes other than those for which the personal data were initially collected should be allowed only where the processing is compatible with the purposes for which the personal data were initially collected. In such a case, no legal basis separate from that which allowed the collection of the personal data is required...'

[50] See WP 203 n 23.

[51] Of course, people tagged within the label of 'data scientist' may still be conceived as researchers within a broad conception of scientific research as, indeed, set forth in the GDPR (recital 159). Moreover, as long as a data scientist's research activities do not lead to measures or decisions regarding any particular individual, it can be argued that neither the omission of prior ethics clearance, nor the lack of availability of the public task lawful basis, should prevent its classification as scientific research from a modernistic perspective.

to meet the informed consent standard, the appeal of being able to satisfy the legitimate interests condition increases under the GDPR.[52] Besides, the Article 29 WP, while being suspicious of legal basis 'shopping', acknowledges the need to let data controllers choose one more time their legal bases due to the coming into force of the GDPR and the applicability of an heightened requirement of consent to processing activities initiated before 25 May. It adds:

> *[i]f a controller finds that the consent previously obtained under the old legislation will not meet the standard of GDPR consent, then controllers must assess whether the process-ing may be based on a different lawful basis, taking into account the conditions set by the GDPR. However, this is a one-off situation as controllers are moving from applying the Directive to applying the GDPR. Under the GDPR, it is not possible to swap between one lawful basis and another.*[53]

For controllers to determine whether they can rely on the legitimate interests legal basis for processing, they need to conduct a balancing test to assess whether their legitimate interests would be overridden by the interests or fundamental rights and freedoms of the data subject. The balancing test requires the controller to understand if the interests of organisations outweigh the fundamental rights and freedoms of individuals. This test must include the consideration of risks and harms, or adverse impacts on individuals – in effect, it requires a risk-based impact assessment to be conducted followed by the putting in place of safeguarding measures (such as anonymisation and pseudonymisation techniques/processes) to mitigate risks to a safe level.[54]

---

[52] Of course, this appeal already exists under the GDPR's predecessor regime, which has seen the standard of consent promulgated by EU-based regulators (such as the Art 29 WP and the ICO) raised increasingly over the last decade. In particular, the ideal consent 'bar' was raised spurred on by the introduction in 2010 of heightened opt-in consent requirements for installing cookies following revision of the E-Privacy Directive 2002/58/EC. In 2012, moreover, the adoption by Google of a new and extremely broad privacy policy around secondary reuse of personal data collected by it, and the regulatory investigations that ensued, illustrate how EU data protection authorities became intolerant of companies assuming extensive permissions to combine and share their customers' personal data on the basis of widely formulated consents and associated privacy policies, which allow individuals little option but to accept if they want to use a company's services.

[53] See WP 259, n 44 at 30.

[54] See, eg, Data Protection Network, Guidance on the use of Legitimate Interests under the EU Data Protection Regulation, 10.07.2017, p. 13, Available at: https://iapp.org/media/pdf/resource_center/DPN-Guidance-A4-Publication.pdf (last accessed 3 March 2018), which uses the expression 'Legitimate Interests Assessment' and insist on the need to document the assessment. The three key stages are: 'identify a legitimate interest', 'carry out a necessity test' and 'carry out a balancing test'. The Centre for Information Policy Leadership goes further in that it suggests that 'legitimate interest may be the most accountable ground for processing in many contexts, as it requires an assessment and balancing of the risks and benefits of processing for organisations, individuals and society' – CIPL, Recommendations for Implementing Transparency, Consent and Legitimate Interest under the GDPR, 19 May 2017, p. 1. Available at: www.informationpolicycentre.com/uploads/5/7/1/0/57104281/cipl_recommendations_on_transparency_consent_and_legitimate_interest_under_the_gdpr_-19_may_2017-c.pdf (last accessed 3 March 2018).

Our claim in this chapter is more nuanced: we argue that consent is not appropriate to ground (type 1) data analytics practices. However, if (type 1) data analytics practices are to be justified legally in pursuit of a legitimate interest under the GDPR, the effects of the principles of purpose limitation

Setting aside the need to affect a balancing of competing interests and rights, the legitimate interest basis does not necessarily mean that the purpose limitation hurdle is eliminated. Hence, the severity of the criticisms expressed from the earliest days of its conception that – by restating the principle of purpose limitation – the GDPR is doomed to fall short of its initial promise on application and may potentially become obsolete. As we argue below, this criticism loses its strength when accepting that the principle of purpose limitation should be interpreted dynamically.

3.2. Data Minimisation and Data Protection by Design and by Default are Antithetic to Data Analytics Practices

The purpose limitation principle goes in hand-in-hand with another fundamental principle of data protection law not so far mentioned, which is also subject to criticism in the context of big data analytics applied to personal data for secondary innovative uses. This is the principle of data minimisation requiring data controllers to only process personal data that are 'adequate, relevant and limited to what is necessary in relation to the purposes for which they are processed' (GDPR, Article 5(1)(c), defined in mirroring terms in DPD, Article 6(1)(c)).

To prevent unnecessary and potentially unlawful secondary data processing, therefore, controllers must carefully consider which data are strictly necessary to perform the desired functionality of their re-usage purpose. Yet again, however, when that purpose is innovative (i.e. premised on the potential for discovering unexpected correlations) de facto this could be difficult to scope out precisely in advance,[55] whereas finding innovative correlations will not retrospectively justify over-using the amount of personal data involved in secondary analysis. The data minimisation principle implies that organisations (including third parties obtaining access to personal data through data sharing) should be able – at the very outset – to determine, articulate, and demonstrate that they are not exceeding what is necessary to achieve their secondary purpose in processing personal data.

The principle of data minimisation is also intimately linked to the principle of transparency in that Article 14 of the GDPR provides that, even in cases where

---

and data minimisation should be calibrated over time. This requirement is necessitated by the fact that satisfaction of the legitimate interest balancing test implies expressly acknowledging that no consequences will be attached to the results of the analytics (unless a second comprehensive assessment will be undertaken to justify these consequences), and also adjusting the amount of data available for processing in proportion to the needs of the analytics (in particular, through pseudonymisation). See also ICO, Guidance on legitimate interests, v. 22 March 2018, Available at: https://ico.org.uk/media/for-organisations/guide-to-the-general-data-protection-regulation-gdpr/legitimate-interests-1-0.pdf (last accessed 23 March 2018).

[55] Similar considerations of necessity and proportionality arise in relation to determining the length of time for which personal data are stored to achieve secondary ends that are not narrowly scoped.

the data has not been obtained directly from the data subject, the data subject should be informed of '*the purposes of the processing for which the personal data are intended as well as the legal basis for the processing as well as the categories of personal data concerned*'. This implies that the data controller has carried out an assessment regarding the categories of personal data it needs for the purpose pre-identified.

Of importance, the hurdle of data minimisation would need to be relativised. Torra and Navarro-Arribas acknowledge that even in a situation of general purpose analysis it is possible to apply data minimisation methods such as masking or pseudonymisation. Other methods could include virtualisation to reduce the number of copies/transfers of data sets.

However, it is true to say the requirement of data protection by design strengthens that of data minimisation. Data protection law obliges organisations to be clear in advance about what their plans for secondary processing of personal data intend to achieve, and how, through a limitative purpose description that is well-defined and comprehensive. Not least this is because the new GDPR principles of data protection by design and default (GDPR, Article 25) also require the upfront design of data processing to demonstrate that this thinking has taken place and to ensure safeguards measures can be implemented to mitigate any notable risk areas identified. In other words, Article 25 provides that data protection principles such as data minimisation should be engineered relative to purposes before the start of processing, at the time of the determination of the means.

The intricacies beholden upon data controllers to satisfy multi-tiered compliance obligations in this way simultaneously is illustrated by the Article 29 WP in its 2013 Opinion on smart device apps[56] discussing DPD compliance issues associated with their design and usage. The WP started by describing the data protection risk related to 'disregard (due to ignorance or intention) for the principle of purpose limitation which requires that personal data may only be collected and processed for specific and legitimate purposes'.[57] It gives the example of personal data collected by apps that are then distributed widely to third parties for 'undefined or elastic purposes'.[58] It subsequently links this concern to a similar disregard for the data minimisation principle, giving the example of apps collecting personal data from smart phones in abundance 'without any meaningful relationship to the apparent functionality of the app'[59] (eg for interest-based advertising and/or analytics) and without the ability of users to revoke their consent. The 'solution', says the Article 29 WP, is described in its following comments:

> *App developers should ensure that function creep is prevented by not changing the processing from one version of an app to another without giving the end users appropriate information notices and opportunities to withdraw from either the processing or the entire service. User should also be offered the technical means to verify statements about declared*

[56] See WP 202 n 43.
[57] Ibid, p. 6.
[58] Ibid.
[59] Ibid, p. 7.

purposes, by allowing them access to information about the amounts of outgoing traffic per app, in relation to user-initiated traffic. Information and user controls are the key features to ensure the respect of the principles of data minimisation and purpose limitation. Access to the underlying data on the device through the APIs gives OS and device manufacturers and app stores an opportunity to enforce specific rules and offer appropriate information to end users. For example, the OS and device manufacturers should offer an API with precise controls to differentiate each type of these data and ensure that app developers can request access to only those data that are strictly necessary for the (lawful) functionality of their app. The types of data requested by the app developer can then be clearly displayed in the app store to inform the user prior to installation.[60]

In other words, privacy-friendly design solutions can be embedded into operations to ensure compliance with data protection law under the DPD, says the Article 29 WP. How much more the difficulties under the GDPR, where data analytics innovation is being created through the secondary usage of data which arguably does not have a clearly defined purpose, and where the innovation does not involve a pre-existing piece of software![61] While this challenge may not be deemed insuperable by the regulator, there is no doubt that it does require constructive thinking and interpretation.[62] As it will be explained below, one key to interpreting the principles of data protection by design and by default in the context of data analytics is to acknowledge that the description of specific data-sharing environments matters for legal qualification and ultimately to adopt a dynamic approach to data protection law. Hence, the need to unfold this approach and reconstruct data protection law to finally overcome its critique.

4. The Dynamic Approach to Data Protection Law

A constructive interpretation of the GDPR may best be reflected in a dynamic approach to the ongoing assessment of both existing and future data protection

---

[60] Ibid, pp. 17–18.

[61] Moreover, the challenges laid down by automated, machine-based data processing can only widen in the future with the uptake of the Internet of Things. As described by Balboni, Cooper, Imperiali and Macenaite 'Legitimate Interest of the Data Controller – New Data Protection Paradigm: Legitimacy Grounded on Appropriate Protection', *International Data Privacy Law*, 3, no 4, (2013): 244–261 at 255: '[i]n such cases, personal data may often be exchanged without the knowledge of data subjects. As 'things' interact and share personal information, security and privacy need to be guaranteed … and built into products and services. Data processing cannot rely on consent as the exchange of data is far too great and fast-moving for data subjects to effectively manage it – or, in many cases, know about it.'

[62] See Art 29 WP, Statement of the WP29 on the impact of the development of big data on the protection of individuals with regard to the processing of their personal data in the EU, 2014. Available at: http://collections.internetmemory.org/haeu/20171122154227/http://ec.europa.eu/justice/data-protection/article-29/documentation/opinion-recommendation/files/2014/wp221_en.pdf (last accessed 3 March 2018) ('The Working Party acknowledges that the challenges of big data might require innovative thinking on how some of these and other key data protection principles are applied in practice. However, at this stage, it has no reason to believe that the EU data protection principles, as they are currently enshrined in Directive 95/46/EC, are no longer valid and appropriate for the

risks involved in secondary data processing, and implementation and evaluation of effective mitigating measures (including but not limited to anonymisation and pseudonymisation techniques/processes). Such an approach requires distinguishing several data protection compliance stages (data collection, data analytics, individual impact), acknowledging the interdependence between the various data protection requirements, as well as the setting up of a robust data governance structure built upon three pillars (ie data quality assurance, purpose preservation, protection adaptation), in order to both ensure that the isolation of certain data protection compliance stages remain legitimate and force the grouping of the different data protection compliance stages in cases in which the impact upon the individuals could be identified before the analytics.

4.1. The Data Protection Principles Should be Interdependent Requirements

We suggest that a dynamic approach to data protection law should first mean taking a seamless perspective on determinations/considerations regarding whether processing data relating to persons falls within the scope of the law *and* whether – if deemed personal data processing – it would then comply with data protection law's requirements. Applying a dynamic approach to achieving data protection law compliance would then require acknowledging that the twin obligations to ensure that personal data processing may be deemed lawful (in a broad sense and not only in the sense of Article 6), and fair, are not distinct but interdependent. Once this interdependence between the different key data protection requirements is accepted, the malleability and adaptability of the GDPR becomes more evident.

The purpose limitation principle is a good example of how this interplay of different data protection law compliance considerations may be gauged in an interdependence fashion. Although the spirit of the Law is arguably more important than its letter, it is interesting to note that the distinction between 'specified' and 'specific' purpose in GDPR Articles 5 and 6 could be seen as supporting the view that the purpose limitation principle's very content, and thereby its effects, should depend upon the nature of the legal basis referred to in grounding the secondary personal data processing at stake.

---

development of big data, subject to further improvements to make them more effective in practice.') and EDPS, Opinion 7/2015, Meeting the challenges of big data, a call for transparency, user control, data protection by design and accountability, 2015, p. 16. Available at: https://edps.europa.eu/sites/edp/files/publication/15-11-19_big_data_en.pdf (last accessed 3 March 2018) ('At the same time, these principles [current data protection principles, including necessity, proportionality, data minimisation, purpose limitation and transparency] must be strengthened and applied more effectively, and in a more modern, flexible, creative, and innovative way.')

As described above, Article 5(1)(b) of the GDPR provides that personal data shall be

> collected for specified, explicit and legitimate purposes and not further processed in a manner that is incompatible with those purposes; further processing for archiving purposes in the public interest, scientific or historical research purposes or statistical purposes shall, in accordance with Article 89(1), not be considered to be incompatible with the initial purposes ("purpose limitation").

Importantly, the purpose limitation principle requires a 'specified' not a 'specific' purpose. A 'specified purpose' should be understood as one that is described with clarity and accuracy. A 'specified purpose' is therefore not necessarily specific in the sense of positively specifying the outcome of the processing to cater for type 1 data analytics situations. However, a negative description of the outcome of the processing should always be present to explain the consequences of the analysis (eg no individual decisions will be adopted at the end of the analysis and the data will be destroyed). Said otherwise a purpose of data-driven general analysis could thus be deemed specified (but not specific) if it is made clear that the processing stops after the general analysis, and a comprehensive assessment would be undertaken at the end of the analysis if the data controller wants to attach consequences to it in order to preserve purposes.

It is true that Article 9 of the GDPR combined explicit consent and specified (and not specific) purpose but this should not necessarily come as a surprise even if Article 9 covers sensitive data, as Articles 6 and 9 should be read together. As a result, this would mean that data analytics practices upon sensitive data would be possible outside the scenarios targeted by Article 9(2)(b)–(j) but only if a legitimate interest was characterised and explicit consent was obtained.

However, a weaker purpose limitation principle would require a much stronger legitimate interest. To characterise a legitimate interest it would then be crucial to assess both the quality[63] and the provenance of the data to be used for the experimentation as much as the standards in place to protect directly identifying or sensitive attributes. As explained by the European Union Agency for Network and Information Security (ENISA) '[i]n the context of big data, where analytics transform raw and distributed data into useful and meaningful outputs, provenance can attest data origin and authenticity, qualify assertions and justify unexpected results. It also forms integral part of an audit-compliance-accountability process …'[64] Data quality metrics are therefore needed

---

[63] On the importance of data quality see D.A. McFarland, H.R. McFarland, 'Big Data and the Danger of Being Precisely Inaccurate', *Big Data Soc*, 2 no 2, (2015): 1–4; Roger Clarke 'Big Data, Big Risks' *Inf Syst J*, 26, no 1 (2016): 77–90; Roger Clarke, 'Quality Assurance for Security Applications of Big Data', Proc. European Intelligence and Security Informatics Conference (EISIC), Uppsala, 17–19 August 2016; Roger Clarke, Guidelines for the Responsible Application of Data Analytics, *Computer Law and Security Review*, 34, no 3 (2018): 467–476.

[64] ENISA – Privacy by design in big data – An overview of privacy enhancing technologies in the era of big data analytics, December 2015. Available at: www.enisa.europa.eu/publications/big-data-protection/at_download/fullReport (last accessed 23 March 2018). See also the IBM white paper:

to evaluate data reliability and relevance as well as the ethics of using certain types of data for non-specific purposes.

If the secondary processing is based upon consent, the 'specified purposes' would still have to be specific as per Article 6(1)(a) of the GDPR and positively specify the outcome of the processing (eg the cleaning of the dataset). Indeed, this is the best way to make consent a meaningful instrument to reduce the asymmetry of power that exists between data controllers and data subjects. Of note, the Article 29 WP does not seem to go as far as to suggest that consent can never be used as a legal basis for general analysis. It nevertheless states that, in the context of profiling, controllers are recommended to 'consider introducing a process of granular consent where they provide a clear and simple way for data subjects to agree to different purposes for processing'.[65] One way of making sense of this comment would be to state that if the purpose is only specified, consent would need to be explicit.

The situation is different when the 'legitimate interests' basis is relied upon. As described above, built into the legitimate interest condition in Article 6(1)(f) GDPR is a test that, if taken seriously, is meant to mitigate the asymmetry of power that exists between data controllers and data subjects. There is, therefore, less of a need to go beyond a requirement of specification and ask for specificity instead. In other words, the 'legitimate interests' ground should not be conceived as an escape to consent and the related requirement of a specific purpose.

How the nature of legal basis may be perceived as having an impact upon the strength of other data protection principles such as the purpose limitation principle is also demonstrated by the above reference to 'archiving purposes in the public interest, scientific or historical research purposes or statistical purposes', which as formulated in this way are not 'specific purposes' but more simply 'specified purposes'. This is confirmed by the choice of the verb 'shall' rather than 'may' and the statement that all these (specified) purposes shall not (which implies a categorical impossibility) be deemed to be incompatible with the initial processing purpose. Research as a purpose is not a specific purpose but only a specified purpose. And yet processing for the purposes of research (in the sense of repurposing) is deemed as not being incompatible with the initial processing. Note that if the application of the doctrine of compatibility of purposes applies, this does not necessarily mean that the principle of transparency will be met as well. In fact, the Article 29 WP recently made the point that the generic reference to research would not be good enough.[66] The principle of purpose limitation in this case should also be interpreted as requiring an identification of the scope and consequences of the research activities, albeit negatively, which would then need to be meaningfully conveyed to data subjects for the purposes of transparency.

Information lifecycle governance in a big data environment. IBM, January 2015. Available at: http://public.dhe.ibm.com/common/ssi/ecm/wv/en/wvw12356usen/WVW12356USEN.PDF (last accessed 23 March 2018).

[65] See WP 251 n 28 at p. 29.
[66] WP 259 n 44 at 27.

Going further, the data minimisation principle could also be interdependent with the principle of lawfulness of processing. This is exemplified by the fact that data minimisation safeguards such as pseudonymisation become of paramount importance in situations of secondary processing when consent is not the initial legal basis and the data controller seeks to demonstrate the compatibility of purposes.[67]

Of note, the choice of the legal basis already has implications in terms of the applicability of different types of data subject rights. Said otherwise, data subject rights apply differently depending upon the nature of the legal basis relied upon by the data controller. For example, the right to portability of personal data under the GDPR[68] is only available when the data subject has consented initially to their personal data being processed or it was processed in performance of a contract.

4.2. The Different Stages of the Processing Activities Should Either be Grouped or Ungrouped Depending Upon a Prior Contextual Assessment of the Data-Sharing Environment

Crucially, acknowledging the interdependence of the principles of purpose limitation and data minimisation, on the one hand, and the requirement of a legal basis in respect of secondary personal data processing on the other, does not necessarily mean weakening the protection of data subjects because a dynamic approach to data protection also requires ongoing and periodic assessments of the data-sharing environment at stake. A data-sharing environment should be understood as a complex data environment[69] involving both several actors and/or primary and secondary processing of personal data. Such assessments should require the setting up of a data governance structure (i.e. the arrangement of processes governing and monitoring the way data is dealt with within and between entities) making the tailoring of the protection in relation to purposes feasible.

Turning to the exercise of conceptualising data analytics practices to explain what a dynamic approach[70] would entail and push further the analyses of policy makers to offer guidance for other types of data analytics (ie when the mere production of statistics is not the expected outcome), it is helpful to distinguish three key times of data analytics practices: data collection undertaken at $t=n$, data analytics undertaken at $t=n+1$, and individual impact taking place at $t=n+2$.

The GDPR implicitly embeds this three-stage approach. As mentioned above, data analytics practices should not necessarily be equated to research activities.

---

[67] See GDPR, Art 6(4).

[68] Ibid. Art 20.

[69] For a conceptualisation of the notion of data environment or data situation see Elliott et al, n 2.

[70] See S. Stalla-Bourdillon and A. Knight 'Anonymous data v. personal data – a false debate: An EU perspective on anonymization, pseudonymization and personal data', *Wisconsin International Law Journal* 34 (2016): 284.

They can be best described as experimentation practices.[71] This could explain why the GDPR uses a different term to describe data analytics: that of 'general analysis', which we understand as targeting type 1 data analytics only. In recital 29, one reads as follows:

> In order to create incentives to apply pseudonymisation when processing personal data, measures of pseudonymisation should, whilst allowing general analysis, be possible within the same controller when that controller has taken technical and organisational measures necessary to ensure, for the processing concerned, that this Regulation is implemented, and that additional information for attributing the personal data to a specific data subject is kept separately.

Building on our previous discussion, one way of interpreting recital 29 would be to state that even if the secondary processing of personal data undertaken for general analysis would hardly meet the requirement of having specific purpose, given it would be difficult to base the processing on informed consent, the requirement of specified purpose could still be met. An alternative legal basis to consent would then need to be found, unless the repurposing is deemed compatible with the initial processing. Compatibility could be characterised if appropriate safeguards were put in place and if pseudonymisation were to be undertaken.

Importantly, pseudonymisation should not be the sole safeguard to consider, in particular if at t=n+1, t=n+2 (individual impact) is not yet anticipated. Purpose preservation mechanisms (to ensure that the processing stops at the end of the general analysis) as well as data quality assurance mechanisms (as a preventive measure), should be built in, even if at t=n+1 no consequences for individuals are yet attached to the general analysis. Indeed, the justification for adapting the effects of the principle of purpose limitation can only lie in the ability to preserve processing purposes and tailor the degree of protection of the data (eg through masking, generalisation or noise inclusion techniques or access restriction, encryption) in relation to each purpose, as well as in the ability to implement preventive measures as early as possible. Yet, at t=n+1 it is clearly possible to assess the quality of the input data.

If the data 'results' of the general analysis (which we may assume are also likely to be personal data, albeit potentially including newly created personal data of a type different from the original personal data collected and secondarily analysed – see below) are at a later stage finally used for decision making targeting individuals, then prior to these decisions being taken another comprehensive legal assessment would need to be carried out by the data controller of the personal data. This assessment would necessarily involve a balancing of the interests of the data controller (or a third party, including potentially a joint controller) with the interests or fundamental rights and freedoms of the data subject. This balancing

---

[71] See, eg, in the context of WiFi tracking, the decision of the French Administrative Supreme Court, Conseil d'État, 10ème – 9ème ch. réunies, 8 February 2017, JCDecaux France. Available at: www.legalis. net/jurisprudences/conseil-detat-10eme-9eme-ch-reunies-decision-du-8-fevrier-2017/ (last accessed 3 March 2018).

exercise would be required to be satisfied and documented. It would indeed be very difficult to rely upon the doctrine of compatibility of purposes for stage t=n+2, if individual decisions are meant to be taken.

Of note, the test for the legitimate interest legal basis necessitates undertaking analysis that goes beyond normal data protection considerations and examines a cluster of fundamental rights. Accordingly, the assessment taking place at (or prior to) t=n+1 will, already, involve the data controller carrying out a data protection impact assessment ('DPIA') style exercise of the type that controllers are mandated to carry out before undertaking high risk processing under Article 35 of the GDPR.

Going further, while the Article 29 WP, in its Guidelines on Automated individual Decision-making and Profiling for the purposes of Regulation 2016/679[72] confirms that profiling can take place at the stage of '*the automated analysis to identify correlations*',[73] the characterisation of profiling at stage t=n+1 should depend upon the type of data analytics at stake (type 1, type 2 or 3). For both types 2 and 3 and depending upon the ultimate purpose already known at t=n+1, profiling could take place very early (either at t=n or t=n+1). When type 1 is at stake, it would make sense to characterise the whole processing activity (ie the three stages) as profiling activity when the output of t=n+1 is finally known.

In the end, at least two different scenarios could therefore be distinguished at t=n+1 (although when it comes to general analysis this might be known only at the end of t=n+1):

- the analysis that takes place at t=n+1 is done at the individual level but is not intended to learn anything from the individuals themselves at this stage, (eg whether company X should produce and sell B on top of C); or

- the analysis that takes place at t=n+1 is meant to create class profiles that will be maintained for application at t=n+2 to the relevant individual such that the inferences thereby made can be acted upon in effecting decision-making about them (eg whether customers from class A should be offered product B as an add-on).

As regards the first scenario, there is an argument that no profiling is taking place even if the data stays at the individual level during the analysis. In the second scenario, profiling should be characterised and another assessment taking place (prior to t=n+2, or at least at the end of t=n+1) therefore becomes of crucial impor-tance. This is because – preceding any individual level inferences being taken – the controller should also address the question whether, in the first place, the output

---

[72] WP 251 n 28. Interestingly, the language of the last revision of the guidelines is less explicit than the language used in the version initially adopted on 3 October 2017. Compare (p. 7): 'Each of the above stages represents a process that falls under the GDPR definition of profiling', with 'Controllers carrying out profiling will need to ensure they meet the GDPR requirements in respect of all of the above stages.'

[73] Ibid. p. 7.

data should be used *at all* to take decisions about individuals, especially if the functioning of the analytics is complex and opaque.

Finally, as hinted above, if the individual impact meant to happen at t=n+2 is actually anticipated at t=n+1, there is a strong argument that the two stages (t=n+1 and t=n+2) should be 'grouped' for consideration so that the full impact assessment is actually undertaken at t=n+1 (or just before t=n+1). A data protection impact assessment is obviously mandatory as per Article 35, when

> a systematic and extensive evaluation of personal aspects relating to natural persons which is based on automated processing, including profiling, and on which decisions are based that produce legal effects concerning the natural person or similarly significantly affect the natural person.

To sum up, building upon Torra and Navarro-Arribas trichotomy, type 1 and type 2 and 3 data analytics practices would lead to the following twofold approach:

Table 11.1 Data analytics practices

Types of data analytics	t=n + 1	t=n+2
Type 1 Data-driven or general purpose	• Legal basis: explicit consent or legitimate interest (unless the data is sensitive and in this case both need to be present) • First impact assessment focusing upon data quality (reliability, relevance, ethics.), data minimisation (eg pseudonymisation) and data security (access restriction, encryption when transfer of data)	• Legal basis: informed consent or legitimate interest (unless the data is sensitive and in this case explicit consent and legitimate interest need to be present) • Second impact assessment focusing upon assessing the consequences following the analysis for data subjects
Type 2 & Type 3 Computation-driven or specific purpose and result driven	• Legal basis: informed consent or legitimate interest (unless the data is sensitive and in this case explicit consent and legitimate interest need to be present) • Comprehensive impact assessment including an assessment of data quality, data minimisation, data security and the consequences following the analysis for data subjects + review of the assessment over time	

5. Conclusion

The GDPR is often depicted as being over-restrictive or unsuited to the era of (big) data analytics. This, however, fails to show that, despite the uncertainty generated by the entry into force of a new piece of legislation certainly aiming at strengthening data subject rights, the GDPR is also intended to be a trust creator and a data sharing enabler for the purposes of innovation fostering. Fundamentally, it intends to achieve this goal through promoting context-driven risk analyses, which in turn requires organisations to be more transparent about their personal data processing practices, including data analytics goals and how they hope to achieve them, and more diligent about carrying out and recording processing-centric assessments on an on-going basis.

We suggest in this chapter that the GDPR does not necessarily undermine the logic of data analytics. By adopting a dynamic approach to data protection law, we show that it remains possible, whatever the type of data analytics practice at stake, to apply key data protection principles, such as purpose limitation and data minimisation and adequately frame plans for future processing activities to ensure data protection compliance. Such a dynamic approach implies acknowledging the interdependence of data protection requirements and the differential impact of legal bases upon data protection principles such as purpose limitation and data minimisation.

Ultimately, reconciling data analytics with data protection requires a strong commitment to purpose preservation over time. For that reason, we argue that the key to unlocking the enabling functionalities of the GDPR edifice is the setting up of robust data governance structures (ie the effective arrangements of processes governing the way data is dealt within and between entities and their monitoring). Three fundamental principles should be at the core of any data governance structure: purpose specification preservation, dynamic protection adaptation, and data quality assurance. Logically, this acknowledgement must go hand-in-hand with the corollary admission that building effective data governance structures for the purposes of GDPR compliance will often be resource intensive, and ensuring compliance requires continuing attention and safeguards applied at every stage of the data life cycle, including data collection, data analytics and individual impact. Finally, and to avoid confusion, this chapter should not be seen as an unconditional celebration of the promises of data analytics. It is acknowledged that in several cases, if not many, the upshot of the assessment to be undertaken prior to the general analysis should lead to a rejection of the practice.

Acknowledgment

This research was funded by the European Union's Horizon 2020 research and innovation programme under grant agreement No 732506. This paper reflects only the authors' views; the Commission is not responsible for any use that may be made of the information it contains.

12

On Boundaries – Finding the Essence of the Right to the Protection of Personal Data

MARIA GRAZIA PORCEDDA

Abstract

In this contribution, I identify the essence of the right to the protection of personal data as understood in EU law. The essence is a fundamental step in defining the permissible limitations of the right; it works as a theoretical border, the trespassing of which leads to the automatic violation of the right. I claim that, to find the essence, it is first necessary to trace the contours of the right to the protection of personal data. In its case law, the CJEU has hitherto followed a substantive approach to the essence of Article 8 of the Charter without, however, providing indications on how it reached its conclusions. I therefore supplement the scant case law of the CJEU with work on indicators developed by the OHCHR, which provides a method for identifying attributes of rights from which I distil the essence. While the final definition of the essence largely depends on the findings of the CJEU, nevertheless this does not imply that discussing the essence is taboo. This is because defining, even if temporarily, the content of the essence and related attributes has relevance beyond the courtroom. The proposed attributes and essence can help in gaining granularity when analysing the intrusiveness of technologies on the right to the protection of personal data (and other rights), and support data protection by design approaches.

Keywords

Essence, right to the protection of personal data, Charter of Fundamental Rights, Article 8, EU law

1. Introduction

The protection of personal data has come a long way and is finally acknowledged as (an almost completely independent) right enshrined in Article 8 of the Charter,[1] which reads:

1.   Everyone has the right to the protection of personal data concerning him or her.
2.   Such data must be processed fairly for specified purposes and on the basis of the consent of the person concerned or some other legitimate basis laid down by law. Everyone has the right of access to data which has been collected concerning him or her, and the right to have it rectified.
3.   Compliance with these rules shall be subject to control by an independent authority.

As with all other rights enshrined in the Charter, the right to the protection of personal data must be read in light of the Charter's horizontal clauses, which command that the essence of the right(s) be respected. The purpose of this paper is to shed light on the notion of the 'essence' of the right to the protection of personal data. It asks why the essence matters, what it is, and whether and how it can be identified.

Such an operation is not as surgical as it may appear: the notion of essence is far from being clear, and the Court of Justice of the European Union (hereafter CJEU) has thus far not committed to a single approach. Furthermore, looking for the essence, or core areas, of the right begs the question as to what constitutes the peripheries of that right – ie tracing its boundaries. Such an operation is both unprecedented and temporary. The latter is due to the fact that our understanding of the right is in a state of (fast-paced) flux dictated by the evolution of the technology underpinning the collection of personal data. Yet, the discussion of the essence is also supported by well-established theoretical debates, because the right to the protection of personal data is of statutory origin[2] and was born as a bundle of principles, the so-called fair information principles or FIPs.

The chapter develops as follows. In section 2 I expound the notion of the essence in the Charter, as well as its theoretical origins. Furthermore, I present two approaches followed by the CJEU with respect to the essence in the case law on Article 8 of the Charter. In section 3 I engage with the literature addressing, directly or indirectly, the essence of the right to the protection of personal data and the logically preceding step, ie the attributes of the right, and I propose a method to identify both attributes and essence. In section 4, I explain the steps needed to find the attributes and essence of Article 8 of the Charter. Section 5, which is

---

[1] Charter of Fundamental Rights of the European Union, OJ C 303/01, Official Journal C 303/1, (14 December 2007).

[2] Lee A. Bygrave, *Data Privacy Law. An International Perspective* (Oxford: Oxford University Press, 2014).

the most substantial, is devoted to the illustration of the attributes and essence; I conclude section 5 with some considerations on the role of sensitive data. After summarising my findings, in the conclusions I discuss the advantages and limitations of identifying the attributes and essence, I identify the potential addressees of this exercise, and engage with the ultimate question of why we should safeguard the right to the protection of personal data.

2. The Essence in EU Law: Rationale, Nature and How to Find it

2.1. The Essence in Article 52(1) of the Charter and in the Literature

The answer to the question 'why does the essence matter' can be found in article 52(1) of the Charter, which is the horizontal clause on permissible limitations to all qualified rights contained therein, such as the right to the protection of personal data:

> Any limitation on the exercise of the rights and freedoms recognised by this Charter must be provided for by law and respect the essence of those rights and freedoms (…)

The Explanations[3] clarify that limitations must be interpreted restrictively and cannot 'constitute, with regard to the aim pursued, disproportionate and unreasonable interference undermining the very substance of those rights'.[4] So, while the formulation of Article 8 would allow for the application of a margin of appreciation, respect for the essence is deemed to be stringent.[5] In other words, a violation of the essence of the right would be impermissible, ie it would be contrary to the rule of law upon which the Charter, and the EU public policy (ideal *ordre public*), rely.

This begs the question of the nature of the essence and, further down the line, how to identify it. The notion of essence contained in the Charter originates from German law,[6] where it is tied to dignity.[7] Brkan[8] argues that the codification of the essence in EU law constitutes a general principle stemming from the constitutional

---

[3] Explanations Relating to the Charter of Fundamental Rights, OJ C 303/02 (Explanations to the Charter), (14 December 2007).

[4] Judgment of 13 April 2000 in *Karlsson and Others*, C- 292/97, EU:C:2000:202, para 45 (2000).

[5] Paul Craig, *The Lisbon Treaty, Revised Edition: Law, Politics, and Treaty Reform* (Oxford: Oxford University Press, 2013).

[6] Ibid.

[7] Maja Brkan, 'In Search of the Concept of Essence of EU Fundamental Rights through the Prism of Data Privacy' in *Maastricht Working Papers, Faculty of Law 2017-01* (2017) 14. She notes this is further demonstrated by Art. 1 and related Explanations. 'The Concept of Essence of Fundamental Rights in the EU Legal Order: Peeling the Onion to Its Core' *European Constitutional Law Review*, no 2 (2018 (forthcoming)).

[8] Ibid, 6–12.

traditions of at least eight Member States, that it is rooted in the ECHR (Article 17) and the case law of the Strasbourg Court, and that it is echoed by early case law of the CJEU, such as *Hauer* (C-44/79), where the Court used the similar notion of the 'very substance' (which is also mentioned in the Explanations to Article 52 of the Charter).

According to the literature surveyed by Brkan,[9] scholarship looks at the essence either in relative or absolute terms. According to the former approach, which she calls integrative, the essence only bears declaratory nature, and can be subject to a proportionality test. For instance, in Alexy's[10] theory of rights, the idea of 'essence' or 'cores' breaks the stalemate that may derive from a pure application of balancing (proportionality). This could be the case when two equally important principles collide, and their relational interference is equally serious. Moreover, although judicial decisions are informed by uniform legal principles, the weight applied to each principle often depends on the right at stake. In a pure balancing scenario, such a clash of principles could only be solved by elevating one set of values above another, with the consequence of engendering a reductionist view of rights that unjustly sacrifices the idea of their classic interrelatedness.[11] The inclusion of 'nuances' avoids such a reductionist view of rights, by supplying additional layers of analysis.

Conversely, the latter approach, which she dubs exclusionary, sees the essence as a limit which cannot be crushed, and cannot therefore be subjected to a proportionality test. An example of the latter is Scheinin's[12] reinterpretation of Alexy's theory of rights. According to him, a violation of the core, or essence, entails the impermissibility of a limitation (and therefore precludes the further application of the test for permissible limitations). The essence is to be seen as a metaphor, in that fundamental rights may hold multiple cores 'defined through a multitude of factors' and 'not preventing contextual assessment.'[13]

2.2. The Essence in the CJEU Case Law on Article 8

Brkan rightly notes that, in its case law, the CJEU 'unjustifiably ignore[s]'[14] making use of the test of the essence, with the notable exception of *Schrems*,[15] the first

---

[9] Ibid.

[10] Robert Alexy, 'Constitutional Rights and Legal Systems' in *Constitutionalism – New Challenges: European Law from a Nordic Perspective*, ed. Joakim Nergelius (Brill); ibid.

[11] As discussed, for instance, in United Nations, International Human Rights Instruments, 'Report on Indicators for Monitoring Compliance with International Human Rights Instruments' in *HRI/MC/2006/7* (2006) 3.

[12] Martin Scheinin, 'Terrorism and the Pull of 'Balancing' in the Name of Security. Law and Security, Facing the Dilemmas' in *European University Institute Law Working Paper 11* (Florence 2009).

[13] Scheinin in Maria Grazia Porcedda, Mathias Vermeulen, and Martin Scheinin, 'Report on Regulatory Frameworks Concerning Privacy and the Evolution of the Norm of the Right to Privacy. Deliverable 3.2, Surprise Project' (Florence: European University Institute, 2013) 43–44.

[14] Brkan, 'In Search of the Concept of Essence of EU Fundamental Rights through the Prism of Data Privacy' n 7 at 13.

[15] Judgment of 6 October 2015 in *Schrems*, C-362/14, ECLI:EU:C:2015:650 (2015).

case ever to be solved, though not without criticism,[16] solely based on the essence. Nevertheless, according to Brkan, the few cases adjudicated on the essence (or the coterminous notion 'very substance') suggest that the CJEU follows an exclusionary approach.[17]

Unfortunately, the case law on Article 8 of the Charter does not offer hints in either direction, because the essence of data protection has not been found by the CJEU to have been breached yet. Nonetheless, the Court has made reference to the essence in four cases relating to the protection of personal data yielding lessons of relevance for this research. In the first and less famous case of *Coty*,[18] the Court found the implementation of Article 8 of the Charter to be affecting the essence of other rights (so this is not, strictly speaking, a case on the essence of Art. 8). In the aforementioned *Schrems*, the Court found the lack of implementation of rules stemming from Article 8 of the Charter to be impacting on the essence of another right. As for the other two cases, *Digital Rights Ireland*[19] and *Opinion 1/15*,[20] the CJEU identified substantive elements of the essence of Article 8 of the Charter.[21] I analyse the four cases in chronological order.

(a) Coty: Procedural Approach to the Essence

Coty, which resulted from a request for preliminary ruling adjudicated by the Court in 2015, concerns the reconciliation of the protection of personal data with the rights to an effective remedy and to property (enshrined in Articles 47 and 17(2) of the Charter) (§33). The case referred to proceedings between Coty Germany GmbH, a company which owns intellectual property rights, and a banking institution, the Stadtsparkasse Magdeburg. The dispute concerned the refusal of the Stadtsparkasse to provide Coty Germany GmbH with information relating to a bank account, ie personal data, necessary to identify a person responsible for the sale of counterfeit goods infringing the intellectual property rights of Coty Germany. In this case, the Court interpreted the requirement of the essence stemming from Article 52(1) of the Charter as meaning that permissible limitations cannot result in a serious infringement of a right protected by the Charter for the sake of fulfilling another right protected by the Charter (§35). Following this reasoning, the CJEU found that a 'national provision which allows, in an *unlimited and unconditional manner*,[22] a banking institution to invoke banking secrecy to refuse to provide, pursuant to Article 8(1)(c) of the Directive 2004/48/EC,

---

[16] 'In Search of the Concept of Essence of EU Fundamental Rights through the Prism of Data Privacy' n 7 at 16–17; 'The Concept of Essence of Fundamental Rights in the EU Legal Order' above n 7.

[17] 'The Concept of Essence of Fundamental Rights in the EU Legal Order' above n 7.

[18] Judgment of 16 July 2015 in *Coty Germany* C-580/13, ECLI:EU:C:2015:485 (2015).

[19] Judgment of 8 April 2014 in Digital Rights Ireland and Seitlinger and Others, Joined Cases C-293/12 and C-594/12, ECLI:EU:C:2014:238 (2014).

[20] Opinion 1/15 of the Court (Grand Chamber), ECLI:EU:C:2017:592 (2017).

[21] Note that *Tele2Sverige* does not figure in this list. Unfortunately the CJEU did not follow the suggestion given by the Advocate General Saugmandsgaard Øe in an *obiter dictum* of his Opinion; see further, sections 3.1 and 4.1.

[22] Emphasis added.

information concerning the name and address of an account holder' (§37) is 'liable to frustrate the right to information recognised in Article 8(1) of Directive 2004/48 and is therefore [as follows from paragraph 29], such as to infringe the fundamental right to an effective remedy and the fundamental right to intellectual property' (§38). This is capable of seriously impairing the effective exercise of the right to intellectual property' (§40).

This approach to the essence of rights in general can be dubbed 'procedural', because protecting individuals by withholding their personal data frustrates the exercise of the right to an effective remedy, which is instrumental to enjoying the fundamental right to property (§29).

(b)   *Digital Rights Ireland: Substantive Approach to the Essence*

Digital Rights Ireland concerns the reconciliation between Article 8 (and 7) of the Charter with the objective of general interest of public security. The case stemmed from a joint request for preliminary ruling raised by the Irish High Court and the Austrian *Verfassungsgerichtshof* concerning proceedings challenging the compatibility of the Data Retention Directive (24/2006/EC) with the rights enshrined in Article 8 (and 7) of the Charter. In order to appraise the compatibility, the CJEU developed a fully-fledged test pursuant to Article 52(1). First, the CJEU ascertained that there was an interference with the rights (§35–36). The Court skipped the legality test, in the clear presence of a legal basis, and assessed whether the interference represented by the Data Retention Directive impinged on the essence of the right (§39–40). In that context, the Court elaborated, *a contrario*, a substantive understanding of the 'essence' of Article 8

> (Nor is that retention of data such as to adversely affect) the essence of the fundamental right to the protection of personal data enshrined in Article 8 of the Charter, because Article 7 of Directive 2006/24 provides, in relation to data protection and data security, that ... Member States are to ensure that appropriate technical and organisational measures are adopted against accidental or unlawful destruction, accidental loss or alteration of the data. (§40)

As is well-known, the Court struck out the Directive on the basis of its threefold lack of limitedness (non-excessiveness) *vis-à-vis* what is strictly necessary to attain the Directive's objectives (§57, 60 and 63), rather than on the basis of the violation of the essence of rights (§48). This is somewhat in contrast with the fact that the CJEU found that the very same provisions of the Directive fulfilling the essence do not 'ensure that a particularly high level of protection and security is applied "... by means of technical and organisational measures" and the fact that those data could be retained outside the EU hinders "compliance with the requirements of protection and security' (§67–68). In sum, the Court identified the essence of Article 8 in data security, which would be fulfilled by the presence of minimum provisions in the applicable law; the assessment of the quality of those provisions was left to the proportionality test, the result of which is that the quality of the law was sub-standard.[23]

(c) Schrems: 'Essential Components' (and Missed Opportunities?)

In *Schrems* the Court invalidated Decision 2000/520, pursuant to which the Safe Harbour Agreement was deemed adequate, because the Agreement impinged on the essence of Articles 7 and 47. The Court found the violation of the essence of the right to an effective remedy (Article 47) to stem from the absence of provisions in the applicable law expressing data subjects' rights, namely 'for an individual to pursue legal remedies in order to have access to personal data relating to him, or to obtain the rectification or erasure of such data' (§95). *A contrario*, elements of the protection of personal data appear to constitute the essence of the right to an effective remedy, but not the essence of Article 8. This approach is problematic, in that it seems to negate the interrelatedness and interdependency of Article 8 and 47, which overlap, as they both express elements of the rule of law (see further section 5.2). Arguably, the approach followed by the Court in *Coty* could have led to confirm such interrelatedness.

The case further raises an important terminological question. In §41, the CJEU said

> The establishment in Member States of independent supervisory authorities is therefore (…) an essential component of the protection of individuals with regard to the processing of personal data (§41).

This quote raises the question as to whether the locution 'essential component' of the right is equivalent to the 'essence'. Three facts constitute arguments against such equivalence: first, 'essential component' is discussed at the beginning of the judgment, as part of the preliminary considerations; second, the quote refers to the wording of recital 62 of Directive 95/46; and thirdly, the CJEU did not explicitly choose to use 'the essence', as it did instead for Articles 7 and 47.

(d) Opinion 1/15: Back to the Substantive Approach to the Essence

Opinion 1/15 was pronounced in response to a request, advanced by the European Parliament, to assess the compatibility of the draft Agreement on the exchange of Passenger Name Record data between the EU and Canada with Article 8 (and 7) of the Charter (as well as to assess the adequacy of the legal basis pursuant to which the Agreement was adopted). Similarly to *Digital Rights Ireland*,

---

[23] This seems closer to what has been termed the integrative (relative) approach to the essence, as opposed to the exclusionary (absolute) approach discussed, and supported, by Brkan. Brkan, 'In Search of the Concept of Essence of EU Fundamental Rights through the Prism of Data Privacy' n 7 at 22; 'The Concept of Essence of Fundamental Rights in the EU Legal Order' above n 7. Note that it is beyond the scope of this chapter to take sides on this debate.

Opinion 1/15 concerns the reconciliation between Article 8 (and 7) of the Charter with the objective of general interest of public security (§149).

Here the Court confirmed the understanding of the essence found in *Digital Rights Ireland* (though with a slightly different wording), and further expanded it. In detail, in §150 the Court found that

> As for the essence of the right to the protection of personal data, enshrined in Article 8 of the Charter, the envisaged agreement limits, in Article 3, the purposes for which PNR data may be processed and lays down, in Article 9, rules intended to ensure, inter alia, the security, confidentiality and integrity of that data, and to protect it against unlawful access and processing.

The Court identified the essence of personal data in rules ensuring the 'security, confidentiality and integrity' (see section 5) of data, which protect it against unlawful access and processing. In addition, it added to the list (also *a contrario*) the well-known principle of 'purpose limitation'. As in *Digital Rights Ireland*, the simple presence of minimum rules, coupled with the existence of an objective of general interest, entails for the Court an automatic fulfilment of the essence (§150). The Court resolves the case instead by means of a classic proportionality test.

For the purposes of this discussion, what matters is that in the case under analysis (as in *Digital Rights Ireland*), which concerns the clash between fundamental rights and objectives of general interest, the CJEU identified the essence as a substantive component of the right expressed in secondary law, the omission of which would be impermissible. The extent to which the entitlement expressed in secondary law is implemented can be further appraised by the Court in the context of a test for permissible limitations.

(e) Lessons Learnt from the Case Law and Open Questions

The four cases converge on some matters, but also diverge on others. *Coty* and *Schrems* have in common the denial of a right to an effective remedy. In the first case, rules implementing Article 8 are found to impinge on the essence of the right to an effective remedy and to property; in the second case, it is the absence of rules in the legal standard stemming from Article 8 that is found to impinge on the essence of the right to an effective remedy. In *Coty*, which concerns the reconciliation of fundamental rights, the Court refers to the essence in 'procedural' terms: the essence (and, *a contrario*, permissible limitations) lies in the ability to exercise a right *tout court*, hence it lies in its guarantees, which in fact become fundamental when a right's enjoyment is limited. Differently, in *Schrems*, the CJEU construes elements of Article 8 as the essence of the right to an effective remedy.[24] Moreover, the Court refers to the 'essential components' of the right, which begs the question

---

[24] This is possibly akin to the ancillary or instrumental approach to data protection proposed by Raphaël Gellert and Serge Gutwirth, 'The legal construction of privacy and data protection' (2013) 29(5) *Computer Law and Security Review*.

of the relationship between this concept and the essence. I will come back to this point in sections 3 and 4, where I discuss the concept of attributes.

In *Digital Rights Ireland* and *Opinion 1/15*, which concern the reconciliation between fundamental rights and objectives of general interest, the Court unambiguously defines the nature of the essence of Article 8 of the Charter in substantive terms. This can be dubbed the substantive approach, whereby permissible limitations must respect the enjoyment of a specific facet of the right, as codified in a legal provision.

In sum, when the Court expressed itself on the essence of Art. 8, it did so in substantive terms. Conversely, the case law on the essence of other rights in relation to Article 8 Charter does not seem to lead to a single approach and leaves several doors open. Ultimately, it is for the Court to clarify which of the approaches is bound to prevail in the case law concerning Article 8. However, this should not imply that discussing the essence is taboo. Pending a clarification by the Court, I will borrow from the lessons drawn from all four cases to identify candidates for the essence and the logically preceding step, the attributes of the right.

3. How to Identify the Essence: The Concept of Attributes

If the right to the protection of personal data were an absolute right, its entire definition would correspond to the essence, a point also made by Brkan.[25] However, Article 8 of the Charter is a qualified right;[26] in this case, talking about the essence, or core areas, of a right begs the question as to what constitutes the peripheries of a right – ie tracing its boundaries. After surveying the literature addressing boundaries of the right to the protection of personal data, I propose a method to identify such boundaries.

3.1. Literature on Boundaries and the Essence

To begin with, it should be recalled that the discussion on 'boundaries' is as old as the question of the independence of 'data protection' from 'privacy', a question kept alive by the inconsistent approach of the Court to Article 8.[27] However,

---

[25] 'In Search of the Concept of Essence of Eu Fundamental Rights through the Prism of Data Privacy' above n 7.

[26] Similarly, to the right to respect for private and family life, personal data protection is not absolute, but must be considered in relation to its function in society. Judgment of 17 October 2013 in *Schwarz*, C-291/12, EU:C:2013:670, para 33 (2013); Judgment of 5 May 2011 in *Deutsche Telekom*, C-543/09, ECLI:EU:C:2011:279, para 51 (2011).

[27] This is discussed at length and convincingly in Gloria González Fuster, *The Emergence of Personal Data Protection as a Fundamental Right in Europe* (Berlin: Springer, 2014); Orla Lynskey, *The Foundations of EU Data Protection Law* (Oxford: Oxford University Press, 2015). Tzanou refers to the Court's incoherent approach as the 'data protection paradox', which stands in the way of the autonomous character of personal data protection. Tzanou (2012) 353.

the discussion on boundaries strongly overlaps with that of fair information principles or FIPs[28] through which data protection was first proposed, as well as the search for principles of privacy, a search which abounds in the literature (akin to most rights which, as De Hert rightly notes, lend themselves to being articulated in terms of principles[29]).

For the sake of this discussion, which concerns the jurisdiction of the EU, I limit myself to attempts made by recent scholarship to identify the boundaries of the right as enshrined in the Charter. A number of attempts, despite their elegance and subsequent success, conflate Article 7 of the Charter with Article 8 under the common umbrella of 'privacy'. This is the case of Finn, Wright, and Friedewald's[30] understanding of the right. The typology proposed by Koops, Clayton Newell, Timan, Skorvanek, Chokrevski and Galic[31] similarly addresses 'privacy', and transcends the boundaries of the EU: the Charter is taken into account, but only as one piece of the regulatory jigsaw puzzle creating regulatory convergence across the two sides of the Atlantic. Nevertheless, the question of regulatory convergence is relevant and acquires particular weight in relation to datafication and the design of technology, issues which, pursuant to the new rules in the General Data Protection Regulation (GDPR),[32] should no longer be an afterthought. I will come back to this point in the conclusions.

Attempts to identify, directly or indirectly, the boundaries and essence of the right to the protection of personal data have been made, in chronological order, by De Hert, Tzanou, Gellert and Gutwirth,[33] Bygrave, Lynskey[34] and Brkan. In the context of the discussion of privacy impact assessments (IA), De Hert[35] appraises the possibility of building a data protection IA, which indirectly entails defining the boundaries of data protection. He argues that the nature of the right to data protection hinders the conclusion of a real IA; the right's nature calls

---

[28] Alan Westin, *Privacy and Freedom* (New York, Atheneum Press, 1967); Robert Gellman, 'Fair Information Practices: A Basic History (Version 1.89)' constantly updated at: http://bobgellman.com/rg-docs/rg-FIPShistory.pdf.

[29] Paul De Hert, 'Data Protection as Bundles of Principles, General Rights, Concrete Substantive Rights and Rules. Piercing the Veil of Stability Surrounding the Principles of Data Protection' (Foreword) *European Data Protection Law*, no 2 (2017) 167.

[30] Rachel L. Finn, David Wright, and Michael Friedewald, 'Seven Types of Privacy' in *European Data Protection: Coming of Age*, edited by Ronald Leenes Serge Gutwirth, Paul de Hert, and Yves Poullet, (Dordrecht: Springer, 2013).

[31] Bert-Jaap Koops et al., 'A Typology of Privacy' (2017) *University of Pennsylvania Journal of International Law* 38.

[32] Regulation 2016/679/EU of the European Parliament and of the Council of 27 April 2016 on the Protection of Natural Persons with Regard to the Processing of Personal Data and on the Free Movement of Such Data, and Repealing Directive 95/46/EC (General Data Protection Regulation), OJ L 119/1.

[33] Serge Gutwirth and Raphael Gellert, 'The Legal Construction of Privacy and Data Protection' (2013) *Computer Law & Security Review* 29.

[34] Lynskey, above n 27.

[35] Paul De Hert, 'A Human Rights Perspective on Privacy and Data Protection Impact Assessments' in *Privacy Impact Assessment* Paul De Hert and David Wright (eds), Law, Governance and Technologies Series (Dordrecht and New York: Springer, 2012).

instead for a compliance check based on the requirements laid down in legislation. He then lists some of the classic principles or FIPs, namely: legitimacy, purpose restriction, security and confidentiality, transparency, data subject's participation and accountability. He does not propose a method to define them, however, or advance a possible notion of the essence. In a more recent piece, De Hert proposes to look at data protection as a bundle of (general and concrete subjective) rights, principles and rules representing a small part of EU administrative law. Adapting a quote from literary author Haruki Murakami, he claims that data protection is inherently hollow: 'Data protection has no vision of the future. It is loosely organized around unfixed principles but has no desire to realize them.'[36]

Conversely, Tzanou originally hinted at a possible method to identify core areas of Article 8 based on positive law, which, however, she abandoned in later stages of her research.[37] In her latest book, she claims that the meaning of Article 8 should be independent from secondary law and be linked instead with the overarching values that the right pursues: privacy; transparency, accountability and due process; non-discrimination; proportionality; and dignity. She rightly acknowledges that Article 8 incorporates a subset of FIPs, each of which could subsume further FIPs, and also notes that FIPs other than those contained in the definition of Article 8 may express the essence of the right.[38]

Gellert and Gutwirth[39] also challenge the idea that we could ever reach the essence of the right to the protection of personal data (and private life). Their approach, which potentially challenges this research, is addressed in the conclusions.

Bygrave[40] discusses the boundaries of 'data privacy', that is the protection of personal data, decoupled from considerations of private life. He identifies seven tenets: i) fair and lawful processing; ii) proportionality; iii) minimality; iv) purpose limitation; v) data subject influence; vi) data quality; and vii) sensitivity. He advances the idea that opposition to automated decisions may be a nascent principle, but he does not articulate this idea further. Besides the fact that, as I will argue, 'sensitivity' cannot be considered a tenet in EU law, his typology is, similarly to Koops et al, also construed in the interest of regulatory convergence.

Lynskey notes that the concept of the essence 'remains elusive'[41] because of the abovementioned confusion of the Court with regards to Article 8, as well as the lack

---

[36] 'Data Protection as Bundles of Principles, General Rights, Concrete Substantive Rights and Rules. Piercing the Veil of Stability Surrounding the Principles of Data Protection (Foreword)' 179.

[37] Maria Tzanou, 'EU Counter-Terrorism Measures and the Question of Fundamental Rights: The Case of Personal Data Protection' (PhD thesis, European University Institute, 2012).

[38] Maria Tzanou, The fundamental Right to Data Protection, Normative Value in the Context of Counter-terrorism surveillance (Oxford and Portland: Hart 2017).

[39] Raphael Gellert, 'Data Protection: A Risk Regulation? Between the Risk Management of Everything and the Precautionary Alternative' (2015). *International Data Privacy Law* 5, no 1.

[40] See Bygrave, above n 2.

[41] Lynskey above n 27, 271.

of consensus concerning which data protection rules are more fundamental.[42] This problem comes partially from the fact that data protection remains intrinsically connected to privacy, a point which I share and elaborate elsewhere.[43] According to Lynskey, the suggestion by the AG contained in the Opinion on *Rijkeboer*, whereby all elements of secondary law which are found in the definition of Article 8 could be seen as 'essential components' of the right, is a possible method to find the essence, though this is not explored in practice.[44] Moreover, she equates essential components with the essence, despite the fact that, as mentioned at the beginning of this section, data protection is a qualified right. When commenting on *Digital Rights Ireland*, which risks embodying the logical fallacy – also observed by Purtova[45] – of distilling the core of a right from secondary law, Lynskey hints at the possibility that the Court claimed data security to be the essence of Article 8 from the perspective of a holistic reading of the right. She suggests that the essence of data protection could actually be privacy, whilst other 'essential components' of the right would play a peripheral role (but does not define them further). In other words, not all elements of secondary law found in the definition of the right would have a fundamental character.

Finally, Brkan proposes a methodology,[46] based on the exclusionary approach to the essence, which is contextual to a case and does not lead to an identification of clear boundaries.

3.2. A Methodology to Identify the Attributes and Essence of Article 8

None of the works surveyed above proposed a working method to define the boundaries of Article 8 of the Charter, and most of them challenge the feasibility of finding its essence. Yet, ascertaining the scope of the essence is of crucial practical application, for instance when developing new technology, assessing its

---

[42] Ibid at 270–72.

[43] The two rights meet at the intersection of identity (and related personality), autonomy and dignity and act in synergy, as I argue in Maria Grazia Porcedda, 'The Recrudescence of 'Security v. Privacy' after the 2015 Terrorist Attacks, and the Value of 'Privacy Rights' in the European Union' in *Rethinking Surveillance and Control. Beyond the 'Security Versus Privacy' Debate*. Elisa Orrù, Maria Grazia Porcedda, and Sebastian Volkmann-Weydner (eds) (Nomos, 2017) 164. See also Maria Tzanou, *The Fundamental Right to Data Protection, Normative Value in the Context of Counter-terrorism surveillance* (Oxford and Portland: Hart 2017).

[44] Lynskey above n 27 at 267–68.

[45] Nadezhda Purtova, 'Default Entitlements in Personal Data in the Proposed Regulation: Informational Self-Determination Off the Table … And Back on Again?' (2014) 1 *Computer Law & Security Review* 30, Quoted in Lynskey, *The Foundations of EU Data Protection Law*.

[46] Brkan, 'In Search of the Concept of Essence of EU Fundamental Rights through the Prism of Data Privacy' above n 7 at 24–26; 'The Concept of Essence of Fundamental Rights in the EU Legal Order' above n 7.

possible use and choosing between policy alternatives.[47] The approach proposed here starts from an identification of the boundaries of the right, using the concept of 'attributes' as the intrinsic and distinctive substantive dimensions of a right. I borrow this concept from the work of the OHCHR[48] (supported by the Fundamental Rights Agency[49]), and the UK Equality and Human Rights Commission,[50] where it was developed in the context of indicators.

Attributes are 'a limited number of characteristics of [a given] right.' (…). To the extent feasible, the attributes should be based on an exhaustive reading of the standard, starting with the provisions in the core international human rights treaties; (…) the attributes of the human right should collectively reflect the essence of its normative content (…). To the extent feasible, the attributes' scope should not overlap.'[51] Attributes represent the synthesis of what would otherwise be the 'narrative' on legal standards of a human right. In the context of the OHCHR work, attributes are the first step to build structural indicators, one of three[52] sub-indicators which measure the commitment of a state towards certain human rights objectives.

In the context of this enquiry, attributes can be used as a powerful instrument to capture the granularity of the intrusiveness into fundamental rights, in that they can help identify core areas of rights, the limitation of which would be impermissible. In this sense, the identification of attributes is a preliminary step toward the identification of essence/core(s), and therefore comes logically before them. The relationship between attributes and essence can be articulated in two ways. On the one hand, the essence can be seen as the core of an attribute. This option seems in line with the Court's case law on the essence of Article 8 reviewed earlier. On the other hand, some attributes may be seen as peripheral, while other attributes could coincide or express a core area. This second option seems to have some traction in the literature, but could lead to conflicts in the application of the law, given the qualified nature of the right to the protection of personal data. Here I follow the first approach and, in line with current case law, submit that there may be multiple essence, or core areas.

---

[47] This was proposed and developed in the context of the SurPRISE and SURVEILLE FP7 projects. I discuss the use of the essence in relation to the fight against cybercrime and the pursuit of cyber security in Maria Grazia Porcedda, 'Cybersecurity and Privacy Rights in EU Law. Moving Beyond the Trade-Off Model to Appraise the Role of Technology' (PhD Thesis, European University Institute, 2017).

[48] United Nations, above n 11 at 3.

[49] Fundamental Rights Agency, 'Using Indicators to Measure Fundamental Rights in the EU: Challenges and Solutions' in *2nd Annual FRA Symposium Report* (Vienna 2001).

[50] Jean Candler et al, 'Human Rights Measurement Framework: Prototype Panels, Indicator Set and Evidence Base' (London: Equality and Human Rights Commission, 2011). I used this to develop the attributes of article 7 of the Charter in Maria Grazia Porcedda, 'Cybersecurity and Privacy Rights in EU Law. Moving Beyond the Trade-Off Model to Appraise the Role of Technology' (PhD Thesis, European University Institute, 2017); 'Privacy by Design in Eu Law. Matching Privacy Protection Goals with the Essence of the Rights to Private Life and Data Protection ', Annual Privacy Forum 2018, Lecture Notes in Computer Science, forthcoming.

[51] United Nations, High Commissioner for Human Rights (OHCHR), 'Human Rights Indicators. A Guide to Measurement and Implementation' in *HR/PUB/12/5*' (New York and Geneva 2012), p. 31.

[52] The other two sub-indicators correspond to the criteria of process and outcome.

To identify the attributes of the right to the protection of personal data, I rely, by analogy, on the method developed by the OHCHR, and focus on its first step,[53] which consists in discerning the applicable legal framework, which includes all applicable instruments, including international ones, case law and authoritative interpretations. Attributes are derived from such a framework; they should be as few as possible, mutually exclusive and able to capture the full meaning of the right. While this exercise is experimental, because the OHCHR methodology requires validation of the attributes by a group of experts, at the same time it benefits from the well-established discussion of (fair information) principles of personal data. Indeed, as noted earlier, the right itself evolved from a series of principles, and the wording of Article 8 of the Charter, which incorporates some (but not all) of the classic principles, testifies to this. The attributes will thus result from a mix of principles, relevant case law and authoritative interpretations.

The OHCHR does not address the notion of the essence (unless we follow the approach whereby some attributes coincide with core areas of the right). As seen, the CJEU has identified two substantive notions of the essence of the right, which must be expressed in a rule, without however explaining the rationale of its choice. Moreover, in at least one case, the Court has adopted a procedural approach to the essence. I suggest supplementing the findings of the Court with a purposive interpretation of the right, whereby the essence should express the elements that aim to fulfil the goal(s) or values of the right.

4. Applying the OHCHR Method to the Right to the Protection of Personal Data

4.1. Step One: The Applicable Legal Framework

This enquiry concerns Article 8 of the Charter of Fundamental Rights: the identification of the attributes and essence of this right is based on the specific hierarchy of norms of EU law,[54] and hence there is no pretence of universal application here.

Attributes should be first distilled from Article 8 of the Charter, Article 39 TEU and Article 16 TFEU, as interpreted by the judgments of the CJEU (ECJ and General Court) *after the Charter acquired primacy* with the entry into force of the Lisbon Treaty (hence since December 2009).[55] Unlike most judgements which

---

[53] United Nations, above n 11 at 3. The second and third steps consist in reviewing the attributes, and validating them respectively.

[54] Allan Rosas and Lorna Armati, *EU Constitutional Law – An Introduction* (Oxford and Portland, Oregon: Hart Publishing, 2010).

[55] Such limitation is justified by the fact that, until the Charter acquired primacy, the Court did not analyse cases concerning the protection of personal data under the light of Article 8 of the Charter, limiting itself to references in passing.

see Article 8 as being joined at the hip with Article 7, I propose that the right to the protection of personal data be interpreted in light of article 52(2) of the Charter, whereby 'rights recognised by this Charter for which provision is made in the Treaties shall be exercised under the conditions and within the limits defined by those Treaties'. There are two intertwined reasons justifying this choice. First, Article 8 is not among the rights deriving from the ECHR listed in Article 52(3), a view AG Saugmandsgaard Øe recently corroborated in an *obiter dictum* to his Opinion on *Tele2Sverige*[56] (though the point was, unfortunately, not taken up in the judgment). Secondly, and in further development to suggestions made by González Fuster,[57] it was first introduced as a right in EU law through Article 286 of the Treaty of Amsterdam.

Reading a right in the light of Article 52(2) of the Charter means, as argued by Craig,[58] that the CJEU should take into sufficient account secondary law, whenever this has extensively refined the purview of a right whose legal basis is found in the Treaty. This could be supported by what the Court said, among others, in *Google Spain and Google*, whereby the requirements of Article 8(2) and 8(3) of the Charter 'are implemented *inter alia* by Articles 6, 7, 12, 14 and 28 of Directive 95/46.'[59]

As a result, the regime contained in rules for the processing of personal data adopted pursuant to Article 16 TFEU and 39 TEU represents a correct implementation of the right, at least until the Court rules the opposite, as it stated in *Schrems*.[60] Hence, such rules should also be taken into account when defining the regime for permissible limitations, to which, as stated above, the right to the protection of personal data is subject (construed – narrowly like all exceptions[61] – in the light of the Treaty and the Charter, and general principles of EU law).

---

[56] 'Article 8 of the Charter, which was interpreted by the Court in Digital Rights Ireland, establishes a right that does not correspond to any right guaranteed by the ECHR, namely the right to the protection of personal data, as is confirmed, moreover, by the explanations relating to Article 52 of the Charter. Thus, the rule of interpretation laid down in the first sentence of Article 52(3) of the Charter does not, in any event, apply to the interpretation of Article 8 of the Charter.' Opinion of AG Saugmandsgaard Øe of 19 July 2016 in Tele2 Sverige and Watson and others, Joined cases C-203/15 and C-698/15, EU:C:2016:572, para 79 (2016).

[57] For a more extensive articulation of this approach, and its implications, please refer to Porcedda, 'Cybersecurity and Privacy Rights in EU Law' n 49 at ch 7. See also Fuster, above n 27.

[58] Otherwise Art 52.2 would be in tension with the idea that the provisions of the Charter enjoy the same legal status as the Treaties, as constitutional provisions could be limited by secondary legislation, whenever the Treaty provisions are formulated in generic terms; it would also conflict with the idea that fundamental rights are used as instruments to challenge the validity of EU law. Craig, *The Lisbon Treaty*, above n 5.

[59] Judgment of 13 May 2014 in *Google Spain and Google*, C-131/12, ECLI:EU:C:2014:317, paragraph 69 (2014).

[60] In an *obiter dictum*, para 52, the court said, 'Measures of the EU institutions are in principle presumed to be lawful and accordingly produce legal effects until such time as they are withdrawn'.

[61] In the context of Article 8, see, for instance, Judgment of 11 December 2014 in *Ryneš*, C-212/13, EU:C:2014:2428, para 29 (2014). Moreover, to ensure that the objective set in secondary law is attained, its provisions §53 'cannot be interpreted restrictively', and they have 'broad territorial scope'. *Google Spain and Google*, above n 59 at paras 53–54.

This approach bears an important consequence for the role of Article 8 ECHR[62] *vis-à-vis* Article 8 of the Charter. In accordance with settled jurisprudence of the CJEU, the case law of the ECtHR holds 'special significance'[63] in the interpretation of the scope and meaning of the right to the protection of personal data (whenever it touches upon the matter), but the latter is not strictly constrained by it. The rationale is to ensure the independence of Union law and its capability of offering greater protection than interpretations pursuant to Article 8 ECHR (which, it should be recalled, represent minimum safeguards that EU law is encouraged to surpass).[64]

Of greater importance in defining the content of the attributes is Convention 108[65] (and its related case law, with the caveats discussed above), an instrument of international law, which has a bearing on the interpretation of EU law.[66] This is for several reasons. First of all, Convention 108 introduced the concept of the protection of personal data as a right. Secondly, it offered the blueprint for the drafting of Directive 95/46, particularly in the part that concerns FIPs (which were, in turn, developed in dialogue with the OECD Guidelines[67]). By extension, any discussion on the attributes of the protection of personal data cannot ignore the FIPs. Finally, because the instrument, and especially the Modernised Convention 108, will provide insight into what represents a minimum threshold of the right. Following recital 105 of the GDPR, adoption of the Convention by a third country is a crucial criterion to decide the adequacy of the legislation of such third country with a view to allow data transfers.

4.2. Step Two: Identification of the Attributes

The purpose of this section is to identify attributes of the right to the protection of personal data, and to propose potential core areas, or the essence, relating to such attributes.

---

[62] Convention for the Protection of Human Rights and Fundamental Freedoms (as Amended by Protocols No 11 and 14), Council of Europe, Ets N° 005, 4 November 1950, (4 November 1950).

[63] Opinion of the Court of 18 December 2014, *Avis* 2/13, EU:C:2014:2454, para 37 (2014).

[64] A second, more far-reaching consequence, is that the case law of the ECtHR should not supersede Union law in case of conflict of interpretation, which has a strong bearing on the scope of the right and hence on permissible limitations. In practice, this may mean that Article 8 ECHR would have a different relevance depending on the difference in scope of private life and data protection, eg, as described by Kranenborg. Herke Kranenborg, 'Access to Documents and Data Protection in European Union: On the Public Nature of Personal Data' (2008) *Common Market Law Review* 45, 1094. For a complete elaboration of this view, see Porcedda, 'Cybersecurity and Privacy Rights in EU Law', chapter 7.

[65] Council of Europe, ' Modernised Convention for the Protection of Individuals with Regard to the Processing of Personal Data' (2016); Amending protocol to the Convention for the Protection of Individuals with Regard to the Processing of Personal Data, adopted by the Committee of Ministers at its 128th Session in Elsinore on 18 May 2018.

[66] See, eg, Judgment of 16 October 2012 in *Hungary v Slovakia*, C-364/10, ECLI:EU:C:2012:630, para 44. This varies on the basis as to whether the EU is a party to the instrument, or not.

[67] Recommendation of the Council Concerning Guidelines Governing the Protection of Privacy and Transborder Flows of Personal Data, Organization for the Economic Cooperation and Development, C(80)58/Final, as Amended on 11 July 2013 by C(2013)79, (11 July 2013).

The CJEU last reaffirmed in *Schrems* that the control performed by an independent authority is an 'essential component' of the right, because it is listed in the definition of the right (§40–41). As expounded in section 2, the 'essential component' is unlikely to constitute the essence; nevertheless, I submit that 'essential component' can correspond to the notion of attributes. By analogy, all elements contained in the definition of Article 8 should be considered an essential component of the right. If we discount the coincidence between attributes and essence (due to the fact that Article 8 is a qualified right), this is similar to Lynskey's argument based on the AG's Opinion in Rijkeboer: all elements contained in the applicable law which are found in the definition of the right should be seen as essential components of the right. As mentioned earlier, in *Google Spain and Google* the Court declared that the requirements of Article 8(2) and 8(3) of the Charter 'are implemented *inter alia* by Articles 6, 7, 12, 14 and 28 of Directive 95/46', which specify further principles; the same must apply to the GDPR. Moreover, in *Digital Rights Ireland* and *Opinion 1/15* the CJEU identified the essence of the right from requirements which are not, strictly speaking, part of the definition (though see section 5.4), but instead are clearly stated in secondary law and the old Convention 108. Hence, and *a fortiori*, it should be possible to identify elements of secondary law that, due to their importance (as testified by their inclusion in the Modernised Convention 108, Opinions or backing by the literature), can be seen as attributes of the right.

As mentioned above, any discussion on the attributes of the protection of personal data must engage with the FIPs. Yet, here it is apt to recall that attributes should be as few as possible, mutually exclusive, and capable of capturing the full meaning of the right. Moreover, the definition of the right does not embrace all principles of the GDPR, which in turn do not coincide with FIPs, as also noted by De Hert.[68] As a result, not all existing principles must necessarily be translated into independent attributes. Moreover, some principles/FIPs representing the duty of a controller are implied in a facet of the right. For instance, the principle of accountability is not contained in Article 8, but is implied by the right to oversight expressed in Article 8(3). Similarly, the principle/FIP of accuracy is implied by the right to rectification.

Table 12.1 illustrates the mismatch between FIPs, principles in the GDPR, and those found in the definition of the right. The top row contains the principles, and the acronym 'FIP' in brackets indicates that the corresponding principle is also a fair information principle (accompanied by the original name when relevant). The left column refers to Article 8 and the GDPR. The presence of the principle in the relevant legal instrument is signalled with the dummy variable 'X' or the corresponding Article (no value means absence).

---

[68] De Hert, above n 29 (Foreword).

Table 12.1 Comparison of data protection principles: FIPs, GDPR and Article 8 of the Charter

Principles / Instrument	Fairness	Lawfulness/consent	Purpose limitation (FIP)	Use limitation (FIP)	Collection limitation (FIP)	Transparency (FIP openness)	Individual rights (FIP participation)	Accuracy (FIP data quality)	Accountability (FIP)	Independent control	Integrity and confidentiality (FIP security)
Article 8	X	X	X			X if with fairness	X	X		X	Notion of protection?
GDPR	Art. 5.1(a.)	Art. 5.1(a.)	Art. 5.1(b) and (e)	Art. 5.1(b)	Art. 5.1 (c)	Art. 5.1(a)	Chapter III	Art. 5.1(d)	Art. 5.2	Chapter VI	Art. 5.1(f)

4.3. Step Three: Relevant Literature

In line with calls from the OHCHR method to supplement the applicable law with what it calls 'authoritative' literature, the identification of the attributes benefits from the elaboration of data protection principles proposed by the literature covered in section 3.1. The work of Bygrave[69] is relevant because, first, he suggests that opposition to automated decisions could be a nascent principle of data protection, and second, he rightly argues that one of the sources of data protection is to be found in the rule of law. Such a source is visible in the formulation of FIPs and the ensuing first limb of Article 8.2 of the Charter: 'Such data must be processed fairly for specified purposes and on the basis of the consent of the person concerned or some other legitimate basis laid down by law.'

The argument advanced by De Hert[70] in relation to data protection impact assessments lends a hand in developing the reasoning concerning attributes that derive from the rule of law, namely fairness, purpose limitation and lawfulness, as well as independent oversight. These are likely to be more easily subjected to a compliance check, rather than an evaluation of their substance; in this respect, those attributes are possible candidates for the essence understood in procedural terms.

Tzanou's and Lynskey's work are of relevance for identifying the essence, to which I move next.

---

[69] Bygrave, n 2.
[70] De Hert, n 35.

4.4. Step Four: Identification of the Essence

As seen, the CJEU has identified two notions of the essence of the right; the existence, in a given legal instrument, of rules protecting the integrity, confidentiality and security of the data, as well as rules on purpose limitation. The Court's choice implies that there can be more than one essence, and that such essence should be expressed in a rule. The Court did not, however, explain the reasoning of its choice. I suggest supplementing its findings with a purposive interpretation of the right, whereby the essence should express the elements of the attribute that aim to fulfil the goal(s) or values of the right. Such an idea is rooted in the law and society approach to rights argued, for instance, by Bobbio and Pugliese.[71]

As noted earlier, Tzanou's proposition that the essence should reflect the ultimate goals of the right also supports a purposive understanding of the essence, though I disagree with her idea that the essence should not be substantively determined. Similarly, Lynskey's suggestion that the choice of the Court to equate data security with the essence follows a 'holisitic' approach to Article 8, could possibly go in the direction of a purposive understanding of the right. I disagree with Lynskey's proposal that the essence of data protection could be privacy. By contrast, I suggest both rights help the individual keep (solid) control of the process overseeing the creation and maintenance of her or his identity and, relatedly, dignity and autonomy, but each does so in a different manner and expresses different core areas.[72]

The right to the protection of personal data provides reassurance that, once a person has expressed her or his (necessarily complex) identity, the integrity of such identity will receive protection. At a deeper level, such protection acts as a filter against direct or indirect attempts to deny the richness of one's personality, allowing the person to evolve and change, that is, to exercise her autonomy. At a more superficial level, such protection tries to pre-empt, or at least minimise, the harms that can ensue from the flattening of one's personality against categories, determined by bureaucratic and economic entities, to (legitimately) provide or deny access to goods and services.[73] The essence should act as the bulwark against the assault on these values.

5. The Attributes and the Essence of Article 8

The table below summarises the attributes discussed here. Attributes I to III derive from the formulation of Article 8. Attributes IV and V do not derive directly from

---

[71] Norberto Bobbio, *L'età Dei Diritti* (Torino: Einaudi, 1997); Giovanni Pugliese, 'Appunti Per Una Storia Della Protezione Dei Diritti Umani' *Rivista trimestrale di diritto e procedura civile* 43, no 2 (1989); Porcedda, above 42 at 149.

[72] For a further elaboration of this argument, and the literature on which it is based, please refer to 'The Recrudescence of 'Security v Privacy' after the 2015 Terrorist Attacks' above n 43 at 164–67. For a quick overview of the essence of Art. 7, see 'Privacy by Design in EU Law', above n 49.

[73] As explained in greater detail, and with the support of rich literature, in 'The Recrudescence of 'Security v Privacy' after the 2015 Terrorist Attacks' above n 43.

Article 8 but have strong backing in legal instruments, case law and the literature. In the following, each section is devoted to a single attribute. I first introduce the attribute, then I discuss the applicable law supporting it and further specifying it, and then I propose the essence; a partial exception is represented by the last attribute, where I follow the opposite route because of the case law of the CJEU. Note that the attributes were identified on the basis of the GDPR only. Further research may include an analysis of the Police Directive and the implementation by its Member States.

Table 12.2 List and sources of attributes, and the essence found by the Court

Attributes from Article 8	Essence unambiguously identified by the Court	Attributes found in secondary law and Convention 108 /literature
I. Legitimate processing (rule of law) • Fairness/transparency • Purpose limitation • Lawfulness	Purpose limitation	
Oversight (partly rule of law) **II. Independent oversight**		Oversight (partly rule of law) **IV. Human intervention (automated decisions)**
III. Data subject's rights • Access • Rectification & accuracy • Objection, including profiling • Erasure (right to be forgotten) • Portability • Restriction	Data security	**V. Data security and minimisation**

5.1. Legitimate Processing (Attribute of the Rule of Law I)

This attribute stems from the first limb of Article 8(2) of the Charter: 'Such data must be processed fairly for specified purposes on the basis of the consent of the person concerned or some other legitimate basis laid down by law'. It refers to the expectation of the data subject that the processing must be legitimate, in all three senses expounded in the Article: in relation to data protection law as a whole (fairness), the interests of the controller in pursuing the processing (purpose specification/limitation), and the legal system/*ordre public* as a whole (lawfulness).

The three principles pave the way to a single attribute because they are not mutually exclusive, but rather cumulative. This is due to their common roots in the rule of law, which effects functional interconnections. To be sure, the three principles only represent some of the tenets of the rule of law as understood in the EU.[74] In detail, fairness stems from legal certainty (and lawfulness), purpose specification from proportionality and non-arbitrariness, and lawful processing from legality. Hence the attribute is called 'legitimate processing'.

Secondary law and interpretations thereof support such interconnections. First, Article 5(1) (a) of the GDPR states that personal data must be 'processed lawfully, fairly and in a transparent manner (lawfulness, fairness and transparency)'. Article 6 of the GDPR on conditions of lawfulness, and particularly its paragraph 3, clearly refers to purpose specification and fairness.[75] Likewise, the conditions whereby processing operations other than those for which the personal data have been collected are compatible with the original purpose, specified in Article 6(4) of the GDPR,[76] read together with recital 50,[77] clearly connect with specification, fairness and consent.

With regards to purpose specification/limitation, the Article 29 Data Protection Working Party noted that it is 'preliminary to several other data protection tenets and contributes to "transparency, legal certainty and predictability", which in turn

---

[74] These are: legality, legal certainty; prohibition of arbitrariness of the executive powers; independent and impartial courts; fundamental rights; and equality before the law. European Commission, 'A New EU Framework to Strengthen the Rule of Law' in (Communication) COM (2014) 158 final (2014). These reflect the constitutional traditions of the Member States and widely correspond to the tenets developed by the Council of Europe's Venice Commission taking into account ECtHR Law. Council of Europe, European Commission for Democracy through Law (Venice Commission), 'Report on the Rule of Law' in Study No. 512/2009 (2011).

[75] In connection to the legitimate aim of the controller, see Judgment of 13 May 2014 in *Google Spain and Google*, n 59 at §74; Judgment of 30 May 2013 in *Worten*, C-342/12, ECLI:EU:C:2013:355, §45 (2013). In the former, the Court stated 'the processing ... can be considered legitimate ... under the legitimate interests of the controller, but that ground ... necessitates a balancing of the opposing rights and interests concerned, in the context of which account must be taken of the significance of the data subject's rights arising from Article 7 and 8 of the Charter.' In the latter, the court ruled that 'national legislation ... which requires an employer to make the record of working time available to the national authority responsible for monitoring working conditions' is not precluded.

[76] The Article follows the recommendations issued by the Article 29 Data Protection Working Party. Accordingly, the legislator prohibits incompatibility; hence, a different purpose may not necessarily be incompatible, and the assessment must be substantive and on a case-by case basis. Article 29 Data Protection Working Party, 'Opinion 03/2013 on Purpose Limitation' in 00569/13/EN WP 203 (2013). See also *ASNEF* and *FECEDM*, where the Court ruled that further processing of personal data in the absence of consent cannot be limited to data that are already available in the public domain. Judgment of 24 November 2011 in ASNEF and FECEDM, joined cases C-468/10 and C-469/10, ECLI:EU:C:2011:777 (2011).

[77] Whereby further processing operations 'should be allowed only where the processing is *compatible* with the purposes for which the personal data were initially collected.' Moreover, to ascertain the compatibility of a further processing with the original purpose, the controller must first meet 'all the requirements for the *lawfulness* of the original processing' and should take into account 'any link between those purposes and the purposes of the intended further processing' and 'the context in which the personal data have been collected, in particular the *reasonable expectations* of data subjects based on their relationship with the controller as to their further use'. Hence, 'the passing of the same data to another undertaking intending to publish a public directory without renewed consent having been obtained from the subscriber is not capable of substantively impairing the right to the protection of personal data, as recognized in Article 8 of the Charter.' Judgment of 5 May 2011 in *Deutsche Telekom*, C-543/09, ECLI:EU:C:2011:279, §66.

enable control by the data subject.[78] Furthermore, the Working Party submits that the purpose must be legitimate, specific and explicit to both controller and data subjects, thus encapsulating fairness.[79] As the Court declared in *Digital Rights Ireland*, using data for several purposes without the data subject 'being informed is likely to generate in the minds of the persons concerned the feeling that their private lives are the subject of constant surveillance.'[80]

The provisions on consent,[81] as defined in Article 4(11) of the GDPR,[82] read in the light of recital 32,[83] also link to fairness and purpose limitation. Consent must be assessed in light of the whole Regulation, in that, pursuant to Article 7(2) of the GDPR, 'consent given in the context of a written declaration … which constitutes an infringement of this Regulation shall not be binding.'[84]

Based on the applicable law just expounded, the functional interconnection of the three principles can be easily explained. If a processing is not fair, then there is no guarantee of purpose limitation, which would void consent or challenge lawfulness. If the purposes of the processing are indeterminate, then the processing cannot be fair, paving the way to uninformed consent and a general disrespect of lawfulness. If the processing is carried out without consent or pursuant to the wrong legal basis, then it is unfair, and there is no guarantee that the purpose is specified and limited as expected.

Perhaps the case lending the strongest support to this attribute is *Digital Rights Ireland*, where the Court ruled, in relation to the Data Retention Directive[85] (focussing on storage limitation), that 'the EU legislation in question must lay down clear and precise rules … so that the [concerned] persons … have sufficient guarantees to effectively protect their personal data against the risk of abuse …'[86],[87]

---

[78] 'Opinion 03/2013, WP 203' at 11.

[79] Hence, a purpose that is vague or general, such as 'improving users' experience', or 'marketing purposes' will not fulfil the requirement of specificity.

[80] Judgment of 8 April 2014 in *Digital Rights Ireland and Seitlinger and Others*, Joined Cases C-293/12 and C-594/12, ECLI:EU:C:2014:238, §37 (2014).

[81] The court ruled that denial of consent to transfer (process) one's data can only be overruled if the potential controller establishes the necessity of such processing (in relation to one of the grounds for lawful processing). Judgment of 29 June 2010 in *Bavarian Lager Ltd.*, C-28/08 P, ECLI:EU:C:2010:378, §77 (2010).

[82] Which reads 'any freely given, *specific*, *informed* and unambiguous indication of the data subject's wishes by which he or she, by a statement or by a clear affirmative action, signifies agreement to the processing of personal data relating to him or her.'

[83] '… Consent should cover all processing activities carried out for the *same purpose* or purposes. When the processing has *multiple purposes*, consent should be given for all of them.'

[84] Moreover, 'where processing is based on consent, the controller shall be able to demonstrate that the data subject has consented to processing of his or her personal data' (Article 7(1) of the GDPR).

[85] Directive 2006/24/EC of the European Parliament and of the Council of 15 March 2006 on the Retention of Data Generated or Processed in Connection with the Provision of Publicly Available Electronic Communications Services or of Public Communications Networks and Amending Directive 2002/58/EC, OJ L 105/54 (Data Retention Directive), OJ L 105/54, (13 April 2006).

[86] See Judgment of 8 April 2014 in *Digital Rights Ireland and Seitlinger and Others*, Joined Cases C-293/12 and C-594/12, ECLI:EU:C:2014:238, paragraph 54.

[87] Moreover, under certain conditions, 'even initially lawful processing of accurate data may, in the course of time, become incompatible with the directive where those data are no longer necessary in

In *Opinion 1/15*, the CJEU clarified that rules on purpose limitation constitute the essence of Article 8. This fulfils the expectation that the data subject's data will not be used to characterize him or her out of context, and create an impact over which he or she has no control.

5.2. Two Attributes Expressing Oversight

Oversight refers to the availability of some form of control to ensure the respect of the principles relating to the processing of personal data and is the counterpart to the pricinple of accountability of the data controller. Oversight is embodied in two attributes.

5.2.1. Independent Supervisory Authority (Attribute of the Rule of Law II)

The first attribute is distilled from Article 8(3) and refers to the availability of an independent public authority monitoring compliance with data protection laws. The existence of a supervisory authority, which is conceived as the guardian of the right,[88] is 'an essential component of the protection of individuals with regard to the processing of personal data'[89] because it is enshrined in 'primary law of the European Union, in particular Article 8(3) of the Charter and Article 16(2) TFEU'.[90]

Like the previous attribute, it has a strong basis in the rule of law, particularly in the availability of independent courts and an effective remedy. Such overlap, also noted by De Hert,[91] should not be seen as implying the redundancy of personal data protection, but, as discussed earlier in section 2, rather as a demonstration of the interdependency and interrelatedness of fundamental rights.

According to Article 4(21) of the GDPR, a supervisory authority is an independent public authority that is established by a Member State. Whereas Member States are free to choose the most appropriate institutional model for the authority,[92] such a model must ensure 'independence'.[93] The essential criteria for independence are

the light of the purposes for which they were collected or processed.' Judgment of 13 May 2014 in *Google Spain and Google* above n 59 §93.

[88] Judgment of 16 October 2012 in *Commission v Austria*, C-614/10, ECLI:EU:C:2012:631, §52 (2012). The Court refers here to the 'right to privacy'.

[89] Judgment of 6 October 2015 in *Schrems*, C-362/14, ECLI:EU:C:2015:650, §41.

[90] Ibid, §40.

[91] De Hert, 'Data Protection as Bundles of Principles, General Rights, Concrete Substantive Rights and Rules. Piercing the Veil of Stability Surrounding the Principles of Data Protection' (Foreword).

[92] Judgment of 8 April 2014 in *Commission v Hungary*, C-288/12, ECLI:EU:C:2014:237, §68 (2014).

[93] The ECJ specified that 'the words 'with complete independence' in the second subparagraph of Article 28(1) of Directive 95/46 must be given an autonomous interpretation, independent of Article 267 TFEU, based on the actual wording of that provision and on the aims and scheme of Directive 95/46 (see *Commission v Germany*, paragraphs 17 and 29). Judgment of 16 October 2012 in *Commission v Austria*, C-614/10, ECLI:EU:C:2012:631, §40.

found in Articles 51 and 52 of the GDPR, which codified the findings of case law,[94] and are the absence of directions and instructions, as well as of political influence (including the threat of early termination), which could lead to 'prior compliance' or partiality. Following *Schrems*, independence, which is intended to ensure the 'effectiveness and reliability of ... the protection of individuals',[95] should be also exercised *vis-à-vis* the Commission.

The provisions on independence serve the ultimate task of supervisory authorities, namely to ensure the appropriate application of data protection rules in order to safeguard data subjects' rights and enable the free flow of personal data.[96] In order to carry out their tasks, authorities are endowed with powers. Those endowed by Directive 95/46 were non-exhaustive;[97] the GDPR codified such findings in Article 58, which harmonizes the powers of supervisory authorities across the Union.

The Court has thus far not indicated whether any facet of this limb of the right is to be seen as the essence. A candidate for the essence is therefore the provision, at a minimum, of *ex post facto* supervision.

5.2.2. Human Intervention

This attribute concerns the right of a natural person to have another natural person, rather than a machine, take decisions based on the processing of personal data affecting a data subject. Such an individual could be the Data Protection Officer (article 37 of the GDPR) or any data controller.

While this attribute is found primarily in secondary law, particularly in Article 22 of the GDPR, and does not correspond to any existing principles of personal data protection, Article 9 (1) (a) of the Modernized Convention 108 recognizes this entitlement. Moreover, the idea that objection to automated individual decisions could be a nascent attribute/principle of the right was also advanced by Bygrave,[98] who discussed it in the context of the principle 'data subject influence' without developing it further. This attribute and its rationale is intimately linked with the attribute 'data subjects' rights' (also highlighted by Bygrave), particularly the right to object (discussed *infra*). Such recognition is not accidental. This attribute embodies one of the key values of personal data protection advanced in this

---

[94] When the Commission sued Germany, Austria and Hungary for failure to fulfil obligations. Judgment of 8 April 2014 in *Commission v Hungary*, n 92 at §51–54.

[95] (Paragraph 41), in that a DPA 'must be able to examine' the adequacy of a transfer of data (in the context of hearing a claim lodged by a person with reference to such transfer) even if the Commission has already issued a decision pursuant to Art 25(6) of the Data Protection Directive (para 53). To do otherwise would mean depriving individuals of their right to a claim.

[96] Case law suggests that for monitoring to be ensured, the data should be stored in the European Union. Judgment of 8 April 2014 in *Digital Rights Ireland and Seitlinger and Others*, n 80 at §68.

[97] Judgment of 1 October 2015 in *Weltimmo*, C-230/14, ECLI:EU:C:2015:639, §48–49 (2015).

[98] Bygrave, n 2, ch 5.

research: that of retaining control over the portrayal of one's identity (and related personality) to society, and the consequences that can ensue from such portrayal.[99]

The GDPR devotes a number of articles and recitals to the subject matter. Article 22 of the GDPR, which is based on Article 15 of Directive 95/46, reiterates the generic prohibition against taking decisions which produce legal effects or significantly affect a data subject when based solely on automated processing, and a reinforced prohibition of taking such decisions when based on the automated processing of special categories of personal data. Examples of negative effects of such decisions on the data subject include the 'automatic refusal of an online credit application or e-recruiting practices without any human intervention' (recital 71[100]).

Article 22(2), read in the light of Recital 71, provides for exceptions to the general prohibition. When automated decisions are taken pursuant to the exception to this norm, the data subject is entitled to know the logic involved in such automatic processing of data to put forward his or her point of view, and appropriate safeguards must be put in place. Indeed, the need to 'lay down clear and precise rules governing the scope and application of a measure and imposing minimum safeguards …. is all the greater where personal data is subjected to automatic processing.'[101] In this case, pursuant to Article 22(3) of the GDPR, the controller must provide safeguards consisting *at least* in ensuring 'the right to obtain human intervention on the part of the controller, to express his or her point of view and to contest the decision'. The provision of information on such automated processing is mandatory pursuant to Articles 13(2)(f), 14(2)(g) and 15(1)(h), which is consistent with the general obligation of fairness and transparency.[102]

An important innovation of Article 22 of the GDPR, compared with Article 15 of Directive 95/46,[103] is the explicit prohibition of decisions affecting the data subject based solely on profiling, which is defined in Article 4(4) of the GDPR (and recital 71) as 'any form of automated processing of personal data consisting of the use of personal data to evaluate certain personal aspects relating to a natural person, in particular to analyse or predict aspects concerning that natural person's performance at work, economic situation, health, personal preferences, interests, reliability, behaviour, location or movements'.[104] Profiling presupposes

---

[99] Which I discuss in Porcedda, 'The Recrudescence of "Security v Privacy" after the 2015 Terrorist Attacks.'

[100] Moreover, it recommends such decisions not to concern a child (in the GDPR, a child aged 13 or under).

[101] Following the reasoning of *Digital Rights Ireland*, Judgment of 6 October 2015 in *Schrems* above n 15 at §91.

[102] The controller must inform of 'the existence of automated decision-making, including profiling, referred to in Article 22(1) and (4) and, at least in those cases, meaningful information about the logic involved, as well as the significance and the envisaged consequences of such processing for the data subject' (see also recital 63 of the GDPR).

[103] The negative change, compared with Directive 95/46, is that Art 22 of the GDPR is subject to the restrictions set by Art 23, as opposed to Art 15 of Directive 95/46, which was not subject to such restrictions. However, Directive 95/46 had limited reach.

[104] See also Art 3(4) of the AFSJ Directive.

monitoring the behaviour of data subjects, which, according to recital 24 of the GDPR, consists in tracking data subjects[105] (on the internet), irrespective of the objective of such tracking. Hence, automated decisions based on profiling are among the processing operations that require conducting an impact assessment (Article 35.3(a); recital 91). Recital 72 clarifies that profiling 'is subject to the rules of this Regulation governing the processing of personal data, and that the future European Data Protection Board should issue suitable guidance'.

The requirement in the law to obtain, at a minimum, the intervention on the part of the controller has the potential of expressing the essence of this attribute, the infringement of which constitutes a violation of the right. The rationale for limiting automated decisions is that such decisions stem from a partial depiction of the individual, which is based on the expropriation of control over one's (digital) identity and the evolution of his or her personality. The proposed essence appears of fundamental importance *vis-à-vis* developments in datafication and the expansion of data science applications (machine learning, data analytics also applied to artificial intelligence, sentiment analysis, etc.), which severely challenge the ability of individuals to control how their data are used to depict themselves, and to take decisions affecting them.

5.3. Data Subject's Rights (Attribute of the Rule of Law III)

Data subjects' rights are the last attribute stemming explicitly from the wording of the right in the Charter. The attribute gives substance to the notion of control over one's personal data. Article 8(2) of the Charter mentions the rights of access and rectification. In line with the interpretation given by the Court in *Google Spain and Google*, that the requirements of Article 8(2) of the Charter 'are implemented *inter alia* by Articles 6, 7, 12, 14 and 28 of Directive 95/46', the corresponding Articles of the GDPR implement and further specify the content of this attribute. Hence, this attribute means that the individual has, as a general rule, at least six entitlements, subject to the restrictions embodied in Article 23 of the GDPR. The Modernised Convention 108 recognises most of them, with the exception of the right to portability. Such entitlements vary in the degree of intensity, and relate to each other as preliminary and subsequent steps, or alternative steps, of a strategy geared at controlling one's data and averting the harms that may result from processing operations.

First, pursuant to Article 8(2) of the Charter, data subjects enjoy the right of access, ie to obtain from the controller confirmation as to whether or not personal data concerning them are being processed, and, where that is the case, to obtain a free copy[106] of personal data being processed (Article 1 GDPR), if possible via

---

[105] The recital refers to the Internet in that it concerns data controllers that are not established in the European Union.

[106] Hence the interpretation given by the Court in X may be tenable only in part: 'In view of the considerations made above in the analysis of Question 2, Article 12(a) of Directive 95/46 must be

electronic means (see also Article 9(1) (b) of Modernised Convention 108).[107] This is particularly the case with health data (recital 63). Such a right to information includes notification of the appropriate safeguards that attach to data transferred outside of the Union. It finds its limits in the potential negative effects it may have on the rights or freedoms of others, including trade secrets or intellectual property, and in particular copyright protecting software (recital 63).

Second, and also pursuant to Article 8 of the Charter, the data subject has the right to obtain from the controller without undue delay the rectification of inaccurate personal data concerning him or her (Article 16 of the GDPR; Article 9 (1) (e) of Modernised Convention 108). As a result, rectification is instrumental in realising the principle of accuracy (data quality), whereby the data must be 'accurate and, where necessary, kept up to date; every reasonable step must be taken to ensure that personal data which are inaccurate, having regard to the purposes for which they are processed, are erased or rectified without delay' (Article 5(d) of the GDPR; Article 5(4)(d) of Modernised Convention 108). The importance of rectification and accuracy can be best understood in relation to the 'personal' criterion of data protection, which links it with a person and her or his identity. To maintain accuracy means to respect and reflect the individual's uniqueness, giving relevance to the individual behind the piece of information.[108] Data which are inaccurate become inadequate and hence, in the language of recital 39, 'every reasonable step should be taken to ensure' that they are rectified, as seen above, whereas data which are outdated become irrelevant, and must be erased. Differently from the Directive, the interpretation given by the Court in *Google Spain and Google*, and the Modernised Convention 108, such a right seems now to limit rectification to the incorrectness of the data, whereas the rectification becomes optional if the stored data 'infringes the Regulation or Union or Member State law to which the controller is subject' (recital 65). However, where the processing is unlawful, then the data subject can claim a stronger entitlement, that of erasure.

This third entitlement of the data subject (the so-called 'right to be forgotten' of jurisprudential origins), means that the data subject has a right, under

---

interpreted as requiring Member States to ensure that the exercise of that right of access takes place without constraint, without excessive delay, and without excessive expense'. Judgment of 12 December 2013 in *X*, C-486/12, ECLI:EU:C:2013:836, §25 (2013).

[107] This includes, for an applicant for a residence permit, access to all data processed by the national administrative authorities in the guise of a full summary of those data in an intelligible form (allowing that applicant to understand those data and check their accuracy and processing in compliance with that Directive), so that the applicant can potentially exercise the other rights conferred by secondary law. Judgment of 17 July 2014 in *YS and others*, Joined cases C-141/12 and C-372/12, ECLI:EU:C:2014:2081 (2014).

[108] The importance of accurate data transcends the field of personal data protection. In the case of *U* (which concerns private life), the ECJ noted that for the information in a 'machine readable personal data page of a passport' to be 'effectively verifiable by the authorities of those States, the form in which the various components of the name of the holder appear must be free of any ambiguity and, therefore, of any risk of confusion' and therefore 'those requirements are not satisfied where, in a passport, the birth name of the holder entered there is indicated by means of an abbreviation which is, moreover, not translated into one of the languages required'. Judgment of 2 October 2024 in U, C-101/13, ECLI:EU:C:2014:2249, paragraphs 44 and 47 (2014).

specific conditions, to request and obtain the erasure of personal data concerning him or her without undue delay, particularly when the data subject withdraws consent, the data are no longer necessary, or the processing is or becomes otherwise unlawful (as in *Google Spain and Google*).[109] If the controller has publicly disclosed such data (or to specific recipients, Article 19 of the GDPR), it has an obligation to take reasonable steps to inform any controllers of the data subject's request to erase such data and any copy thereof.[110] The Modernised Convention 108 recognises a generic right of erasure when data are processed contrary to the provisions of the Convention (Article 9 (1) (e)). Similarly to rectification, erasure also ensures accuracy, as well as purpose specification. In *Digital Rights Ireland*, the Court considered 'the obligation to erase or make those data anonymous where they are no longer needed for the purpose of the transmission of a communication' to be an important element of the 'the system of protection of the right to privacy established by' secondary law (§32).

The fourth entitlement consists in requesting the restriction of processing (known as 'blocking' in Directive 95/46). Restriction means 'the marking of stored personal data with the aim of limiting their processing in the future' (Article 4(3) of the GDPR), for instance by 'temporarily moving the selected data to another processing system, making the selected personal data unavailable to users, or temporarily removing published data from a website' (recital 67). Such a restriction can be demanded, pursuant to Article 18 of the GDPR, in cases where the data subject has requested the rectification of their personal data, during the time necessary to verify their accuracy, or similarly when the data subject has objected to processing (see *infra*), during the time necessary to ascertain whether the legitimate interests of the controller can override the rights of the data subject. It can also be requested as an alternative to the erasure of unlawfully processed data, for instance because the controller no longer needs the personal data for the purposes of the processing, but they are required by the data subject for the establishment, exercise or defence of legal claims. In this case, the only processing allowed is storage, unless the data subject requests to lift such restriction, or some restrictive conditions apply (Article 18(3)).

The fifth entitlement is new, and consists of 'receiving the personal data concerning him or her, which he or she has provided to a controller, in a structured, commonly used and machine-readable format and have the right to transmit those data to another controller without hindrance from the controller to which the personal data have been provided', where the processing is performed on grounds of consent and also by automated means (Article 20 of the GDPR).

---

[109] Recital 65 clarifies that such a prerogative is particularly important in the case of data subjects who are, or were, children, at the time of the processing of their personal data.

[110] This obligation, however, must be commensurate with the costs of implementation and available technology, and must be reconciled with the right of freedom of expression and information, reasons of public interest in the field of public health, archiving purposes in the public interest, scientific or historical research purposes or statistical purposes, and to fulfil a legal obligation or for the performance of a task carried out in the public interest or in the exercise of official authority vested in the controller.

Although the so-called right to portability does not lay down an obligation to develop interoperable processing systems, recital 68 encourages data controllers to use compatible formats for data transfers, particularly to enable the direct transfer from one controller to the other (Article 20(2)). Article 20 provides for the independence of the right to portability and the right to erasure, which should not be mutually prejudicial.

The final entitlement, already contained in Directive 95/46 and interpreted by the Court in *Bavarian Lager Ltd.* and *Google Spain and Google*,[111] enables the data subject to object to processing on grounds relating to the particular situation of the data subject, when automated processing relates to the performance of a task carried out in the public interest or in the exercise of official authority vested in the controller, or to the legitimate interests pursued by the controller[112] or by a third party (Articles 6(1)(e) and (f), and 21 of the GDPR). Pursuant to Article 21 of the GDPR, read in the light of recitals 69 and 70, data subjects are endowed with the prerogative of objecting to the automated processing of personal data consisting in profiling, including for marketing purposes[113] (with limits consisting, for instance, in ensuring public health[114]). The innovation, compared to the corresponding Article 14 of Directive 95/46, is that the former referred to direct marketing, whereas the GDPR refers widely to profiling (based on Article 6(1)(e) and (f)), a point that was anticipated in the discussion on human intervention (*supra*). In this particular connotation, objecting to the processing means allowing an individual not to be characterised solely by a machine. Article 9(1) (d) of the Modernised Convention 108 incorporates these innovations.

The explanation to this attribute is contained in Recital 75, whereby, '… where personal aspects are evaluated, in particular analysing or predicting aspects concerning performance at work, economic situation, health, personal preferences or interests, reliability or behaviour, location or movements, in order to create or use personal profiles', there is a 'risk to the rights and freedoms of natural persons' which could lead to 'physical, material or non-material damage'.[115]

In sum, this attribute takes substance[116] in the control exercised by natural persons on their own personal data, which can be exercised through six different avenues. Such entitlements vary in the degree of intensity, and relate to each other as preliminary and subsequent steps, or alternative steps, of a strategy geared

---

[111] See Judgment of 13 May 2014 in *Google Spain and Google,* C-131/12, ECLI:EU:C:2014:317, §99.

[112] As for the legitimate interests of the data subject prevailing over those of the data controller, in the context of access to freedom of information, see Judgment of 29 June 2010 in *Bavarian Lager Ltd.,* C-28/08 P, ECLI:EU:C:2010:378, §77.

[113] Pursuant to Article 6.1(f) and recital 47, marketing is considered a legitimate interest of the data controller, which can nonetheless be overridden as described in the main text.

[114] Recitals 46, 52, 53 of the GDPR.

[115] It is in this light that profiling of children is inadvisable, as they 'may be less aware of the risks, consequences and safeguards concerned and their rights in relation to the processing of personal data' (Recital 38 of the GDPR).

[116] Based on indications of the OHCHR, at validation stage this attribute may need to be split into two.

toward controlling one's data. In detail, following access, an individual could resort to restriction with a view to either demand rectification or object to the processing; he or she could request the portability of his or her personal data and, as a more drastic measure, their erasure.

No case law has, thus far, given indication of the essence. The strongest candidate for the essence is the presence, in the applicable law, of rules which allow to access, at least indirectly (eg via the supervisory authority), one's data. Lack of access, in fact, would prevent the right holders from taking any further actions to protect themselves.

Milder candidates for the essence include the existence in the applicable law of provisions enabling to have one's data (at least indirectly eg through the supervisory authority) rectified, and the possibility given by the applicable law to challenge profiling, understood as the retention of the individual over his or her identity (and related personality).[117]

5.4. Security and Minimisation

In §40 of *Digital Rights Ireland* the Court ruled, *a contrario*, that the adherence to minimum safeguards of data security is the essence of personal data. Such a view was confirmed in *Opinion 1/15*, with a slightly different wording that better reflects information security principles used in the GDPR and other instruments of EU law.

Prima facie, the Court derived this understanding of the essence from secondary law, though data security is one of the original FIPs. Yet, it could also be argued that it stems from the right itself, namely either from Article 8 (1), or from a holistic reading of the right (as proposed by Lynskey). Indeed, the very notion of protection in 'data protection' refers to securing data against risks stemming from processing operations,[118] risks which could lead to more or less severe consequences for data subjects.

If the Court found a provision of secondary law to be the essence, then, *a fortiori*, the principle it refers to can be seen as an attribute. The idea that security can be an attribute is corroborated by the GDPR, where security features among the data protection principles ('integrity and confidentiality'). This finds substance in the expectation of the right holder that the data controller (ie the duty holder) implements measures proportionate to the risks of varying likelihood and severity for the rights and freedoms of natural persons (Articles 5(f) and 32 of the GDPR; see also Article 7 of the Modernised Convention 108).

---

[117] Porcedda, above n 43.
[118] Indeed, secondary law is underpinned by a risk-based approach. Article 29 Data Protection Working Party, 'Statement on the Role of a Risk-Based Approach in Data Protection Legal Frameworks' in 14/EN WP 218 (2014).

This begs the question of the scope of the attribute of security. A first option is to consider that the essence embodies minimum rules of security, whereas the attribute encompasses the full suite of security measures commensurate to the level of risk,[119] whereby risks are often inherently tied to the nature of the processing.[120] Article 5(f) contains an indicative and non-exhaustive list of the risks, i.e. unauthorised or unlawful processing and against accidental loss, destruction or damage, which is complemented by recitals 75 and 83: for instance, identity theft or fraud, financial loss, loss of confidentiality of personal data protected by professional secrecy, unauthorised reversal of pseudonymisation, accidental or unlawful alteration of data, which 'may in particular lead to physical, material or non-material damage'. Examples of measures to avert risks are provided in Article 32 of the GDPR, and include pseudonymising and encrypting personal data, ensuring the ongoing confidentiality, integrity, availability and resilience of processing systems and services; in case of an accident, swiftly restoring the availability and access to personal data, and regularly testing, assessing and evaluating the effectiveness of technical and organisational measures implemented.

A complementary option is to consider that the attribute of data security includes fulfilling the principle of data minimisation, whereby the data processed must be those that are 'adequate, relevant and limited to what is necessary in relation to the purposes for which they are processed' (Article 5(c) of the GDPR; Article 5(4)(c) of Modernised Convention 108).[121] The rationale for including data minimisation in the attribute is that it is intimately connected to security: the fewer the categories of data disclosed by the data subject, the lesser the risks of breaches of security within a single processing operation.[122] Data minimization as part of security also links to accuracy and purpose limitation, in that a suitably carved identification of purposes leads to a more targeted collection of personal data, and also good data cleansing practices. In this last respect, the Court declared in *Google Spain and Google* that 'initially lawful processing of accurate data may, in the course of time, become incompatible with the Directive where those data are no longer necessary in the light of the purposes for which they were collected or processed. That is so in particular where they appear to be inadequate, irrelevant

---

[119] I discuss the different notions of risks, particularly with reference to data breaches, in Maria Grazia Porcedda, 'Patching the Patchwork? Appraising the EU Regulatory Framework on Cyber Security Breaches' *Computer Law & Security Review* 34, no 5 (forthcoming (2018)).

[120] Such as where the processing may: give rise to discrimination, damage to the reputation, or loss of rights and freedoms; concern sensitive information or children; effect profiling; or involve a large amount of personal data and affect a large number of data subjects. Other risks are tied to the security of the data.

[121] In previous versions of this study (Porcedda, 'Cybersecurity and Privacy Rights in EU law. Moving beyond the Trade-off Model to Appraise the Role of Technology' (PhD Thesis, European University Institute, 2017)), data minimization was treated as a standalone attribute. The choice made here is justified by the desire to economize the number of attributes that overlap, as opposed to providing the greatest number of nuances.

[122] As I elaborate in Porcedda, n 120.

or no longer relevant, or excessive in relation to those purposes and in the light of the time that has elapsed.'[123]

This attribute expresses the idea that data should be secured in relation to the risks of varying nature and likelihood entailed by the processing, risks which could effect physical, material and non-material damage, as well as harm the rights and freedoms of data subjects. It also expresses the legitimate expectation of an individual to be required to communicate the minimum amount of personal data necessary for a given purpose. The attribute finds substance in the adoption of best organisational and technical practice, but also in the collection of as few data as required upfront, or good data deletion, because data which are not collected are not at risk.

The Court unambiguously stated that the presence of minimum rules ensuring 'integrity, confidentiality and data security' embody the essence of Article 8.

5.5. Considerations on Sensitive Data

Bygrave[124] considers the protection of sensitive data as an essential tenet ('core principles') of the right to personal data protection. Thus far, the Court has not directly addressed the matter of sensitive data in the case law on personal data protection. The only reference was contained in *Schwarz*, where the court mini-mised the risks involved by the use of biometrics. In particular, it declared that 'taking two fingerprints "is not an operation of an intimate nature ... nor does it cause any particular physical or mental discomfort" and that "The combination of two operations designed to identify persons may not *a priori* be regarded as giving rise in itself to a greater threat to the rights' in Article 8 (§48 and 49).

From the perspective of identifying attributes, sensitive data cannot constitute an autonomous attribute: to propose the opposite would defy the tenet whereby all personal data deserve protection irrespective of their sensitivity (in relation to the potential risks for the rights and freedoms of data subjects).[125] According to Simi-tis, the point of sensitive data is to highlight the inefficiency of normally applicable law in ensuring adequate protection, which carries with it the possibility, but not the obligation, of a ban on processing.[126] Rather, sensitive data should be seen as a type of personal data that transversally affects all attributes, and calls for height-ened safeguards or a higher threshold for permissible interferences. In this respect, it could be seen as a specification of the rule of law (proportionality) enshrined in the test for permissible limitations: when the interference is potentially greater, the threshold of permissibility is increased.

---

[123] Judgment of 13 May 2014 in *Google Spain and Google*, above n 59 at §93; Porcedda, above n 43.
[124] Bygrave, above n 2 at 145–67.
[125] As stems from the combined reading of the judgments in *Bavarian Lager (Judgment of 29 June 2010 in Bavarian Lager Ltd.*, C-28/08 P, ECLI:EU:C:2010:378, §61.) and *Google Spain and Google* above n 59 at §96).
[126] Spiros Simitis, 'Revisiting Sensitive Data' in *Council of Europe* (1999).

6. Conclusion

This chapter proposed how to identify the essence of the right to the protection of personal data as understood in EU law, which is a fundamental step in defining the permissible limitations of the right. The essence works as a theoretical border, the trespassing of which leads to the automatic violation of the right.

The approach of the CJEU to the essence in the case law on the protection of personal data which, as stressed several times, remains elusive, may raise more questions than it answers. The reader is left wondering whether the approach to the essence will depend on the nature of proceedings (the clash between an objective of general interest and a fundamental right, as the case of *Digital Rights Ireland* or the reconciliation of two fundamental rights, as the cases of *Coty*) or whether the exercise of the right to an effective remedy is at stake, as in both *Coty* and *Schrems*.

Thus far, the Court seems to have favoured a substantive understanding of the essence of Art. 8, seen as the presence of minimum rules that guarantee the exercise of the right, rules which cannot be omitted or limited. Yet, we cannot discard the case of *Coty*, whereby the essence is not identified in a specific facet of a right, but consists in guaranteeing the exercise of a right *tout court*. In this case, attributes I and II would be fundamental to ensure such understanding of the right, and instrumental in guaranteeing respect for the essence.

It may be possible that both the procedural and the substantive approaches could be used, depending on the issue at stake, or that the Court may find a third way altogether. Pending more enlightening case law by the Court, I have borrowed a methodology developed by the OHCHR in its work on indicators, which aims to identify attributes of rights. This is because, to find the essence, it is first of all necessary to trace the contours of the right to the protection of personal data. This exercise builds on the understanding, distilled from case law of the CJEU, that the essence of the protection of personal data can be both a substantive and procedural requirement.

The result of this exercise is summarised in the table below. The first column on the left contains the attribute. The column next to it, on the right, summarises its content. The last two columns contain a summary of the essence. The first one displays an idea of the essence openly identified by the CJEU, whereas the second contains suggestions for core areas that I have identified experimentally. Empty cells correspond to the absence of cores.

In these pages I mentioned that the proposed methodology is experimental; a fully-fledged implementation of the OHCHR methodology to find the attributes requires validation by a wide community of experts. Moreover, the tenability of the model largely depends on the Court, which has the final word on the nature of the essence.

Nevertheless, this research hopes to open up the debate on both the attributes and the essence, in the belief that the question is too important not to be

Table 12.3 Summary of attributes of the right to personal data protection

Attribute	Description	Essence (CJEU)	Essence – (proposed)
I Legitimate processing (attribute of the rule of law)*	In sum, this attribute refers to the expectation for the data subject that the processing must be legitimate, which refers to three interconnected principles stemming from the rule of law: • Fairness and transparency • Purpose limitation (includes storage limitation) • Lawful legal basis	*Substantive:* Purpose limitation	
Oversight* (II & IV)	It refers to the availability of oversight concerning data processing and the respect of the principles relating to the processing of personal data. It paves the way to two attributes.	N.A.	N.A.
II supervisory authority*	This attribute, which stems from the rule of law, means that the individual can claim without hindrance the intervention of an authority for the protection of his or her right.		Ex post supervision
IV Human intervention	This attribute means that decisions (significantly) affecting an individual cannot be taken by a machine, and that a human being must be involved in the process		*Substantive:* Obtain human intervention on the part of the controller, to express one's point of view and to contest the decision
III Data subjects' rights	This attribute substantiates the notion of data subjects' control over their personal data, enabling them to intervene in the processing. It includes the following steps, which should be seen as a range of options available to the data subject depending on the situation: • Accessing the data and obtaining a copy • Rectifying inaccurate data • Objecting to processing, including profiling • Restricting the processing of one's personal data • Erasing data • transferring one's data		*Substantive:* Indirect Access Rectification? Objection to profiling?

(continued)

Table 12.3 *(Continued)*

Attribute	Description	Essence (CJEU)	Essence – (proposed)
V Security and minimisation	This attribute means that the individual can trust that personal information is protected against risks of a varying nature and likelihood which could affect physical, material and non-material damage, as well as expect to communicate the minimum amount of personal data necessary for a given purpose	*Substantive:* the provision of security safeguards in the legal basis	
Sensitive data: affects the threshold of permissible interferences			

* attributes likely to consist of a checklist, and to embody a procedural understanding of the notion of the essence.

discussed in the interim. This is because the Court is not the only addressee of this discussion. Having an understanding of the attributes and essence would benefit the analysis of the intrusiveness of technologies on the right to the protection of personal data (and other rights); in this case the addressees are public authorities. Clarifying the notion of attributes and essence would also enable tech companies and their end users (ie the addressees) to develop better approaches to so-called 'privacy by design' or, more correctly, data protection and information security by design, which determine, in many ways, the creation of material permissible limitations.[127]

This point calls into question whose standard will prevail: will it be that imposed, *de facto*, by the dominant tech companies? Will it be that imposed by a broad territorial application of the GDPR? Or else, will it be in everyone's interest to find regulatory convergence, thus developing an understanding of attributes and the essence that are acceptable on both sides of the Atlantic, and beyond, hence favouring the approach taken by Bygrave, as well as by Koops et al.? The next few years are likely to determine the answer to these questions, but whichever approach will be better suited to safeguard the right should merit full support.

This calls into question the 'durability' of the attributes and essence proposed in these pages. Besides the need, called for by the OHCHR methodology, for validation by a wide community, I submit that any definition of the attributes and essence should be conceived with an expiry date. In this respect, I agree with Gellert and Gutwirth, as well as De Hert. Defining once and for all the attributes and essence of

---

[127] Which I discuss in Porcedda, n 49. Note that the attributes and essence defined here concern the right, but by no means the standards necessary for the protection of personal data in a technological environment; for the sake of developing 'by design' approaches, a similar matrix can be created for the duties of data controllers. The most fundamental duties of data controller would correspond to the rights of data subjects, and vice versa.

the protection of personal data may not be possible,[128] unless we move the clocks back to the early twentieth Century. The right's unfixed principles[129] are a direct consequence of the attempt to keep up with technological disruption (and flow logically from purposive interpretation). One may even look at the architecture of data protection as a matrix, whereby the essence sealed in the attributes stemming from the definition of the right is enriched and enforced by secondary law, and is matched by corresponding principles which express the duties of the data controllers.[130] Such a 'bundle of rights, principles and rules'[131] may not look as elegant as the construction of other rights in the Charter, but is nonetheless worth defending. Safeguarding the independence of Article 8 as a right endowed with an essence is in fact instrumental in retaining control over one's identity and the free development of one's personality *vis-à-vis* the pressure of a data-driven society, and allow for autonomy to be cherished.[132]

Acknowledgments

I wish to express my sincere gratitude to the organisers of the 11th edition of the CPDP, in the course of which this chapter was presented. The dialogue with the contribution from one of my co-panelists, Maja Brkan, has enriched this paper. I am very indebted to the anonymous reviewers of this contribution, whose acute remarks led to the substantial improvement of this draft. I also wish to thank Catherine Jasserand-Breeman, Gloria González Fuster, Marta Otto and Olivia Tambou, as well as the editors of this book, for the thought-provoking questions, suggestions of literature and encouragement to publish this chapter. Many thanks, as always, to Martyn Egan for the support in writing the article and linguistic advice. Earlier drafts of this chapter appeared in a project deliverable (2013) and my PhD thesis (2017), partly funded by the FP7 SURVEILLE project (grant agreement no. 284725). Completion of this chapter was funded by the EPSRC research project 'Combatting Criminals In The Cloud' (CRITiCal – EP/M020576/1).

---

[128] See Gutwirth and Gellert, n 33.
[129] De Hert, n 29.
[130] Discussed in Porcedda, 'Privacy by Design in EU Law. Matching Privacy Protection Goals with the Essence of the Rights to Private Life and Data Protection'.
[131] De Hert, n 29.
[132] As I discuss in Porcedda, n 43.

13

CPDP 2018 – EDPS Side Event 26 January 2018 'Privacy by Design – Privacy Engineering'

GIOVANNI BUTTARELLI

EDPS

EUROPEAN DATA PROTECTION SUPERVISOR

CPDP Closing Speech 26.1.2018

Ladies and gentlemen,

My congratulations to Paul and the whole CPDP team on another triumphant CPDP.

Over 1000 participants, multiple stakeholders, with a need for a big second venue, and now running now for 5 days, including the Privacy Salon event tomorrow for the true diehards.

The range and depth of panels here present an embarrassment of riches.

And now, with many of the sessions being filmed, you can watch them after conference at your leisure.

At this rate of expansion, Paul, I may need to put you in touch with the managing director of the National King Baudouin Stadium

A big year lies ahead – Probably the biggest year ever for EU data protection.

Of course we are going to celebrate GDPR Day on 25 May.

It will be a great achievement for the DPAs who for years have called for updated rules, for civil society organisations who have campaigned for it, and for the legislators who had the courage to stick to the principles and values of the Charter.

It is even an achievement for the lobbyists who, I am sure, helped improve the text in many ways with their 3999 amendments.

(By the way, what a disappointment that no one had the creativity and ambition to table amendment number 4000!)

The EDPB will soon launch, and all eyes will be on the effectiveness of the One Stop Shop and the Consistency Mechanism, as DPAs seek to cooperate closely while respecting each authority's independence.

The internet has been with us for only a couple of decades.

It has evolved in weird and wonderful ways, but also in very bad ways.

'Connecting people' should not mean following them around and recording their movements, words, actions and thoughts for eternity.

'Convenience' and making life's chores quicker or easier should not make people less safe or less free.

So at least as important this year is the work to adopt the ePrivacy Regulation.

Constant monitoring of behaviour is not the only business model for digital products and services, nor is it the most desirable business model. And it shouldn't be the most profitable.

The ePrivacy regulation is the law which will do more than anything else to persuade companies and investors that there is a better way to connect people and services.

So let us make 2018 the year where Europe says "Enough! No more covert opaque and ubiquitous surveillance of people in the digital environment."

Let us also make 2018 the year where the EU adopts rules, obligations and rights where EU bodies process personal information consistent with the GDPR.

It is, ultimately, a question of integrity.

We claim to lead by example – so therefore we need to ensure that all EU bodies, including those dealing with the most sensitive and complex issues like Europol, applying consistent and reliable standards.

Don't forget, this year will be five years after the Snowden revelations.

We may have made great progress on data protection, but on surveillance it is a very different story.

The Privacy Shield is a sticking plaster.

What we need is for the European Council to make good on its commitments, particularly those in its conclusions, particular in October 2013, undertaking to find a sustainable approach to intelligence sharing with strategic partners.

Apparently last year was the moment over 50 per cent of the world's population became connected to the internet.

Meanwhile another 10 or so countries around the world adopted data privacy laws last year.

The total according to our oracle for such questions, Professor Graham Greenleaf, is now 121 countries.

But this extraordinary growth is uneven.

There are huge numbers being left behind.

Women tend globally to have less access to the internet.

And that means poor urban communities suffer in particular.

Our children are being surveilled like never before – take the example of the schools in California which, for lack of public funding, have chosen to allow their pupils to be monitored in exchange for private capital.

And then there are massive data protection deserts around the world – imagine a gigantic arc from southern Africa through to central Asia and China – where there are no formal privacy protections, or at least no independent regulator protecting individuals from the risks of digitisation.

In too many parts of the world, data protection is treated as a proxy for national security. We in this room have a lot of work to do.

Everybody deserves to be respected, not only those who can afford to pay for the privilege.

Later this year, from 22 to 25 October, here in Brussels, I will host the next International Conference of Data Protection and Privacy Commissioners.

You might think that the biggest sporting occasion this year will be the World Cup.

I disagree – and not, I insist, because I am a bad loser.

This year, for those not familiar with this annual jamboree, Olympic Games for privacy are coming to town.

We can promise unmissable events including mental gymnastics, legal marathons and of course the corporate lobby steeplechase.

I promise that this is going to be an event unlike any other.

We will have over 700 places in the hemicycle of the European Parliament, each seat equipped with microphones and headsets. It is going to be a big and spectacular conversation about technology and ethics in the age of artificial intelligence and the internet of everything.

In our closed session we will determine the future of the conference: how we can be more inclusive to global partner authorities while preserving the integrity of the community of independent regulators.

2018 is going to be a big year.

You should count on us DPAs to be focussed, and single minded, like a squad of human-rights-obsessed Jose Mourinhos.

Thank you – and see you at the Olympics in October.

INDEX